COMPARATIVE PUBLIC POLICY

The Politics of Social Choice in Europe and America

COMPARATIVE PUBLIC POLICY

The Politics of Social Choice in Europe and America

SECOND EDITION

ARNOLD J. HEIDENHEIMER
Washington University

HUGH HECLO
Harvard University

CAROLYN TEICH ADAMS
Temple University

ST. MARTIN'S PRESS
NEW YORK

Library of Congress Catalog Number: 82–60471

Manufactured in the United States of America.
76
fedc

For information, write St. Martin's Press, Inc.
175 Fifth Avenue, New York, NY 10010

Book design: Robert Bull
Cover design: Myrna Sharp

paper ISBN: 0-312-15366-X
cloth ISBN: 0-312-15367-8

PREFACE

When we published the original edition of this book in 1975, we sought to enable students "interested in public policy and the social sciences to surmount disciplinary and national boundaries" so that they might gain a better understanding of "the scope and substance of major public policies affecting the United States and Western Europe."

Then as now, we emphasized that the temporal dimension ranked in importance with the spatial one. By focusing effort on explaining how and why national programs in various policy areas have developed as they have, we hoped to provide a platform to "permit the study of public policy to become both more comparative and more meaningful."

We were surprised and gratified that our colleagues in the American Political Science Association selected it as the best book on public policy published that year. Usually such awards are given to scholarly monographs, and rarely to books aimed directly at undergraduate readers. In its willingness to jump some boundaries of its own, the prize committee seemed to reciprocate the spirit in which we had planned and written the book.

Tokens of its reception elsewhere proved equally gratifying. Many reviewers appreciated the novelty of our undertaking. The book was adopted in a variety of courses in public policy, comparative politics, urban studies, and social policy, both here and abroad. The growth of interest in this emerging field seems to derive most broadly from an urge to probe how party and other forms of political activity "matter" in their impact on society and the economy. The "policy approach" is not the sole means of pursuing this aim, but for many political scientists it has become a relatively congenial and fruitful one.

The recognition granted our initial endeavor encouraged plans for preparing a new edition, while also making us conscious of the different and higher expectations which this new volume would have to meet.

Some difference in expectations arises from the fact that the policy climates of the 1980s differ from those prevailing in the mid-1970s. Examining how resource constraints relate to choices in public policy did not seem to command as high a priority then as now. This recognition has led us to introduce several new chapters—such as those on Economic Policy (ch. 5) and on the Capacity of Local Governments (ch. 9)—as well as sections in other chapters that deal with problems of program effectiveness and cost controls. Similarly, the greater urgency of policy problems like unemployment has had to be recognized more explicitly in our discussions of education, income maintenance, and other policy sectors.

Another symptom of the changed climate is the greater attention given to policies that advocate substituting private for public activities. In recognition of the shift in policy debate we have dealt more explicitly with private or market alternatives to prevailing policies, especially in the "Scope and Thresholds" sections of each chapter. Some of the public-vs-private discussion rests on facile labellings of very mixed cases which are not uniform on a cross-national basis, but we have surmounted methodological misgivings to illustrate the options for political choice on this dimension.

Still, if we had wanted only to update our discussions we would not have rewritten almost the entire text of the book. A gratifying stimulus for doing so was the availability of much more extensive comparative research from other social scientists. The number of policy areas where our colleagues have filled lacunae in comparative studies of high quality in the past eight years (particularly in housing, health, and local finance) exceeds those where they have not yet done so (in taxation, for example). This has permitted us to draw on a more extensive and sophisticated literature than before, and we can only hope that we have done justice to the opportunity. Indeed, the wealth of the recent literature is reflected in our bibliographical references now being both more extensive and more selective.

Given the variations in recent policy experience and the new richness of sources, we faced a challenge of maintaining the readability of our book for undergraduates. Resisting the temptation to "write down" to them, we have adopted several devices which we hope will make their learning experiences less difficult. One consists of introducing each chapter with a perspective section, *Choices in Policy*, to provide an overview of the major policy choices faced in each field. Another is to organize the materials in each chapter in terms of a uniform set of sub-headings which introduce discussions pertinent to choices of *Scope and Thresholds, Policy Instruments, Distribution,* and *Restraints and Innovation.* In addition to providing greater continuity throughout the book, this schema should allow the reader to more easily relate the policy discussion from one chapter to the next. The concepts for these sections are discussed and illustrated in Chapter One, along with a discussion of how the authors perceive their value and methodological positions with reference to those of other tendencies in contemporary social science research.

* * * * *

In the previous edition we listed some problems which students of comparative policy ought to be aware of if this field of research was heading where we hoped it might. We would like to briefly return to these themes, and reflect with our readers how the situations have changed:

The Uniqueness of Policy Experiences. The problem in a nutshell is that a majority of the world's political scientists are Americans, and the majority of these have not regarded foreign experiences as relevant to their research. This is changing slowly, with more Americans undertaking comparative studies, and some Europeans beginning to include American policies within their comparative framework. Volumes comparing welfare state growth, or particular policy endeavors in both Europe and America, have begun to appear, and considerable progress has been made in comparing policy outputs within Western Europe. Slowly the research effort is becoming more multilateral.

The Distinctness of Policy Concepts. The similarity in policy labels across nations—"education," "housing," etc.—initially suggested comparative research since the units appeared to be similar. As researchers are becoming more sophisticated, however, they are finding that such labels can be deceptive and that classifications sometimes need to be closely examined. More sticky is the problem of how one distinguishes between *politics* and *policy* in various language traditions. For English-speaking political scientists the present problem is how to bridge the conceptual moat separating phenomena which are distinguished under the two labels. But those writing in French, German, and most other languages have to use the *same* word (in German, *Politik;* in French, *politique*) to refer to *both* politics and policy. Thus their problem is logically just the reverse of their English-speaking colleagues. This could engender confusion, which might be avoided by a better understanding of both the causes and consequences of this terminological conundrum.

The Parochialism of Policy Specialism. Since policy studies have such a strong "applied" anchor, the danger that policy researchers will define their interests narrowly with regard to policy area and/or nation are considerable. Can cross-national and cross-policy comparison serve a broadening function in this regard? Here one can discern countervailing tendencies. On the one hand, comparative lessons have been brought to bear even on mundane policy areas like waste disposal. On the other, increasing trends toward the sectoral control of research funds in particular bureaucracies, as well as the repercussions of funding cutbacks in general, may tend to reinforce the parochial tendencies.

* * * * *

We would like to alert readers to a number of conventions and usages employed in this book. First, as to collective labels. Since our book focuses exclusively on the democratic capitalist systems of Western Europe, it is the residents of that area which we mean when we refer to "Europeans." Often we use the term for a particular sample of European nations referred to in that particular context. Germany in this sense presents a microcosm of Europe, and since we do not deal with East Germany, we have usually used the term *German* to refer to the West German cases. A somewhat parallel practical usage is employed when we use the shorthand *American* to refer to actors and events in the United States.

When we employ monetary measures we often translate pound or mark amounts into dollars at the rate prevailing on the date that the data refer to. But readers will be aware that Western currencies have fluctuated rather sharply in their exchange value against each other over the past decade. This means that the comparative implications of such data must be read with an additional grain of salt: Whenever possible, we have employed such measures as Percent of GNP, which are less subject to these short-term fluctuations.

Finally, a few words about the chapter bibliographies. For easier reference, these are placed together, so to speak as a bibliography chapter, at the end of the book. There the volumes referred to in the text are listed by alphabetical sequence of the name of their authors or editors. Also included there are additional titles which are relevant to the subject of that chapter. Because this way of organizing the references and bibliography facilitates the task of finding works by particular authors, an index of authors' names seemed less useful, and thus has not been included in this edition.

* * * * *

We have in this edition again both merged and differentiated our efforts. Thus the chapters are usually the fruit of efforts by one, or sometimes two, of us. The responsibility was assumed as follows: One, The Politics of Social Choice (Heclo and Heidenheimer); Two, Education

Policy (Heidenheimer); Three, Health Policy (Heidenheimer); Four, Housing Policy (Adams); Five, Economic Policy (Heclo); Six, Taxation Policy (Heidenheimer); Seven, Income Maintenance Policy (Heclo); Eight, Urban Planning (Adams); Nine, the Capacity of Local Governments (Adams); Ten, Policy Contrasts in the Welfare State (Heidenheimer and Heclo).

We received assistance from numerous colleagues, who either provided information for our use or commented on the drafts of various chapters. Hence we would like to express our thanks especially to the following: Brian Abel-Smith, James E. Alt, Douglas E. Ashford, Samuel Barnes, Nicholas Barr, James Brasfield, Lawrence Brown, Ole Berg, David Cameron, William Glaser, Harry Gourevitch, Byran Jackson, Lillemor Kim, Rudolf Klein, Anneliese Mennel, Richard Merritt, Joyce Mushaben, Rune Premfors, Lee Rainwater, Martin Rein, Cedric Sandford, Alberta Sbragia, Vito Tanzi, and John Woolley.

Several institutions should be thanked for providing opportunities for our interpretations to be scrutinized by our colleagues. Thus in 1978–79 the University of Stockholm and the London School of Economics invited Arnold Heidenheimer to conduct seminar series in which both policy makers and academic colleagues commented on our interpretations of their policy experiences. Hugh Heclo and Heidenheimer are grateful for the opportunity to learn from their colleagues in a research group on The Development of Welfare States in Europe and America, especially Jens Alber, Peter Flora, Theodore Marmor, and Harold Wilensky, whose joint publication provided invaluable data for several chapters in the present volume.

Valuable preparatory work for several of the chapters was provided by both European and American graduate students at Washington University and at Harvard, including Maja Arnestad, John Barnes, Gerd Braitmaier, Holger Dürr, Mack Garder, Hirobumi Ito, John Layson, Henrik Madsen, Jürgen Meinert, Maryska Suda, and Peter Wong. We would also like to acknowledge the efficient assistance of librarians Margaret McDermott, Kenneth Nabors, and Victoria Witte.

We are very appreciative of the contributions of yet another group of good spirits, especially Tina Maines and Emma Dankoski, who fed successive versions through the word processor and offered many helpful suggestions along the way. Credit for the quality of the index must be given to Emma Dankoski. Finally, we are grateful for the skillful editing of Marilyn Moller at St. Martin's Press, who heartened us with her patience and concern for the quality of the end product.

Arnold J. Heidenheimer
Hugh Heclo
Carolyn Teich Adams

CONTENTS

A List of Tables

A List of Figures

1 THE POLITICS OF SOCIAL CHOICE

Many of us frequently compare public policies in everyday conversation. At election time we often compare one candidate's or party's stands on given policy questions with those of another. We move from one state or city to another and observe how high taxes are here compared to there. We move from cities to suburbs and compare carefully which area has the best schools, or which neighborhoods have the safest streets.

If we were living in Western Europe, we might assess education, employment, and retirement opportunities in terms of the taxation levels and social benefit policies of the various nations. We might consider pursuing university study in a country that gives students grants rather than loans, accepting a job in a country with lower income tax rates and higher family benefits, or retiring to a country with good and nearly free services for the elderly. These options would require greater linguistic skills and cultural adaptation than would moving from one American state to another, but we would weigh the costs and benefits in the same way. A working person considering a move to the Sunbelt might weigh the advantages of better job prospects against the more limited housing and other social benefits in most of the southern states.

These everyday comparisons of public policies have one important thing in common with more systematic, academic efforts at comparative policy analysis. Both informal and formal approaches seek a deeper understanding than could be gained by looking at only one thing at a time.

By assessing one situation against another, we gain a fuller perspective of both options and constraints. This kind of perspective is effectively achieved by comparing policies across national boundaries.

While informal comparisons generally serve some personal end, the academic study of comparative public policy has a broader agenda. One aim on this agenda is to learn why some governments seem to fare better than others at coping with similar problems. Though most cities have come under increasing financial pressure in recent years, some political systems seem to have managed with these pressures without crisis while others have not. All the western democracies received severe economic shocks from oil-exporting countries in the 1970s; but some nations seemed to handle the strains with less inflation and unemployment than did others. Why? By comparing the political management of similar problems, useful lessons might be learned. Some of these lessons may be positive, providing guidelines for what to do. Others—perhaps most—may be negative, telling us what *not* to do. Many will suggest alternatives which would be difficult to implement in some political systems, but which might nevertheless become viable options if certain variables were to change.

A second aim in comparing public policies is to gain a deeper understanding of government institutions and political processes themselves. Aristotle asked three seemingly simple questions: Who governs? How do they govern? What are the results of their stewardship? These remain the fundamental questions of politics, and in today's world the raw materials for answering them can be found in the vastly expanded activities undertaken by governments. To examine who governs, it is not enough to know who votes or who is elected to office or appointed to the bureaucracy. It is necessary to know what people in and at the fringes of government actually do. As the scale and activities of governments have grown throughout the West, more and more of this "doing" takes the form of making and remaking public policies.

Hence comparative policy analysis is not only a means of acquiring a broader understanding of particular policy problems and their lessons. It is also a window onto the practical operation of politics: the different roles of political parties, bureaucracies, interest groups, and public opinion. Above all—and this is the central theme of this book—comparative public policy illuminates the various ways in which politics works to produce choices of a collective or social nature. Sensitivity to that process allows us to begin to see beneath the surface of politics and of our everyday comparisons of public policies.

WHAT IS COMPARATIVE PUBLIC POLICY?

Comparative public policy is the study of how, why, and to what effect different governments pursue particular courses of action or inaction. While this definition may seem straightforward, it contains a number of important conceptual distinctions. But before plunging into the subject matter, we might consider how to think about the subject. In essence, there are two schools of thought.

One approach is basically deductive. Though it is often identified with the work of professional political economists, the deductive approach is followed by many schools of political thought. From certain behavioral premises we deduce the policy patterns and relationships that can be expected to result. Marxists, for example, begin with the premise that society is always divided into social classes based on who owns and does not own the means of production. Following from this view it is possible to argue that government policies are simply an expression of the dominant underlying economic class interests. In today's capitalist democracies this may sometimes imply repression or it may lead to various welfare programs to buy off mass discontent (O'Connor; Piven and Cloward).

Much of the recent conservative counterpressure against the growth of government is based on a similar deductive approach to public policy. Theorists using rationalistic models, for example, often begin with the premises that all bureaucrats seek to expand the size of their programs, that all politicians seek to manage the economy so as to ensure their reelection, or that all citizens are biased to vote for the benefits of government spending programs but against the taxes necessary to support such programs. These and other premises have been used recently to show why democratic politics leads to bigger government, higher deficits, and more inflation (Borcherding; Brittan; Buchanan and Wagner; Nordhaus).

This deductive approach to public policy is a powerful intellectual tool. It makes manageable a huge number of complex details that otherwise can overwhelm any analysis. It reduces uncertainty by showing the constants that underlie transitory and seemingly contradictory events. Above all, this approach corresponds with many people's assumptions about what the policy-making process is like. Surely governments make policies by deciding on objectives and then trying to find appropriate means to attain them. If that is the case, then it seems reasonable to begin by identifying the source of those objectives—whether it is class interests, ambitious bureaucrats, or insecure politicians.

The second approach is inductive and is most closely associated with pluralist schools of political thought. In this case, behavioral regularities are not posited at the outset but are inferred by observing the many interactions among partially opposing interests that occur on any public policy issue. Policy does not result from a given set of objectives; rather, objectives are discovered and changed in a never-ending process of conflict, bargaining, and compromise (Lindblom; Wildavsky). Since some groups obviously have more power than others, the policy results are skewed toward the goals of the powerful. But power itself is not constant, and some groups can gain power while others in seemingly dominant positions can lose it. Differing political structures, events, and other factors can heavily influence the play of group interactions and hence the eventual policies. In one place and time welfare programs may indeed be a form of social pacification, whereas in other places and times they may stem from poor people themselves demanding newly felt rights. Some bureaucrats may want to build empires, while others prefer the security of the status quo or specialize professionally in budget cutting.

In contrast to the deductive approach, inductive approaches to public policy highlight complexity, uncertainty, and ambiguous relations between ends and means. Our approach tends toward the inductive, pluralistic school of thought. The role of government bureaucrats, the monopoly power of professional groups such as doctors or teachers, the effects of party competition for votes—these and similar issues are seen as questions to be explored rather than subsumed under axioms to be taken for granted. Yet it is impossible to study public policy making without realizing that certain inherent orientations often seem like virtual "givens" in any situation. By and large most bureaucrats are more committed to carrying out existing policy than to policy innovation. Specialized professions do attach a high priority to maintaining their autonomy from those in government who are not part of the professional fraternity. Elected politicians are almost always more sensitive to immediate political pressures than to the long-term plans of experts.

In other words, the real world of policy making shows a constant interplay between purpose and unexpected consequences, between objectives that exist *a priori,* and objectives that are discovered *a posteriori,* between the respective utility of deduction and induction. To capture something of this reality, our analysis will concentrate not on pure forms of any sort, but on the complex, often ambiguous political interactions through which policy development actually occurs. Comparison shows how public policies are both structured in common ways and varied across time and nations.

We can begin to bring some order to these complex interactions by returning to the definition of comparative public policy and sorting out its major terms: the study of *how, why,* and *to what effect* different governments pursue particular *courses of action and inaction.*

To ask *how* governments choose to act focuses our attention on what goes on inside and at the fringes of the state. It requires learning aspects of the structures and processes through which governmental decisions are reached. In a generalized, almost deductive sense, we say that the United States and West Germany are federal states while Britain, Sweden, and France are more centralized unitary states. Hence, we might expect the policy approaches to differ in the two sets of nations. But when we look closer we see that federalism takes on different meanings, depending not only on the country but also on the policy in question. So too do the connotations of centralization in countries such as Britain and France (Ashford). Hence, if we wish to go beyond clichés regarding federalism and centralization, it is necessary to examine in some detail how different governments and their related constellations of parties, interest groups, and bureaucracies actually work through various policy problems. This approach is pursued in Chapter Two, which deals with the development of national education policies in the five countries just mentioned.

To ask *why* governments pursue particular courses of action is obviously as difficult to answer as it is important to ask. Why has the United States followed Europe in adopting some social policies but preceded Europe in other social programs? Why have some countries preserved their major cities as a national resource while others have tolerated more urban decay? Why is the social security "safety net" a subject of quiet, consensual politics at one place and time and an ideologically charged political issue at other places and times?

Answers to "why" questions such as these can depend on historical developments in the distant past which current policy makers may well be unaware of, on the underlying political culture of a nation and subsections of its population, or even on a changing state of public consciousness that makes something a problem for policy attention rather than simply a condition to be accepted. For example, the French and the Germans may be especially sensitive to policy questions about the uniformity of school curricula because of nation-building experiences that occurred between the sixteenth and nineteenth centuries. But here we cannot trace such complicated linkages, nor can we unravel the subtle interactions between political culture and public policy predispositions.

What we can do is keep in mind the importance of these ultimate determinants of policy choices when we discuss the various policy instruments that nations select in areas such as education, health, and economic management. And so we will regularly refer to these background influences even as we concentrate on the more proximate sources of policy development. These closer factors consist of the interactions of politicians, bureaucrats, interest groups, public opinion, program beneficiaries, and any other elements that bear on policy making. The ideas policy makers present, no less than the power they seek to exercise, constitute the raw materials for explaining why policy similarities and differences occur.

The third element in the definition of comparative public policy—*to what effect*—is for many people the payoff. Apart from political scientists, few people are likely to be interested in studying government for its own sake. But almost all people care about what government is doing to them and for them. In other words, they care about its policies. Studying comparative public policy, rather than comparative government or political behavior, gives special attention to the effects of government action on peoples' lives. Rarely are the results exactly what governments intended when adopting a policy; sometimes, the result is a new round of political debate and choice. Assessing governments' capacity for coping with unintended consequences and learning from different experiences in policy development makes the subject matter both complex and fascinating. And, in our view, an approach that anticipates and explicitly deals with surprises and adaptation leads to more realistic analysis than one which emphasizes deductions based on behavioral premises.

We are left with two components of the original definition. When we refer to *different governments* we are being intentionally vague, so as not to exclude comparisons that go outside the normal country-by-country approach. Although all of the chapters in this volume deal with contrasts among different national governments, it is equally useful to compare public policies among various local units of government. Indeed one can often find as many interesting differences between local jurisdictions of the same country as between different countries (Fried and Rabinovitz). Even more differentiated comparisons can be made by considering voluntary organizations and other private groups that also affect public policy (Sharkansky; Graham).

What is needed, what is seriously lacking in the scholarly literature, is a comparative approach that can cover levels of government as well as different nations. Interactions among policy makers in the different national capitals are important, but rarely do they tell the whole story. This has become particularly true in recent years as national governments have increasingly sought to cope with their financial problems by shifting policy burdens to local jurisdictions and semi-public groups. Perhaps more than ever before, public policy has become a mosaic pieced together by government authorities at different levels and semi-public groups with public policy responsibilities. The comparisons in subsequent chapters try to capture some of this reality, but there is still much work to be done in the comparative study of subnational policy making.

That leaves us with the final element of our original definition: A *course of action or inaction* is a policy. It is not enough to identify this or that decision and how it was made. What matters for purposes of comparative public policy is the string of decisions that add up to a fairly consistent body of behavior on the part of the government. In this regard studying comparative public policy is much like trying to analyze weather patterns. The local TV announcer records how particular interactions between clouds and temperature variations produce particular sequences of rain or sunshine during a specific day. But the serious meteorologist, who understands the long-term variations, is more interested in identifying whether continents are likely to have colder or wetter winters or even decades. In making his prognoses he must allow for the introduction of variables, such as agricultural patterns or the effects of particular kinds of industrial pollution.

Like comparative policy scholars, meteorologists differ about how to weigh and evaluate the factors that produce a colder or warmer winter. But what general weather patterns are to the one, policies are to the other: namely, an *overall configuration of movement and activity.* Both must be flexible observers, concerned primarily with the larger, general trends.

What then about decisions that a government does not make, or issues that it refuses to face? Are these also public policy? Clearly it would be absurd to think that everything a government does not decide about is *ipso facto* a policy. Few modern governments have made explicit decisions regarding styles of dress between the sexes (Iran and China are the exceptions); likewise, no country has decided to impose special immigration quotas on interstellar visitors. This does not mean that the countries therefore have a policy condoning sexist differentiation in clothing or a policy discriminating against earthling immigrants vis-à-vis the interplanetary variety. Yet it would also be absurd to deny that by studied inaction in certain situations governments are expressing something that is just as much a public policy as any big spending decision. Thus for many years the United States national government did have something of a civil rights policy when it steadfastly refused to intervene in matters of racial discrimination occurring under state laws. Similarly, until the 1960s brought stronger demands for reducing inequalities, U.S. health policy was defined largely by an absence of interference with private enterprise in stimulating and meeting a growing demand for health care.

Government inaction, or non-decision, becomes a policy when it is pursued over time in a fairly consistent way against pressures to the contrary. It is never easy to say just when government passivity begins to assume the characteristics of a public policy, but the growth of controversy is one good clue. Certainly by the 1950s, for example, there was a spreading feeling that by doing nothing Washington was condoning and thus supporting racial discrimination throughout the South. Likewise, by the 1980s it became clear to more and more Americans that by *not* regulating hospital prices, the government was pursuing a public policy of restricting demand by making consumers pay more for health care. In these and other cases, what matters for purposes of identifying "policy in repose" is that the issue be perceived by at least some major participants as being on the political agenda. At that point it becomes possible to compare meaningfully one government's hands-off attitude to another government's hands-on approach to the same issue. The discussion in Chapter Three of how the West German government came to institute health cost controls while similar American efforts failed is an example of this kind of comparison.

From the way we have now defined the subject, it should be clear that pursuing comparative public policy studies demands individual judgment, as much as it does skills for measuring objective social conditions. When does a non-decision become a policy? What policy trends should be compared against each other? How deeply should one delve into history and political culture for explanations of differences and similarities? Answers to these and similar questions do not depend entirely on scientific theory or measurement and hence will always be in some degree a matter of interpretation and judgment. In this text we have attempted to be "scientific" in applying careful reasoning to the best available empirical evidence. But the reader should bear in mind that the subject of this book is framed by questions upon which judgments are necessarily subjective at least in part.

Likewise, comparative public policy can never become a self-contained specialized discipline, for the subject draws elements from many different disciplines. The "how" part of our definition draws heavily on work in comparative government, public administration, and political science generally. The "why" portion often extends to topics covered in political sociology, history, social psychology, and other fields. The "to what effect" questions are strongly related to policy analysis, economics, and ultimately—when we evaluate results (as we must) in terms of the kind of society we would like to live in—social philosophy.

Comparative public policy is located at a busy crossroads in the social sciences. It provides a setting where political scientists, sociologists, historians, and economists are learning from one another. The premises each brings can be tested against the perceptions of others. At the pedestrian level the subjects of study—Title IV here, the 1983 amendments there—may differ from month to month. But from their elevated viewing stands, experienced policy watchers will be able to recognize continuities of form, style, and substance and to discern when the wind blows fair for bolder goals in education or housing, or why similar economic stimulus proposals may encounter more turbulence in one national setting than in another.

POLITICS AS CHOICE

"To govern is to choose." Hidden within this familiar saying lies a profound insight. To appreciate the insight involved in linking politics and choice, we need to pass beyond the image of a few individual governors and encompass many people and groups. We must think not of this or that newsworthy decision, but of many streams of decisions and interactions that cumulate into processes of choice. These are choices made on behalf of society, not because politicians and leaders necessarily act in the public interest, but because the outcomes of such choices authoritatively sanction certain social arrangements but not others. Perhaps, then, we might say that "to be governed is to have choices made for you"; but that statement overlooks one important reality—namely, that leaders do not act unrestrained and that they are engaged in reciprocal influence processes with those they lead. A much more persuasive image comes from Hermann Hesse:

> The expedition did not, in fact, proceed in any fixed order with participants moving in the same direction in more or less closed columns. On the contrary, numerous groups were simultaneously on the way, each following their own leaders and their own stars, each one always ready to merge into a greater unit and belong to it for a time, but always no less ready to move on again separately. . . . (Hermann Hesse, *The Journey to the East*)

If this seems unduly abstract, consider some of the collective, or social, choices that have been made through politics over the past one hundred years:

Schooling, at public expense, has grown from a kind of charity offered to relatively few children for a few years to a right provided each generation into adulthood. Selection criteria which used to be most powerful at the entrance to secondary school have been moved "up" the educational ladder to the doors of graduate and professional schools. (Education policy is considered in Chapter Two.)

Health care, once universally thought to be of little governmental concern, has everywhere been elevated to the level of public policy. While in earlier periods of power politics the strength of nations was measured in terms of battalions and armaments, now societal indicators such as infant mortality or the capacity to deal with drug addiction are often perceived as equally or more important. As life spans have lengthened, governments have been drawn more deeply into questions of health care financing generally, but especially for the larger elderly proportion of the population. (Health care policies are dealt with in Chapter Three.)

The shape of cities and the nature of people's housing have always been byproducts of market forces. But whereas they were once thought of as natural and inevitable results of economic realities, they are now regarded as subjects for forethought and governmental intervention. (How Europe and the United States have shaped relevant policies is examined in Chapters Four and Eight.)

As societies, we have decided that much of what a person earns shall be taken from him or her in taxes, that certain kinds of income and spending shall be taxed differently from others, and that people will receive various kinds of public income whenever they cannot meet basic needs as we have defined them. (Policies pertaining to these questions are examined comparatively in Chapters Six and Seven.)

These and other topics are dealt with in the subsequent chapters of this book. In 1881 the first great national program of social insurance was initiated by the German Emperor William I. Given the current expansion in the agenda of public policy, we might well call the hundred years since then the century of the welfare state. The data are far from perfect, but the overall trends in Europe and the United States are clear and consistent for the last hundred years: A rising share of total economic resources has been absorbed by taxation and devoted to public spending. Of all public spending, a growing share (except in years of war) has gone to social programs; of all these programs, more and more have involved income security programs (Flora and Heidenheimer). As we shall see, national variations within these trends are important, but the overall movements stand out as long-term themes for every developed nation.

The generation since 1960 has, if anything, seen these same trends become more prominent. Obviously there are many differences among the political systems examined in this text. But for all, the period from 1960 to 1980 may indeed have been a golden age in the long history of welfare state spending and taxation.

But are we really justified in calling these developments examples of collective choice? Surely public spending has grown as a proportion of the economy without anyone consciously choosing what the level or ratio should be; the aggregate patterns have just happened.

Again we must beware of thinking that choices can be made only deliberately by some individual decision maker. Choices can also be made through complex processes of interaction. Politics serves as a mechanism of social choice in much the same sense that markets serve as means of making aggregate economic choices that no individual participant in the market may have intended or decided to make. Changing prices signal the movements in supply and demand and in doing so yield two types of overall aggregate economic choices: namely, choices about how scarce resources will be allocated to produce a desired mix of products from all the possible mixes that could potentially be produced, and distributive choices about who will have the money incomes to purchase these products. This allocation of resources and distribution of income may be seen as the warp and woof of economic life.

For better or worse, political life is even more complex, and deductions based on such political economy concepts take us only a little way toward understanding the complexity of political choice. In the 1970s, for example, many writers used such concepts to show that democratic policy and politics were headed inexorably toward hyper-inflation and political disaster. Public demands revealed a preference for government spending but against the taxation to support such spending. Reinforcing this tendency was the fact that bureaucrats engaged in the "supply" of public services—and using taxpayers' money—had no "cost" constraint to limit their ambitious programs. Such economic concepts were useful in capturing some general tendencies, but they scarcely offered a full portrayal of political reality. By the beginning of the 1980s, government expansion seemed to be slowing down; moreover, hyper-inflation and massive government deficits did not develop in most Western democracies. Politicians such as Ronald Reagan and Margaret Thatcher won popular followings by promising to reduce government spending and taxation levels. With somewhat different rhetoric and methods, many Social Democrats in continental Europe similarly acted to cut back public budget trajectories. All of these developments were of course part of the politics of social choice.

What separates a choice from a mere result is the fact that a significant number of people believe that the political process can be managed so as to produce a desired result. It is this growing awareness of the possibilities and implications of choice that, perhaps more than anything else, distinguishes our time from earlier periods of policy making. Thus a conservative such as Ronald Reagan entered the Presidential office with a blueprint, not only for balancing the budget, but also for reducing the federal government's share of Gross Domestic Product (GDP) from 21% to 19.6% by the end of his first term, for cutting inflation, and for achieving a high and stable level of employment. While economists in his administration differ strongly about how these goals might be achieved, it is striking that no one questions the idea that these goals are, potentially at least, within the power of the policy-making process to achieve. Such assurance would not have been felt by most people of earlier generations. How could it? No one could argue about the size of the government in relation to the economy because only in this century has there been widespread political debate on the concept of managing a national economy; and only in the 1940s were the first reliable measures of economic size and movement (Gross National Product) made. Unemployment and inflation were largely accepted as part of the natural order of things; hard times alternated with good times as a matter of course, just as the weather fluctuated beyond anyone's control.

Once a condition is given a name and accepted as a problem rather than simply as part of the natural order, then it is only a short step to interpreting any unemployment or inflation level as something that government has created through policy or chosen to countenance. That willingness to recognize choices is what marks our times, and it applies to much more than the economy. To grant or refuse federal funding for abortions becomes for many people pro- or anti-abortion policy. The area of technological change (nuclear power, chemicals use, natural resources development, genetic engineering, and so on) is especially rich in examples of declining willingness to let developments take their own course and greater willingness to try to control trends—which is to say, to become mobilized in the politics of social choice. Though we cannot hope to cover all these fields in this volume, we shall see that tendencies show up clearly in those social policy fields we do cover.

CHOICES AS FRAMEWORKS

What choices of a collective nature has politics served to make? Earlier in this chapter, we pointed out that markets make two types of economic choices—allocational and distributive. The possible array in politics is much larger, but in this book we concentrate on four types of choice applicable to each policy area. These four types of choice fall short of the macro-choices between equality and inequality or liberty and security, but they are major choices all the same. And, as we shall see, they are subject to constant change and adaptation.

Choices of Scope

This type of choice concerns whether and where lines shall be drawn between public and private responsibilities. For example, is the purchase of health care strictly a private matter between health care providers and those with the money to pay for it? If the government does take part, how far should it go in setting requirements for doctors and hospitals that provide the service? How much responsibility should the person in need of health care bear? Some scope choices may also exist within public policies themselves rather than between public and private sectors. Should housing policy be concerned mainly with increasing the physical supply of buildings, or should it also be used as a part of anti-poverty or economic management policies?

Choices of Policy Instruments

Given that government accepts a responsibility to intervene, what structures and tools will it use? Does it want to retain policy-making power at the national level, or delegate the power to sub-national levels of government? Does it want to let local or regional governments shape educational or social assistance policies, or does it value homogeneity sufficiently to transfer such jurisdictions to higher levels? Further options relate to the manner of public interventions—by maintaining public schools and housing estates, by granting subsidies to non-profit or for-profit builders or hospital operators, or by using licensing power to assure that some regulatory standards are met. Though such choices are not mutually exclusive, most national systems tend to give priority to some instruments over others. But these choices need not be consistent across policy areas.

Choices of Distribution

Whereas economic markets arrive at distributive choices by letting costs and benefits lie wherever they happen to fall, the political process normally makes such choices in a much more self-conscious manner. Is it fair that children from wealthy families should be able to buy their way into better private schools? Is it fair that their families should have to pay taxes to support public schools their children do not attend? How shall the burden of taxation be distributed among households, between individual income earners and business profits, between income and consumption?

Choices of Restraints and Innovation

These choices become particularly applicable when significant change in the character of constraints poses questions about how to continue, terminate, or adapt policies which had been implemented in light of the preceding choices. In one direction choices can go toward toughening the prevailing rules regarding the extension or extraction of resources and benefits; in the other they can go toward experimenting with new techniques. Recourse to severity can allow for fewer deviations or loopholes in the administration of prevailing rules, or it can adjust the rules to tighten selection criteria for public assistance, abortions, or housing subsidies.

Without being too ritualistic, we will use these four dimensions of choice to trace the major lines of development in each of the subsequent chapters.

THE POLICY AREAS

The subject matter of these chapters covers a broad field, from education to economic management, and it is a field that is anything but arbitrary. The public policies which we will be comparing concern government's role in economic and social affairs, for these are the sectors in which national governments have carved out important functions in this past century of welfare state development. The national departments which administer these policies are generally of more recent origin than those that handle the more traditional governmental functions, such as of defense or public works. Let us commence by looking at public policies involving services.

The services considered in Chapters Two through Four—education, health care, and housing—were in earlier centuries left mainly to commercial and philanthropic agencies. Today these services are often regarded as vital social goods in whose allocation governments must play a key role. In different nations the governmental role has developed at different times. Germany and Austria preceded Britain and the United States in the introduction of health insurance and public pension programs and today devote larger shares of their budgets to these programs. Compared to the United States, European nations have generally also been leaders in the provision of public housing. But with regard to the provision of post-primary public education, it was the United States that preceded the major European countries by a generation or more.

In contrast to its lag in the health sector, the United States has been ahead of Europe in the education sector. The American public education policy was first established during the early decades of the twentieth century. In 1890 the United States had proportionately only half as many full-time secondary students in public schools as Germany; by 1899 it had an equal proportion; and by 1930 its secondary school attendance rate was more than three times that of Germany or Britain. During this period in the United States a new public high school was established every day of the year. A 1935 article in the *Encyclopedia of the Social Sciences* noted that education in the United States was still "the only fully developed social service" (Comstock). In contrast to Europe, where academic secondary schools were maintained for a small elite of children from middle- and upper-class families, the American high school by the 1920s came to be attended by children from all social, economic, and intellectual groups.

In Chapter Five we turn to economic policy and look at governmental influence on the overall performance of the economy. The purpose of this chapter is to examine differences and similarities in the ways that democratic nations have coped with common problems of economic management. Compared to other topics in this book, economic policy is distinguished by widespread agreement, not only on its aims, but also on the specific ways in which progress toward these goals should be measured. Progress toward these goals is everywhere measured in terms of widely accepted statistical constructs: unemployment rates, price indices, and gross national product. Policy makers can hence be much more clearly identified with results, even though the underlying economic processes may be largely outside their control. Since no one can deny bad news contained in economic statistics, there is a strong political incentive to engage in or at least appear to engage in problem solving.

In Chapters Six and Seven we turn to taxation and income maintenance policies, two topics that are appropriately grouped together if we think of social policy as being concerned with a distribution of both benefits *and* costs. Income maintenance programs allocate cash payments; taxation distributes tax extractions. In practical terms, a cash benefit received and a tax cost avoided may be indistinguishable in their effect on a family's disposable income. Special tax provisions can support the income positions of some persons by leaving untouched money which would otherwise go into the national tax coffers, while other groups may receive aid from overt cash payments made through social security, public assistance, or other income maintenance programs.

Compared to education, health, and housing programs, these two areas are obviously much more concerned with cash transfers to and from citizens. For a variety of reasons, this difference would suggest that income maintenance and taxation policies are subject to more direct and exclusive goverment control than any of the other three policies, partially because negotiations with professional groups supplying services and time-consuming capital projects are not normally required for income maintenance and taxation policies.

Though income maintenance programs and taxation are largely monopolistic activities under direct government control, powerful inertia may still affect basic policy change. Moreover, possibilities for change may also be constrained by certain political contexts. A pluralistic political setting with a weak central administration will offer considerable opportunity to specialized groups interested in policy changes. Once a policy is established, advocates of general change are likely to have little leverage compared to that of coalitions of particularized interests. In less fragmented political systems, policy makers, without disregarding the special interests of particular groups, are able to deal from positions of greater strength with those broad policy guidelines affecting everyone in general and no one in particular.

In Chapters Eight and Nine we turn to the role of local governments. Our focus in these chapters is on the interaction between national governments and local jurisdictions in the policy areas of urban renewal, city planning, and urban transportation. The patterns of intergovernmental relations in these policy areas are quite varied in the nations considered in this book. Some national governments of Europe, such as those of France and Britain, have historically taken great interest in planning and building cities, especially the great capital cities. In other European nations the planning and control of urban growth, involving the sensitive interface between public authority and private property rights, is a policy area where local prerogatives have been more protected.

Chapters Eight and Nine emphasize how important the extreme jurisdictional fragmentation in the American political system is for policy implementation. Local communities in the United States have consistently rejected proposals to create supra-local planning agencies that would have the authority to enforce zoning and transportation decisions. In contrast, European national governments have used their leverage both to promote reform at the local level and to mediate conflicts among local jurisdictions.

In the European patterns of intergovernmental relations, we find that as a rule a larger proportion of local revenues is contributed by national treasuries than in the United States. This allows European governments to promote a spatial redistribution of public revenues—a feat which encounters enormous difficulties in the jurisdictional maze of American intergovernmental relations. Moreover, the system of national financing increases the national administrators' control over the implementation of programs at the local level. In many cases the combination of strong financial leverage and close administrative scrutiny by national agencies makes local authorities mere agents of the national administration.

In Chapter Ten we relate our study of policy arenas to a discussion of the dynamics that underlie the expansion and contraction of the welfare state. Here we consider the longer-term perspective through a discussion among four of the politicians who played key roles in the development of the welfare state on both sides of the Atlantic. We also look at patterns of policy change, with special consideration of how much such patterns have varied across nations, across policy sectors, and across different historical eras. How and why support and evaluation of government programs varies by nation and policy sector is then examined cross-sectionally on the basis of survey findings from the 1970s in the United States and three European countries. The factors determining different degrees of voter support for policy expansion or tax reduction are also considered and then related back to the opportunities for social choice in different kinds of Western systems. We conclude by placing in perspective the effective choices facing the Western electorates in a period such as the 1980s in which there is a growing awareness of scarcity.

THE COUNTRIES

Attention in this volume is focused on the developed nations of Western Europe and the United States. Wherever possible we have tried to include information on as broad a range of countries as possible, while looking in much greater detail at the United States, Britain, France, the Netherlands, Sweden, and West Germany.* Our rationale for this selection is based on economic, political, and historical factors.

The five European countries exhibit overall economic and political profiles similar to that of the United States. They are rather alike in their reliance on mixed economies and in their level of economic development; Sweden and Germany are slightly ahead of the United States in per capita GNP, while the Netherlands, France and Britain are somewhat behind. The six nations' political systems have also remained similar during the second half of this century in exhibiting a continuity of party-based governments selected through competitive elections. During the thirty-five years since World War II, their political and economic elites have had to act within parameters bounded by a liberal international economy on the

*As already stated in the Preface, we are utilizing the following conventional abbreviations: *Americans* for citizens of the United States; *Europeans* for citizens of Western Europe; *Germany* for the Federal Republic of Germany, or West Germany; and *Britain* for Great Britain.

one hand, and by well-organized domestic electorates on the other. It is partly because these characteristics have held true more for the northern-central region of Western Europe that we have chosen to study systems from that stable and prosperous region, and neglected the Mediterranean area. Cavils that might be raised about the exclusion of Italy or Spain might also be raised with regard to Canada or Japan, but our resources were not sufficient to include these somewhat distinctive national policy experiences into our framework in a meaningful way. Even so, we make some references to these countries' policy records, and to those of other small European nations.

Though we focus in this book on contemporary policy problems, we also concern ourselves with how the historical structures of institutions and roles shape current policy responses. The nations discussed here exhibit basic differences in inherited attitudes toward governmental initiatives and intervention. On the one hand British and American traditions favor limits on government power, as is reflected both in individualist values and in the sharp borders perceived between private and public spheres. By contrast, in Sweden, France, the Netherlands, and Germany, traditions allow governments more freedom to devise innovative solutions for problems caused by industrialization, urbanization, and other facets of socio-economic development. To understand this basic difference between Anglo-Saxon and Continental patterns—as well as the variations that occur within these two groups of nations—one needs to appreciate the way historical development has structured today's policy-making systems (Moore; Rokkan; Dyson).

France, Germany, and Sweden, despite their many differences, are all countries that entered the modern era with strong carry-overs from the feudal institutions of the past. Living uneasily with the republican impulses of the Revolution, the French aristocracy never quite lost its grip on French society and a large rural sector steeped in traditionalism. The German nation was founded in the late nineteenth century on a Prussian version of feudal authority patterns. Sweden saw itself as a nation organized into four great social estates, a concept that was only gradually abandoned in the late nineteenth century.

These countries each entered the modern era with a well-developed state bureaucratic apparatus that predated both large-scale industrialization and widespread commitment to democratic participation. From the earliest phases of economic and political modernization, the state was an accepted presence and, moreover, an unavoidable independent force in the affairs of each nation. The German and French legacies of statism are undoubtedly the most familiar. Sweden offers another example. After the Crown and local government councils, the national bureaucracy is the oldest Swedish political institution and has played the central role for centuries in linking Crown and *kommune*. Modernized in the nineteenth century according to the model of Prussian bureaucracy (but without the resources or opportunity for territorial aggrandizement), Swedish bureaucracy has played the most enduring role in modernizing a nation that was at the beginning of this century still agrarian and pre-democratic.

Another common historical strand these nations share concerns industrialization. In each country industrialization occurred after economic modernization was well under way in a growing international economy. Any industrial revolution is of course a complex process with few clear beginnings or endings, but it is important to note that France, Germany, and Sweden all went from being predominantly agricultural to being predominantly industrial around the beginning of this century. What early industrializers could do with relatively little competition, small amounts of capital, and rudimentary transportation systems was later thought to require collective protection, concentrations of capital, and public investment. The result was a natural mutuality of interest between relatively large-scale business concentrations, banking interests, and a preexisting, well-developed state apparatus that could provide the needed protection and investment aids. A traditionalist, non-commercialized agricultural sector in these countries had no less an interest in state protection.

It would be a very lengthy and probably foolish exercise to try to determine which of these three factors was most important in shaping the domestic basis for current policies. Indeed, economic, political, and historical factors have to form a complex web. The legacy of feudalism carried with it a commitment to established authority patterns and an expectation of coherent status hierarchies. The legacy of statism brought an established administrative apparatus confident of its ability to exercise such authority. And the legacy of late industrialization provided an incentive for concentration of economic power that would work comfortably with an equally powerful public authority.

The contrast of the United States and Britain is striking. Feudal institutions scarcely ever existed in the United States, and in Britain the early commercialization of agriculture in the eighteenth century effectively undercut forever the economic and social base for such authority. The early development of parliamentary institutions in Britain and democratic government forms in the United States represented a severe restriction on the executive power of the state. In both countries national bureaucracies developed afterward and were forced to accomodate themselves to preexisting forms of popular political participation. Relatively early experiences with industrial production and commercial agriculture were seen to demonstrate the virtues of free market approaches and fairly small-scale enterprises.

TABLE 1.1 The Nations of Western Europe and North America Ranked Among 141 Countries with Regard to Some Resources and Public Policy Indicators, 1978

	POPULATION		GNP		PUBLIC EXPENDITURES					
	Total (millions)	Density (per sq. kilometer)	Total ($ billion)	Per Capita (U.S. $)	Military per capita (U.S. $)	RANK	Education per capita (U.S. $)	RANK	Health per capita (U.S. $)	RANK
North America										
Canada	23	2	200	8531	174	24	688	8	469	9
United States	219	23	2133	9752	499	8	565	10	341	13
Western Europe										
Belgium	10	328	97	9878	322	13	589	9	399	10
Britain	56	299	312	5578	262	17	297	23	268	18
Denmark	5	119	55	10830	259	19	752	3	806	2
France	53	97	475	8902	350	11	512	12	546	6
Ireland	3	47	12	3695	59	53	232	26	220	21
Italy	57	188	265	4669	112	30	215	28	211	22
Netherlands	14	340	131	9396	304	15	730	4	560	5
Norway	4	13	39	9528	322	13	729	5	633	3
Spain	37	73	146	3996	67	48	86	45	116	26
Sweden	8	18	87	10379	365	10	927	2	883	1
Switzerland	6	155	88	13948	280	16	710	6	486	8
West Germany	61	246	643	10479	350	11	491	14	591	4
World										
Developed	1038	19	7204	6937	309	—	382	—	284	—
Developing	3276	42	2076	635	30	—	24	—	10	—

SOURCE Ruth Leger Sivard, *World Military and Social Expenditures, 1981* (Leesburg, VA: World Priorities, 1981), pp. 25–30.

* * * * *

Comparing policies cross-nationally, then, can utilize certain conceptual orientations which are closely related to empirical data about how public policies and programs have come to help determine the allocation of countries' resources. The data presented in Table 1.1 give a bird's eye view of how nations compare on some measures of resources and policy emphasis. These data and rankings will become more meaningful as the reader becomes more familiar with the various policy areas. In the next chapter we focus on education policy, beginning with an examination of governmental roles in education developed in consonance with the emergence of state institutions.

2
EDUCATION POLICY

Citizenship in democratic countries involves obligations, some of which are legally prescribed. Voting in national elections is compulsory in some countries, and non-voters may even be fined. In other countries the practice of an occupation or profession entails compulsory membership in a chamber of artisans or physicians. But in *all* these countries compulsory education laws require parents to send their children to accredited schools for about a decade of formal education.

Why is it that states have chosen to concentrate their power to compel behavior on adolescents rather than on adults of voting age? Partly because the responsibility for ensuring that youth achieves a certain level of literacy and mathematical proficiency has come to be transferred from the family to the government; partly because governments see schools as an opportunity to inculcate regime values into future citizens when they are still at an impressionable age; partly because future voting rights presuppose a socialization process in which schools play an important part. In these ways adult society tries to legitimize its choices for the next generation and to reduce the opportunities for deviating radically from them.

Extensive state intervention in education can be justified in that the knowledge and credentials achieved in schools broaden the choices that youth can make at later stages of their education and employment. Thus the choice to "drop out" of education is especially restricted where national goals stress "equality of opportunity"; nations must make sure that youth stays in the education system long enough to be offered this opportunity.

In democratic capitalist systems, social stratification is the main mechanism to implement and legitimize economic and social inequality during adult life. A nation's commitment to allocating "life chances" rests heavily on education, particularly on access to higher education, where the nation's social and professional elites are trained. Some health and housing policies are also relevant, insofar as poor health or crowded housing may affect a child's performance in school. Most important, however, are the quality of education offered in the various kinds of schools and the equality of access to them.

CHOICES IN EDUCATION POLICY

The Scope of the State Education Monopoly

Although no Western democracies directly prohibit churches or private groups from operating non-public educational institutions, they encourage or discourage them in varying degrees. The techniques with which they implement their education policy choices rest largely on their power to license or charter institutions and to assist them financially. The preponderance of public education varies from nation to nation. The de facto dominance of public institutions is most thorough in Scandinavia. Though only a few Continental countries offer extensive support to private institutions, Britain has a significant private school sector. The largest number of self-supporting religious and other private schools and universities is found in the United States.

Generally, more than four fifths of all pupils and students in these countries attend public institutions. Two controversial questions are whether the minority attending private schools should receive public subsidies, and whether it is just for them to get better educations largely because of their parents' higher incomes. The diversity of American practice is illustrated by the fact that in some states—Colorado and Tennessee, for example—no private college students receive state grants, while in others all receive some public support. Such regional differences would probably violate national constitutional rules in West Germany, where few private schools and no private universities exist.

The Instruments of Education Policy

How centralized should national education systems be, and how much leeway should local or regional authorities have to make deviating decisions? The polar choices here lie between the powerful American local school boards within a decentralized federal system, on the one hand, and the centrally run school systems of unitary polities such as Sweden and France, on the other hand. In the latter countries powerful national boards enforce similar rules and curricula throughout the nation. Uniformity is lower in Germany, by contrast, because the primary power is exercised from the *Land,* or state, level and not the national level. But Land officials assign teachers and stipulate curricula in ways that would arouse outrage in the even more localized American system.

In Britain local education authorities (LEAs) have inherited stronger traditions of self-government than in Germany, one result of a more pluralist public system. In Britain and in the United States the emergence of supra-local public school systems has been incremental; in both countries similarity of curricula is still induced indirectly through nationally set examinations, and less through direct bureaucratic prescription. But in Britain dominant reliance on national financing and party control of LEAs serve as nationalizing influences which have caused education policy choices to become polarized on a partisan basis, sometimes between national and local education authorities.

The Distribution of Educational Opportunity

That goals such as social equality and social mobility until recently held low priority in European countries was reflected in their secondary school systems, which were tripartite in being divided into academic, technical, and general schools. The academic high schools educated only a small elite, selected through what in Britain was known as the "eleven-plus" exam, for rating children at the ages of eleven to thirteen on their abilities. Because the school diploma was something of a ticket to a lifetime journey, the distribution of places was important. As was once said about this system: "The man with the third-class ticket who later feels entitled to claim a seat in the first-class carriage will not be admitted, even if he is prepared to pay the difference" (Marshall, p. 113).

This early selection system limited the number of children from lower social strata who achieved social mobility by graduating from elite schools and going on to the university. In America greater equality of educational opportunity encouraged broader class recruitment to the secondary schools and universities, causing these levels of schooling to become more universal.

In recent decades in Europe, left-wing parties such as the Social Democrats have sought to reform both the secondary and university systems. Such impulses have coincided with strong expansions of both sectors, so that the proportion of European youth going on to higher education has begun to approach American levels. Whereas about half of American youth now start college, the proportion in Europe is about one quarter.

Restraints and Innovation in Education

Higher education is an appropriate place to examine potential restraints and innovation in education policy, for the variable length and quality of degree courses present complex choices in resource allocation. American students usually study four years to earn an undergraduate degree, British students three years. Over the last fifty years the length of study in medicine has grown more than that in engineering or social work, reflecting choices by universities and employers about how and where specialized training should be extended. Occasionally, curricular innovations have shortened study time; more frequently they have extended it. But when vastly enlarged numbers of students have coincided with the imposition of fiscal restraints, as has been the case in Europe since the early 1970s, resulting policies have meant restraining educational opportunities for at least part of the student population.

Admission and graduation requirements inevitably color the allocation process. Should "ability" be the sole criterion for allocation, or should allocation be affected by the experience and histories of applicants, or by their capacity to contribute financially to their education? If "ability" must be determined, then by what kinds of previous school or test scores should it be measured? If tuition-paying capacity helps the well-to-do, then should this be balanced by special affirmative action programs for members of "disadvantaged" social or ethnic groups? Should the projected "needs" of labor markets be the chief determinants of how many should study what subject?

POLITICAL CHANGE AND EDUCATION DEVELOPMENT

SCOPE AND THRESHOLDS

Education has long been a concern and responsibility of governments, both local and national. And though education histories tell of no abrupt changes such as the 1946 nationalization of British health care (a takeover that was facilitated by the lack of opposition from the private sector, local governments, and religious groups and that was due partly to special conditions during the preceding wartime period), there have been numerous initiatives for changing and nationalizing school systems. Their implementation, however, has usually been gradually extended over the course of several generations.

Evolution of the Public Systems

In the period of nation building, national governments usually followed several different strategies to increase their influence on private or locally run schools. Two groups who might have resisted governments' actions included educators and church leaders. Educational administrators and teachers often constituted a subsystem whose compliance political leaders could not take for granted. Church leaders also held great power and could retaliate if governments eliminated religious prerogatives in education too abruptly. The way that national governments came increasingly to influence education policy was through financial leverage. (Until the 1960s the United States remained an exception, because conservatives blocked all federal aid to education.) With the extension of citizenship and franchise rights in the nineteenth century, moreover, bringing educational institutions more under public control became a prime national concern.

In Europe, churches allied with certain higher social groups had tightly controlled admissions and curricula. Those seeking to erode this quasi-monopoly tended to pursue a *restrictive* strategy of discouraging church schools if they had access to the governing elites and could convince them that religious educational control was politically undesirable. This strategy was pursued in Prussia in the early 1800s, for example.

A *substitutive strategy* of providing alternative education facilities was better suited to reform groups, which were stronger in economic rather than political resources, and could use these gradually to devalue the existing educational monopoly (Archer, Part One). This strategy was optimally pursued in nineteenth-century Britain by middle-class reformers to undermine the stultifying control held by the Anglican Church over schools and universities. Not politically strong enough to legislate large-scale changes, they instead started their own less traditionally oriented schools, which came to compete with the Anglican-controlled schools. In time these plural networks were incorporated into a directly state-run system, though not until 1870 for primary schools and 1902 for secondary schools.

As major school types came to be *unified* within a state-run system, they gradually dropped fees and became increasingly dependent on public financing. Thus, the terms of financing largely determined the long-term viability of church-run or other private schools. In countries where private schools lost state aid, as in Sweden, they eventually became almost extinct. But in countries where religious schools can still qualify for state support on the same terms as secular schools, as in the Netherlands, they still exist. These European systems do not adhere to a U.S.-style "separation of church and state" doctrine. Partly because of this constraint, the American school development pattern followed the substitutive model with an especially strong decentralist bias. This has led to *both* an unusually large public school system and a comparatively large private school and college sector. Compared to Europe, most American states have remained very permissive in allowing communities and private groups to charter and establish schools and colleges.

In the more centralized European states, unification of the educational system resulted in tight central control, as manifested in detailed curricula which determine what is taught in schools throughout the country. Thus, French ministers of education could tell that at a given hour fifth-grade *lycée* classes everywhere in the country were reading Livy. In the more pluralist systems, unification came about more erratically as a byproduct of public financial support and legal recognition of school diplomas. Thus, around 1900 the British Education Ministry acted more as a central paymaster than as a ministry, a description that remained apt for the U.S. Office of Education even in recent decades.

The process through which education became anchored in the public sphere reflected the different policy priorities of centralized political systems, such as those of France and Prussia-Germany, and of decentralized ones, such as those of Britain and the United States. In the former, the king and the bureaucracy developed earlier and more complete control over national and local administration, whereas in the latter, national control long remained more circumscribed. French and Prussian-German policy consequences included the tendency to go beyond school system unification to *systematization,* through which types of schools and curricula were made uniform; and the tendency to give priority to *university-level* public institutions, since these were expected mainly to train candidates for the extensive bureaucracy. The more circumscribed national control in Britain meant that it long had fewer universities, and in the United States that the school system remained much more heterogeneous.

Public and Private Schools Today

When systematization was attempted early in democratic political systems, as in some American states, the result was "several systems and subsystems, each comprising institutions of varying degrees of publicness . . ." (Cremin, p. 152). There, attempts to set national standards were repeatedly repulsed. A U.S. federal university was proposed in the early 1800s, but its advocates scared off support by suggesting that its graduates then be the only ones eligible for high federal appointive offices. Since then, "no one has challenged the principle of high academic standards across the whole system because no one has proposed it; there have been no common standards, high or otherwise. Indeed, if Europe's slogan for higher education has been 'nothing if not the best', America's has been 'something is better than nothing' " (Trow, in Gans, p. 276).

In most countries public schools serve 90 percent or more of the student population. If one automobile manufacturer were to supply cars for as large a proportion of adult drivers as public schools provide education for a nation's youth, it might be deemed a monopoly. Of course the educational programs vary considerably within the different public institutions, and at some levels there is considerable competition among them.

In the lower school levels, pupils are usually assigned to a particular school near home; but their range of choice increases as they progress to the higher levels. At the university level there is considerable competition among public universities to attract students. In Europe this has been less overt, tied less to varying rates of tuition than to relative attractiveness of courses, programs, degrees, and locations. As in American public universities, European universities cater to students outside their immediate location, but what is not found in Europe are differential tuition levels, with higher charges for out-of-state students, as exists in the United States. Such variations would violate the equality guarantees of national citizenship in a federal system such as West Germany's, even though German universities, like American public universities, are run by the individual states.

Countries differ considerably in the proportions of youth in various age groups attending school full-time. Since most countries require full-time attendance until age 15 or 16, almost all youths in the 6–15 age group are enrolled full-time. But national policies differ considerably in the inducements used to keep students in full-time schooling in the upper secondary levels—the 16–18 age group. Recent statistics show some 77 percent of Americans of this group as full-time students, whereas the corresponding proportions show 56.8 percent for Sweden, 63.1 percent for the Netherlands, and only 35.2 percent for Germany. For most others, the alternative has been employment, usually as apprentices, with part-time schooling. Countries also differ from one another in the proportion of young adults at university-level study during their early twenties. Sweden retained about 15 percent of this age group as students in 1976, compared to 24 percent in the United States, 13.9 percent in Germany, and 7.1 percent in Britain, as Figure 2.1 illustrates.

The relative proportion attending private institutions is comparatively high in the United States and the Netherlands, limited in Germany and Britain, and virtually nil in Sweden. In Europe private institutions become fewer as one ascends the educational ladder, which does not hold for the United States, with its large private university sector. But if we look at direct *public* expenditures on *private* education, the contrast is sharp again. The Netherlands spends about 5 percent of its GNP on such support, whereas Sweden spends only one hundredth of 1 percent of the GNP. For Germany and the United States the proportions are between one tenth and one fifth of 1 percent (OECD 1981, p. 174).

REFORM MODES AND CENTRALIZATION

INSTRUMENTS

The instruments which governments develop to make and implement education policy are determined partly by the governments' own struc-

FIGURE 2.1 AVERAGE ENROLLMENTS BY AGE GROUPS IN SIX NATIONS

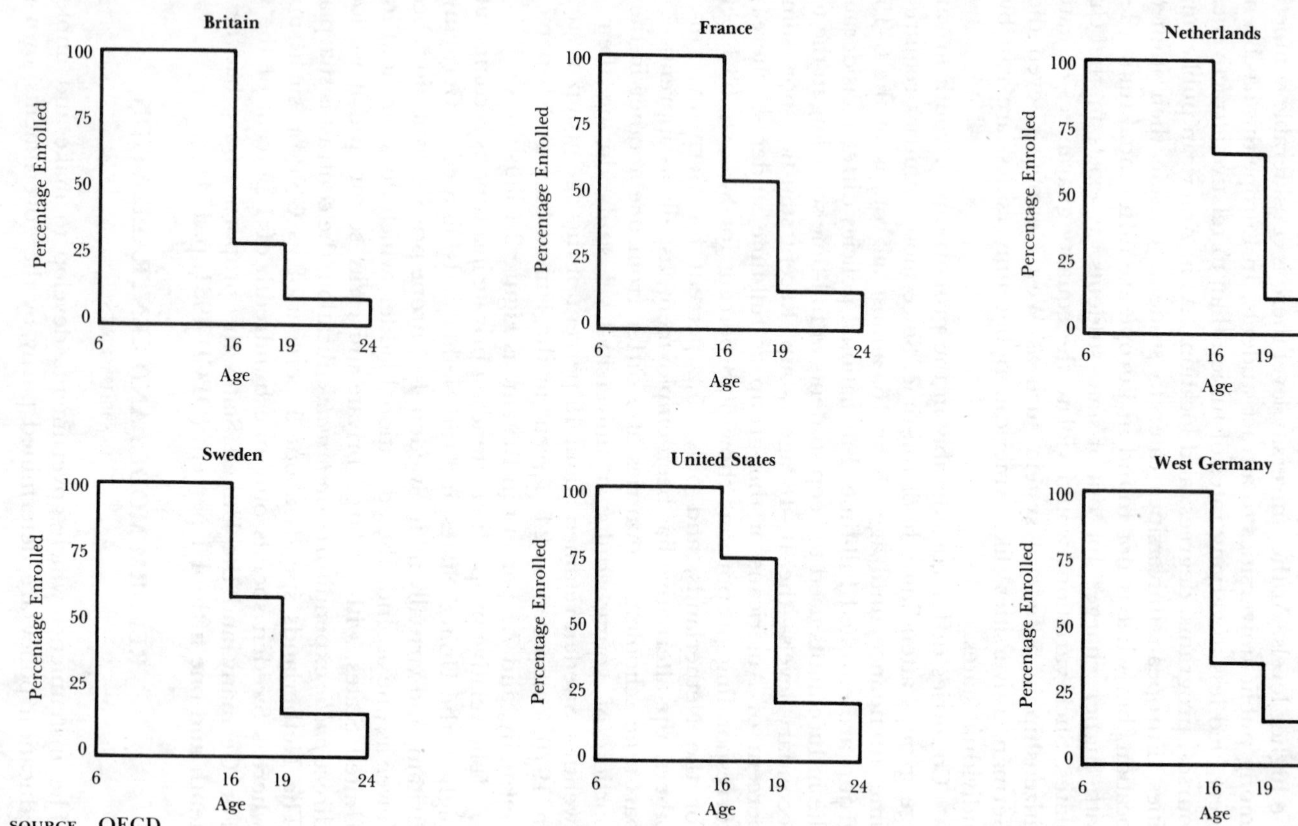

SOURCE OECD

tures and partly by the traditions of state-school relations. A federal system may tend to entrust education policy to local structures, while unitary systems tend toward centralization of power. But within each category we can identify gradations. Thus, among federal systems, the United States has a more decentralized educational system with autonomous local officials, while Germany has greater homogeneity with less local initiative. Among unitary systems, France's education system is more centralized, and Britain's is less centralized.

In centralized political systems educational policy attention is focused predominantly on national legislation and decrees, because implementation problems are minimal. In decentralized systems the relevant decision-making arena is much broader, since it includes state and local, as well as national, government organs. Moreover, some education policy changes are negotiated autonomously within the educational institutions themselves. This has been especially true in the United States, where some crucial changes in curricula and credentialing have been implemented with little reference to general government. Only when education decisions arouse the ire of outside interests do politicians veto school policies. But those who seek to mobilize protest against controversial subjects or textbooks can do so more easily in the American system than in other decentralized systems, since the responsible policy makers tend to be more accessible and more susceptible to pressure (Church).

Even today local policy structures such as U.S. school district boards and British LEAs remain more significant than in more centralized systems. Local officials have power to appoint principals and teachers, which in Bavaria is done by ministry officials in the state capital. French and German systems have no elected school officials at the local level, only appointed ones who generally have civil service tenure. By contrast, American school superintendents usually serve at the pleasure of a locally elected school board, which raises the bulk of school finance through taxes which are not only local, but are usually raised separately from the general municipal revenue. The amount of revenue that school boards receive from state and federal sources varies, but is, on the average, lower than in Europe. As British education has become systematized, it also has to rely more on national financing, currently about 60 percent. The British LEAs differ from American school district boards, however, in that their members are local town councillors, are usually elected on party tickets, and have commitments to national party education platforms.

As public education services expanded in the centralized European systems, choices had to be made about which groups in society should get priority. The central governmental bureaucracy had top priority; next highest priority was given to other political elites; then came lower-status social groups who supported the regime. But as long as resources and institutional capacity were limited, there was a "severe tailing off of educational services to other sections of the population" (Archer, p. 231). Of course this deprivation was in part deliberate, since rulers did not want lower-class children to develop ambitions unsuitable to their future positions in the labor force.

What distinguished American education policy making in the mid-nineteenth to mid-twentieth centuries from that in most European nations was the greater attention paid to demands from the middling parts of the population. School and college opportunities became so plentiful that even some poorer American youth could make their way to some college.

In American society at the turn of the twentieth century, class lines were more fluid than in European society, and formal education credentials permitted more members of working-class families to rise to middle-class status. Sometimes, of course, this mobility was costly to the mobile member's own family, as in the case of a Chicago teamster family around 1900. There a working-class father had

> . . . encouraged his daughter's ambitions to become a school teacher only to find his own self-respect jeopardized: he was forced first to rent a new flat and buy new furniture; he was then expected to entertain his daughter's status-conscious white-collar friends; what is more, as the result of his added expenses the father was forced to send out his younger children to supplement his now inadequate wages; finally, his teacher daughter threatened, at every sign of opposition from her father, to leave her home for more congenial surroundings. (White, p. 178)

In this American social model, family resources were mobilized to enable the individual of working-class background to acquire the status symbols of the middle class.

In Europe the educational opportunities of the working-class were until the most recent decades low and not rising. In fact, the opportunities of workers' children actually decreased in the course of nineteenth-century industrialization. Growing centralized bureaucratic structures then tended to limit access. Whereas middle-class groups found more of the alternatives they sought, the lower-class children lost some scholarship opportunities which had been more available *before* the systems were unified (Kaelble, in Flora and Heidenheimer).

Proponents of educational reforms often strengthen their positions by relating their structural or curricular goals to broad political ideologies. In earlier European periods dominant ideologies were perfectly consonant with the idea that public universities should serve the interests of the ruling class, but in the present era strong ideological support can be marshaled for arguments that "equality of opportunity" shall also extend, or even especially extend, to the lower classes. Attacks on selective secondary schools have recently been more effective when used with socialist and other egalitarian ideology, for example, to show how retaining Latin as a prerequisite for university study perpetuated the bias in favor of admitting the children of social elites.

That European leftist parties long did not give education policy much attention was due in good part to the difficulty of converting parliamentary influence into policy change. For European universities and schools were shielded from direct influence by strong traditions of both professional and bureaucratic autonomy. Thus, European secondary schools remained very distinct from the primary schools, because they too employed admissions barriers that kept out children without the "right" kind of cultural background.

Political Change from Within and Without

It is fruitful to examine comparatively how similar changes—such as the adoption of new subjects in the curriculum, or the integration of several kinds of secondary schools—may come to be initiated in several different systems. For example, the *internal initiation* of school policy change—by educators, without reference to political policy makers—takes on a wider scope in decentralized systems. Extra-educational interests such as local businesses or union groups may also be more successful in influencing policy in decentralized systems. Appeals to ideology to promote or oppose change, on the other hand, tend to be weaker in decentralized systems and to come later than they might in centralized or unitary systems. (Some of these concepts are developed in Archer, Part One.)

The initiation of policy change from within the education sector is more feasible in *decentralized* systems because the educators are usually more autonomous and can draw on their own financial resources. The public education sector in these systems usually developed through the integration of regionally and/or religiously diverse local school types. Professional educators benefit from this residual pluralism in that they retain important powers outside the central bureaucracy. Consequently, a new type of curriculum or instructional technique can be tried in a few schools or school systems, then generalized to others without reference to central government. Education leaders can ally with philanthropists, leading to such phenomena as the Carnegie Foundation's tremendous influence on American higher education (Selden). These arrangements have no equivalent in the centralized Continental systems. There teacher organizations are important mainly in negotiating with the central bureaucrats, but they are less able to generate and filter demands from parents, business people, and other consumer groups so as to help structure policy alternatives (Ringer).

Educational change in *centralized* systems arises more from negotiations among political, bureaucratic, and social elites at the national level. For example, reduction, then termination, of public subsidies to private schools in Scandinavia occurred largely as a result of pressure exerted by Social Democrats during the inter-war period. This campaign not only led to the virtual elimination of private schools (in contrast to Britain), but also was followed up in the 1950s with efforts to combine parallel secondary schools into a more homogeneous system of comprehensive schools.

Some examples are found in university-level policy. When France urgently moved to reform its university system after the student revolt of 1968, initiatives also centered on the national Ministry of Education. Overnight, the University of Paris became the University of Paris IV and the University of Paris VI, as the huge parent institution was split up by administrative fiat. Thus, one advantage of centralization—speed—is illustrated by this case. Never could this have occurred at the University of London, for the constituent colleges of that university had remained freer to run their own affairs. Public universities in the decentralized American system provide yet another contrast: There the upgrading of former teachers' colleges could force a dominant state university, such as the University of Wisconsin at Madison, to share *its* name with the newer institutions.

Educational change may sometimes involve conflict between different segments of the profession, as when in 1970 German primary school teachers sought to narrow their status differentials from secondary school teachers. In 1970, when the education ministers of the *Länder* (the German states) sought to introduce a unified scheme for teacher education, the secondary teachers' organization rejected it, insisting that upper secondary teachers continue to study at least ten semesters at the university, while primary teachers be trained at teachers' colleges for only six semesters. In addition to enlisting allies from other professional unions affiliated with the civil servants' federation, they mobilized middle-class parents' associations to defend the quality of *Gymnasium* education. Building on these alliances, the secondary teachers were able to defeat reform proposals, even while their colleagues in Sweden were losing similar struggles. There the opponents were less willing to exclude themselves from the ongoing reform negotiations by taking an explicitly opposing stand (Heidenheimer, 1974).

Policy Choices Between Center and Periphery

An observer of the turbulent education controversies of the early 1970s would have been much better able to follow German developments from Bonn than American ones from Washington. Why was this so, since both federal governments played only secondary policy roles to those of the states? It is because German education politics is both federal *and* centralized. The German Land education ministers' battles were fought out largely on a party basis, with Land ministers confronting one another directly in the national parliament (*Bundesrat*) and the Council of Education Ministers. Changes made in Hamburg schools concerned Bavarians much more than changes made in Georgia concerned Minnesotans. Whether Bavaria would accept the school diplomas from Hamburg concerned the politicians in Bonn much more than any such conflict between regional accrediting associations troubled officials in Washington.

In decentralized systems such as the American, change occurs all the time; it is constantly initiated, imitated, modified, reversed, and counteracted at some level in some school district, state, or national arena. Much of it is monitored in Washington by only one bureau of the Department of Education. Many of the changes in curriculum, teacher training, and accreditation, are negotiated autonomously in one of numerous commissions, which might meet in Cincinnati one year and in New Orleans the next. Not all proposals even have to be passed up to the national level—only those that ask for federal funding or require federal monitoring. In fact, the issues where federal involvement has made headlines—whether concerning free lunches or school busing—have often been quite marginal to the educational enterprise as such. The appearance of federal marshals to force the acceptance of black students at the University of Alabama was seen as high drama, but most decisions affecting access of socio-economic groups are incremental. A decade later some committee may study the results, and outsiders are often quite surprised to see the trends that have materialized.

In systems which are both centralized and unitary, such as the French, demands for change accumulate over a longer time while awaiting centralized attention and approval. Since all negotiations involve the all-powerful national ministries, the negotiation process is more distinctively patterned. If teachers in Lyons have salary or curriculum grievances, they have to ask their union representatives to negotiate with bureaucrats in Paris, although this has begun to change in the 1980s. In the German federal system they would go to the Land capital. But if the teachers in one Land get many more concessions than those in another, the issue will soon be raised by a national union or a politician. Uniformity of standards gets much more support in Europe than in the United States, where attempts to require states to equalize funding, so that per-capita school revenue becomes more equal, have not gotten too far, even within one state. As for inter-state differences: If Scarsdale wants to pay its teachers three times as much as El Paso pays, it is perfectly free to do so.

EQUALIZING SECONDARY SCHOOL OPPORTUNITIES

DISTRIBUTION

Questions of distributional equity in education policy are closely linked to practices determining when and how pupils shall be assigned to schools or programs having different curricula and prestige. Until recently, European students at the secondary level were generally differentiated by tests at about age eleven, with those assigned to the more selective schools receiving a much greater share of teaching and other resources. In practice very few children from working-class families have been assigned to these schools, and in the 1950s some European governments began to reform the prevailing tripartite structure of academic, technical, and general schools in order to provide equal educational opportunity for all children. In this section we will examine the factors that determine the success of similar parties in carrying through reforms intended to redistribute such opportunity.

The first country to initiate such a reform was Sweden, where the Social Democrats "comprehensivized" secondary schools. Comprehensivization means that all students are enrolled together in one school, which is created by merging previously distinct school types. The Swedes were able to implement this reform fairly rapidly, for theirs is a centralized system where the Social Democrats held continuous control of national power. But what were the outcomes of similar implementation drives in countries with different distributions of political control at either the national or the sub-national level? To answer this question we will compare similar initiatives in Britain, which has a unitary system with strong decentralist traditions in education, with those in Germany, where component states exercise stronger education policy powers than either the national or the local government.

Introducing Comprehensive Schools

Just as they had in Sweden, the Social Democrats and Labour supported reform in Britain and Germany, endorsing comprehensivization as a means of overcoming class barriers to educational opportunities and of postponing school selection decisions. Children from their working-class following came from families with lower cultural attainments than did middle-class children. Thus the Social Democrats reasoned that if selection were to take place at age eighteen rather than age eleven, the children from lower social strata would then have had more formal education that might compensate for their family background. Most reformers also thought that keeping youth together in the same classes and schools was socially beneficial. Pro-selection parents disagreed, feeling strong attachments to the selective schools (called *grammar schools* in Britain and *Gymnasien* in Germany), which challenged students with a more demanding curriculum. In time the issue became party-polarized, with the British Conservatives and the German Christian Democrats opposing the comprehensive schools and defending the separate school types. Prior decisions about the location of education powers, as in the West German Constitution of 1949 (which gave these to the Länder), greatly influenced the success of their resistance.

It is important to note that in its initial phases, comprehensivization had the backing of the Social Democrats in Sweden and Germany, whereas it occurred in Britain without apparent partisan promotion. From the 1930s through the 1950s, initiation from the British educational professions themselves led to the establishment of some comprehensive schools. "Comprehensive education began as an ideal within the teaching profession, mainly activated by socialist thought. . . . It did not gain the active support of the main radical party except in formal terms in the 1951 and 1959 Labour party statements" (Kogan, p. 222). Some comprehensives were started in London, a Labour party stronghold, but many more were initiated in rural counties. Although the 1944 Education Act gave the central government potential power to promote them, comprehensives remained few during the Labour government of 1945–1951. Hence, in the 1950s, the "local assault on central tripartism" emanated from rural counties such as Leicestershire, where one model school received more than one thousand outside visits in two years. The result was that insiders became convinced that the system was workable and "influential educationalists from outside" perceived that the model could be generalized throughout the system (Kogan). The Conservative-controlled British ministry tolerated local initiatives, with the result that by 1964 LEAs were educating about 8 percent of secondary students in comprehensive schools. When the Labour party returned to national power in 1964, the ratio of comprehensive schools to grammar schools was about 1:7. By 1971 the ratio of comprehensive schools to selective schools was only 1:20, with most of the extant 100 schools in only 2 Länder.

In Sweden and Germany the experimental phase was initiated with more direct support from national or state bureaucracies. Sweden not only started earliest, but added new schools most quickly, so that after a decade of experimentation half of all lower secondary students were in comprehensives, which in 1961 became the sole authorized model. German attempts to initiate comprehensives were squelched in the 1950s, and it was not until the 1960s that the Social Democratic government of the Land of Hessen introduced them. As in Britain, this occurred primarily in rural areas, where their establishment did not threaten selective schools. Other German Länder did not follow the Hessen lead, however, as other British LEAs had followed the Leicestershire example in the 1950s.

Although both the British and the German political systems were dualistic, in that the national government shared policy-making power with sub-national governments, the diffusion pattern we have sketched illuminates some crucial differences. In Britain neither the national ministry nor the LEAs had as large a share of the education decision-making power as did the Länder in Germany. If a Land was determined to resist an innovation, the countervailing influence of either the higher national, or the lower communal, organs was very limited. But since in the mid-1960s even conservatives recognized that Germany had lagged in educational provision, a number of structural adjustments were made. One of these was a constitutional change which gave the federal government some explicit influence in education policy. Also came the establishment of the *Bildungsrat,* a council of educational researchers and administrators set up to coordinate reform impulses, and of the Federal-State Commission for Educational Planning (BLK), through which politicians and bureaucrats were supposed to coordinate various government plans and produce periodic Overall Education Plans spelling out the projected policy developments.

Given these circumstances, we might expect different strategies of pro-reform Labour and Social Democratic leaders when they came to power in Britain in 1964 and in Germany in 1969. Would they emphasize new legislation? What variety of comprehensive school models would they project? Would they highlight or downplay the comprehensive school issues in relation to the many other policies on the governmental agenda, for example, the Educational Priority Areas in Britain (Banting, Chapter Four)?

The British Labour government might have used its parliamentary majority to pass legislation obliging LEAs to follow ministry directives on school reorganization, but in fact new legislation was not adopted until twelve years later. Instead the Education Ministry was asked to send the LEAs an administrative directive, called Circular 10/65, urging them to submit plans for comprehensivizing their schools. In Germany the Social Democratic Party (SPD) placed education reform near the top of the party platform on which Willy Brandt became chancellor in 1969. At that point school issues were controversial and attracting great interest, and so ambitious SPD deputies vied to get on the *Bundestag* education committee. They had to cool their heels, however, for SPD and Christian Democratic Union (CDU) education ministers were to wrangle in the BLK and other forums for four years before finally producing the Overall Education Plan for parliament and the governments. By its rules decisions required the approval of nine of the twelve ministers and were binding only on those Länder that had approved.

Decision makers in both Britain and Germany had to consider which curricular, class, and physical characteristics to adopt for their comprehensive school models. The British authors of Circular 10/65 followed the incrementalist pattern of their predecessors. Rather than prescribing *one* model, they requested LEAs to select among six different school types

FIGURE 2.2 THE BRITISH EDUCATIONAL SYSTEM

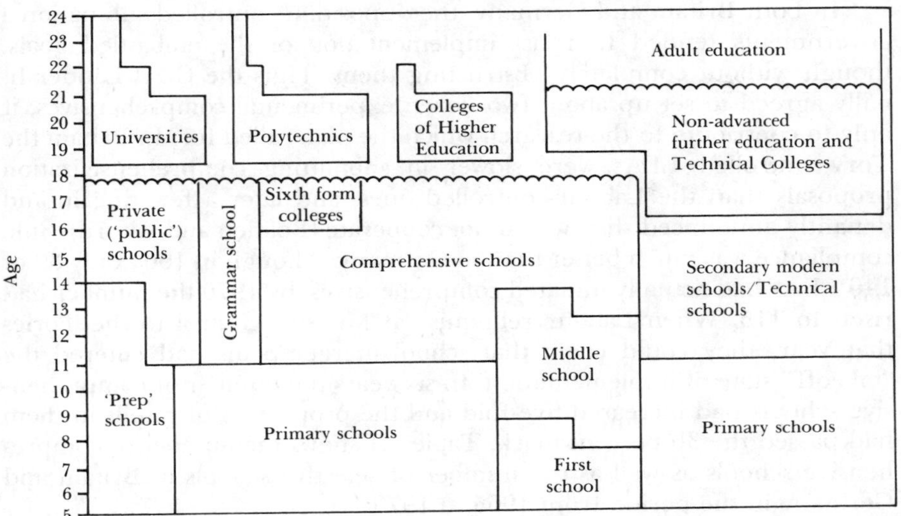

which already existed among the thirty-nine LEAs which were operating comprehensive schools. These included: (1) An "all-through" comprehensive school, for ages eleven to eighteen, where students study all seven years at the same school. This was the model favored by most Labour activists and given special endorsement in the circular. (2) Several lower-tier and upper-tier plans, based on a division like that between American junior and senior high schools. (3) Several plans for age groupings at either the lower (ages nine to thirteen) or the upper (ages sixteen to eighteen) end of the secondary range. Figure 2.2 shows the various types of schools in the British system.

In the corresponding German negotiations the SDP and FDP (Free Democratic party) majority in the BLK had to try to get the agreement of the CDU minority to the crucial specifications. In addition to calling for a fifth- and sixth-grade observation stage, during which student assignments would remain in flux, their model called for an "integrated" comprehensive school (where students take similar courses and are assigned to different classes only with respect to their differing abilities in a given subject) and for less or later differentiation in tracking and curricula than in some British models. They asked for large-scale financing to make possible hundreds of comprehensives during the experimental phase. The CDU Länder resisted all these demands, but did finally agree to establish some comprehensive schools as long as plans included both the "integrated" model, and a more permissive "cooperative" comprehensive model, which provided for three secondary tracks within one school.

Local Resistance to Reform

In both Britain and Germany, the opposition-controlled sub-national governments tended to resist implementation of the embattled goals, though without completely obstructing them. Thus the CDU Länder finally agreed to set up about two dozen experimental comprehensives, if only to contribute to the research which the plan called for. In Britain the Tory-controlled LEAs were slower in submitting comprehensivization proposals than the Labour-controlled ones, and later a few dug in and defiantly announced they would not cooperate (Boaden and Alford). Still, compliance was much better than in Germany. Though in 1964 only 39 of 146 LEAs had actually initiated comprehensives, by 1970 the number had risen to 115. When Labour relinquished Ministry control to the Tories that year, they could claim that school merger plans had entered the "takeoff" state of implementation. In six years the number of comprehensive schools had increased five-fold and the proportion of pupils in them had passed the 30 percent mark. Table 2.1 shows the number of comprehensive schools as well as the number of selective schools in Britain and Germany in the period from 1965 to 1979.

In Germany a very conditional commitment to comprehensive school experimentation had been made by the time Willy Brandt left office in 1974, and 183 comprehensive schools had been established. But when the big push of the 1969–1972 period failed to win a breakthrough, much of the political impetus diminished. Educational goals became embattled within the SPD itself, their priority on the party agenda was diminished, and the party was unable to make a potentially strong issue pay off in Land-level elections. Although at one point in the early 1970s the SPD had marked education as the policy area which was to get the largest budget increase in the decade, their own finance ministers did not follow through on this commitment when they actually made up their budgets.

TABLE 2.1 British and German Secondary Schools, 1965–1979

	1965	1970	1975	1977	1979
Selective Schools					
Britain (Grammar Schools)	1180	975	547	390	254
West Germany (*Gymnasien*)	1926	2311	2415	2448	2464
Comprehensive Schools					
Britain	221	1016	2398	2875	3203
West Germany	—	—	216	221	242

NOTE The data for Britain include England and Wales.

SOURCES *Statistiches Jahrbuch der BRD, 1979* (Stuttgart, 1979), p. 338.
"Schools in England and Wales," *Statistics of Education, 1979,* Vol. 1 (London: HMSO, 1979).

Close association with the comprehensivization issue had different effects on the political fortunes of leading Swedish and German politicians. In Sweden the effect was apparently very positive, insofar as the two education ministers most closely identified with the reform, Tage Erlander and Olof Palme, subsequently became both leaders of their party and prime ministers. In Germany, on the other hand, none of the federal or Land ministers has since risen to high party or government office, and some who have remained ministers (Hildegard Hamm-Brücher, Klaus von Dohnanyi, and Rainer Jochimsen) have shifted laterally to quite different policy responsibilities.

To understand fully how these distributional choices were formulated, we must clarify patterns of party control at the national and subnational levels. In Sweden the Social Democrats led the national and most local governments throughout the decades of educational reform, from 1950 to 1970, and by 1976, when the non-Socialists won national government power for the first time since 1932, almost all education decisions had been made. In Germany, for the fifteen-year period from 1966 to 1981, all the Länder except for Lower Saxony remained in control of the same party or party coalition. In Britain, by contrast, there was more frequent shift of party control not only at the national, but also at the local level. Thus many of the 146 LEAs shifted from Labour to Conservative, or vice versa, at least once. Since the British tended to use local elections to voice protest against the party in national power, many local areas had a much more checkered party control than did the German states. Surprisingly, this tended to favor progress toward comprehensivization, because it discouraged Tory attempts to undo what Labour had promoted during its phases in power.

The greater significance of private school alternatives in Britain, compared to Germany, also eased the movement toward comprehensives. Margaret Thatcher was the first Conservative prime minister to have graduated from a grammar school; all her predecessors had been educated at private independent schools (there called *public schools*), most of them at the especially prestigious schools, such as Eton, Harrow, and Winchester, which have for generations educated the sprigs of the English upper and upper middle classes. Even the 1979 Thatcher cabinet included only two grammar school graduates among a majority of private school graduates. This pattern might be contrasted with the CDU leadership, who had all graduated from public institutions, since Germany has only a very few prestigious private secondary schools. Indeed, it has been observed that the Conservative leadership had an easier time acquiescing in the movement to make the grammar schools less elite, since members of their social strata could after all afford more selective education for their children outside the public sector.

When Edward Heath, leading the Conservatives back into power in

1970, appointed Margaret Thatcher to the Education Ministry, he did not realize that he was giving national exposure to the woman who would take the Conservative party leadership away from him five years later. Indeed if Maggie Thatcher came to win the hearts of the right-wing Tories, it was not because she reversed the ongoing comprehensivization patterns. She did replace her predecessor's Circular 10/65 with her own Circular 10/70, which essentially directed the LEAs to submit comprehensivization proposals if they wanted to, but not to feel compelled to do so. She also scored some points in the private v. public question by cutting back on free school milk and meals. But otherwise she did not try to block any of the pending school reorganization proposals or to veto the additional ones that came to the Ministry from the LEAs (where Labour regained control in the 1972 local council elections). Consequently the proportion of secondary students in comprehensive schools did not decrease during the 1970–74 Tory period in government, but actually increased from one third to over one half (Bellaby, p. 11).

During the late 1970s an anti-comprehensive backlash spread through the conservative parties in both Britain and Germany as a result of economic change. The energy crisis of 1973–1974 ushered in a period of low growth, causing the skilled job market to stagnate, which in turn affected the expectations parents held for their children's future. Middle-class parents became less willing to yield accustomed education advantages, and right-wing politicians built on these fears to launch more strident attacks on the "leveling" strategies they attributed to their leftist opponents. In Germany this produced a decline in the number of comprehensive schools to be founded to only about ten a year during the 1974–1978 period; and in Britain it caused Conservative "hold-out" LEAs to become bolder in their defiance of the Ministry.

Thatcher's Labour successor in the Education Ministry replaced her order with his own Circular 4/74, which gave the twenty-four hold-out LEAs until the end of 1974 to submit reorganization proposals. When some still refused to do so, Labour pushed for parliamentary endorsement through the Education Act of 1976, which clearly asserted the LEAs' obligation to implement comprehensivization. It also forbade LEAs to use public funds to pay for some students' education in selective private schools. This move was aimed at the private, but publicly subsidized, "direct grant" schools which had helped to perpetuate the problem of "creaming-off" talented students (Bellaby, p. 15).

It was at this point in both Britain and Germany that the courts entered the thicket, with different consequences in each nation. In Hessen middle-class parents turned to the courts to argue that the Constitution guaranteed them a choice of sending their children to any of the various school types, including the selective one. The courts affirmed this right, and thus handicapped the state's power to merge Gymnasien out of existence. Similar court appeals in Britain were defeated, however, so that the LEAs gradually reduced the number of situations where parents were faced with a difficult choice between sending their children to selective or comprehensive schools. During Labour's 1974–1979 period in office, the number of LEAs that had fully implemented comprehensivization grew greatly.

In Germany the numerous coordinating structures that had been bridging intergovernmental differences in education came to be severely tested in the late 1970s. The Bildungsrat, which had outlined the educational reforms, was abolished at the behest of the CDU Länder. Then, in 1978 the federal government provoked strong CDU reaction by issuing its Report on Structural Problems in the Federal Education System and proposing that questions of the mutual acceptance of educational degrees be transferred to the jurisdiction of the federal government. Since this would have required a two-thirds majority of both chambers, it of course had no chance of passage (Bericht). The BLK was unable to compromise the positions and accomplished little other than issuing a 1979 report that listed the opposing views. The CDU Länder held that experience did not support proposals to add the comprehensives as a regular school type, while the SPD Länder pointed to both German and foreign experiences as justification for just such a step. Even this "agreement to differ" was undermined when Franz-Josef Strauss asserted that Bavaria would not tolerate its acceptance as a regular school type anywhere else in the nation. When Hamburg did so anyway, it risked the possibility that its graduates might not be accepted into Bavarian universities. The determination of Bavaria and Baden-Württemberg to use their veto authority to the utmost alienated even their fellow CDU education ministers, and the education minister of Lower Saxony resigned from the chairmanship of the BLK because of their intransigence. In addition, the more progressive CDU trade union and youth group leaders spoke out against their party's position.

In this atmosphere the Länder research findings on the functioning of comprehensive schools which were supposed to be released in the late 1970s came to be fodder for partisan exploitation. The ministries allowed only commissioned researchers into the schools. Though researchers in the SPD-ruled North Rhine-Westphalia attested that comprehensive schools worked well and recommended that they be legally adopted as one standard school type, the CDU opposition encouraged a competing study which claimed that students who passed the final exams (*Abitur*) did better if they attended the Gymnasien rather than the comprehensive schools. Still others pointed out that only 18 percent of the pupils in the differentiated schools completed the upper secondary level, compared to 27 percent in the comprehensives. Electoral outcomes seesawed: When teachers and parents managed to initiate referenda with education as the

FIGURE 2.3 PROPORTION OF PUPILS ENROLLED IN COMPREHENSIVIZED SCHOOLS, 1950–1980

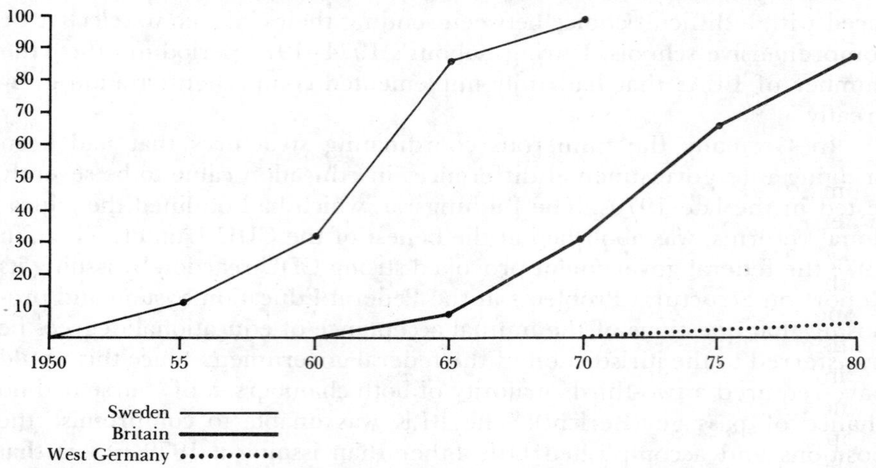

SOURCES *Utbildningsstatistisk arsbok, 1978* (Stockholm: Central Statistical Bureau, 1978). *Statistiches Jahrbuch der BRD, 1979* (Stuttgart, 1979), p. 338. "Schools in England and Wales," *Statistics of Education, 1979,* Vol. 1 (London: HMSO, 1979).

sole issue, they sometimes halted reform proposals, but in general elections they were less successful.

Education and Parties' Reform Capacity

Clearly, the three countries were able to adopt and implement the comprehensive school model at different rates. Sweden was quickest to enact reforms, followed by Britain and then by Germany. Figure 2.3 compares developments in the three countries over the decades following similar take-off points. If Britain did not fully match the Swedish reform pace, it has come reasonably close to approaching it: Fifteen years after reform proposals were first placed on the national agenda, about two thirds of the students were in comprehensives, and after twenty-five years the proportion can be expected to lie between 85 and 90 percent. Germany's implementation pace, however, was much slower than Britain's: After fifteen years only about 2 percent of German secondary pupils were in comprehensives. Moreover, while most British grammar schools were converted to comprehensives in the 1970s, the number of German Gymnasien showed no decrease, indicating that the 242 comprehensives there at the end of the decade were newly established schools.

The incremental strategy employed in Britain, with its tolerance of six alternative schemes minimizing the initial adjustments which LEAs had to make, helps explain the more rapid progress there. It also raises questions on the comparability of the data, for adherents of tighter definitions would accept only some of the six types as genuinely comprehensive. Still, these reservations do not cloud the basic pattern.

To refine our conclusions about party influence on education reforms, we must sharpen our understanding of differences in *context.* In making the distributional choice of whether to comprehensivize or not, what mattered ultimately were the instruments available to national governments to press comprehensivization, and the power allowed to local governments to resist it. The obstacle presented by the great Land powers in Germany's federal system was stronger than the potential obstruction by the British LEAs. Equally important, in terms of the cyclical nature of support for education reform, were factors of *timing.* It was easier for British reformers to marshal ideological support during the affluent and optimistic 1960s than it was for the Germans ten or fifteen years later. Sometimes nations may enjoy certain "advantages of lateness" in policy adoption, but in the pessimistic late 1970s it was the opponents of comprehensive reform who managed to pinpoint and capitalize on the shortcomings of comprehensivization in pioneering countries such as Sweden.

What do these comparisons suggest about the capacity of political parties to carry through education reforms like comprehensivization? The Swedish case illustrates that under optimal conditions a party such as the Social Democrats can provide leadership—for allies in the trade unions, in the bureaucracy, and in other parties—to carry reform through thoroughly in a period of economic growth. In Sweden as well as in Britain, the Left had the advantage of operating within a unitary system, which meant that the national party leaderships held strong positions. Thus, even though local British Conservatives could delay LEA introduction, they did not control arenas which could compete for national attention in the way that the German CDU education ministers did. Moreover, the incremental strategy allowed the center to wear down the hold-out LEAs by waiting until local opponents declined in electoral or financial support. As the number of hold-out LEAs diminished, the Conservative national party tended to lose interest and the issue dropped on the national agenda. And though after their 1979 victory Convervatives changed the law to restore local option, they offered no encouragement to LEAs who sought to reconvert their comprehensives to the tripartite system.

In Germany entrenched CDU power in several Länder prevented the Social Democrats from making any measurable progress, even though they had held national government control from 1969. During this period they failed to win control of any of the CDU-controlled Länder, and toward its end they lost control to the CDU of many city governments as well. Any prospects that they might enter the "take-off" phase of implementation later in the 1980s dimmed. Moreover, the CDU-led Länder did not stop the reformers with a stand-pat position, but instead they met the demand for greater educational opportunity by opening wider the Gymnasium door, so that a larger proportion of students was encouraged to enter these now somewhat less selective schools. Thus, even where their diffusion was most limited, the comprehensive schools exerted pressures which made the remainder of the tripartite system more accessible.

UNIVERSITY PROGRAMS AND SOCIETAL NEEDS

RESTRAINTS AND INNOVATION

From the 1960s, European universities were inundated by greater numbers of secondary school graduates and thus faced questions of how to alter admissions and graduation requirements and, later, how to stretch reduced resources to cover vastly expanded functions. In the name of university reform, all manner of innovations were tried—ranging from the leveling of admission requirements to the imposition of tight quotas even at the department level. Novel allocation mechanisms ranged from centralized national student assignment agencies, as in Sweden and Germany, to the adoption of lottery-based admissions procedures in the Netherlands. At issue were questions also controversial on American campuses—for example, how much admission criteria for medical schools should differ from those for other professional schools. Where high school graduates could enter any faculty of their choice, as in Italy, some faculties were immensely overloaded. But where bureaucrats sought to stem student flow with "limited capacity" arguments, their rules were sometimes invalidated by the courts as infringements on students' rights to train for a profession of their choice (Merritt).

Besides the rapid growth, university problems in Europe were aggravated by the absence of the hierarchies of institutional prestige and tuition levels which served to balance student demand with institutional capacity in the United States. In order to rationalize their selection procedures European authorities tried to balance student preferences against societal goals and needs. To promote egalitarian recruitment the Swedes counted work experience in with high school grades in the admissions process. Societal needs could most persuasively be defined in terms of the anticipated future needs for different kinds of skilled labor power. Official brochures in effect advised students to select university subjects less with reference to their high school academic experiences, and more in accord with suitable career opportunities.

One context for choices was the question of how predominantly and directly the anticipated labor market requirements should determine the kinds of university programs governments would finance with tax funds. Were the humanities and liberal arts becoming a luxury which less prosperous societies could no longer afford? If so, then perhaps more American students would find themselves funneled more into professional and vocational programs directly from high school.

FIGURE 2.4 SCIENCE ACHIEVEMENT SCORES (IEA)

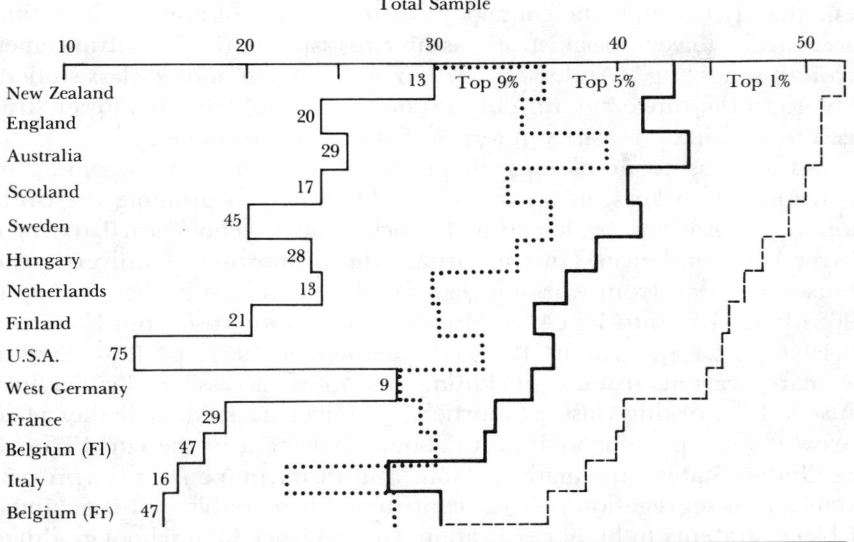

Mean Science Scores for Total Samples of Pre-University Students and for the Top 9, 5, and 1 percent respectively. For each country the size of the pre-university population as a percentage of the total relevant age group has been indicated.

SOURCE Husén et al. (1973), p. 146.

Another big question was whether broadening access to previously selective institutions lowered the achievements of the most able students. If that were indeed the case then the more equality-oriented countries might risk losing out in the international competition to produce innovative ideas and products.

Critics of broadened access to higher education have little difficulty finding data showing that standards of learning have been declining. *Average* test scores can be expected to drop drastically as the less gifted students are encouraged to stay longer in high school and the university. The key question is whether the most able 1 or 5 percent achieve more highly in countries that have retained selective school structures. Figure 2.4 shows the *mean* scores in science tests for high school seniors to be lower in countries like the United States and Sweden, where larger proportions of an age group reach the senior year, than in more selective countries such as Germany. But if we look at the average grades of the top 1 and 5 percent scorers, then we find little evidence that the achievement of the most able is held down in countries that distribute education opportunities more generously (Husén).

How do working-class students become the first in their families to reach the university? According to those who stress motivations, it happens mainly through the contagious diffusion of aspirations. "Over time, successively lower social strata assimilate aspirations for advancement through schooling" (Anderson 1979, p. 413). While middle-class students may go to the university for cultural motives, those from the lower strata need to anticipate rewards in terms of status improvement.

As long as economic growth promised to create more openings for professional workers, governments could choose to promote the contagion of aspirations by lowering financial and psychological barriers to university attendance. Thus in Britain the proportion of university students who came from working-class families increased in the prosperous 1960s from 1 in 6 to 1 in 4, and in Sweden the ratio rose from 15 percent in 1956 to 21 percent in 1969 (Heidenheimer 1977, p. 426). Even in Germany various routes—including the more accessible Gymnasien—caused the working-class proportion of university student bodies to increase from 4 percent in 1952 to about 15 percent in the late 1970s. In the United States "affirmative action," meant to compensate for previous exclusion or segregation policies, contributed to a doubling of the number of black students in higher education. Indeed black high school graduates tended to become *more* likely to attend college than whites.

But often the fit between the universities' curricular offerings and the expectations of a changed student clientele was poor. The new students often sought courses teaching skills which would be directly rewarded in the labor market and avoided those in the humanities and other cultural areas. Colleges with rapid shifts from middle-class to working-class and ethnic student bodies saw extreme consequences. At New York's City College, for example, in 1981 the department chairman of Germanic and Slavic languages taught neither Russian nor German, but courses in English as a second language.

In European universities somewhat different conflicts developed between the pressure of student numbers, the anticipated needs of the labor market, and the content and structure of university curricula. In centralized systems such as Sweden's, bureaucrats went furthest in rationalizing university systems against the strong opposition of many students and professors; a radical reorganization of universities has mandated that all course offerings be related to programs leading into the various labor markets. For instance, courses in Latin could be accommodated if they promised to be of use to medical students. And, to reduce the danger of large numbers of unemployed graduates, the universities in the 1980s extended *numerus clausus* to admissions policies; that is, they set national admissions quotas for the various fields of study and admitted only as many students as planners projected could be utilized in the foreseeable future. Unfortunately, this policy taxed the forecasting ability of planners almost as much as it did the adaptability of students and professors (Premfors, Chapter Six).

With student numbers quadrupling in two decades, Europe found itself in an era of mass higher education much more suddenly than had been the case in America. Table 2.2 shows the comparative growth figures. The centralized Continental systems found it difficult to replicate the somewhat subtle American selection mechanisms through which students are not shunted in or out of higher education, but instead are channeled into institutions of varying quality when they enroll in colleges and graduate or professional schools. The highly systematized Continental systems lack the flexibility which makes these informal rankings possible, and hence their bureaucrats were forced to devise generalized rules to deal with problems of student selection. At one extreme was the rule of "open admission" to any university faculty for students who had secondary certificates; at the other was a system of assigning first-year places in all faculties solely according to computerized rankings of high school grades. Operating close to the latter model, central Swedish and German assignment bureaus in Stockholm and Dortmund allocate students to particular departments, often in universities other than the ones students have actually requested (Teichler). To study their subject in a university of their preference, students must advertise to exchange places with someone with the opposite preference (if there is one).

Centralized student assignment systems presume of course that the grade/test ranking criteria further meritocratic equity in terms of societal needs. But is society best served if the high achievers apply disproportionately to high prestige professional schools, leaving to other departments only those with lower scores? In an era of declining research funds, recruitment of the best students to basic science disciplines worsens relative to applied fields. Looking at employment prospects, many abler students

TABLE 2.2 Annual Percentage Increase in Full-time Students in Higher Education, 1955–1975

	1860–1960	1955–60	1960–65	1965–70	1970–75
Britain	2.7	7.0	8.2	6.8	2.3
France	3.2	6.1	13.2	9.8	5.3
Netherlands	3.7	9.0	8.6	11.0	4.9
Sweden	1.8	7.1	14.2	12.7	−0.7
United States		6.9	10.8	10.8	6.3
West Germany	2.9	9.3	8.2	7.0	17.4

SOURCES Rune Premfors, *The Politics of Higher Education in Comparative Perspective* (Stockholm, 1980), p. 100.
E. G. Edwards, "An Analytical View of Trends in Student Enrollments in Western Europe," *Higher Education in Europe* (July, 1981), p. 47.

decide that they cannot "afford" to study biology or physics and opt for medicine or engineering instead (Neave, p. 148).

Are health care needs really best served if most medical students are selected from the top 5 percent of high school graduates? Will those high achievers make good primary care physicians, if that is what is going to be needed most ten years later? Some countries think the answer is no and have therefore chosen to allocate medical school places by lottery. The Netherlands operates a weighted system under which all applicants who pass a moderate grade threshold in specified subjects participate in the lottery, but those with higher grades have more entry forms put in for them (Karstanje, in Neave, p. 205). Germany in 1980 also began to allocate some of its medical school places in this way, responding to a suggestion from its constitutional court that such a selection method might serve to extend the protection of the constitutional right to choose freely a profession or place of training (Merritt).

Sometimes when education ministries try to nudge university professors and students toward the apparent needs of the labor market or of society, the quality of education declines. In 1976 the French tried a variant of the Swedish approach by passing a decree aimed at revamping university curricula so that all programs would have clear outlets into the labor market. Since no additional funds were provided, however, the universities felt pressured to close down those programs that were of less vocational relevance. This decree led to the largest French student demonstration since 1968; in contrast to Sweden, the ministry backed down and agreed to continue all existing programs. But argument about the unemployability of graduates had raged for six months, leaving the universities under a "pall of demoralization." Then, a policy of fiscal austerity engendered a "widespread feeling that the universities had been singled out for especially severe treatment because of their intransigence" (Geiger, p. 269).

Student resistance against official *dirigisme,* strong in the period of mobilization during the early 1970s, weakened somewhat as the strength of post-materialist values diminished among students entering in the late 1970s (Inglehart). But governments had to contend with tenured faculty resistance against the closing of departments or schools. Trying to avoid closing entire schools, officials instead pressed for reorientation of university goals or mergers between similar programs. In the decentralized British university system this was easier said than done. One example was the effort to induce some mergers among the thirteen medical schools of the University of London, whose teaching hospitals were inopportunely located, given the declining population in inner London. But since these units enjoyed much greater autonomy than those in France, merger proposals were repeatedly defeated in the London University Senate, even though the fiscal drain was playing havoc with the budgets of the non-medical parts of the University.

The Thatcher government's drastic cut of subsidies forced vast tuition increases, and fewer foreign students could pay what then became the world's highest tuition fees (apart from some American medical schools). The government's imposition of a 17 percent cut of university budgets in the early 1980s caused the universities to plan for the termination of several thousand lecturers, even though their claims to tenure made their dismissal very difficult and costly.

The problem of reducing excess capacity was handled more easily in the United States, with its large number of small private colleges. Declining demand has led many to close their doors without causing sleepless nights in Washington, or even in any state capitals. Of 136 higher-level institutions closed in the course of the 1970s, only one was a public four-year institution, and the great majority were private ones like Eisenhower College, a memorial to the former President which closed in 1982.

Degree Value and Career Expectations

How have countries varied in the way they have encountered and coped with an oversupply of university graduates, and what lessons have they drawn from other cases? In 1976 the German Education Ministry commissioned a study of how its situation compared with that of other countries, resulting in the analysis shown in Figure 2.5. It distinguished countries which had by then resolved, were then grappling with, and would yet anticipate problems of excess graduates, coding countries on the degree to which they were facing four problems of labor market integration. Sweden was identified as most successful partly because academic unemployment and vertical substitution seemed to be diminishing, whereas all other countries except Japan were facing escalation of these problems. Britain and the United States were rated as having serious and intensifying problems in three out of four problem areas, largely as a byproduct of lower economic growth. For the Continental countries unemployment and inferior employment were coded as of moderate or weak intensity, but were expected to become more problematic as the larger groups of graduates would be seeking positions; thus Germany and the Netherlands were warned to anticipate a worsening overall problem. Almost everywhere university graduates seemed destined to lose more of their relative income advantages, compared to the less skilled work force. In fact, the reason Sweden was coded differently is that the graduates had been forced to accept such a reduction already in the early 1970s (Heidenheimer 1976).

In comparing the past employment patterns of their own graduates with those in countries such as the United States, the Germans noted that a much higher proportion—about 60 to 70 percent—were going into professional jobs in the public sector. Many of these were teachers, for

FIGURE 2.5 HIGHER EDUCATION GRADUATES IN THE LABOR MARKET, 1976

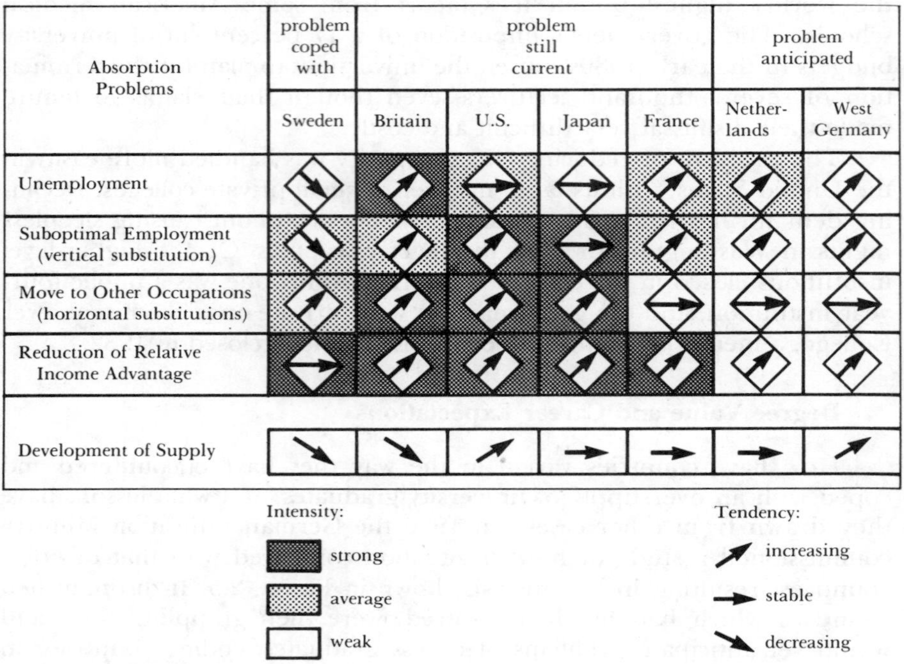

Absorption Problems	problem coped with	problem still current				problem anticipated	
	Sweden	Britain	U.S.	Japan	France	Netherlands	West Germany
Unemployment	weak, decreasing	strong, increasing	average, stable	weak, stable	average, increasing	average, decreasing	weak, increasing
Suboptimal Employment (vertical substitution)	average, decreasing	average, increasing	strong, increasing	strong, stable	average, increasing	weak, increasing	weak, increasing
Move to Other Occupations (horizontal substitutions)	average, increasing	strong, increasing	strong, increasing	strong, increasing	weak, stable	weak, stable	weak, stable
Reduction of Relative Income Advantage	strong, stable	strong, increasing	strong, increasing	strong, increasing	strong, increasing	weak, increasing	weak, increasing
Development of Supply	decreasing	decreasing	increasing	stable	stable	stable	increasing

Intensity: strong; average; weak

Tendency: increasing; stable; decreasing

whom there would be less need because of the smaller number of school-age children in the 1980s. Because of the fiscal consequences of lowered growth and tighter public budgets, they also anticipated many fewer positions developing in other public service areas. They considered cutting back university enrollments, but the unions and other groups protested that this would cause high school graduates to compete for white-collar jobs and simply push unemployment down the skill scale.

The German ministers chose rather to let student enrollment rise toward the one million mark, but emphasized that degrees would no longer constitute quasi-entitlement to public sector professional positions. They pointed out that if the United States and Japan could absorb two thirds of their graduates into the private sector, this should also be feasible in Germany. But prerequisites were that private employers fill more positions with graduates, and that the universities cease regarding more mundane occupations as beneath the dignity of their graduates. After all, if prestigious (even Ivy League!) American universities could train youth for hotel and motel management, why shouldn't European schools likewise stoop to conquer new labor markets?

American efforts toward universalizing not only secondary but also higher education led considerable numbers of college-trained youth to enter not only white-collar but also blue-collar employment. This phenomenon was quite alien to European perceptions. Inevitably the downgrading of students' job expectations had an effect on enrollment in a way which tended to undo some of the gains made in attracting more able working-class youth to attend universities. For them more than for middle-class youth, the lowered prospects of professional-level jobs reduced the incentive to pursue further studies. Why invest more years in study, and incur debts, if the job one expected to get with a degree would not be clearly superior in pay and status to what one could find directly from high school?

But even in the more permeable American system, many college-trained people had to accept jobs in which they would not utilize all their abilities. As the large age group born around 1960 moved through college and into the job market, many had to accept lower-level positions. Even with the broader definitions of what constituted an "acceptable" job for American graduates, the U.S. Bureau of Labor Statistics anticipated a surplus of college graduates during most of the 1980s.

Universities were especially subject to the repercussions of economic and fiscal policies in the United States and Britain under programs pursued by the Reagan and Thatcher governments, as these sought fitfully to attain their primary goals of containing inflation. As they reduced public education expenditures, they reduced the subsidies to higher education. On the other hand, their monetary and credit policies allowed unemployment to balloon, thereby sharply reducing the number of less skilled jobs which young adults could enter from high school. Thus universities risked becoming under-financed parking places for students who could neither get full-time jobs nor be optimistic that their prospects would improve measurably if and when they received their degrees.

* * * * *

In education policy, then, we can identify some convergence between American and European policies with regard to the distribution of educational opportunities. Institutional policy instruments and selection mechanisms effect considerable national variations in the way that opportunities are allocated and linked to labor market requirements. Variations in demographic patterns and social demands, together with an unusually complex pattern of conflicting interests, help shape strong cyclical patterns in the priority accorded this policy area. But education enjoys relatively strong political agenda support, and is an area where, as further discussed in Chapter Ten, popular satisfaction with public programs is relatively similar in both Europe and the United States. We turn attention in the next chapter to health policy, often a strong competitor of education for public resources.

3
HEALTH POLICY

The incidence of illness is different from that of ignorance, and the clients of health care systems are age-skewed in a way drastically different from that of school populations. Whereas one caters predominantly to the young, the other is more concerned with the elderly. In both cases increased supply generates additional demand for services. The provision of more and better secondary education, if accompanied by a "contagion of aspirations," leads to demand for more university places. Breakthroughs in the treatment of disease creates additional patient need among those who otherwise would have died at an earlier age.

Families would hate to have to decide that Grandpa should forego life-prolonging care so that Junior can go to college. In earlier days that choice was usually accentuated by market mechanisms, and sometimes softened by charity opportunities. Then the growing free provision of public services transferred the locus of choices, since demands in both fields were so highly legitimized. Education and health were both among the fastest-growing public sectors when economic growth provided ample public budgets, as in the 1960s. Since then, education expenditures have been suppressed in a way that health expenditures have not, partly because the elderly have become relatively more numerous as both clients and organized voters, and also because governments find it more difficult to implement tough decisions in the health sector.

Of course all age groups have some need for health care, and this has increased the incentive for governments to become financers of last resort at the minimum, and general providers of care at the maximum. Providing health insurance for industrial workers so that medical treatment could help them to resume their productive lives (as Chancellor Otto von Bismarck led Germany to choose in 1883) implied economic benefits for the whole society. Thus national legislation began to transform the mandate which the health system was given by society (Field). No longer were governments content to license certain practitioners to give orthodox medical treatment; now they began to use various incentives and compulsion mechanisms to prescribe where, to whom, and, increasingly, how such care should be provided.

CHOICES IN HEALTH POLICY

Scope and Thresholds

The legislative initiatives as to which social groups in an industrial society should be assured health care have been clearly the results of political choices, not merely the products of socioeconomic development. For example, consider the British introduction of national health insurance of the German model: Had it been determined solely by the pace of industrialization, such a system should have been adopted a half-century before Germany, and not a quarter-century later, as it was. The governments which led public intervention into the health delivery sphere—paternalist monarchies in countries such as Germany and Sweden—sought to anticipate the demands which working-class parties were later to press directly (and to implement when they in turn came to power). In the United States, the relative slowness in public health legislation can be strongly attributed to the later and weaker political organization of labor (Flora and Heidenheimer, Chapters 2 and 3).

As they function today, the West European systems reflect different varieties of government intervention due to political choices made in earlier eras. German political leaders from the 1920s to the 1950s transformed their insurance-based arrangements into a *corporatized* system, under which health providers and recipients regulate themselves and one another in accordance with rules prescribed by the state. The British in the 1940s chose to have the national government assume direct responsibility for health care, thus creating a truly *nationalized* system. A more decentralized version of the British model was implemented in Sweden. American decisions to delay intervention produced a *segmented* system, under which several public subsystems—for the poor, the elderly, and military veterans—coexist with a myriad of other privately financed activities.

Instruments of Health Policy

The choice of legislative and administrative health policy instruments has produced varying patterns in different countries. In contrast to the near monopoly of the British National Health Service, Sweden relies on the counties to operate most health facilities as well as to finance them from their own taxes. In Germany hospitals are financed and operated by the state governments, though most health licensing and insurance powers rest with national agencies. In the United States, federal legislation has established the larger public programs, while state and local governments have maintained limited roles; some programs, in fact, are jointly financed by federal and state governments, though some states choose to stay out of such arrangements (as Arizona has done with regard to Medicaid, for example).

The constraints on governmental choices are greater where certain kinds of health delivery functions are already being performed by private or sub-national public organizations. Although the British case illustrates that national governments can sometimes preempt such activities, in the 1960s the Swedish national government provided a different example, yielding important ground to regional governments.

Governments also make choices, directly or through delegation, regarding which kinds of personnel may provide what kinds of medical care. Should osteopaths and homeopaths be allowed to compete with orthodox medical school graduates? Should primary care be reserved to general practitioners, and specialists limited to practicing mainly in public hospitals?

Britain and the Netherlands give general practitioners (GPs) a monopoly of primary care. Germany gives that monopoly to all privately practicing doctors, in contrast to Sweden, where much of the primary care is provided in hospital outpatient clinics. There and elsewhere in Europe, hospital practice is limited to specialists on fixed salary, while in the United States doctors usually look after their patients both in their offices and in hospitals.

The Distribution of Health Care

Governmental choices pertaining to the distribution of health care face greater constraints than do those about education. Definitions of illness are subject to interpretation by both doctors and patients, and involve a vast battery of standardized tests. Governments can give priority to research on certain diseases, but delivering the resulting remedies—for example, to those who need it but do not know they do—poses great problems. One thing governments can do is influence the geographical and social distribution of hospitals and physicians' offices.

Let us consider the geographical distribution of doctors. Problems of under-doctoring in rural areas and inferior services in poverty locations are especially evident if private purchasing power is the strongest magnet for hospital and physician location, as in the United States. An instrument like Medicaid, for example, which is targeted only at the poor, invites abuses which are less likely to occur where public funding supports care for both the middle and lower classes. But even in nationalized systems equalized health care access may be a problem, because doctors, more than other professionals, prefer to practice in urban centers and university towns. Whereas in some countries teachers are assigned to both a given school and town, physicians have to be induced, mainly through payment mechanisms, to provide the care that is needed where it is needed.

In recent decades governments have chosen to give less emphasis to hospital treatment, and instead to encourage the formation of smaller health centers. Here American policy makers have sometimes had more effective options to create new structures—as in the case of prepaid health programs—than have the more homogeneously organized European systems.

Restraints and Innovation in Health Policy

How should governments ascertain the efficiency and effectiveness of health services, in both the public and private sectors, and what strategies should they follow to improve deficiencies? These goals and options, which frame a fourth set of governmental choices in the health sector, are complicated by general disagreement over the criteria that determine which patients are getting "too much" or "too little," or "better" or "poorer" health care.

In order to devise more effective and efficient health care delivery methods, planners have suggested innovations ranging from pilot projects to large-scale reorganizations. They have been asked to ascertain where medical resources have been distributed in an ineffective or inequitable manner, and to suggest remedies. Their recommendations have been most easily implemented in the more homogeneous systems such as the British and Swedish ones. In the segmented American system, recommendations about allocation have been more difficult to implement, and hence their effectiveness has been more tenuous. Perceiving a choice between improving health care planning or stimulating competition, the Reagan administration has opted strongly for the latter.

Proposals for restraints or innovations to bring down the costs of the total health sector have received top priority. Those seeking to improve efficiency by increasing competion have proposed manipulating modes of payment for doctors and hospitals. Planners are dubious that such "a discipline of the market place" can be applied in the health sector; hence, they have focused more on rationing expensive new technology and related specialities in their efforts to keep health facilities more within their budgets.

STATE CONTROL AND THE MEDICAL PROFESSION

SCOPE AND THRESHOLDS

The road to revolution may have been paved in some nations' classrooms, but hardly ever has it begun in their hospitals. Partly as a result of the realization that health services are difficult to allocate in accord with uniform bureaucratic rules, nations have varied about whether and how far to transform health systems into public monopolies. The directness of state control—whether it relies mainly on regulation, financing, or actual management of medical care—has varied more in health care than in education.

The Extent of Government Intervention

Though all Western systems have gone beyond mere licensing to assume financing responsibilities, most prominently through compulsory health insurance programs, the scope of their programs varies. Whereas in Britain health insurance was a stepping stone to a nationally managed health service system, in Germany it was not. Even where financing has become predominantly public, some countries have let both financing and management remain at the regional level, as in Sweden. Of the nations we are considering here, the United States has only grudgingly expanded the public finance component, and has shown the least tendency to expand the direct health care delivery role of public institutions.

This degree of variation is somewhat surprising, because the scientific knowledge and techniques of health services are probably much more uniform among Western countries than is the content of school curricula, or perhaps even of housing construction programs. Let us therefore now look at the development of national health policies, starting with that of Britain.

In Britain, public health jurisdiction developed rapidly and consistently, taking place in three stages, as shown in Table 3.1. Several factors facilitated the establishment of a nationalized public health system there. For one thing, extensive benefit systems were developed voluntarily by trade unions and the Friendly Societies and later utilized by public programs. For another, local public health bureaucracies—similar to the county governments in Sweden or the Sickness Funds in Germany—did not oppose nationalization. Last, the medical profession itself was somewhat divided on the whole insurance issue and so did not present the unified opposition which organized medicine in the United States did.

In 1948 the National Health Service (NHS) Act gave the British gov-

TABLE 3.1 The Development of the Public Health Sector in Britain

Date	Stage of Development	Specific Developments
Late 19th century	Infrastructure growth	Friendly Society insurance for physicians' services Strong local government health responsibilities
1911	Public health financing prototype	Compulsory health insurance—at first only for low-income workers, later expanded
1948	Full National Health Service	Free medical treatment for all residents National operation of all hospitals Standardized remuneration schemes

ernment, especially the Ministry of Health, greater direct control of more health subsystems than has been achieved by any other Western government. It made Britain the Western model for a system which was not only collectively financed, but *nationalized;* its components were directly run by the national government. From an administrative point of view, the most dramatic aspect of the British NHS reform was the virtually complete takeover by the national government of voluntary as well as municipal hospitals, and their integration within larger regions that superseded local and county borders. Moreover, the NHS financed the health system largely from general revenue, thus moving away from reliance on insurance contributions.

In the United States, public health insurance came closest to adoption between 1915 and 1920, when compulsory health insurance was one of the most widely debated social policy issues. Bills that would have established a public health insurance program similar to Germany's were introduced between 1916 and 1917 in eighteen state legislatures and were discussed in Congress, supported by a president of the American Medical Association (AMA), and hailed by the AMA *Journal* as "the inauguration of a great movement which ought to result in an improvement in health." A ground swell of opposition rose from state and local medical societies, however, based on the defense of professional autonomy, and coinciding with American entry into World War I. By November 1918, when California voters were asked to approve a constitutional amendment establishing public health insurance, it was soundly defeated with the help of a pamphlet bearing the Kaiser's picture and the message: "Made in Germany: Do you want it in California?" (Lubove, pp. 67, 83).

In twentieth-century America, public health long remained limited to the predominantly preventive and sanitary preoccupations associated with it in the nineteenth century. Within the segmented system, the public sector ranked low in prestige, scientific interest, and financial support. Public hospitals in the United States continued to cater mainly to the poor, especially in the cities, and public health expenditures increased at a snail-like pace, from 0.4 percent of the Gross National Product (GNP) in 1913 to 0.7 percent in 1932. In 1964 expenditures still stood at less than 1 percent of the GNP. Not until 1965 did the federal government even assume the role of compulsory insurance administrator, which the British government had assumed in 1911 and used as an entering wedge for growing public responsibilities.

The first bitter campaign against U.S. health insurance convinced advocates in subsequent unsuccessful attempts in 1936 and in 1947 to 1948 that "the less identification with Europe, the better." After one debate on Medicare, the British Medical Association's *Journal* deplored "the vulgarity and cheapness of the AMA's past and present attacks upon the National Health Service" (Skidmore, pp. 354–355). Starting early in the 1950s, U.S. health insurance protagonists shifted to an accretionist strategy of relating their proposals to the earlier popular social security programs. Whereas most European countries had initiated health insurance programs by providing coverage for low-income workers, in the United States the initial group was the aged, first covered in 1965 by Medicare. Like Bismarck's original sickness insurance program of 1883, Medicare has operated as a *categorical* program, for which only a small population group is eligible. With a coverage of some twenty million Americans aged sixty-five and over, Medicare insures about ten percent of the population, a proportion similar to the German one of the 1880s.

How countries differ in their public and private emphasis can be measured in a number of ways. Table 3.2 shows the sources of health

TABLE 3.2 Public and Private Sources of Health Care Finance (1974–75)

	Britain	Sweden	Germany	France	Netherlands	USA
General Taxation	87.3	78.5	14.6	7.0	15.1	31.0
Public Insurance	5.3	13.1	62.5	69.0	56.0	11.7
Total Public	92.6	91.6	77.1	76.0	71.1	42.7
Direct Consumer Payments	5.8	8.4	12.5	19.6		27.1
Private Insurance	1.4	—	5.3	3.0	27.3	25.6
Employers, Other	0.4	—	5.1	1.4	1.6	4.6
Total Private	7.6	8.4	22.9	24.0	28.9	57.3

NOTE Direct consumer payments include non-prescription drugs. For detailed definitions see source.

SOURCE Robert J. Maxwell, *Health and Wealth* (Lexington, Mass.: Lexington Books, 1981), p. 61.

financing, though it should be pointed out that some of the public financing may flow through private health care structures. The two most public systems, Britain and Sweden, finance the bulk of health expenditures from general taxation, relying only modestly on either public health insurance or private sources of any kind. In the systems which rely primarily on health insurance financing—France, West Germany, and the Netherlands—the dependence on public sources is still predominant, though not as many of the health care facilities are publicly operated in these countries as in Britain and Sweden. The American system, by sharp contrast, draws its predominant financing from the private sector, even though public sources have increased greatly since the 1960s. Its segmented character is reflected in the fact that taxation, private insurance, and direct consumer payments each accounted for between a quarter and a third of revenue, with public insurance like Medicare and Medicaid running behind.

The role of both private voluntary insurance systems and of private delivery systems is much more extensive in the United States than in other countries. It is significant to note, however, that the country which first introduced national health insurance, Germany, is relatively similar to the United States today in terms of the role still played there by church-related hospitals and privately practicing physicians. Though they are not public institutions in the way that German Sickness Funds are, American third payers such as Blue Cross and Blue Shield are becoming similar to these in their functions. Whereas private health insurance plans still loom larger in American health finance, their role in Germany is marginal compared to the role of the publicly mandated systems.

The Medical Profession and Self-regulation

Of all the major social service occupations, medicine has since the late nineteenth century sustained the fastest rate of scientific and technological improvement. As scientific breakthroughs increased certainty about the causes of contagious diseases and the effects of antiseptics and vaccines, the correlation between physician treatment and patient recovery greatly increased. The doctor's ability to eliminate pain effectively and delay death has helped to rank medicine among the most prestigious professions.

In some American states, medicine was so well entrenched that the medical societies were trusted as the state boards of health. Elsewhere state governors were constitutionally required to appoint health board members from slates submitted by the state affiliates of the AMA. Such provisions were not implemented to the same degree for boards regulating the less prestigious occupations.

Medical claims for self-regulation became stronger as physicians were able to claim a growing monopoly of knowledge of increasingly esoteric and specialized techniques. American doctors for some time did not fully share in this status gain, mainly because of an American lag in phasing out marginal, second-echelon healers and the schools that claimed to train them. In Britain and Germany improved bureaucratic capabilities had matched scientific advances; rigorous official licensing had helped gradually to raise the standards for physicians.

Scientifically minded American medical leaders for a while supported the idea of giving strong licensing and other powers to the federal government, just as some of them favored following Europe in the extension of public health insurance. Then the alternative of using their own professional association, the American Medical Association (founded in 1847, nationally integrated in 1902), to serve as the key instrument of self-regulation became attractive. Responding to a call from the 1903 AMA convention, medical leaders initiated a vigorous weeding-out process among medical schools on the basis of Abraham Flexner's Carnegie Foundation-sponsored report.

Implementation of the Flexner Report's recommendations, backed up by the "blackballing" powers of the professional elites, led within two decades to a sharp reduction both in the number of medical schools, from 162 to 76, and in the number of doctors, from 157 to 126 per 100,000 (Kessel; Stevens, 1971).

In some European countries, health care consumers were for a time more effectively organized than physicians. In the nineteenth century British Friendly Societies organized some three million largely working-class users of health services and exercised strong bargaining power in contracting physicians to treat their members. Germany had similar organizations, known as Sickness Funds, which became the intermediaries for implementing the first compulsory health insurance for workers in the world introduced by Bismarck in 1883 (Abel-Smith, p. 225).

But small-scale consumer groups, led by volunteers with limited education, often were ineffective in the face of the "scientific revolution" in medicine and improved management techniques. Unless government experts stood at their side, the consumer advocates were increasingly at a disadvantage as the knowledge-status gap between them and better-trained physicians widened. Friendly Societies were outmaneuvered in 1911, then proved unable to hold their own as insurance intermediaries against commercial carriers. One official noted: "The Friendly Society people were such an extraordinarily thick-headed crowd. They were immensely worthy . . . but oh! they were so difficult—often so suspicious—and always so unintelligent and unacceptable. . . . But why did they not get good advice? Why did they allow themselves to be outwitted every time? Every time!" (Bunberry, p. 92).

In Germany the Sickness Funds received better bureaucratic and scientific help from their allies in the trade unions and in the Social Democratic party and became a prime example of institutionalized *third payers,* which contracted physicians and institutions on behalf of their members. American medical practitioners, on the other hand, successfully combated the creation not only of state-sponsored but even of voluntary third payer groups. Until the 1940s, AMA membership was declared incompatible with treatment of patients under prepaid health insurance plans, and in many instances the use of hospital facilities was denied physicians who defied this rule. In fact, when the third payers Blue Cross and Blue Shield were introduced, they were controlled by hospitals and the medical profession, not by consumers.

Government policies toward the medical profession's claims of autonomy have varied extensively. Sometimes governments have supported medical associations in their quest for tighter professional monopolies. At other times they have undermined the licensing and professional practice rules so as deliberately to place physicians under greater competitive pressure. Since the early nineteenth century, American policies have shifted between the two alternatives more than European ones have (Berlant).

In Europe the modern governmental tendency has been to recognize and support the attempt of physician associations to share responsibility for health care, but to coopt them by making them instruments of official policies. Means to this end have included compulsory membership in medical associations, granting of franchises to professional associations for certain kinds of care, and recognition of established professional groups as exclusive negotiating partners of governments. At the level of the individual practitioner, this has tended to make the physician less an independent entrepreneur and more a civil servant, although subject more to peer rather than to hierarchical pressure.

Thus in Germany membership is obligatory in quasi-public organizations such as the Chamber of Physicians and the Insurance Doctors Association. The physicians who belong to them share legally recognized monopolies in the market for ambulatory medical care, as well as in the formulation and enforcement of rules regarding the practice various groups of doctors can engage in. Office- and hospital-based doctors therefore are subject to quite different constraints. In return for these powers, the medical associations must monitor their members' claims under the health insurance program, and see to it that opportunities for medical treatment are available and publicized at all times. It is this type of system which we label a corporatized one, since it features a deliberate incorporation of public functions with professional and private functions (Heidenheimer 1980b).

A comparison with Britain shows that more direct national control of the health system does not necessarily diminish professional autonomy. For since the British national health system has greater financial control than is the case in Germany, the authorities can tolerate greater physician self-control of some conditions of practice. In addition to bargaining exclusively with the British Medical Association over doctors' remuneration claims, the government allows the Association informally to regulate physicians' conditions of practice. But the profession's power to assert itself is limited by direct state management of hospitals, as well as by the general splintering of interests among the physicians. Thus the less prestigious doctors have been able to narrow the income level between themselves and the senior specialists, which has weakened the natural authority pyramids through which the specialists used to exert more distinctive leadership within the profession as a whole (Honigsbaum).

In the United States the monopoly power of the American Medical Association long remained greater than that of its European counterparts because it indirectly controlled the licensing of graduates of AMA-approved medical schools. Leaders of the AMA county affiliates could also determine which doctors were admitted to the staffs of hospitals. Osteopaths and other non-orthodox medical practitioners were denied entry to AMA-recognized hospitals, and so they built their own, though in some states they have come to be blanketed into the AMA after public acceptance made them difficult to boycott. But other potential competitors to physicians, such as chiropractors and optometrists, were combated by the medical association, whose ethics code until recently forbade members from accepting or referring patients from or to these other practitioners (Feldstein, pp. 53–57).

A vigorous attack on the profession's restrictive practices has been pursued since 1975, when the courts ruled that learned professions did not enjoy exemption from antitrust laws. Since then the Federal Trade Commission has sought to strengthen competition between doctors by attacking the legal basis on which medical associations employed ethics codes to prevent doctors from advertising. Also successfully attacked through the courts were the AMA's accrediting powers, the profession's control of some medical insurance programs, and boycotts against physicians who participated in prepaid health systems not approved by the medical societies.

The divesting of the medical association's monopolistic controls was pursued less as an end in itself than as a means of developing potential competitive market pressures. Thus, "If one concludes that antitrust law can in fact be established as a meaningful check on the profession's power to shape its economic environment . . . the entire drift of health policy toward increasingly heavy regulation begins to seem less inevitable" (Havighurst). Though this thrust was consistent with the Reagan administration's aims of dismantling regulations and, instead, seeking to further competition, it encountered strong resistance in Congress.

POLICY GOALS AND IMPLEMENTATION INSTRUMENTS

Just as countries vary in the structures and techniques they use to implement health policy, so their choice of policy instruments leads in turn to different patterns in different countries. One important element in any nation's health policy is the personnel involved; as we shall see, countries vary also in their policies regarding the training and utilization of physicians.

Policy-making Structures

As the various health care financing and delivering responsibilities assumed by governments suggest, health care is a system to a different extent in different countries. In Europe the agreement of a few ministers and bureaucrats may suffice to set implementable policy goals, whereas in the United States the fragmentation of responsibility requires policy makers to follow carefully considered strategies, with the success of most policies contingent on a long string of conditions. A Congressional mandate *may* be implemented, *if* the federal bureaucracies cooperate, *if* they can enlist the cooperation of local officials, *if* the private interests offer support, and so on. Both systems have specialists called health planners, but their ability to implement a program differs greatly.

In Britain decisions by committee are endemic. When vested interests are strongly entrenched (as they were with the closing of some London University medical schools mentioned in Chapter Two), it may take years to reach agreement. But once several options crystallize, decisions in the health sector proper can be made rather quickly. If the Minister of Health and his top bureaucrats agree, and if the necessary funds are agreed to by the Treasury, a new set of rules can be issued with some confidence that officials in the health system and local governments will carry them out. (Examples include the decisions to expand health centers and to limit the acquisition of CT scanners, discussed later.)

In Germany no significant policy could be finalized by just two ministries. Policy deliberations must include not only the Ministries of Health and Finance, but also the Labor Ministry, which supervises the health insurance system, and all the Land Ministers of Health. On some issues the Chamber of Physicians might claim veto power and, if offended, might resort to the threat of a doctors' strike (as in the case of the Cost Limitation bill described later in this chapter). Although German health policy has been less party-polarized than its secondary education policy, changes are very difficult to push through the corporatized German decision-making system (Stone 1980, Chapter 2). Thus, to help bring about consensus, the Germans have augmented the official machinery by setting up a broader National Health Conference to set annual health policy goals. Even so, the Germans have made much less progress than the Swedes in projecting and implementing, for instance, a set of medical manpower planning objectives.

In Sweden health planners have been more effective largely because of a policy of *regionalizing* responsibility for the public health delivery systems. The counties were given a virtual monopoly, including jurisdiction over some mental hospitals and district doctor systems which the national government had previously run. Another step was to reduce competition between the twenty-five counties, which meant instituting a uniform national pay scale for all hospital employees and placing all hospital doctors on a "salary only" remuneration basis (Carder and Klingeberg, in Heidenheimer and Elvander 1980). Furthermore, it meant developing a system through which all counties would cooperate to fit their hospital staffing and training policies into one national framework. This scheme was in turn further developed through a "health regionalization" program, through which various kinds of hospitals were assigned duties which carried with them quotas regarding the various medical and other health personnel. Building on this framework, then, Swedish health planners were able not only to announce goals of producing fewer surgeons and more specialists in geriatrics, but actually to implement these goals by coordinating the control mechanisms of hospitals, medical schools, and counties (Heidenheimer and Elvander 1980).

In the United States the federal government has been given greater policy-making leverage in return for the increased financing it has provided since 1965, which has led to a whole new variety of standard-setting mechanisms designed specifically to fit into the segmented American health system. These new mechanisms included the Health System Agencies (HSAs), Health Maintenance Organizations (HMOs), and Professional Standards Review Organizations (PSROs). Created in the 1970s, these structures increased the national government's influence, bypassing established state and local agencies to set up brand new structures at local and regional levels.

Typical were the Health System Agencies (HSAs), which were set up on the basis of the 1974 Health Planning and Resources Development Act. The country was divided into 206 regions, most comprising a portion of a state or a metropolitan area, and each regional HSA was provided staff and powers to develop plans to match local needs and resources, with special reference to the investment plans of hospitals. Consumer representatives outnumbered providers on the HSAs, but the law did not specify how their boards were to be elected. If the local HSAs thought that hospital proposals to add new capacity or equipment did not merit certificate-of-need endorsement, the major federal funding agencies could withhold support from them. Thus the attempt to introduce even *some* decentralized planning into local systems involved *many* conditions, all of which had to be satisfied before federal planners might try successfully to oppose the expansion plans of a locally influential private hospital board. Starting in 1982, however, HSAs began to be dismantled on a state-by-state basis as part of the Reagan administration's attack on federal regulation. The last state to enact relevant legislation, Missouri, was one of the first to dismantle its HSAs.

Techniques of Intervention

In a nationally administered health system like Britain's, the instruments through which government affects health policy are largely identical with the administrative subdivisions of the National Health Service—for example, ambulatory, hospital, and preventive services. In a corporatized system like Germany's, instrumental powers are more scattered among various public, private, and professional bodies. In a segmented system like the United States', where the national government operates only a few facilities (such as Veterans Administration Hospitals), the government pursues a series of loosely related strategies of intervention aimed at different components of the health delivery system.

U.S. federal health policy of the 1970s was aptly described as a four-ring circus, with four sets of techniques pursued within as many rings (Brown 1978). One technique of intervention tried to determine the quantity, quality, and distribution of medical and other health manpower. Another aimed to support and control the actual health care facilities, including both traditional ones such as hospitals and newer ones such as health centers and prepaid health care centers. A third technique focused on regulating health care services (as in the efforts to control technology described later in this chapter). A fourth technique involved channeling subsidies to groups such as the elderly and the poor.

The Reagan administration has been trying to alter this pattern by merging funds for many programs into block grants whose dispersal among various programs is left more to the states' discretion. Four such block grants set up in 1981 covered preventive health services, primary care, maternal and child health, and mental health.

Those involved in health politics find that their options are affected by how loosely or tightly the four rings are interconnected. Favoring the medical profession is the fact that doctors dominate a public service whose aims are often ill defined; consequently, they are in a particularly strong position to promote their own policy preferences. Moreover, where methods of payment and administration do not contain it, health care is one service whose supply tends to determine demand, rather than vice versa. Studies have shown that when additional hospital beds become available, patients are found to fill them.

Physician Training and Utilization

Health policy choices are conditioned by a country's physician-to-population ratio, and also by the proportion of medical students who are trained as generalists or specialists. The difficulty of entering medical training has varied over time and among countries. In the 1960s the United States, like most of Europe, expanded the number of medical students. Yet even with this expansion admission was more selective than in most European countries, where, apart from Britain, a relatively higher number were allowed to start studies. Often this has resulted in crowding in clinical training, because the number of patients in university hospitals and the number of lab places are limited. This problem has proved severe in Germany, and even more so in Italy, where an already high physician to population ratio has grown yet higher, as Table 3.3 suggests.

Starting in 1963, the U.S. federal government began to subsidize both medical schools and medical students heavily in the belief that increasing the number of doctors was the key to improving health delivery. From then to 1973, federal subsidies to medical and other health professional schools acquired a preferred status, since such aid was not given to schools of law, engineering, or business. While first-year enrollments increased from 8,760 to 1965 to 14,500 in 1975, the proportion of medical school income covered by tuition decreased from 17 percent in 1948, to 7 percent in 1960, to 4 percent in the 1970s.

The criteria by which medical students are selected has come to vary cross-nationally. In some countries secondary school grades and entrance test scores count heavily. But high achievers do not necessarily make the best doctors; and so the Netherlands and Germany now rely partly on lotteries to select from those basically qualified. The financial barrier in the United States, where annual tuition fees exceed $15,000, has made family wealth a stronger criterion, with the percentage of students from

TABLE 3.3 Medical Education in Six Countries

	Britain	USA	Sweden	France	Germany	Italy
Annual intake of new medical students, 1970s	3,700	16,100	1,050	8,900	11,000	27,100
Percent increase, 1960–1970	NA	94	99	31	83	874
Entering medical students per 100,000 population	6.7	7.5	12.7	16.7	17.9	47.9
Number of medical schools	30	124	6	38	28	28
Physicians per 10,000 population, 1975	13.1	16.7	17.1	14.6	19.2	19.9

SOURCE Bundesministerium fuer Bildung und Wissenschaft. Die Ausbildungs-situation im Studiengang Medizin in der Bundesrepublik Deutschland und in neun vergleichbaren Laendern (Bonn, 1979).

lower middle-class families (with an income of $10,000 to $20,000) declining from 34 to 26 percent between 1974 and 1977, as federal subsidies were reduced. Medical school leaders are now concerned that medicine is going to become even more markedly a profession for the rich. In Europe, where fees are not a barrier, more weeding out occurs. Thus France has tightened the test which screens out many after the first year, while in Germany a new second-year multiple-choice test threatened to eliminate 56 percent of the class in 1981. In that case, however, massive student protest led to a revised procedure, and to a lowering of the failure rate.

In advanced medical training the U.S. system is tilted toward the production of specialists, since there are more residency training positions than there are candidates in most specialties. In Sweden manpower planning has restricted the number of residency positions in specialties which are deemed less needed. In Britain and Germany young doctors know that the number of full-time senior hospital specialist positions is limited, and so, rather than earn specialty credentials which may not lead to promising careers, more of them are deciding to work in general practice and primary care.

In most European systems, the crucial role of the "gatekeeper," who determines which patients shall have what kind of hospital care, is played by the specialist, to whom GPs refer patients for more complex diagnoses. Such doctors impose a somewhat higher criterion for hospital admission than would most American physicians, who can arrange admission for their own patients. Once they get to a hospital, the large majority of European patients, in contrast to American ones, "are treated by hospital physicians in whose choice they have no part. The relationship of patient to doctor is not a private one, fortified by a personal financial transaction, but rather a social one in which the institution takes responsibility for providing the needed medical care" (Roemer and Friedman, p. 55). With hospital appointments a mark of great prestige, European hospitals have tended to develop a "closed staff" system, in contrast to the freewheeling "open staff" hospital typical of the United States.

By 1974, American politicians comparing British and American physician distribution noted that in Britain 74 percent of the doctors were primary-care physicians and only 8 percent were in surgery, while in the United States' free-market system about 47 percent of the physicians were in the primary-care specialties (including internal medicine, pediatrics, and obstetrics) and 24 percent were in surgery. As Senator Edward Kennedy asked: "Why do we have the same number of neurosurgeons in Massachusetts, with a population of five million, as they have in England, with a population of forty million? . . . Why do we have twice as many operations in the United States as in England? Could it be because we have twice as many surgeons? Could it be because we have a Parkinson's Law for surgery, which says that the amount of surgery performed in

America expands to fill the time of the surgeons available to do it?" (*National Journal*, 17 August 1974).

Clearly, the quality of surgery depends on the skill of those who are allowed to perform operations, though the reason for surgery must also be considered. In the United States, for example, surveys have shown a high percentage of unnecessary hysterectomy and appendectomy operations. Half of all American operations are performed by doctors without either surgical specialization or board certification—a function of the fact that individual hospitals set their own standards. In some teaching hospitals, patients have not been told that residents in training were operating on them, triggering the following criticism based on reports by a New York State medical task force:

> Consumer advocates say that if the surgeon he selects is not going to perform the operation himself, he ought to tell the patient who is . . . Increasing numbers of patients believe that they have a right to know what is going to be done to them, who is going to do it and why . . . Although many physicians and surgeons consider such views as unwarranted interference in their practice of medicine, legal and ethical trends are clearly siding with the patients . . . Doctors are not entirely reconciled to the idea of legislatures and courts telling them how to practice their profession. But it is a trend to which . . . the medical profession must adapt. (*New York Times*, 6 February 1978)

Surgeons have also had to accept the fact that health insurers encourage patients to get a second opinion before agreeing to proposed surgery. Studies have shown that in more than one quarter of cases there was disagreement in the advice given by two surgeons.

While maintaining higher standards for surgeons and other specialists, Britain has also managed to resist the general decline in the supply of GPs. In both the United States and Sweden the proportion of GPs in the total physician population has decreased sharply in recent decades. Table 3.4 gives the figures for 1967. The British have prevented the erosion of

TABLE 3.4 Distribution of Physicians by Type of Primary Activity, 1967

	United States	Sweden	England
Patient Care	93%	91%	98%
General practice	23	35	48
Specialties	70	56	50
Medical	(21)	(26)	(14)
Surgical	(27)	(17)	(20)
Other	(22)	(13)	(16)
Administrative	7	9	2

SOURCE Odin W. Anderson, *Health Care: Can There Be Equity? The U.S., Sweden, and England* (New York: Wiley, 1972), p. 124.

general practice through both health insurance (from 1911 to 1948) and the National Health Service (from 1948 to the present). These programs have helped to "encapsulate" general practice, protecting it against technological and professional pressures by providing it with a "clearly defined administrative and professional function" (Stevens 1966, p. 356).

The degree of health financing by public insurance has little relationship to a patient's choice of primary physicians. In an insurance-based system like Germany's, patients enroll with a physician of their choice and may change doctors on three months' notice. A similar choice of physicians is available under the British NHS. Affluent American suburbanites have more choice than Europeans in specialist and hospital care; but, for many Americans in rural areas and inner cities, choice is inhibited not only by cost, but by the availability of physicians and medical facilities.

In Britain the distribution of general practitioners is influenced by the various incentives for locating practices in different areas. GPs are offered an additional income for settling in under-doctored areas, while areas with a surfeit of doctors are declared closed to new practices. Even entries into intermediate areas are screened.

The United States' health manpower legislation contained similar incentives, based on the cancellation of student loan debts, for those choosing to practice in under-doctored areas. The hope of guiding medical graduates to rural areas enjoyed little success: Over a ten-year period only 146 of 170,000 loan recipients chose this option.

ACCESS TO HEALTH CARE AND HOSPITALS

DISTRIBUTION

The question of distribution concerns the access that a population has to health care—specifically, to physicians' offices, hospitals and health centers, and health plans. In formulating health policy, governments have, to varying degrees, concerned themselves with its geographical and social distribution.

Inequalities in Health Care Access

A cross-national study of medical care utilization in the United States and Sweden, emphasizing the role of income and class, found that in the early 1960s the utilization of physician services was strongly related to income in the United States—but not at all in Sweden. Whereas the percentage of Swedes seeing a doctor during 1963 was fairly constant for all income groups, in the United States there was a large spread between the low-income group, of which 53 percent had seen a doctor, and the high-income group, of which 72 percent had. Moreover, Americans who carried health insurance were much more likely to utilize both physicians and hospitals than those who did not. In their overall comparison, the authors of the study "judged the accessibility of the population to the Swedish system to be greater than to the system of the United States because the proportion of the cost of services paid by the consumer at time of service is lower in Sweden" (Anderson *et al*, p. 12a).

Initially, some students of the British National Health Service argued that, even though there was no cost barrier, medical care benefits were more accessible to the middle class than to the working class. However, studies suggest that the lower-class groups have learned how to take advantage of the benefits to which they are entitled, that they make the greatest use of physicians and in-hospital medical services, and that the care they receive is as good as that secured by the other social classes (Rein).

In the United States, the Medicaid and Medicare programs, implemented in the late 1960s, have increased the access of lower-income groups to medical care. In 1970, 65 percent of people with incomes below $3000 saw a physician, compared to only 56 percent in 1963. Whereas in 1930 high-income patients averaged twice as many doctor consultations as low-income patients, by 1970 low-income patients were seeing doctors as frequently as high-income patients, and their hospital admission rate was higher.

Information on how frequently Americans in various income groups saw doctors in the course of a year is given in Table 3.5, and presumably the greater equalization between 1963 and 1974 reflects the influence of the Medicare and Medicaid programs. Notice, however, that the figures in the first column do not reflect the relative need of patients. This aspect is built into the information in the second column, which gives data on doctor visits as they relate to sickness incidence as measured by disability days. Since the lower-income groups experienced relatively more disability, it was concluded that the distribution of medical care when measured in this way had *not* significantly improved.

TABLE 3.5 Physician Visits of Americans by Income Level and Disability Status, 1963 and 1976

Income Levels of Patients	Mean Number of Annual Visits Per Person		Number of Visits Per 100 Disability Days	
	1963	*1976*	*1963*	*1976*
Low	4.3	5.4	19	20
Middle	4.4	4.8	30	31
High	4.8	4.9	36	39
All patients	4.6	5.0	28	29

SOURCE Ronald Anderson, "Health Status Indices and Access to Medical Care," *American Journal of Public Health,* May 1978, Vol. 68, No. 5, pp. 458–462.

A more recent American study examined the effects of social factors and sources of health care on the utilization of preventive medicine measures. Only 28 percent of the young children in the survey had received medical examinations during the preceding year. The five most important variables, in order of their importance in affecting the probability of getting examinations, were social class, regular source of care, health insurance status, sex and race, and age. Those children with access to regular sources of care, such as health centers, were more likely to get exams and immunizations, as were those covered by public or prepaid insurance (Wan and Gray).

Medicaid is the embattled safety net through which public financial support reaches the non-elderly poor. In 1981 some 20 million Americans, including 8 million children, received Medicaid benefits. About 56 percent of the $31 billion spent under the program that year came from federal funds, with the remainder coming from the states. Most recipients lived beneath the poverty level, and the median income of Medicaid households (in 1980, $6,100) was barely one third that of all American households. The trend in the late 1970s was toward a concentration of benefits such as Medicaid and food stamps on the poorest households. However, because it could find no other way of containing the startling annual cost increase of 15 percent, the Reagan administration in 1982 sought to make Medicaid patients pay for each doctor visit. Some officials thought this might deter hypochondriacs, but others observed that if the charge deterred visits at an early stage of illness, the government might eventually end up paying more later for more numerous consultations required at later stages of illness.

Since the European systems mostly bypass financial charges to the patient, they rely more on waiting lists and office routines to deter patients who might not really need care. Time spent in doctors' waiting rooms can also be costly to American patients. A U.S. study found that American patients waited an average of 29 minutes to see their doctor; in hospital out-patient clinics this rose to an average of 45 minutes, with a striking difference between 41 minutes for whites and 61 minutes for blacks (National Center for Health Services Research). The same report found that in 1978 the number of Americans who had no health insurance at all—26.6 million or one eighth of the civilian population—was much larger than the number of Medicaid-supported Americans. Nonwhites were half again as likely to be uninsured as whites; but most vulnerable were young adults, since 3 out of 10 in the 18–24 age range had no coverage.

Education may in part have replaced income as the major determinant of variation in health care utilization. One study showed that level of education had both direct and indirect effects on health care consumption. The direct effect was that the better-educated were more inclined to utilize services, because they knew where to get appropriate treatment. But more education also happens to be associated with fewer and less severe chronic conditions (for reasons that are related to income and standard of living); thus, the indirect effect of education was to reduce health care utilization. In brief, the direct and indirect effects of education tended to cancel each other out (Berki).

Hospitals and Health Care Delivery

Hospital emphasis tends to vary from country to country. In 1975, for example, Britain spent 3.8 percent of its GNP on hospitals, thanks mainly to its highly centralized administration and the virtual monopoly of hospital practice held by a small and hierarchically organized group of specialists, who provided efficient gatekeeping at the hospital door. Sweden, by contrast, spent 6 percent of its GNP on hospital expenditures, twice that of Germany or the United States (Maxwell, pp. 83–86).

In the 1960s Sweden constructed some of the world's largest and best-equipped hospitals, which proceeded to rotate world health care records among themselves. The costs of construction and maintenance were borne predominantly by the counties, of whose budgets health care constituted about 80 percent, and which were free to set their own tax rates. Expansionism was encouraged by the National Health Board chairman, who in commenting on British health care wrote, "it is not likely that a contraction of investment like that of the English would be accepted in our country, nor would we recommend anything like that for Sweden" (Mechanic, p. 135).

In the United States, the AMA's resistance to prepaid group insurance indirectly caused hospitals to emerge as the preferred institutions for health care extension. The Blue Cross Association, which became the profession's preferred health insurance instrument in the 1940s, was under producer and not consumer control and, until 1972, was linked to the American Hospital Association.

Federal grant-in-aid programs also gave overt preference to hospital investment, offering special advantages for rural and voluntary hospitals. Besides bolstering voluntary hospitals and their self-perpetuating boards, these programs "laundered" the funds through these private institutions and so made the use of public money ideologically more acceptable. Thus financing practices, along with fairly lax gatekeeping and the question of physician convenience, made the hospital the organizational hub of medicine in the United States.

While general hospital beds increased markedly in the United States, from 3.3 beds per 1,000 in 1950 to 4.5 beds per 1,000 in the mid-1970s, the ratios in Britain and Sweden declined slightly, though Sweden has long had a high bed-to-population ratio compared to other industrialized countries. In all three countries, however, admissions to general hospitals increased over this period, growing from 110 to 157 per 1,000 in the United States; from 113 to 156 in Sweden; and from 64 to 104 in Britain. The average hospital stay in the United States has declined slightly, to about 8 days; in Sweden it fell from 16 to 10 days; and in England from 15 to 10 (Anderson and Bjorkman, in Heidenheimer and Elvander 1980, p. 231).

In Sweden, one effect of the highly developed and well financed hospital system was that half of all doctor contacts with ambulatory patients occurred in hospital out-patient departments. When in the 1960s some Swedes questioned whether such a system was either economically or medically justified, health planners gradually leaned toward health centers as less expensive sites for the delivery of health care. By 1970 the National Health Board chairman officially stated that the board "would favor an exodus of specialists from hospitals into health centers," both because this would "relieve some of the need for hospitalization," and because it would "restore the confidence of patients in the health care system by making specialists more accessible" (*The Swedish Health Service System* 1971, p. 209).

The local health centers in Britain, though hailed in 1946 by Health Minister Aneurin Bevan as one of "three main instruments" of the new NHS, did not flourish at first. Two decades later, however, another Labour government finally initiated a significant health center trend. Tensions between GPs and specialists had become acute, and the government looked to health centers as one solution to the struggle. Thus the Ministry greatly encouraged the development of health centers, subsidizing rents and increasing their number from 29 in 1959 to over 300 by 1972.

American critics of the British health care system tend to deplore British priorities as soft-headed, urging them to cut back on ambulances and to invest more in high technology. While admitting that Britain enjoys the service of many more GPs and furthermore that they perform services not always available in the United States—house calls, for example—Americans point out that the British system pays the price. "If community health services seem lavish by American standards, hospital services seem skimpy. Over 750,000 people are now waiting to enter British hospitals" (Goodman). The long waiting lists are characteristic of the NHS, since the absence of a price mechanism tends to make queuing an informal rationing device. Patients with non-critical problems often have long waits; in fact, evidence presented to the 1979 Royal Commission on the NHS showed that one fifth of all surgical patients had been on a waiting list for more than two years.

The 1979 commission identified a high degree of consumer satisfaction and dismissed claims that the system was near collapse. It proposed some changes, however, including the elimination of one tier of NHS authority that had been introduced by the Tories in 1974 and that most agreed had not paid off. Another suggested reform was a change in the hospital doctor structure in order to attract and hold younger doctors. With a non-medical majority, the commission failed to make even a strong case for more money and was therefore criticized for its "seeming acceptance of financial famine as an irremediable fact of life" (Klein).

The hospital doctors felt themselves insufficiently appreciated if put politely in their place. One specialist commented: "The commission thinks we are upset because our status has been eroded by modern democracy. Our morale is not important for its own sake. . . . When I read this breathtaking snub I had to cool off by walking around my lawns and kicking the peacocks."

Another commission recommendation which aroused doctor dissent was that free service for all residents be continued. "I am not convinced that this sacred cow should be kept at pasture and not sent to the slaughterhouse . . . I do not see why non-UK citizens should be provided with benefits 'without restriction' " (Drife). Shortly afterward, in 1981, the Thatcher government moved to charge non-British users fees for non-emergency hospital treatment (unless they were EEC nationals), which the Minister thought might raise five million pounds per year. This eliminated one of the hallmarks of the NHS, with the Tories arguing that Britain could no longer afford this universalist gesture toward visitors.

Launching a New Health Care Delivery Model: HMOs

American health planners in the 1970s also wished to move the health care emphasis away from hospitals both because they are more costly than other treatment sites and because they tend to stress curative, rather than preventive, treatment. In this context the HMO concept was introduced and has since won widespread adherence. In an HMO, or Health Maintenance Organization, members are offered full medical coverage on a prepaid basis. Though the concept of group health care had earlier been attacked as radical, the HMO delivery model came to be actively promoted by both the Nixon and Ford administrations. It promised more efficient treatment and lower costs, without the stigma of outright public ownership.

HMO memberships vary in size from 10,000 to 1 million. Employers, unions, and individuals can enroll in HMOs, which provide both preventive and crisis medical coverage as well as in-patient hospital care. They differ significantly from parallel European health delivery structures, regarding not only formal ownership, but also their position in the medical care market. Specifically, HMOs can compete with one another for clients; typically, there could be several HMOs in any one community..

Promoters of HMOs were able to take advantage of the greatest single difference between the segmented American and the quasi-monopolistic European health systems—namely, the diversity and privatism of American insurance carriers, which theoretically permit extensive competition. Some competition has occurred to a very limited extent between the two dominant groups, the commercial stock and mutual insurance companies and the quasi-public insurance carriers Blue Cross and Blue Shield. Otherwise, private carriers, who usually "pass through" health insurance costs to employers, have lacked incentives to resist cost increases: The higher their payouts, the higher the reserves they can maintain as a source of investment income. Such a set-up of course makes "inflation and the insurers natural allies, whereas the welfare of the public might be better served if they were natural enemies" (Krizay and Wilson, pp. 34, 53–57, 91).

But when the federal government placed limits on reimbursement of hospital costs, in an attempt to hold down Medicaid expenditures, the private insurers complained of increased "cost shifting" from patients under public programs to those privately insured. In 1979 hospital payments on behalf of the former were $198 a day, compared to $239 for the latter; by 1983 the differential is expected to reach $100 per day. Thus the privately insured might have to shoulder a "hidden tax" of nearly $5 billion a year as a consequence of federal budget cutting (*National Journal*, 21 November 1981).

Comparisons of patient utilization and cost performance of the prepaid HMO systems with insurance-reimbursed fee-for-service systems have generally shown the HMO systems in a good light. Their costs are lower, due mainly to their members' shorter hospital stays. Naturally, this advantage is clearest where the participating physicians have the strongest financial incentive to keep hospital referrals to a minimum. It must be added, though, that usually when enrollees had an option between the two kinds of plans, only a minority chose the prepaid plan. Even by 1980, considerable efforts to publicize the plans failed to boost the number of HMO members above 5 percent of the population, and about half of those are in California, mostly in the Kaiser Permanente programs.

Although legislative promoters expected federal encouragement to lead to some 1700 new HMOs, by the early 1980s only some 250 had become established. An optimistic forecast is that their number might double by the end of the 1980s, to about 20 million members—still less than 10 percent of the population. Why have they not caught on? The main reason is that their architects did not pay enough attention to overcoming both the conflicting interests of other health providers and the deeply ingrained habits of most health consumers. "The fundamental weakness of the HMO proposal was that it rested on an uncritical application of the concept of incentives. . . ." The economists who developed the model tended to take institutions for granted and overestimated the influence that their rational model would have on hospital executives and union leaders. Thus, up to 1981, the failure of HMOs to take off demonstrated "a central irony and limitation of the economics-based policy analysis, namely that an orientation that takes so little direct account of the institution-building process generates so often and so enthusiastically recommendations that presuppose heroic institution-building efforts" (Brown 1981, p. 151).

In contrast to the Nixon health message of 1971, which touted HMOs without even mentioning the word *competition,* Reagan advocates of competition have based their strategy squarely on developing a toughened HMO model, seeking to make evident that some of the amenities of fee-for-service practice—such as free choice of physicians or hospitals and short waiting lines—imply costs which may be beyond their utility to consumers. In this regard they share the judgment of the NHS managers in Britain; but, instead of steering toward a monopoly, they want to engender a "duelling HMO model," in which the more efficient would survive. To ensure survival of the really efficient requires that the competing HMOs all meet some fairly high standard of service. Otherwise, free-riders would shift from high-option to low-option plans whenever they anticipated lower health risks (Enthoven). Then the more expensive treatments would still have to be borne by others.

PLANNING, COMPETITION, AND COST CONTAINMENT

RESTRAINTS AND INNOVATION

One of the most important issues in health policy today concerns soaring health care expenditures. Policy makers fall into two camps: those favoring planning and those favoring competition. The issue at hand is whether costs can best be held down by improving health care planning or by stimulating more market competition.

Physician Payment Systems and Cost Controls

Physician remuneration systems are one focus in the debate. They can be distinguished according to the payment mode utilized. The *fee-for-service* mode is used for most general practitioners and specialists in the United States, Germany, and France. The *salary* system is used for hospital specialists in Britain and Sweden, as well as for many American medical school hospital staffs. In Britain and the Netherlands general practitioners are paid on the *capitation* system. Under this system doctors are paid according to the number of patients enrolled with them. How *often* patients consult them does not affect their income, whereas it does for doctors practicing under the fee-for-service system. In Britain most general practitioners favored the capitation system at the time of the creation of the NHS. German doctors, on the other hand, negotiated a shift from a capitation to a fee-for-service system in the 1960s (Stone 1981).

Payment systems can be deliberately used to influence medical practice. By "weighting" a doctor's income more or less favorably for various services—preventive checkups, drug prescriptions, house calls, and so forth—the payment system can encourage some treatment techniques over others (Glaser 1970). Insurance-based health systems which use the fee-for-service format, such as those in Germany and Japan, have had the highest frequency of doctor visits. The introduction of a compulsory health insurance program does not necessarily trigger basic change in the physicians' remuneration mode, but in time such change may occur. Britain and Sweden are countries where change has taken place, Germany and France where it has not.

Related to cost containment is the concept of peer review.

Peer Review. When government agencies contract for the services of road- or building-construction firms, acceptance of and payment for the work depend on certification by qualified government officials that the finished construction fully meets the specifications of the contract. The same procedure is not applied to health services, because a strong taboo inhibits federal agents from making medical judgments on a patient's care; the government is not allowed to infringe upon the self-regulation of an established professional organization. Professional control, then, implies that only professional peers can evaluate the quality and cost of the services rendered. Since 1974 peer review groups have begun to be established in American communities, known as Professional Standards Review Organizations, or PSROs.

In 1972 Congress passed a bill providing that PSRO membership be open to all licensed physicians, not just to medical society members. This provision made medical societies ineligible as operators of review schemes, but still allowed them to sponsor local PSROs, which they proceeded to do in many places. Some 187 PSROs, each including 300 or more physicians from any one locale, were operating in 1981.

PSROs are intended to substitute peer monitoring of services for bureaucratic monitoring, which has proved distasteful to physicians in both the United States and Europe. In this way PSROs are the counterparts of organizations such as the German Insurance Doctors Associations, which review contractual services provided by physicians who are not full-time government employees. One researcher who examined both systems found that "PSROs put government procurement decisions in the hands of the producers . . . Disciplinary authority, which medical societies and licensing boards have never vigorously exercised, is now firmly institutionalized among the same people with a different organizational home. Unlike the West German system, there are no organized adversaries to monitor, challenge and bargain with the PSROs" (Stone 1974, p. 12).

Does utilization review as operated through PSROs help to control costs? Several studies of their operation in the late 1970s suggest that the savings PSROs initiated were modest (around $50 million) and barely matched the funds expended to maintain them (Newman). In view of these cost-benefit findings, and in keeping with its general drive to eliminate regulation, the Reagan administration in 1981 proposed to phase out support for PSROs, but Congress supported further funding. Health advisors for large employers also argued that the PSROs' record warranted improvement rather than eradication.

An important reason that doctors' fees have gone up faster in the United States than in Europe is that they are seldom fixed in advance or visible to patients. "Almost every economic transaction in the world occurs only after the provider has exhibited his price list or has negotiated a unique price with the customer. American medicine is one of the few situations where the customer rarely knows or understands his obligations in advance" (Glaser 1978, pp. 183–189). Whereas most countries have tended to place professional services on set fee schedules, in the United States even third payers such as Blue Shield have tended to abandon the set fee schedule. Attempts to introduce them under Medicaid have caused physicians to refuse to accept Medicaid patients.

As Europe and America entered the 1980s, the proportion of GNP claimed by health expenditures was in most countries near the 10 percent mark. This constituted a vast proportional increase, since only two decades earlier the proportion was hovering around the 5 percent mark. In Sweden the jump was from 4.7 percent in 1960 to 9.4 in 1980; in the United States it was from 5.3 percent to 9.6; and the figures for Germany and the Netherlands were similar. In fact, it varied somewhat by calculation method and year just which of these was the current recordholder. Systems as distinct as the public insurance-based European systems, the county-based public system of Sweden, and the private American one were all similar in failing to halt the cost inflation. Generally, the wealthier the society, the greater the proportion spent on health. But management and political control also matter, as Figure 3.1 illustrates. Thus the British were able to hold the lid down better than the others.

The major determinants of the growing health expenditures have been identified as the following: demographic changes involving the increasing needs of aging populations and related changes in disease patterns; advances in medical technology extending the range of particularly acute medical treatment and raising public expectations; raised skill levels in health sector occupations leading to higher labor costs, which prevailing financing systems, public or private, have generally not been able to afford.

But the key question in health cost control may be how many actors, public or private, affect investment and other expenditure decisions. In

FIGURE 3.1 HEALTH CARE EXPENDITURES IN TOTAL, 1975

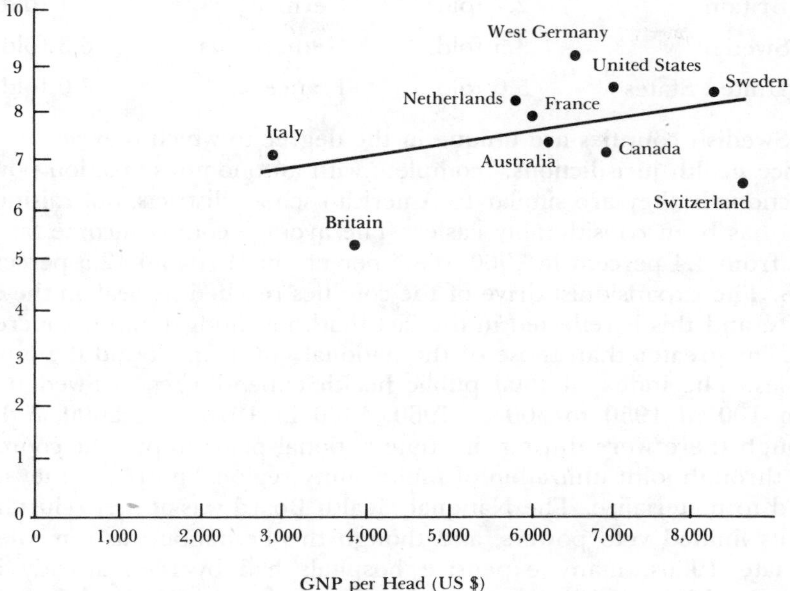

SOURCE Robert J. Maxwell, *Health and Wealth* (Lexington: Heath, 1981), p. 39.

Britain the dominant control exercised over health expenditure by the national treasury and health ministries permitted a tighter limit on costs than in Sweden. The awareness that doctors' pay levels and all other big-ticket items must fit into one annual budget is the major reason that Britain delivers good medical care for a below-average proportion of a below-average per capita GNP. True, doctors have complained noisily about pay increases awarded by the British income review boards, but this has often given the public a misleading impression. "Many Britons—and the Americans who read their selective news coverage of British affairs—assume that the entire medical profession is desperate and that 'socialized medicine' is about to collapse" (Glaser 1978, p. 178). In fact, over time the various groups of British doctors have come to accept that they cannot maintain the large lead over incomes of other professionals like lawyers and engineers which doctors have preserved in the United States and Germany.

In most countries the gap between the average doctor's income and the average worker's income increased in the 1960s, a period of expanding health care demand. The degree of income inequality varied considerably, however. Thus, in 1973–1974 the average physician's income exceeded that of the average production worker by the following ratios (Maxwell, p. 77):

Britain	2.7 fold	Germany	6.1 fold
Sweden	3.5 fold	Netherlands	6.3 fold
United States	5.6 fold	France	7.0 fold

Swedish counties are unique in the degree to which they act as "uni-service health jurisdictions," complete with autonomous taxation powers. Functionally they are similar to American school districts, but raising tax rates has been considerably easier: The average county income tax rate shot from 4.4 percent in 1960 to 8.6 percent in 1970 and 12.5 percent in 1978. The expansionist drive of the counties reached its peak in the early 1960s, and this is reflected in the fact that their budget and tax increases were far greater than those of the national government and the municipalities. The index of total public health expenditures in Sweden rose from 100 in 1950 to 300 in 1960, 1400 in 1970, and 2600 in 1975. Though there were during this time national plans to provide coordination through joint utilization of multicounty regional hospitals, they often failed to materialize. The National Health Board was at first reluctant to use its limited veto powers, and though this hesitation was remedied in the late 1960s, many expensive hospitals had by then already been erected, with each 100 crowns of investment requiring 63 crowns of annual operating expenses.

In the United States most recent attempts at health care cost containment have emphasized micro-level interventions through HSAs and PSROs, where selected groups of providers and consumers became subjects of experiments with utilization and pricing mechanisms. At the same time the resource constraints of the 1980s have encouraged attempts among decentralized political systems to achieve the degrees of macro-level budget control which have sometimes been possible in centralized systems like Britain's, and the Reagan administration's 1981 budget cutting strategies were one example of such an effort. But in the health sector it was Germany that led the way, creating in 1977 a framework which allowed the expenditure policies of numerous public authorities and Sickness Funds to be guided by an overarching budget which was indirectly imposed on most purchasers and third payers of non-hospital health care.

The effort to create this macro-mechanism was triggered by the inability of German legislators to check the vast cost increases of the predominantly public system. Health care expenditures had grown at an annual rate of about 10 percent in the 1960s and rose by almost 20 percent in the early 1970s. This was three or four times the parallel figure for the consumer price index, and it caused German total health expenditures to claim about one tenth of the GNP by 1975.

To brake this trend the federal government introduced and passed—over the strong opposition of the medical profession—the Health Care Cost Containment Act of 1977, which created a National Health Conference, in which all major governmental and private groups engaged in the health sector are represented. It is charged with issuing annual recommendations for ambulatory health development; on the basis of these projections, it fixes annual limits for the total remuneration due to physicians under the insurance system, as well as on total drug expenditures If the prescription increases attributed to certain doctors grows disproportionately, the excess can be taken out of the funds from which doctors' fees are paid (Landsberger).

In its first year of operation, the Conference got unanimous agreement that payments to physicians should increase by 5.5 percent, of which 2.5 percent was to cover rising prices, and 3 percent was for projected increases in physicians' services. From 1977 through 1979 the rate of health cost increase was kept below the rate of increase of GNP, at about 5 percent. The contributions which employers and workers paid to the insurance fund, which had risen from 8.2 percent of wages in 1970 to 11.4 percent in 1977, were stabilized. The budget controls worked less well in 1980 and 1981, when it proved difficult to make some of the limits stick, but even then the increases were well below what they had previously been. One major drawback can be attributed to opposition from the Christian Democratic Union and some *Länder* (states), which delayed extension of the controls to the hospital sector.

Though some physician associations strongly opposed the act and were on the brink of strike action in their campaign against the bill, even right-of-center opinion rejected their case. Organized business pointedly refused to back the physicians' struggle, giving its anti-inflationary goals priority over its anti-control proclivities (Landsberger, p. 53). Thus physicians also came to participate in the corporatized system, through which negotiation machinery became more centralized.

One American attempt at hospital cost containment was backed by the Carter administration but defeated in the House of Representatives in November 1979. Even though it contained many loopholes, the bill could have saved $40 billion over 5 years, according to the administration. Unlike their counterparts in the Bundestag, the American legislators broke party ranks, with two fifths of the Democrats responding to intensive hospital interest lobbying to vote against mandatory controls.

Hospital rate-setting legislation has been passed in New York State and five other states, mainly in the Northeast. As a result, hospital rates there rose by 11.2 percent between 1976 and 1978, compared to an increase of 14.3 percent in the other forty-four states. Nationally the voluntary schemes for holding down cost have proved ineffective, especially after the Reagan victory caused the health industry to ease up on self-restraint. From 1980 to 1981 the rate of health cost increase almost doubled—to 18 percent, much more than the general inflation rate.

Technology Control and Health Planning

In the 1960s most health agencies, public and private, were unambiguously in favor of any new medical technology; its cost-effectiveness was seldom in question. By the 1970s, however, uncontrolled technological development and diffusion began to seem less desirable. Some of the new technologies were very expensive, and with third payers absorbing the costs, demand was enormous even when benefit was marginal. Administrators concluded that public agencies had to decide how much of each new, expensive technology could be afforded and who should receive treatment—and then find a way to enforce their allocations.

In the United States the growing federal health financing role led to the creation of the Health Systems Agencies (HSAs) in 1974, charged with studying local needs and doing the necessary planning. Various forms of federal aid to hospitals and for hospital construction were then tied, sometimes directly and sometimes through state agencies, to the "certification of need" given by the local HSA.

The first significant technology issue faced by HSAs involved the computer tomography (CT) scanner. The CT scanner uses a moving x-ray tube and a computer for a cross-sectional picture of the internal structure of a body or body part. As of 1981, these scanners cost about $500,000; at full capacity the cost per scan is between $150 and $300. The potential users are almost unlimited. Some recent studies have shown that though CTs can be highly cost-effective, their widespread use could draw funds from other priorities in and outside the health sector. How, then, can the CT scanner be restricted to those uses to which it is genuinely better-suited than any less expensive method (Brasfield)?

Some HSAs established definite criteria for "certificate of need" clearance, requiring hospitals to justify the addition of a scanner. They could refer to federal standards, which required that every scanner already in an area should be performing a minimum of 2500 scans per year. The actual controls often remained weak, however, as planners learned the hard way that the American local level was the toughest setting in which to try to stem the technological tide. Localism, commercialism, and boosterism combined to overwhelm the controllers.

By 1980, 80 percent of large hospitals had scanners in operation. In 1981 a report by the Office of Technology Assessment concluded that the left hand of the federal government had in effect undermined the curtailment efforts of its right hand. For "the stance assumed by the federal government toward other stages of development and use of scanners has tended to foster diffusion and widespread use . . . through its reimbursement policies it continues to assume an almost open-ended commitment to pay for CT scans" (Office of Technology Assessment, 1981).

The CT scanner has been deployed much less widely in Britain than in the United States, even though it was a British invention, and the original leading manufacturer was British. This can be attributed to an explicit policy of holding down NHS costs, which resulted in strong resistance to the acquisition of anything so new and expensive. Usually the central contracting arrangement, as handled by the Scientific and Technical Branch of the Department of Health and Social Services, has made it possible to make restrictions stick.

Private philanthropy has permitted some circumvention of the tight restrictions, and hospitals are sometimes able to get a scanner with the help of donors. Since hospitals pay maintenance, however, the NHS sometimes has to pay to operate a scanner where it did not want one. Even so, by March 1979 CT installation had been contained in Britain to one per million people (compared to 5.7 per million in the United States).

In Sweden there were only two scanners in place and one on order when the national plan for controlling the CT scanner came out. The Swedish preference for broadly supported corporatist decision making led them to early regular consultations with doctors about the scanners and largely precluded major attempts to circumvent the emergent policy. Sweden stressed replacing equivalent, equally expensive, and much more dangerous techniques with CTs, allocating scanners mostly to those regional hospitals already doing a great deal of work in the relevant area. This policy thus allowed the new technology to be introduced while maintaining the intended restraints on diffusion.

Germany got a later start at regulating hospital technology, which has allowed the scanner to diffuse much more freely. Hospital purchases are supported with federal or Land funds, though hospitals have financed scanners by holding fundraising drives. In addition, private physicians are permitted to buy the equipment. Consequently, Germany has many more scanners per capita than Britain or Sweden, with 30 percent—an unusually high proportion—installed in the offices of specialists in private practice. By 1979 the tentative planning goals of 160 to 200 scanners had already been surpassed.

As Table 3.6 shows, CT scanners diffused faster in the United States and Germany than in Britain or Sweden. In both the United States and Germany authority over new technology is more divided between federal and state governments, providing more loopholes for adroit hospital administrators to exploit. Furthermore, the structure of payment has accelerated diffusion by creating profitable private markets for CT scanners.

TABLE 3.6 Diffusion of CT Scanners

	Number of Scanners		Scanners per Million Population	
	March 1978	*March 1979*	*March 1978*	*March 1979*
United States	1005	1254	4.6	5.7
West Germany	93	160	1.5	2.6
Britain	52	57	.9	1.0
Sweden	13	14	1.6	1.7

SOURCE Erik H.L. Gaensler, Egon Jonsson, and Duncan vG. Neuhauser, "Controlling Medical Technology in Sweden," *The Implications of Cost-Effectiveness Analysis of Medical Technology*, OTA Background Paper Number 4 (Washington, D.C.: Office of Technology Assessment, October 1980).

The Swedish record in holding CTs down shows that on some capital investment issues the Swedish system, though formally less centralized, can operate almost as well as the British.

Utilization of costly technology for dealing with kidney failure offers another example of differing national allocation procedures. Here, too, Britain had led in setting up a system of treating renal patients through dialysis or transplants but came to limit hospital dialysis much more than other countries, with the consequence that people over age 50 were much less likely to be accepted for treatment there than in Germany or the United States. A leading British authority makes an illuminating comment on the equity choices involved:

> The choice of whom to treat and whom not to treat is, of course, a very hard one in ethical and human terms. Too much medical intervention is a real hazard when resource constraints are not apparent, and treatment can then become inhumane . . . What is apparent is that resource constraints have influenced the pattern of provision of end-stage renal failure in the United Kingdom. The choices made seem logical within the resource constraints (Maxwell, p. 95).

Competition and New Health Care Models

In the United States during the 1970s the debate about the introduction of a national health insurance program waxed hot. In that context we asked, in the previous edition of this book: "Will the American health delivery system in 1984 be significantly different from what existed in 1974, or will a basically similar system be selling similar sets of services, with the federal government paying a higher price than private patients did earlier?"

The answer, we can now ascertain, has come out more in terms of the second alternative, though only partly, for the overall range of public programs has not been extended. Under the Carter administration, policy makers looked closely at foreign models of health insurance development, particularly in Canada and Germany. But differences between the very cautious proposals of the administration and the more expansive proposals of Senator Edward Kennedy and his labor allies allowed opponents to lobby successfully against the pending bills. Limited progress was made in developing the regulatory techniques; somewhat more was accomplished in pursuing preventive health measures (Kelman). However, then the Reagan administration veered far in the other direction, proposing to phase out many of the regulatory programs. Its hostility toward insufficiently cost-conscious reformers was symbolized by the head of the Occupational Safety and Health Administration, who ordered the destruction of 50,000 government booklets on cotton dust because he believed the cover photograph was overly sympathetic to victims of brown lung disease.

These American developments reflect, much more sharply than those in Europe, a realignment of forces in health politics. For more than a generation the politics of health care was polarized largely around the issue of national health insurance, with one coalition led by the Democratic party, and another coalesced around the AMA. Both of these institutions have become weakened over the past decade. For the Democrats, the failure to "run with" the health insurance issue reflected the general decay of the New Deal coalition. For its part, the AMA has lost many members, and has been on the defensive in many respects.

The multiple pressures on the AMA were reflected in the new code of ethics which it adopted in 1980. The new code drops the bans on advertising as well as dealings with nonorthodox practitioners (which had cost the AMA more than $1 million per year in lawsuits). The premier role previously assigned to physicians has been replaced by a more modestly phrased statement stressing respect for patients and other health professionals. However, it still defends the doctor's freedom "to choose whom to serve and with whom to associate."

Partly because the United States has not developed effective structures to monitor and guide income and price policies, American business organizations have tended to remain relatively uninvolved in health issues. Whereas German business organizations supported health cost controls legislation, equivalent American groups such as the Business Roundtable opposed similar legislation in 1979. Although financing their workers' health benefits is costly, amounting to some 7 percent of the wage bill in the automobile industry, industry has not yet collaborated with government on this issue. Whether they are likely to become more involved is uncertain (Sapolsky *et al.* 1981). However, a Washington, D.C., business lobby on health issues opposed the Reagan administration's proposals to dismantle control instruments like PRSOs and HSAs, at least until the proposed alternatives were firmly in place.

The Reagan administration's health policies have centered on dismantling regulation and promoting competition between alternative suppliers of health care. But because medicine has for so long been enmeshed in practices that restrain competition, these policies are very difficult to design. Various experiments with financial incentives—for example, payment schemes for both patients and providers—are being tried. But as the growing pains of HMOs illustrate, strong systemic resistances have held back progress. Not least are those in Congress. As Budget Director David Stockman's former legislative assistant wrote in 1981: "The legislative future of competition is not necessarily bright . . . Legislation contemplating a market solely composed of prepaid plans . . . is the *least* likely outcome of congressional deliberation over injecting competition into the health care field" (Moran, p. 193).

Skeptics continue to insist that the infusion of market forces into health care is limited by the atypical nature of deeply set attitudes in this sector. "People want health insurance and they want it without deductibles or coinsurance . . . They don't wish to be forced to make rational trade-offs when they are faced with medical care consumption decisions." The pro-competition plans would shift the burden of regulation from the providers to the insurers, and critics argue that this would merely shift, and not displace, regulation. Indeed, the offensive against regulation put forth by economists may obscure deeper-lying policy choices: "The current hostility toward regulation (and the converse promotion of competition) owes little to dispassionate intellectual analysis. Rather it arises from a conjunction of short- and long-term political forces with the tendency of health policy makers to adopt new fads every two or three years" (Vladeck, p. 209).

In 1981 the British Tory Social Services Secretary sent several officials to Europe and the United States to examine health insurance models which might be considered as alternative finance models to the National Health Service. The information they returned with was not encouraging for those wanting to devise competitive insurance-based modules in order to begin replacing the National Health Service. In a poll, those who thought that the idea of switching to an insurance-based system of finance was a good idea were outnumbered three to two by those who judged it a bad idea. The idea of privatizing the system, so as to have "everyone choosing and paying for the service they want," was rejected by more than six to one. When asked whether the NHS represents "value for money to the taxpayer," 71 percent said yes, and only 21 percent said no (*The Guardian,* 21 December 1981).

* * * * *

There are numerous reasons why we cannot provide a confident bottom-line assessment which fully contrasts the costs and benefits of national systems. This is so partly because we do not yet have fully reliable

TABLE 3.7 Cross-national Rankings of Health Care Expenditures and Measures of Health Status, 1975

	Health Care Expenditures as Percentage of GNP	RANK	Patient Access to Specialists	Health Status Based on 17 Mortality Rates	RANK
West Germany	9.4	1	Uncontrolled	1.23	6
United States	8.7	2	Uncontrolled	1.17	5
Sweden	8.5	3	Uncontrolled	0.73	1
France	7.9	4	Uncontrolled	1.10	4
Netherlands	7.9	4	Referral only	0.79	2
Britain	6.1	6	Referral only	0.93	3

NOTE The index employed in the health status column reflects how the average of that country's rates for 17 age- and sex-specific mortality rates relate to the mean of the above 6 countries plus 4 others (Australia, Canada, Italy and Switzerland).

SOURCE Robert J. Maxwell, *Health and Wealth* (Lexington, Mass: Lexington Books, 1981) pp. 52, 90.

comparable cost data, but even more because there is no consensus about how to assess the benefits that medical care brings. With these reservations we nevertheless present figures in Table 3.7 which show at least an initial approach with one set of plausible data. This table relates health expenditure rates of 1975 to indicators of health status, as reflected in a variety of mortality rates, which treatment might be presumed to have affected to some degree. From them one can extract the following theses for further consideration:

Both the segmented American and the corporatized German systems exhibit relatively poor cost-benefit profiles. They lead the other countries in expenditure ranking, and yet exhibit the poorest health status indicators.

The decentralized Swedish public system, though also costly, is accompanied by the most favorable health status measure.

The more fully nationalized British system achieves middle-rank health status through by far the lowest level of expenditures.

Systems which do not seek to control access to specialists may engender more costly waste, though this conclusion hinges rather strongly on the British case.

These findings are not conclusive. At the present stage of comparative policy analysis, they must be regarded as suggestive only. Indeed, we must repeat that health status is only partly determined by treatment, and vastly by social conditions affected by other policies. One of the most important of these is housing, to which we turn in the next chapter.

4
HOUSING POLICY

Most people would agree that a roof over one's head is as vital a human as any of the other goods and services discussed in this volume, including education and even health care. Although housing has not achieved the status of an entitlement in most Western societies, all Western governments have taken some responsibility for assuring that all citizens, including the poor, have access to decent housing. But housing policy, as we shall see in this chapter, is not simply a matter of seeing that every citizen has a roof overhead.

Housing programs have profound effects on a nation's economic health, on individual families' financial security, and on the shape of urban areas. In all Western economies, the construction industry is a major economic sector whose fortunes seriously affect overall levels of employment. By manipulating tax and credit policies and production programs to raise or lower the volume of housing construction, a national government directly influences the jobs of hundreds of thousands of construction workers, suppliers of building materials, real estate brokers, and others who depend on the industry. For many families, buying a house is the largest single investment they ever make. Thus the financial calculations of millions of households are affected by government actions regarding housing. Moreover, unlike some social policies, housing policies have effects that cannot easily be modified or reversed, because they are literally cast in concrete. Housing developments influence transportation, commerce, and the location of many kinds of community facilities for years after they are built.

CHOICES IN HOUSING POLICY

Scope and Thresholds

Despite the similar considerations affecting housing policy makers in the industrialized countries, the choices they have made in formulating national housing programs have by no means been uniform. In establishing the scope of responsibility for housing, national governments face the basic choice of whether or not to limit aid to those citizens who cannot secure even minimally decent housing through the private market. Some governments have supplemented the housing offered by the private market, chiefly to the poor, the elderly, and the handicapped, while others have intervened in broader ways by trying to plan and control the provision of housing to all groups in the society. However, even governments that have chosen the broader approach have eschewed the nationalization of housing that has occurred in communist countries. As mixed economies, all the Western nations maintain strong private housing markets, primarily to serve middle-income households. It has become distressingly clear, however, that private housing markets cannot produce sufficient quantities of decent housing for low-income people. That task has fallen increasingly to the national governments, which typically have worked through either nonprofit producers or local governments to build low-cost housing. In several European nations the nonprofit sector, composed of housing cooperatives, trade unions, and nonprofit corporations, builds most of the low-income housing, in cooperation with both national and local governments. In other nations, local governments themselves operate as builders and managers of low-income housing. The degree to which housing programs faithfully reflect national intent thus depends on the degree of leverage that national governments have over local governments and nonprofit builders. As we shall see, that degree of leverage differs from nation to nation.

Housing Policy Instruments

The selection of policy instruments by national governments presents a choice between two strategies that can be broadly labeled "supply-side" and "demand-side" strategies. That is, policy makers can opt for subsidies either to builders (profit-making or nonprofit) or to consumers—or for a combination to both. The balance between these two main types of subsidy has differed in the six nations under study, although in the last fifteen years a general shift in all six toward consumer subsidies has occurred. The relative advantages of the two options are sharply focused in public debates over which should be used to assist poor families. Are the poor better served by public housing projects, or by allowances that send them into the private market to find their own housing? Naturally, such debates are conditioned by the interests at stake in the housing field. Predictably, producer lobbies on both sides of the Atlantic have preferred construction subsidies, and have shown little enthusiasm for subsidies to consumers. Despite their preferences, however, consumer subsidies are increasing in most Western nations.

Distribution of Costs and Benefits

The distributional issue facing policy makers can be simply stated: Who should benefit from housing subsidies? This issue, as we shall see, is closely related to the choice of policy instruments. Proponents of the supply-side strategy have met increasing opposition from critics who argue that government programs to subsidize producers are ineffective in helping low-income citizens. The filtering effect in urban housing markets has been called into doubt; governments cannot be certain that by enlarging the total housing stock, they are creating vacancies for all income groups in the population. In American cities, residential segregation patterns prevent many families from moving into neighborhoods where better housing opportunities exist. European housing markets have their own built-in rigidities created by rent control. Even when governments subsidize producers to build housing specifically for the poor, it is extremely difficult to ensure that the housing will ultimately be occupied by the intended beneficiaries. Such distributional considerations have certainly contributed to the shift by all six governments toward direct subsidies to consumers.

Restraints and Innovation in Housing Policy

Without doubt the single most important factor limiting housing improvements at the present time is inflation. The steep rise in housing costs since 1970 is common to all of the countries under review. In addition to preventing many consumers from upgrading their housing situation, this rise limits governmental options in the housing field. To blunt the impact of inflation on housing consumers public officials have experimented with certain policies, including various types of rent control and new ways to facilitate home ownership. The common criticism of both of these experimental strategies is that they risk creating long-term problems in exchange for short-term relief.

GOVERNMENTAL RESPONSIBILITY FOR SHELTER

SCOPE AND THRESHOLDS

Legislative rhetoric regarding governmental responsibility for housing is remarkably similar throughout the industrialized nations. Every national government has produced policy statements pledging its commitment to a decent home for every citizen. Moving beyond the rhetoric, however, we discover important differences in the role that national governments have chosen to play, as well as differences in the extent of local governments' responsibility for, and control over, housing programs.

Public Intervention in the Private Housing Market

Shelter is one of humankind's basic requirements. Yet until the twentieth century the governments of Europe and the United States took almost no direct responsibility for housing their populations. Even the horrifying accounts of working-class living conditions contained in the popular works of writers such as Emile Zola and Charles Dickens stimulated little immediate action by governments. And when, in the late nineteenth century, governments did begin to take action, it was usually in the form of regulatory legislation prohibiting slums and requiring tenement owners to upgrade housing on their properties. Such legislation placed greater demands on property owners, forcing them to raise rents and making it increasingly difficult for low-income families to afford housing. A limited amount of housing for special groups had of course been provided by private charities. Governments, however, were not in the practice of building houses, even for the poor. Before 1900, the provision of housing by some local governments in Europe was limited to special-purpose institutions, such as the British foundling homes and workhouses.

The housing sector has, of course, always depended to a certain extent on government economic policies. At a minimum, the functioning of the housing sector requires that government enforce some consistent set of agreements regarding property rights. In addition, government must maintain a stable economic environment in which permanent financial institutions can survive, for housing is a durable, high-cost commodity which requires long-term investment. But before 1900 most direct public involvement in housing was limited to encouraging self-help schemes through cooperatives and unions, in order to build and maintain a limited amount of working-class housing. Even the social reformers of the 1890s tended to agree with the banks, the landowners, and the building industries that government intervention in housing would constitute an unhealthy form of paternalism.

Despite this bias against public intervention in housing which prevailed on both sides of the Atlantic in 1900, the combined impact of two world wars and a major depression in the first half of the twentieth century brought all Western governments into the housing field. While many nations began experimenting with housing programs during the interwar period, it was not until after World War II that most of these programs really "took off" and began to assume their present dimensions.

Even up to 1950, many governments assumed that their housing responsibilities were temporary, seeing their role as a response to the emergency conditions created by the war damage, by the 1930s collapse of private capital markets, and by the abnormally high construction costs that stemmed from war-related shortages of material. Once the private housing market was reestablished, governments expected to withdraw.

Several socioeconomic trends, however, conspired to expand rather than reduce government involvement. Postwar demographic changes produced larger populations of elderly people and an increase in marriage rates. These trends, combined with widespread prosperity in the 1950s, led to a greater tendency for households to subdivide, thereby creating pressure on housing markets. In addition to providing greater opportunities for the establishment of separate households, the postwar economic expansion drew large numbers of migrant workers into growing industrial centers, especially in northern Europe. At the same time, governments were recognizing the need to modernize and upgrade much of their older housing stock. Urban renewal on a large scale was thus added to the public agenda. Finally, in addition to all of the problems confronting governments with regard to the housing stock itself, the question of distribution also came to the fore in the postwar period. Governments now intervened to try to reduce the huge disparities in the housing situations of different income groups in the population.

During the 1960s, observers of housing policies in Western Europe and the United States began to use the labels "comprehensive" and "supplementary" to distinguish between policies which aimed at planning and controlling the total volume of housebuilding and policies which aimed only at bolstering the private housing market and providing housing for those groups that could not be served by private builders. Those governments with *comprehensive* policies took responsibility for the housing needs of the entire population; those with *supplementary* policies relied on private industry to plan for the vast majority of the population, while they planned only for the minorities unable to obtain housing on the open market (the poor and the elderly, for example).[1]

Surprisingly, the scope of government responsibility for housing is not necessarily most comprehensive where it is most visible. The presence of large government-owned housing stocks in British and American cities does not mean that government in those two nations takes a greater

[1]For examples of the use of the labels "comprehensive" and "supplementary," see D. V. Donnison, *The Government of Housing* (Baltimore: Penguin, 1967) and United Nations, Economic Commission for Europe, *Major Long-Term Problems of Government Housing and Related Policies,* Vol. 1 (Geneva, 1966). A recent study which uses these categories in a modified form is Bruce Headey, *Housing Policy in the Developed Economy: The United Kingdom, Sweden, and the United States* (New York: St. Martin's Press, 1978).

responsibility for housing. In fact, the reverse is true. Those governments of Europe which plan for the entire housing market have usually chosen *not* to build government housing, but instead to subsidize private builders of both the profit-making and the nonprofit variety. The scope of governmental responsibility tends therefore to be most comprehensive where it is least visible.

Under this scheme, the housing policies in Britain and the United States are classified as supplementary. In both nations, the growth of the housing stock has taken place very gradually, within the framework of long-established trends toward urbanization and industrialization. In these countries, the building industry and the private credit market have for the most part been adequate to sustain a large volume in construction.

In Britain during the years immediately following World War II the Labour government assumed a very large share of the responsibility for financing and distributing housing. In retrospect, however, that spate of housing activity appears to have been an exception, dictated by the acute postwar shortage, and the 1950s saw the Conservative governments returning to the position that government housing activity should be a supplement to rather than a replacement for the private market.

Given the fact that the Labour party has furnished the most consistent support for expanding public housing, it is surprising that the Labour government which took over in 1964 did not strongly contest the Conservative position. In fact, the Labour government's 1965 *White Paper on Housing* was explicit on this point:

> Once the country has overcome its huge social problem of slumdom and obsolescence, and met the need of the great cities for more houses let at moderate rents, the programs of subsidized council housing should decrease. The expansion of the public programme now proposed is to meet exceptional needs . . .

Not unexpectedly, we find this view reinforced in the Conservatives' 1972 Housing Finance Act, which aimed to limit public housing to the needy, and once again in the Labour government's 1977 *Green Paper on Housing,* which explained planned cutbacks in government investment by arguing that the need for it was finally declining. The government would therefore confine its activity to certain housing stress areas, leaving the private market to supply the housing needs of the majority (Department of Environment).

The history of American housing policy presents an even clearer illustration of the traditional belief that government activity should merely supplement private activity. One recent commentator on U.S. housing policy even argued that "in a sense, U.S. housing policy is to have no policy and rely on private enterprise" (Headey, p. 175). The cornerstone of federal housing policy is the mortgage guarantee program, which operates through the Federal Housing Administration (FHA) and the Veterans Administration (VA). Far from interfering with private enterprise, the mortgage guarantee program has greased the wheels of the private credit machine so as to promote private transactions. The FHA and the VA furnish insurance on the risks that private credit institutions take in lending money to finance housing purchases; both agencies agree to make good any approved loan if the home buyer should default on payments. By thus allowing private banks and savings associations to lend money to home buyers without bearing the risks involved in normal lending transactions, they have facilitated home ownership.

Nor has American public housing ever occupied a position of competition with the private rental market. So strong were the pressures against undermining the private housing market by building cheap government housing that Congress wrote into the original 1937 legislation an "equivalent elimination provision," which stipulated that for every public housing unit built, a substandard dwelling must be removed within five years, via condemnation or demolition. The anxiety expressed by American housing officials that "the indiscriminate production of new subsidized housing could lead to sharp diminution of the demand for privately financed housing" (Kristof, p. 91) hardly seems justified, given the record of the public housing program. Never since the 1930s has public housing constituted more than 3 percent of the total housing stock in the United States.

In contrast, the housing policies of Sweden, France, West Germany, and the Netherlands are classified as comprehensive, even though none of these governments has directly built as much government housing as Britain (see Table 4.1). All have explicitly committed themselves to a policy of channeling the flow of national resources in the housing field in ways that will maximize the welfare of the entire population. By means of relatively shallow subsidies to a very broad spectrum of housing investors, the governments of these countries are able to exercise significant control over the volume, timing, and even the location of residential building for all income levels and by almost all types of builders.

Sweden presents the most dramatic example of a comprehensive housing policy. Although public programs played a marginal role in Sweden's housing sector up to World War II, the Social Democratic government undertook from 1946 to 1948 a series of measures which vastly extended the government's control. Here the comprehensive approach to housing encompassed planning for all income levels, not just for low-income Swedes. The government's ability to carry out its plans rests on its mortgage loan program, which has expanded so dramatically since 1946 that in recent decades as much as 90 percent of all housing construction in the country has involved government loans.

In West Germany at the end of World War II, there was an undeniable need for the government to take a major role in rebuilding that nation's devastated housing stock. Yet in the postwar climate, officials declined to create a massive government-owned housing stock; instead, they chose to influence the housing supply by providing interest-free loans to any individual or enterprise desiring to build, provided the housing was to be rented at a moderate sum. By this means, as well as with low-interest loans and tax concessions to homeowners, the government was able to bring the nation from a 35 percent housing shortage in 1950 to a national vacancy rate of 3 percent (considered optimal) in 1975 (Hallett, p. 12).

Similarly, France builds almost no housing directly but wields enormous influence over the entire construction industry. All construction is channeled through a government licensing system. And not only does the French government closely control the principal lending agencies, but it manipulates tax privileges on repayment of building loans in order to lure investors in directions it favors.

Overlaps and Conflicts Between National and Local Responsibilities

The administration of housing programs invariably requires some reliance on local agencies. Decisions made at the national level must be filtered through the prism of local politics, always with the possibility that the interaction between national purposes and local interests will significantly alter the shape of a program.

To produce housing, national governments rely either on local governments as builders or on private producers, both nonprofit and profit-making. One might assume that choosing local governments as producers would give national policy makers more centralized control over the production process than would a decision to rely on non-governmental producers. Such a view would be overly simplistic.

For one thing, many of the non-governmental builders in Western Europe are large, highly professional nonprofit enterprises with far-flung interests throughout a particular country. Working through such companies gives governments more leverage over costs and building standards in a greater number and variety of projects than they could gain by working through local governments. The outstanding example is West Germany's Neue Heimat, which began in the 1920s as a union-sponsored nonprofit builder in Hamburg. As a national and even international organization, Neue Heimat not only builds an enormous amount of housing but also furnishes planning, zoning, and urban renewal assistance to cities all over the country. This nonprofit has pioneered prefabricated housing technology in Germany, and its computerized information system provides a unique national data base with which to analyze housing market trends. In Sweden, similar roles are played by the two major national housing cooperatives, HSB and Svenska Riksbyggen, and by SABO, the peak organization of the nonprofit corporations. Such national organizations serve to structure what would otherwise be a highly fragmented housing market, and hence they act as coordinating points for housing policy.

Nor is it as easy as it might seem for national governments to control the housing programs of local authorities, even in the unitary political systems of Europe. When local governments take the major responsibility for housing production, they must normally go to the private capital markets for some substantial portion of the investment funds, just as nonprofits and other developers must do. Hence the size and timing of their building programs are affected not only by national priorities but also by the requirements of the private credit market. Furthermore, the partisan complexion of local governments, relative to the national administration, may play an important role in determining local cooperation with national objectives. So, for example, the ability of Sweden's Social Democrats to gain local cooperation in implementing their housing program after the war was undoubtedly related to the fact that the main cities were also controlled by Social Democrats. And in Britain a number of studies have shown that local authorities controlled by the Labour party pursue more vigorous building programs than Conservative-controlled localities (Boaden; Boaden and Alford; Davies).

Normally, local governments can be expected to respond positively to national production incentives when it is a question of housing their own population. It is more difficult, however, for central governments to persuade localities to build housing for people outside their boundaries, especially low-income families. When the prevailing national policy is to promote the movement of low-income households across local government boundaries, then national-local power relationships quickly come into play.

Perhaps the most striking examples are found in American cities. Since its inception in 1937, American public housing has been concentrated in central cities. Under the legislation that created this housing program, localities were free to request federal subsidies to build low-rent housing in their municipality. By 1970 only about 15 percent of the eligible jurisdictions had chosen to participate (Fried, p. 72). Among those who did were all American cities with populations over 250,000. Small towns and suburbs, on the other hand, have been notoriously resistant to any public housing for low-income families; what little they have constructed has been designed for elderly tenants.

In passing the 1974 Housing and Community Development Act, Congress seemed to provide national housing officials with more leverage over recalcitrant suburban jurisdictions. Under the 1974 Act, in order to receive the block grants to which they are entitled, all localities must submit to the

Department of Housing and Urban Development (HUD) a Housing Assistance Plan that acknowledges that a specified number of low- and moderate-income residents can be expected to reside in their community in the future. Moreover, the 1974 legislation gave HUD the option to contract directly with private developers to build low-income housing in the suburbs, rather than wait for the local government to apply. In practice, however, these changes have made little difference in national-local power relationships. First, HUD's only weapon against non-complying jurisdictions is to withhold funds; and suburban communities have turned down federal Community Development funds rather than comply with the requirement to include low-income housing. Second, even if HUD tries to bypass local government to work directly with private developers, local officials can still use zoning laws, building codes, and other local ordinances to obstruct the development. Few profit-oriented developers are willing to sustain lengthy court battles against local governments in order to build low-rent housing in suburban communities.

American cities are not alone in facing suburban resistance against the influx of low-income renters. The city of Stockholm faced a similar problem in the post-World War II era. But in Stockholm's case, the power of the national administration was sufficient to force city-suburb cooperation. Like many other European cities in 1945, Stockholm suffered from a housing shortage. To attack the problem, the city, with financial encouragement from the national government, created in 1947 a set of three nonprofit public utility corporations to build and manage new housing units. There was, however, a scarcity of undeveloped land in the city itself, severely limiting the amount of new construction possible within its jurisdictional boundaries. Surrounded by twenty-eight other municipalities, each of which exercised autonomy in regulating construction inside its borders, Stockholm had by 1956 acquired a waiting list of 100,000 for new housing, and had a limited number of sites on which to build.

To get the cooperation of the suburbs in tackling this housing crisis, the city launched a vigorous campaign at the regional level, using a double-edged strategy. Socialist city officials persuaded suburban leaders to join in a metropolitan planning agency, the Greater Stockholm Planning Board, to coordinate housing production throughout the region. But, in addition to cultivating the formal cooperation of suburban governments within the planning board, the city also used its land-purchase powers to gain informal leverage over suburban officials. Stockholm has pursued a land-purchase policy since the turn of the century; but the purchases made in the 1960s far exceeded the total acreage that had been acquired from 1904 to 1959. The city's acquisitions ranged over the entire metropolitan area, some parcels lying twenty miles or more from the city's center. By aggressively pursuing this land-acquisition policy, the city managed to gain control over large land parcels located in suburban jurisdictions; and city ownership of suburban property then provided a bargaining edge when the city sought out suburban cooperation in housing production. Numerous bargains were struck, in which suburban governments agreed to accept city building companies as partners in the construction of new housing projects on suburban sites.

However, it soon became apparent that the distribution of these newly built units was a potential source of conflict between the city and the suburbs. One of the great risks run by suburban politicians in cooperating with the city on housing production was that the city could choose to steer large numbers of low-income families to suburban housing units. Since Swedish municipalities gain most of their revenues from personal income taxes, they could not be expected to welcome an influx of low-income residents. The suburbs therefore resisted handing over their power to distribute new apartments to a regional housing exchange.

Their resistance was overcome only when the national government intervened to force an integrated solution to Stockholm's housing crisis. A royal commission created in 1962 to study the question produced a final report which left only two options open to the suburbs: Either they would cooperate voluntarily in a regional distribution scheme for allocating new housing, or the national government would impose a common housing exchange. As a follow-up to the commission's report, the national government announced in 1966 that its loans in the region would henceforth go only to municipalities which were participants in the housing exchange. The impact of that announcement is obvious, if we remember that 90 percent of Swedish housing construction depends on government loans of some kind.

INTERVENTIONS INTO HOUSING MARKETS

INSTRUMENTS

Just as in the delivery of health care each nation has developed its own system for deploying and paying doctors, so different nations use various strategies for producing and distributing housing. Nonetheless, we can broadly distinguish two kinds of strategies: subsidizing producers, and subsidizing consumers. These two strategies can be characterized respectively as the supply-side strategy and the demand-side strategy.

Supply-side Strategies

Offering subsidies to housing suppliers is the most direct method of stimulating housing production. It is therefore the favored strategy for meeting a nation's need for additional dwelling units. The need to stimulate housing construction may arise from a number of different causes, the most obvious being a dramatic population shift. In Sweden the proportion of the population living in urban areas shot up from only 38 percent in 1931 to 73 percent in 1961 (Donnison, p. 160). Naturally, such rapid urbanization created an acute housing shortage in the cities. The Dutch present the clearest case of a postwar housing shortage that stemmed from the effects of demographic change: In addition to very rapid population growth, the Dutch experienced a sharp upturn in the proportion of marriage-age citizens and older people. Such shifts have multiplied the demand for housing units. West Germany's postwar shortage was of course related to war damage. For the French, the postwar housing problem was caused less by an absolute shortage of units than by the overcrowded, substandard conditions prevailing in a large proportion of French households. The French lagged far behind most other European countries in such measures as the number of rooms per person or bathroom facilities per dwelling, as well as in the overall modernity of the housing stock.

A somewhat different motivation for governments to adopt production subsidies comes from a general need to stimulate the economy. In the United States, for example, the Depression of the 1930s lowered the living standard of a great segment of the population but did not actually create a housing shortage. On the contrary, the postponement of marriage and child-bearing plans, coupled with the doubling-up of unemployed families, led to the abandonment of many homes. The federal housing programs created under the New Deal were motivated more by the desire to create employment in the construction industries than by the need to enlarge the housing stock.

The two primary instruments for pursuing a supply-side strategy in housing are: (1) construction programs in which the government builds its own housing for rent, usually to low- and moderate-income people, and (2) subsidies to private producers of either the profit-making or the nonprofit variety. Britain has used the first instrument, public construction, more vigorously than any other Western nation. From 1945 to 1948, Britain moved from a negligible volume of public construction to over 190,000 units of public housing completed in one year (1948). Even under the Conservatives in the 1950s and early 1960s, the annual completion rate never dropped below 100,000. In fact, from 1946 to 1976, Britain built at the impressive rate of 143,000 public housing units per year (Merrett, Chapter 9). Public housing is so prominent now in Britain that it contains a quarter of all British households. Its widespread acceptability is based on the fact that it was not confined to low-income tenants, but open to tenants at all income levels.

Since the early 1970s, however, the view of public, or council, housing held by both the British government and the public has been gradually changing. The largest single step toward change was taken by the Conservatives in the 1972 Housing Finance Act, which forced local government councils to charge higher rents across the board, while instituting special rent relief only for those who could demonstrate need. Defenders of public housing charged that the result would be to force out the more prosperous residents who would find it cheaper to live elsewhere. They invoked the grim images of public housing in America as evidence of the problems that governments encounter when they limit public housing to the poor. Interestingly, though, America's public housing program was not originally created to serve the welfare poor only.

The initial political pressure for government housing in the United States came from the large, relatively articulate population of "deserving poor" created by the Depression, the millions of people who had been reduced in the 1930s from middle-class to low-income status or worse. However, Congress's determination to limit public housing to the poor gradually transformed the composition of the tenant population in the housing projects. The Housing Act of 1949 gave priority to families displaced by urban renewal, and prohibited local housing authorities from refusing to accept families merely because their incomes were derived from public assistance. Twenty years later, Congress reaffirmed this view of public housing as an assistance service to the poor by passing the Brooke Amendment of 1969, which stipulated that public housing tenants could not be required to pay more than 25 percent of their monthly incomes for rent. This made public housing accessible to many families that previously had not been able to afford the rent levels.

As the projects have been transformed into poverty enclaves in the last thirty years, they have become increasingly unacceptable to all but the lowest socioeconomic group. Life in public housing exerts so little attraction that even those families who are poor enough to qualify (maximum acceptable income varies widely from state to state) frequently reject this alternative. As the program's clientele has narrowed over the years, so that now it serves only problem families and the elderly, the reservoir of political support for public housing has shrunk. Labor unions such as the AFL-CIO, which played a key role in the legislative battles over the program in the late 1940s, provide a good example of public housing's political problem. Union enthusiasm for the program has dampened markedly over the years; although union spokesmen still support the program in principle, they have little stake in its expansion. Given their income levels, the skilled and semiskilled members of unions are unlikely to benefit from public housing. On the contrary, in speaking for their members as housing consumers, the unions are much more interested in the expansion of the FHA mortgage insurance program than in large-scale government-sponsored rental programs. The gradual disenchantment exhibited by the program's original supporters, combined with local hostility to the construction of new projects, has meant that "very few people are pushing [public housing] as a vitally important program, the way they were in the 1930s" (Wolman 1971, p. 35).

Rather than building a stock of public housing, most Western European nations have opted to stimulate production by sudsidizing private builders. When offered to profit-making enterprises, such subsidies are commonly restricted to dwellings that will be moderately priced. For example, West Germany's postwar policy of offering interest-free loans to private builders stipulated that the housing constructed with the subsidies must be offered at a prescribed "cost-covering" rent to households that met certain eligibility requirements based on income and family circumstances. Similar restrictions were imposed by the U.S. Congress when it included the Section 221(3) program in the 1961 National Housing Act. This program provided below-market interest rates to private developers who agreed to build or rehabilitate apartments for low- and moderate-income families. In accepting the subsidy, the developer committed himself to limiting rents.

Needless to say, the success of such programs rests on the degree to which they are competitive with other forms of investment that profit-making developers might make instead. In the case of the Section 221(3) program, relatively few units have actually been produced, precisely because profit-motivated developers could earn higher returns by investing in housing for middle- and upper-income families.

Several European governments have avoided this problem by relying more heavily on nonprofit builders. The category of "nonprofits" includes a variety of investor types, from semi-public utility companies whose directorship is part public and part private, to labor unions, housing cooperatives, nonprofit corporations and associations. Typically, these various nonprofit enterprises sell limited-interest membership shares in order to acquire starting capital, on the basis of which they can then apply for government loans. Once backed by government loans, they are able to secure further loans from private credit sources. Since they are partially backed by low-income government loans, they extract no profits from their buildings; and, as they usually pay no taxes, they are able to rent their units out at prices below the private market.

Sweden made nonprofit builders the core of its post-World War II housing policy. Unlike Britain's postwar socialist government, Swedish socialists avoided building a large volume of public housing. Instead, they gave favorable treatment to nonprofits, both corporations and cooperatives, thereby helping them to build about two thirds of all postwar housing. As Table 4.1 shows, thirty-four years after the war, Sweden's nonprofits still occupy a prominent position in the nation's housing market.

In France, nonprofits currently represent about a third of building starts. As in Sweden, the HLMs (*habitations à loyer modéré*) are not owned by the government itself but by independent housing societies. They do, however, receive government subsidies in the form of long-term Treasury loans at low interest rates, permitting them to charge rents that are typi-

TABLE 4.1 Dwellings Completed, by Type of Investor, 1969 and 1979

Country	National, County, and Local Governments	Nonprofits**	Private Builders
Sweden			
1969	5.2%	56.1%	38.7%
1979	1.9	31.9	66.2
Netherlands			
1969	19.0	31.7	49.3
1979*	2.7	27.7	69.6
France			
1969	0.7	34.7	65.3
1979	0.9	48.7	50.4
West Germany			
1969	2.5	22.1	75.4
1979*	1.8	7.7	90.5
Britain			
1969	50.5	—	49.5
1979	35.1	9.7	54.0
United States			
1969	2.6	—	97.4
1979	0.1	—	99.9

*Figures are actually for 1978.

**This category includes cooperatives, nonprofit corporations and associations, and trade unions.

SOURCE United Nations Economic Commission for Europe, *Annual Bulletin of Housing and Building Statistics for Europe 1970* (pp. 40–43) and *1979* (pp. 38–40).

cally only two thirds the rents on comparable private housing. Another important parallel to the Swedish system lies in the breadth of French subsidies; in recent years, less than a quarter of French construction has been undertaken without some form of government subsidy.

Demand-side Strategies

The second major strategic option available to governments is to stimulate housing demand by subsidizing housing consumers. The two most common instruments used to subsidize consumers are: (1) tax concessions, which most often go to owner-occupiers, and (2) cash allowances, most often used to subsidize renters.

Most Western governments encourage owner-occupation by giving home owners important tax breaks that are not available to people who do not own their own homes. Normally, home buyers pay no tax on income which has gone to pay interest on their mortgage. Similarly, capital gains which they realize when they sell their house are not taxable. Because these tax concessions represent revenue which the government has foregone, they are in effect subsidies to consumers for buying houses. Moreover, in several Western countries, including the United States, the government regulates interest rates on mortgages, keeping them lower than the interest rates for other kinds of borrowing. Such regulatory measures, while they do not directly transfer money to consumers from the public treasury, nevertheless yield them financial benefits.

Renters, on the other hand, receive subsidies in the form of cash payments known as "housing allowances." Virtually all Western European governments now provide housing allowances in one form or another, and the United States has recently begun to experiment with this instrument as well. When they were first introduced, these direct assistance programs were usually structured to meet the needs of particular groups in the population, especially those unable to obtain decent dwellings without subsidy (for example, large families, the elderly, the handicapped). These programs take different forms, depending on the target population. In the case of the elderly, governments may channel the recipients of the allowance into apartment units designed specifically for older tenants. But when the target population has been low-income groups, European authorities have seldom encouraged the construction of projects specifically for them. Instead, the most common form of subsidy has been a direct cash transfer, which permits the tenant families to choose among the housing alternatives available on the open market. In some countries, most notably Sweden, the idea of the housing allowance has gradually reached beyond specific target populations to embrace the majority of households in the nation.

As a policy option, the housing allowance has the distinct advantage of being acceptable both to socialists, who like its redistributive potential, and to conservatives, who like its applicability to the free housing market. Thus governments controlled by parties as widely divergent as the French Gaullists and the Swedish Social Democrats have, since World War II, given the housing allowance an important role in their housing subsidy programs. That role has increased markedly in recent years, as the pressure of housing shortages in most European nations has diminished, reducing the emphasis on housing production. Analysts have increasingly perceived difficulties in tying government subsidies to particular buildings rather than to people. In offering production subsidies, governments can never be absolutely certain which households will be the beneficiaries of their largesse. As we have already seen, production subsidies hold down the housing costs of the tenants living in dwellings whose construction has been supported by government loans or grants. Once they are built, however, the government loses control over just how the subsidized units are to be allocated. Families originally qualifying under the established eligibility requirements may experience changes in their circumstances over time; and when their incomes rise or their children leave home, they often opt to stay in the subsidized unit. Without an elaborate, permanent monitoring system, governments cannot guarantee that their stock of subsidized housing will be optimally allocated. Because of the difficulty of targeting the aid to particular kinds of households, production subsidies are a relatively inefficient, and therefore expensive, instrument for meeting the housing needs of particular groups in society. This inefficiency became a more pressing issue for most governments in the 1970s, as soaring construction costs and tighter national budgets forced all Western governments to reassess their spending priorities. An additional criticism of production subsidies is that they restrict the resident's freedom of mobility: He enjoys the subsidy only so long as he lives in a particular unit. British Conservatives have even charged that the practice of attaching subsidies to council houses acts as an impediment to national economic growth, for the subsidized rents and the long waiting lists for council houses discourage British workers from relocating for the sake of job opportunities. (*New York Times,* 8 June 1980, p. 1) Yet another objection is that production subsidies have helped to compartmentalize urban housing markets; subsidized tenants are concentrated in certain kinds of buildings in certain parts of a city, instead of being dispersed throughout the housing market.

Conscious of these shortcomings and no longer faced with the severe shortages of the postwar years, European governments have gradually expanded housing allowances so that in recent years they have constituted a growing proportion of national housing expenditures (Howenstine). For example, in 1967 the Netherlands began a process of gradually reducing interest subsidies on its construction loans, while raising rents in subsidized buildings at an equivalent rate. But, to cushion the impact of these increases on low-income families, the Dutch government also introduced a housing allowance. Sweden in 1968 raised interest on government mortgage loans to equal market interest rates. Thus, even though the national government continued to be a major lender, it was no longer subsidizing production with low-interest loans.[2] At about the same time, Sweden began extending housing allowances to cover families with children, pensioners, unmarried mothers and fathers, and finally even single people without children. Similarly, West Germany raised its *Wohngeld,* or housing allowance, in the early 1970s. Housing allowances had been available on a limited basis since 1956, but legislation in 1970 extended them to all housing. They supply the difference between what a family actually pays for its

[2]Headey argues that mortgage subsidies were not really abolished by the 1968 measure, because the government took other compensating measures which diluted the impact of this action (p. 84).

housing and the so-called "tolerable rent" for that same family, based on its size and income. By 1975 such allowances amounted to about half of what Germany was spending on production subsidies (Hallett, p. 33).

As we have said, housing allowances appeal to conservatives as well as to politicians on the left. Britain's Conservative party provides a good example. In their 1972 Housing Finance Act, they took the dramatic step of imposing a "fair rent" scheme on the nation's public housing stock, which said that public housing tenants would henceforth be charged rents which were roughly comparable to the rents paid by private sector tenants. The Labour party had introduced a fair rent scheme in the private sector in 1965, designed to assure that landlords would receive no more than a "fair" return on their investments and that all landlords with comparable units would charge similar rents. Contrary to what the Labour government had expected, rents were raised in many buildings, rather than lowered (Headey, p. 152). In the early 1970s, Conservative critics of public housing increasingly argued that the system of rents in council houses was a hodgepodge. Rents differed widely, depending on the age of the building, and many tenants were paying much less than they could afford to pay. In one sweeping move, the Conservatives brought public housing rents up to a fair rent standard, thereby effectively eliminating the benefits to renters of the initial construction subsidies. At the same time, they directed local governments to offer allowances to tenants in both public and private accommodations, according to their income and family size. The Conservatives' intent was to change the subsidy to public housing tenants, from a subsidy attached to the particular building in which they lived, to a housing allowance dependent on their family circumstances. The effect of the change, however, was diluted by the Labour government, which replaced the Conservatives in 1974. Perhaps because of their earlier experience with fair rents in the private sector, Labour repealed the provision that rents in council housing had to conform to a fair rent standard, while leaving in place the system of cash allowances for both public and private tenants.

France's conservative Gaullist party has also enthusiastically advocated the extension of housing allowances. Since its origin in 1939, France's housing allowance has traditionally been linked to the more general family allowance, and both have been systematically manipulated by the government to encourage higher birth rates. As a response to the demographic problems associated with a low birth rate, the French government stipulated that neither allowance was to be available to families with fewer than two children. Since 1971, however, benefits under the housing allowance program have been extended to almost a million more French citizens whose circumstances warranted aid: the elderly, the handicapped, single persons, and young couples without children.

The move to extend benefits was part of a housing reform program advanced by the controversial Minister of Housing and Equipment, Albin Chalandon. Like the Swedes, Chalandon had decided that direct payments to families would in the long run provide greater benefits for low-income groups than would government subsidies to construction. The special designation of some housing complexes as low- and moderate-rent units, a practice which fosters social segregation, would be unnecessary, Chalandon argued in 1971, if housing allowances could be increased for those who needed them most. In addition, Chalandon justified greater reliance on the housing allowance as an effort to allocate the nation's housing stock more equitably by eliminating the distortions introduced by production subsidies. A self-styled champion of *désétatisation* (literally, "degovernmentalizing"), Chalandon frequently during his public career found himself at odds with other members of his own party. Far more than most other Gaullist politicians, he wanted to move in the direction of decreased government intervention in the urban economy. In both economic and social ways, he contended, the private market can be made to function more effectively if the government simply provides cash subsidies to help low-income groups obtain standard housing, rather than herding them together in low-rent projects.

In the United States, the housing allowance has been promoted recently by conservative Republicans as an alternative to the Democrats' low-income housing programs of the 1960s. Although the allowance idea had been advanced periodically by American social reformers since the 1940s, it was not given serious consideration until the Nixon administration introduced and passed legislation in 1970 which included a $30 million authorization for a nationwide experiment with housing allowances. The trial runs, carried out between 1972 and 1980 in a dozen American cities, were described by HUD officials as a possible vehicle for a radical redirection of the entire federal housing program.

The need for such a redirection was undisputed, even by critics of the Republican administration. By the early 1970s, the image of the federal public housing program was so tarnished by the massive deterioration of the projects and by the shoddy construction and real estate profiteering which had marked the experimental programs of the late 1960s that little dissent was heard to President Nixon's observation that "all across America, the federal government has become the biggest slumlord in history."

The design of the national Experimental Housing Allowance Program was complex, incorporating three main components—a supply experiment, a demand experiment, and an administrative agency experiment. Over 25,000 American families participated in the program, receiving housing allowances that averaged $75 per month, calculated as the difference between what the family would have to pay for adequate housing and what the family could afford to pay (assumed to be 25 percent of the household income). Allowances were paid directly to the consumer, who was free to spend them on housing or not, so long as he was living in a unit that met certain minimum quality standards. The massive data collected over the seven years of the experiment are still being analyzed, but preliminary findings are quite positive, suggesting that the U.S. government could profitably follow the European lead and shift its emphasis from housing production for the poor to housing allowances for the poor (Frieden).

Interest Group Politics and the Choice of Policy Instruments

One reason the United States lags behind Western Europe in adopting housing allowances is the opposition mounted by the producers' lobby. The National Association of Homebuilders has been joined by the AFL-CIO building trades unions and the National Association of Housing and Redevelopment Officials in resisting any program that would divert federal support from new construction toward cash allowances. Interestingly, two other trade groups have publicly supported the allowance concept: The National Apartment Association and the National Association of Realtors see allowances as an instrument that will increase demand for older units, bolstering rents and increasing property turnovers by giving more tenants and prospective owners the resources to compete in the housing market.

In analyzing the influences shaping housing policy in Europe and the United States, we find some important differences in the roles played by producer groups. All Western governments, whatever the public-private mix in their housing sectors, and whatever their strategic choices as to subsidizing producers or consumers, have had to deal with housing producer groups to implement their policies. In the field of health care, most babies are delivered by obstetricians who are not civil servants; similarly, few construction workers are permanent government employees. By and large, government activity in the housing sector has been channeled through the private house-building industry. But in their dealings with governments, producer groups, as we shall see, have wielded varying degrees of influence over policy.

A reading of the history of national housing policy in the United States suggests that the house-building industry has played the largest single role in formulating the policy. The effort to create a federal subsidy for home ownership in the 1930s was spearheaded by the major financial institutions connected with the housing industry (the Mortgage Bankers Association, the American Bankers Association, the United States Savings and Loan Association, and the National Association of Mutual Savings Banks), and by the major building industry organization (the National Association of Home Builders). These same lobby groups, along with the Chamber of Commerce and the National Association of Real Estate Boards, organized the vociferous opposition to the public housing program envisioned in the 1937 Wagner Act. Their well-orchestrated attacks forced the Wagner bill's sponsors to limit eligibility for public housing to persons who lacked the resources to bargain for housing on the open market, thus stamping public housing as an assistance program.

This housing industry coalition, formed in the 1930s, has persisted with few basic changes up to the present day, and it continues to operate as a clientele group supporting the FHA and as a veto group opposing public housing in any form. Its continuing influence on federal housing policy is evident, for example, in the drafting of the 1968 National Housing Act (Wolman 1971, pp. 91–92). The role played in that process by a presidential blue ribbon commission on urban housing (the so-called Kaiser Committee) is a classic example of the tendency of the American government to place a major share of policy-making responsibility in the hands of organized groups whose interests are directly engaged by the policy. The total membership of the Kaiser Committee was eighteen; out of that total, nine members represented the construction industry, while three more represented financial institutions. Given that composition, it should have surprised no one that the committee drafted a proposal (which ultimately became Title IX of the 1968 act) based on the assumption that the solution to the nation's housing crisis was for private builders to produce twenty-six million new houses over the next decade. The example of the Kaiser Committee is revealing, not only of the way in which federal policy is formulated, but also of the reasons why federal policy promotes home ownership rather than public housing. One Congressional staff member summed up the powerful influence of the building lobby on the 1968 Housing Act this way: "That's why they are builder programs. They are oriented toward housing production—units, starts, and property—with people being secondary considerations" (Lilley in Pynoos *et al,* p. 37).

It has sometimes been argued that such lobbying activity has accomplished little more than to echo the mainstream of American public opinion and reinforce the beliefs already held by federal policy makers. Lobbying to expand federal support for suburban construction of single-family dwellings, it is argued, coincides with the preferences held by American consumers (Headey, p. 194). Other analysts contest that interpretation, claiming that the pattern of suburban development has less to do with consumer choice than with a series of agreements between large residential builders and federal housing officials (Checkoway).

Compared with the United States, the more direct control exerted by most European governments over their domestic credit institutions and their larger share of the total investment in residential construction have placed them in a stronger bargaining position vis-à-vis private builders. Sweden furnishes the most striking example of a government that moved in a few years from a very limited role in the housing sector to a position of undisputed dominance over the private building industry. Up to World War II, private enterprise completely overshadowed public activity in planning and building Swedish housing. Yet, within a decade after the war, the national government had "assumed control over the planning, financing, and construction of Swedish housing" (Wendt, p. 68). The autonomous activity of building firms was substantially curtailed by the Social Democratic administration's decision to hold down the interest rates that could be charged on mortgage loans, while permitting interest rates on other forms of commercial lending to rise normally. Naturally, private credit migrated out of the mortgage market, leaving building firms dependent on government credit for a large part of their investment capital. Once it had gained this leverage over construction, the government proceeded to give preference to local governments and nonprofit housing associations in distributing loans. This policy of reducing the opportunities for speculative building ventures was firmly and speedily imposed.

An important byproduct of Sweden's postwar housing initiatives was the establishment of the nonprofit building corporations that are grouped together under SABO, as well as the massive expansion of the cooperatives, HSB and Svenska Riksbyggen. In a sense, the Social Democrats created Sweden's producer lobby by sponsoring the growth of these organizations with the building loan program, thereby guaranteeing that there would be a pressure group for the maintenance and expansion of production programs (Headey, p. 81). This coalition of nonprofit builders, along with Swedish construction workers' unions, formed a permanent alliance with the Social Democratic party on housing issues.

TARGETING HOUSING SUBSIDIES

DISTRIBUTION

The transition from production subsidies to consumer allowances is directly related to distributive issues. Since World War II Western governments have shifted from a focus on absolute housing deprivation caused by shortages to a focus on equity in the distribution of housing. With this shift has come an increased determination to use subsidies to improve the relative position of the neediest families in the housing market. Housing administrators have long recognized the difficulty of using production subsidies to benefit the neediest directly. For reasons discussed in the preceding section of this chapter, the production subsidy is an ineffective instrument for targeting expenditures to specific groups. By 1970 administrators in various European nations were estimating that 20 to 50 percent of all social housing was occupied by households that no longer met the income eligibility criteria that had prevailed when they moved in (Frommes).

Moreover, rising building costs in the 1970s made it more difficult to subsidize construction enough to produce an affordable rent for needy families. Thus, it has been common for housing units supposedly built for the needy to be occupied instead by the not-so-poor, who are more able to afford the rents. For example, German production subsidies have in theory been confined to units built for low- and moderate-income tenants. But in fact the eligibility ceilings have risen faster in the 1970s than average incomes have risen, so that in one province in 1975 the ceiling on social housing was set high enough to include 70 percent of the province's population (Hallett, p. 34). Needless to say, these increases in eligibility limits are strongly supported by the nonprofit builders, who want to improve their chances of collecting a reasonable rent from their tenants.

Another case in point is the Swedish government's growing awareness in the 1960s that while Sweden boasted the highest rate of annual housing production per capita of any Western nation, the construction program was favoring the middle class. Systematic investigations of the tenant population in new units showed that new buildings contained disproportionately large numbers of middle- and upper-class families. For example, a study of four new developments in Stockholm built from 1966 to 1968 revealed the income distribution shown in Table 4.2. Obviously, the units in these new developments tended to go to more affluent families.

As we saw earlier, the Swedish government has since 1967 been gradually replacing the interest rate subsidy to builders with an expanded housing allowance that will single out low-income families for special help. Sweden's experience to date suggests that a housing allowance program is not necessarily less expensive than a production subsidy program. The advantage, however, lies in the government's ability to concentrate housing expenditures on low-income families with children. From a base rate of about $140 a year per child, the amount of the allowance varies, depending on the number of children in a recipient family and on the household income. Thus, although the allowance program provides be-

TABLE 4.2 Distribution of Stockholm Households, by Income Group

Household Income (in kroner)	Percentage of Total Number of Households	Percentage of Households in Four New Developments
9,000 and under	16.4%	0.0%
10,000–19,000	26.5	4.3
20,000–29,000	22.8	18.7
30,000–39,000	14.4	27.8
40,000–59,000	13.5	40.4
60,000 and over	6.3	8.9

SOURCE International Confederation of Free Trade Unions, *The Housing Situation of Low Income Groups* (Brussels, 1970, p. 51).

nefits for a large proportion of Swedish families (an estimated 40 percent of families in 1969), the largest allowances go to the neediest families.

The widespread adoption of housing allowances reflects the fact that housing policy has become primarily an income redistribution issue rather than a shelter issue. Debate no longer centers on whether all citizens should possess minimally decent shelter; with the dramatic exception of the homeless found in certain areas of American and British inner cities, virtually all citizens in the industrialized West now live in minimally decent homes. The political question now is whether low-income citizens should have to pay substantially larger proportions of their income for housing than do higher-income households. Housing allowances are everywhere based on the premise that a family's housing expenses should not exceed some specified percentage of its income, which varies from nation to nation. In Sweden, for instance, national subsidies have succeeded in bringing workers' rents down from 27 percent of their income in 1950 to 17 percent of their income in 1974 (Headey, p. 58). In a comparison of Britain's rent allowance program and the United States' Experimental Housing Allowance Program, the Urban Institute concluded that "the main effect of the allowance payments in both countries has been a reduction in housing costs relative to income" (Trutko, p. *x*). In other words, most recipients in both nations have used the allowance, not to buy more housing (by making improvements in their existing unit or by moving to a more expensive unit), but instead to obtain budgetary relief. In short, they have used their allowance as an income supplement. This finding prompted urban economist George Sternlieb to label the housing allowance "an income transfer thinly masquerading as a housing device" (Sternlieb in Sternlieb, p. 549).

While it is clear that governments have used housing allowances to target aid to the needy, it would be wrong to identify consumer subsidies in general only with aid to the poor. In fact, the tax concessions to home buyers offered by most Western governments represent a massive subsidy to the middle class. So significant is this form of consumer subsidy that it has created a "second welfare state" coexisting with the more widely recognized "first" welfare state (Headey, p. 24). The tax concession to home buyers is regressive in that the size of the benefit increases in rough proportion to the home buyer's income. The higher an individual's income, the higher his tax bracket and therefore the more a major deduction is worth to him. Ironically, the more steeply progressive the tax structure of the country, the larger the proportion of interest payments that is deductible in the higher tax brackets. Even in the category of home buyers, favorable tax treatment has a differential distributive impact on existing owners and new buyers. By stimulating the demand for houses, tax subsidies have inflated house prices to the benefit of those who already own a home and to the disadvantage of first-time buyers (Lansley, p. 136).

Not surprisingly, then, this favorable tax treatment afforded to home buyers is strongly supported by the property-owning electorate. Few politicians in any of the Western nations have dared to suggest limiting or reducing this subsidy. One exception is Sweden's Social Democratic party, which openly addressed the question in 1974, thereby risking alienating Sweden's middle-class electorate. Like other nations, Sweden has allowed home buyers to deduct interest paid on their mortgage loans. Sweden's policy in this regard is actually less advantageous to home buyers than either Britain's or the United States' because it combines the tax deduction of mortgage interest with a capital tax levied each year on the amount of the home owner's accumulated equity. In the early years of ownership, when the home buyer is accumulating little equity, this tax is small; but as equity grows it grows. In a sense, these capital taxes in later years help to compensate the government for the tax revenue it has foregone in the earlier years. Yet even with this provision, Sweden's steeply progressive tax schedule makes the interest deduction a highly regressive instrument. It was calculated in 1972 that the tax subsidy represented a 33 percent reduction in the cost of the average new home, and that this reduction gave new owner-occupiers a 7 percent increase in their real income (Kemeny 1978, p. 319). In response to a growing controversy over this undeniable subsidy to the middle class, the government in 1974 decided to act. But rather than eliminating the tax concession to home buyers, it offered an equivalent benefit to renters in the form of lower interest rates on the money that builders borrow to construct rental housing. Apartment developers would henceforth pay less interest on their building loans than the rates charged for owner-occupied housing. This would enable them to charge renters less, and the renters would save an amount approximately equivalent to the benefits derived by home buyers from favorable tax laws. This solution to the problem may appear to have been a cowardly and expensive way out of the dilemma, since it cost home buyers nothing and merely provided an increased subsidy to renters. But in fairness it must be acknowledged that Sweden is virtually alone among Western governments in facing this crucial equity issue at all (Headey, p. 88).

By comparison, Britain's socialists have had much less stomach for the battle over tax concessions to home buyers. This is surprising, since Labour came to power in 1974 on a platform that included a commitment to end "the scandal whereby the richer the person and the more expensive the house, the greater is the tax relief." Anthony Crosland, who was to become Labour's Environment Minister, declared during the 1974 election campaign that "we are determined to stop this situation where the richest men in our society get their houses on the cheap" (Weir, p. 15). Once in office, however, Labour spokesmen got unfavorable press reports every time they raised the issue of mortgage interest relief. But more important in discouraging Crosland from pursuing this election pledge were the conflicts he encountered with the Treasury and with Labour's overall economic strategy in the 1970s. First, the government wanted to hold down housing costs as part of its incomes policy; raising housing costs by withdrawing the interest deduction would help to stimulate wage demands. Second, the proposal to eliminate tax relief for home buyers in the higher brackets was opposed by the Treasury because it would unnecessarily antagonize Britain's middle-management class, a segment of society whose confidence the Labour government was trying to win. The *Green Paper on Housing* finally issued by Labour in 1977 did not simply postpone reform; it rejected it outright, arguing that the continuation of mortgage tax relief was vital to the growth of home ownership and that its elimination would lead to a decline in investment (Department of Environment).

We have explored the change taking place in housing policy throughout Europe and the United States over the past fifteen years—an increasing emphasis on subsidies to consumers and a declining emphasis on subsidies to producers. Without doubt, this shift is related to the gradual elimination of postwar housing shortages, which had obliged Western governments to concentrate on production. As we have just seen, however, the two main forms of consumer subsidies now in use in Western nations are likely to have quite different distributive consequences for housing consumers. In the rental sector, housing allowances have a significant redistributive impact, since the size of the benefit is inversely related to the recipient's income. Over the long run we can expect such a system to improve the housing position of the lowest-income families, relative to the rest of the population. In contrast, measures to promote home ownership through tax subsidies and programs that increase the flow of credit to home buyers appear more likely to widen the gaps between income groups. Such policies will encourage those already in the market to trade upward; but, by fueling housing inflation, they may actually make it more difficult for first-time buyers to get into the market.

The new emphasis on consumer subsidies has emerged in spite of strong producer lobbies in most countries, which have long favored subsidies to production instead. The powerful producer lobby in the United States, for example, was unable to prevent Congress from creating, as a key element of the 1974 Housing and Community Development Act, a new rent subsidy program, called Section 8. This program is a modified form of housing allowance in which the allowance is paid not to the tenant, but to the landlord on the tenant's behalf. Strictly speaking, Section 8 is a voucher program, not a pure housing allowance. It is only a step away from an allowance, however. The impact of the Experimental Housing Allowance Program has yet to be felt in Washington; but Congressional willingness to spend $160 million on this nationwide experiment reflects the interest which federal housing officials now have in the idea of a cash allowance. Another example of a powerful producer lobby is Sweden's nonprofit builders. Despite their consistent support for government programs to promote the construction of high-rise rental housing, the Swedish government has, through the instrument of the tax concession, subsidized a growing stock of single-family detached housing in the suburbs. Alongside these well-organized producer lobbies, the consumer lobbies in all of these nations look puny.

How then do we account for the universal trend toward consumer subsidies? It can be explained largely by the political acceptability of consumer subsidies to both the political left and right. Politicians on the left see allowances as a way to equalize access to housing. Politicians on the right are prone to support allowances because they provide a more direct way than production subsidies to target government aid to the neediest. In times of scarce resources, therefore, they represent a cost-effective method for allocating housing aid. Moreover, they assign the task of building housing to the private sector and give recipients the money to go out and buy their housing on the open market. Thus, they take government out of competition with the private sector.

COPING WITH INFLATION IN HOUSING

RESTRAINTS AND INNOVATION

There is currently no more consistent and universal trend in the nations under discussion than inflation in the housing market. A national task force on American housing lamented:

> The high cost of housing is now a major problem of millions of American families. Costs of acquiring or occupying decent housing have increased dramatically in recent years . . . the high cost of shelter is not merely serious, it is too often an insurmountable crisis. (Task Force on Housing Costs, p. 1)

Despite the dramatic tone adopted by the task force, inflation in America's housing market in the 1970s has actually been moderate when compared to other Western nations. Of the six countries in Table 4.3, only West Germany shows a lower rate of increase in new housing costs, and the United States experienced the lowest rate of increase in the rental market. That disposable income is rising at rates that keep pace with housing prices is not necessarily comforting. It simply reflects the interpendence between wages and housing costs; workers demand higher wages in part to cover higher housing costs, and wage increases in turn drive up housing prices.

What have been the governmental responses to this universal inflationary trend? In this section, we will examine governmental responses in the two main sectors of the housing market, rental and owner-occupied.

TABLE 4.3 Average Annual Rates of Increase in Cost of New Housing, Rents, and Disposable Income, 1970–1977

	Rate of Increase in Cost of New Housing	Rate of Increase in Rents	Rate of Increase in Disposable Income
France	10.3%	8.3%	13.3%
West Germany	6.1	5.5	8.1
Netherlands	10.4	9.0	11.2
Sweden	10.6	7.4	9.7
Britain	17.1	12.6	14.7
United States	8.5	4.9	8.8

SOURCE E. Jay Howenstine, *Housing Costs in the United States and Other Industrialized Countries, 1970–1977* (Washington, D.C.: HUD International Division, September, 1979) pp. 2, 15.

In both sectors we will see that the responses which offer short-run political gains to public officials may have even more important long-run drawbacks.

The Rental Sector

If renters as a group represented a cross-section of all income levels in the population, then they would not have fared as badly as home owners in the inflationary period of the 1970s. As Table 4.3 shows, in all six nations in the 1970s disposable income was rising on the average faster than rents were increasing, appearing to improve the position of renters in the housing market. We cannot, however, take the figures in Table 4.3 at face value. For in most countries, renters as a group have lower incomes than owner-occupiers. The lowest-income families in almost all Western cities are renters, for whom any increase in rents is difficult to manage. That is why rent control has such political appeal in inflationary periods. One such period was during and immediately following World War II, when housing shortages across Europe threatened to drive rents beyond the means of all but the wealthy. At that point all six nations in this study enacted some form of rent control. And, although all six governments have subsequently moved toward decontrol, three of them encountered a revived pressure for controls in the 1970s. Before examining these three, let us look at the nations where rent control has all but disappeared.

Sweden and the Netherlands have had somewhat similar experiences in the years since World War II. Both governments retained controls until 1967; in that year, both legislated a gradual decontrol. In Sweden rent controls finally disappeared altogether in 1975, while in the Netherlands controls now exist only in the densely populated Randstad and only for buildings constructed before 1940. Why was the process of decontrol relatively painless in these two nations? In effect, both governments replaced traditional rent control with rent limitation provisions, which are part of the loan agreements they negotiate with all nonprofit builders who borrow from the government. Because government-subsidized nonprofits have built such a large proportion of postwar housing, the governments have been able to provide their citizenry with a growing stock of rental housing at minimal rents.

Rent decontrol also came rather easily to France. With a history dating to 1914, rent control in France was codified in 1948 in a bill which called for gradual decontrol of rents in existing buildings and exempted all new construction entirely. The 1948 law gradually reduced the rent-controlled sector in France to only 16 percent of all rental units (Brenner and Franklin, p. 21). Following World War II, the French government had the unusual problem of finding politically acceptable ways to increase the proportion of income that families spent on housing, which in 1948 was only about 4 percent. Decontrol was one way to accomplish that aim. Hence, the French government has walked a relatively easy path toward decontrol compared to some other European governments.

The public pressure favoring rent controls has been much greater in the 1970s in Britain, Germany, and the United States. In Britain, wartime controls covered all unfurnished units. Through the 1950s piecemeal efforts at decontrol by the Conservatives created a dual private rental market in British cities—a controlled and a decontrolled market. But most of the decontrolled portion of the market was brought under a new form of regulation in the mid-1960s, when the Labour party's "fair rent" scheme produced rents that were higher than those in rent-controlled buildings but still lower than market levels. Thus, at present, most of Britain's private rental market still falls under some form of regulation. The political penalties to be paid in Britain for any serious steps toward decontrol are so high that even the Conservatives have pursued decontrol only in a halting and piecemeal fashion.

In postwar West Germany, the Christian Democratic Union's position on rent control was consistent with its overall policy of promoting a "socially responsible market economy." Rent regulation was viewed as a necessary emergency measure to cope with the acute shortages of the 1950s. But by 1960 the Christian Democrats were ready to eliminate controls, which they regarded as inconsistent with their pro-market ideology. The 1960 Housing Controls Act called for the phasing out of rent control, county by county, as the housing shortage fell below 3 percent. By 1966 only Munich, Hamburg, and West Berlin still had rent control. But in 1971 the Social Democrats reintroduced rent control in a modified form, in an attempt to stem the rent spiral. Under this second generation of rent control, the landlord may initially charge the tenant as much as he can get, but all subsequent increases are regulated so that they do not exceed what is being charged for comparable units in the local area (Hallett, p. 28).

In the United States the national government initiated rent control in 1942 in a number of port and inland cities where the defense build-up was putting sudden pressure on housing markets. But as early as 1947, Congress passed a bill to start the process of phasing out federal rent control in cities. Simultaneously, the governments of many states enacted their own rent control legislation to replace federal controls as they expired. Even these state statutes lasted only a short time, and by the mid-1950s all states except New York had eliminated rent control (Lett).

For almost two decades, New York City was an anomaly—the only American city to retain controls. But the inflation of the 1970s brought renewed pressure on local and state governments to enact rent controls. Big cities such as Boston, Washington, Los Angeles, and Baltimore, as well as smaller communities, including over a hundred municipalities in New Jersey, have recently joined New York City in enforcing rent control.

Most economists who have studied the effects of rent control say that politicians in these communities are buying short-term relief for tenants at the cost of long-term deterioration. Rent control, they argue, not only discourages investors from building new units; it also discourages them from maintaining and repairing existing buildings. Also, it encourages them to convert their rental properties to condominiums or, in the worst circumstances, simply to abandon them. Since local taxes on apartment buildings are usually based on rent receipts, rent control can reduce a city's tax base (Sternlieb and Hughes in Sternlieb, p. 283). Moreover, it has other drawbacks that are similar to those that apply to production subsidies. That is, rent control produces benefits for the tenant so long as he occupies a specific unit and thereby discourages mobility. Furthermore, its benefits cannot easily be targeted to those who need them most. Rent control may protect very affluent tenants who do not need protection, or it may encourage families to hold on to more space than they really need.

In the United States, the growing acceptance of rent control by local governments may bring them into direct conflict with the federal housing establishment. Federal priorities, strongly influenced by the house building lobby, have traditionally stressed housing production, whereas the actions of many local governments in adopting rent control are perceived as inhibiting production. It is not surprising, therefore, that in the spring of 1981, Senator Alfonse D'Amato (Republican, New York) sponsored a bill in Congress to withhold federal housing funds from all cities that have rent control laws. His rationale was that local rent control ordinances stymie new construction and therefore operate not only to the short-run disadvantage of builders but also to the long-run disadvantage of renters.

Promoting Home Ownership

Inflation has two important effects on housing which may at first appear mutually contradictory. On the one hand, inflation puts home ownership beyond the reach of an increasing number of families; on the other hand, it enhances the appeal of home ownership as the best hedge against inflation. It leads, in fact, to a shift in the perception of housing from shelter to investment. Inflation dramatically increases the advantage of home ownership over renting. Mortgage payments, remaining constant over a twenty- or thirty-year period, in reality decrease because of the gradual erosion of currency. The conventional mortgage, in effect, allows the buyer to pay off the debt with cheaper and cheaper money. This benefit for home buyers is separate from, and in addition to, any tax benefits. Thus, inflation increases the demand for home ownership while at the same time making home ownership more difficult for the average family to achieve (Grebler and Mittlebach).

Not surprisingly, opinion surveys throughout Europe and the United States demonstrate an increased preference for ownership over renting. In a 1975 British poll, for example, nearly seven out of ten respondents named owner occupation their first choice among the different forms of housing (British Market Research Bureau, Harrison and Lomas). The survey evidence from Germany in the 1970s is ambiguous, but a 1975 EEC poll found that 40 percent of citizens, when asked how they would spend a sudden increase in income, said they would buy a house (Hallett, p. 71). Perhaps most surprising of all is the marked turn toward home ownership in Sweden, which until the 1970s built very few single family houses. In recent surveys of housing preferences, as many as 80 to 90 percent of Swedes have said they would prefer owning a house to renting a flat (Daun; Michelson; Kemeny 1978).

Governments have responded to this increased demand for home ownership in a number of ways. First, they have authorized a series of new mortgage types involving a graduated rise in payments over the life of the mortgage. One type levies a fixed rate of interest, but sets up a schedule of payments so that lower payments in the early years are balanced by higher payments in the later years. Such schemes are now used in most of Europe and in the United States (OECD 1974). Another type is the variable-interest rate mortgage, in which the rate of interest is indexed to the rate of inflation; as inflation increases, the lender may either increase the borrower's monthly payment, or extend the length of the loan over a longer pay-back period. Variable-rate mortgages are used in Britain, Germany, the Netherlands, and now the United States (OECD 1975).

Governments have also created "special circuits" of housing finance to divert a specified portion of the nation's savings into institutions that specialize in mortgage lending and that are sheltered from other segments of the credit market. Examples are France's *épargne-logement* and Germany's *Bausparkassen,* both of which are savings societies in which individuals who deposit savings according to a specified schedule earn moderate interest and an entitlement to a mortgage loan at an interest rate below the regular market. A variation on this model is Britain's building societies, which pay depositors a more competitive rate of interest but do not necessarily guarantee that each depositor will get a mortgage loan (OECD 1974, pp. 33–41). In all three cases, the national government foregoes taxes on all interest earned by the depositors. A more limited variant of this strategy is the action taken by the U.S. Congress in 1981 to authorize the "all savers' certificate," whose tax-free status was designed to boost the supply of available housing credit by attracting deposits to savings and loan associations.

Yet another approach to facilitating home ownership has been suggested by Britain's Conservative party: They want to sell public housing units to the tenants who occupy them. The proposal is not new to Britain; the idea of selling council houses was first approved by the Conservative government in 1952. That party introduced a campaign in 1972 to encourage sitting council tenants to buy, actually succeeding in selling 25,000 units that year (Headey, p. 156). Sales tapered off again under the Labour government in the mid-1970s. But within two weeks of their election victory in 1979, the Conservatives announced that they would revive the campaign, this time offering tenants discounts of 30 to 50 percent, depending on the length of time they had lived in council housing. In addition, if the prospective buyer were unable to secure a mortgage from a conventional source, the local government was encouraged to lend up to 100 percent of the purchase price. Labour opposed this new initiative, arguing that the most desirable units would be sold off, reducing the choices for future tenants and moving council housing one step closer to being a last resort. One Labour MP warned in parliamentary debates that Britain's housing problem could not "be solved by easy application of free market forces. Mr. Milton Friedman has only to take a short cab ride from his university in Chicago to see what free market forces have done to some districts of that city" (Katz, p. 464).

A major difficulty with all of these efforts to facilitate home ownership is that, like rent control, they are short-run remedies that may actually exacerbate the problem in the long run. And, by pumping more money into the housing market, they may fuel inflation even further. In the jargon of the economists, such policies are "procyclical" rather than "countercyclical"; that is, they reinforce rather than counteract the inflationary spiral.

Government initiatives to promote home ownership may be criticized on other grounds. Their long-term impact, according to some critics, may be to lead nations to over-invest in housing relative to other sectors that also need capital investment. Some observers believe this has already happened in the United States. Tax laws and other incentives to ownership have encouraged citizens to invest all of their earnings in housing and to abandon other forms of saving and investment. The result over time has been to draw savings and investment away from more productive uses—for example, financing new capital and equipment—and ultimately to reduce national economic productivity (Tuccillo; Sternlieb and Hughes in Sternlieb, Peterson in Solomon). A similar trend worries economists in Britain, where the proportion of personal wealth in housing and land almost doubled between 1960 and 1974—from 27 to 47 percent—while the proportion held in stocks dropped in half—from 23 to 11 percent (Lansley, p. 137).

Others fear that increasing levels of home ownership will generate intolerable costs in resources and energy. Housing built at low density requires more extensive infrastructure (roads, water, and sewer lines) than does high-density housing. Typically, single-family detached housing consumes more fuel and water per person than multi-family housing, and trip lengths of residents are systematically longer than the lengths of trips made by people living in higher-density housing (Struyk, p. 37). Sweden's Social Democrats have been particularly vocal in expressing these objections to the suburban-style housing that is preferred by owner-occupiers.

Yet another criticism focuses on the relationship between housing policy and social policy in other spheres. One possible consequence of government programs to encourage home ownership is that in the long run they will inhibit the growth of various kinds of social welfare programs and will thus contribute to "privatizing" the economies of Europe. The logic of this argument is as follows: Because of the irresistible incentives to home ownership, more and more young families are persuaded to assume a substantial burden of debt early in their adult lives. This step determines, to a very great extent, their pattern of consumption for years afterward. Such households necessarily display a strong preference for maintaining private control over the pattern of family expenditures, so that they can manipulate their budgets to allocate a very large proportion of income to house payments in the early years, with a gradual easing of the burden later on. They can therefore be expected to resist government taxation for the purposes of providing more collective welfare benefits. "Owner occupation, then, acts as a powerful force to maintain or increase privatization in other spheres of life" (Kemeny 1980, p. 380).

* * * * *

As with health care, policy makers in the housing field are confronted with choices that hinge on the relationship of government programs to private sector alternatives. With the exception of Britain, the governments under consideration here have chosen not to build large stocks of public housing but instead to work through the private market, both by providing loans, grants, and tax concessions to builders, and by offering subsidies to consumers in the form of cash allowances to renters and mortgage support to owner-occupiers. Since World War II the trend has clearly been away from subsidizing producers and toward subsidizing consumers. While this shift has undoubtedly enabled governments to target their aid more directly to the intended recipients, it may also have contributed to an "over-investment" in housing. Critics charge that like government health insurance, consumer subsidies for housing have inflated prices and encouraged families to consume more housing than they otherwise would. Whether or not we accept this last argument, it serves to remind us that housing policy is closely tied to wider policies of taxation, income maintenance, and economic management, and can never be made in isolation from these other spheres.

5
ECONOMIC POLICY

All of the world's industrial democracies have met with severe economic problems in recent years. Declining rates of economic growth, productivity slowdowns, trade deficits, inflation, and higher unemployment have struck Western Europe, the United States, and Japan. In each case, trends that appeared merely worrisome in the late 1960s became much more disturbing in the 1970s.

In retrospect, it seems clear that post-World War II economic development can be divided into two general phases (Feldstein 1980; OECD 1980). From the initial period of reconstruction of wartime damage through the 1950s and 1960s, the industrial democracies enjoyed unprecedented high rates of economic growth amid general price stability. At the end of the 1960s and in the early 1970s, this first phase gave way to a second, as economic fluctuations became more erratic and severe. In most countries the onset of the second phase was marked by tight labor markets, increased strike activity, higher wage settlements, and student unrest. At the same time, inflation began to increase, fueled by major U.S. spending in Vietnam without accompanying tax increases. Mild recessions in the Western nations and Japan during 1969 and 1970 were followed by a booming economic expansion in 1972 and 1973. An oil embargo in late 1973 and the quadrupling of OPEC oil prices stoked these inflationary fires; and the anti-inflation policies of 1974 and 1975 produced the worst economic downturn in most nations since the Great Depression of the

1930s. After 1976 came a weak economic recovery, which was followed by more inflation, another oil price shock in 1979, and another recession in 1981 and 1982. Throughout most of this period, and contrary to almost all professional economists' expectations, successive bouts of recession-induced unemployment did little to reverse the inflationary trend. Figure 5.1 gives a rough indication of how, during the recent period of slower growth, most Western democracies managed to get the worst of both worlds: higher inflation and higher unemployment.

All in all it was a sorry economic record. At the same time, however, we must consider this period in perspective. Seen against the background of rapid postwar growth during phase one and in the light of economists'

FIGURE 5.1 CHANGES IN INFLATION AND UNEMPLOYMENT RATES, 1960–1980

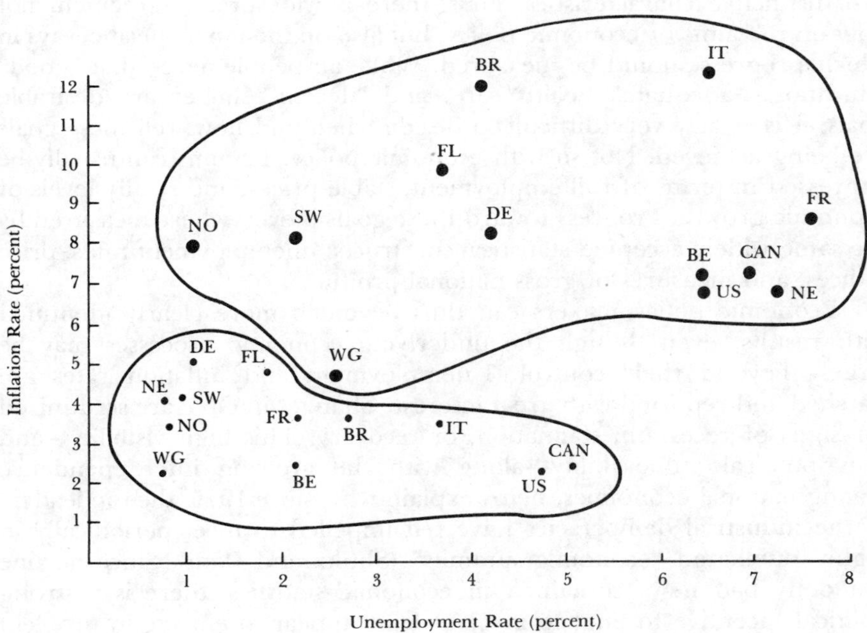

• Average rates for 1960-1969

● Average rates for 1970-1979

BE	Belgium	IT	Italy
BR	Britain	NO	Norway
CAN	Canada	NE	Netherlands
DE	Denmark	SW	Sweden
FL	Finland	US	United States
FR	France	WG	West Germany

confidence that they had finally learned the lessons of economic management, the performance of the 1970s and early 1980s looks bleak indeed. But viewed in relation to the longer history of the last century or more, the recent record is far from disastrous. In their severity and duration, these modern economic downturns have been much milder than the panics and depressions that preceded World War II. And recent inflation, though troublesome, has not expanded into the speculative bubbles that once brought down whole banking and financial systems.

In this chapter we will not try to explain different inflation, unemployment, or growth rates among nations. Such differences depend on a highly complex interaction of economic, political, social, and even cultural factors. Instead, we will examine differences and similarities in the ways that democratic nations have coped with common problems of economic management.

Compared with other topics in this book, economic policy has at least two distinctive characteristics. First, there is widespread agreement not only on the aims of economic policy, but also on the fairly specific ways in which progress should be measured. While all people agree that "good" education, "adequate" health care, and "decent" shelter are desirable goals, it is clearly very difficult to decide when and how well these goals are being achieved. Not so with economic policy. Its aims can usually be expressed in terms of full employment, stable prices, and steady levels of economic growth. Progress toward these goals is everywhere measured by the same widely accepted statistical constructs: unemployment rates, price indices, and measures of gross national product.

Economic policy makers can thus be much more clearly identified with results, even though the underlying economic processes may be largely beyond their control. Unemployment and inflation rates are watched and reported with great interest. Changes in GNP are scrutinized for signs of recession, stagnation, or recovery. This high visibility—and thus political vulnerability—along with the growing interdependence among national economies, helps explain why, since 1975, the top leaders of the industrial democracies have felt impelled to meet periodically in highly publicized "economic summits" (Shultz and Dam). Since no one can deny bad news contained in economic statistics, there is a strong political incentive to engage in or at least appear to engage in problem solving.

The second distinction of economic policy is that in every country, a specialized profession has developed to advise on problems of economic management. Professionals in other policy areas, such as educators or doctors, may or may not be consulted for their views on health or education policy; but professional economists are everywhere regarded as legitimate sources of guidance on economic policy matters. This reliance on economists has increased over time, as economics in the postwar period has become more theoretically complex and data-rich (through the advent of computers). The result is that ideas—expressed in the ebb and flow of debate among economists—play a particularly important role in shaping, though never entirely determining, policy choices in economic management. The influence of ideas has been felt throughout the various dimensions of choice in economic policy.

CHOICES IN ECONOMIC POLICY

The various managerial strategies in economic policy can be grouped in terms of the familiar fourfold set of choices; recent economic history has in fact facilitated this kind of comparative policy analysis. The shared economic problems of recent decades, such as the oil price increases of the 1970s, have provided a natural testing ground, illuminating each nation's particular capacities for political management and economic adjustment.

Scope and Thresholds

Regardless of the party in power, every central government in the industrial democracies is now assumed to have responsibility for overall economic management. There is little question that economic performance in terms of jobs, inflation, and growth is within the legitimate bounds of government activity.

Because it is so obvious, it would be easy to overlook the similarity among nations in this basic commitment to economic management. In every advanced democracy, the government's own taxing and spending policies and its control of the money supply are today considered the key factors involved in managing the economic activity in the private sector. Yet as recently as the 1930s the national budget was regarded simply as a means of paying for the government's own operation, not of regulating overall economic activity. The boundary between public and private sector responsibilities for the economy has thereby become increasingly fuzzy—but fuzzy in different ways in different nations.

Instruments

Western democracies apply a complex but not wholly dissimilar mix of fiscal and monetary tools in economic management. For example, in response to the 1981–1982 recession, government spending and tax policies were everywhere used to prop up domestic demand, while central banks manipulated financial levers such as interest rates to curtail inflationary increases in the money supply. The widespread reliance on these "big levers" of macro-economic management demonstrates the common influence of economic ideas and the professional economists who expound them.

Distribution

The choices of economic policies imply major distributive consequences. Despite political rhetoric to the contrary, measures to fight inflation have produced significant increases in unemployment. Many persons complaining about inflation are not the ones most likely to suffer from the effects of sustained unemployment. Distributive consequences are also produced by efforts to spur economic growth through increased investment and capital accumulation. Given the existing structure of economic ownership, government incentives to increase investment and savings tend to reward those who are already the largest owners of capital and those with the greatest capacity to accumulate resources for new investment. Thus the debate on "trickle down" theories has followed rather different contours, depending on the distributional sensitivities of the political system in question.

Restraints and Innovation

During the first several decades of the postwar period, a gradual consensus emerged on the role of government in the economy. Essentially, this view was Keynesian: Government must manage aggregate demand so as to assure high levels of stable employment.

Events of the 1970s eroded this consensus without putting any comparable consensus in its place. Each nation has embarked on a search for innovations in economic policy making, although each has done so in its own way. This recent agitation for economic policy innovation in the midst of constraints provides an exemplary case study in what has been termed "structured variation."

THE WILL TO INTERVENE

SCOPE AND THRESHOLDS

Since World War II, every industrial democracy has seen the creation of central executive organizations run by personnel with professional economic training to advise on policies for managing the economy. Likewise, in every nation, central government banks nowadays consciously attempt to control the supply of money and other financial aspects of the economy—an endeavor that simply would never have occurred to central bankers before 1940 (Schnitzer and Nordyke; Woolley). As a consequence of these and other factors, the boundary lines between public and private sectors of the economy have become increasingly blurred. With little apparent intention of doing so, modern democratic governments of every political persuasion have effectively converged to blot out the time worn distinction between government and a self-regulating economy. Private economic relationships and self-managing market mechanisms continue to operate, but they do so everywhere within the larger designs of government economic policy.

Several factors help to explain these overarching similarities. First is the sheer size of today's public sector in relation to the rest of the economy. (The particular categories of spending and taxation are considered at greater length in other chapters of this book.) All of these government commitments have—largely inadvertently—cumulated into a government presence that easily overshadows any other actor in the economy.

In every industrial democracy, government is the single largest purchaser of goods and services (teachers' salaries, school buildings, hospitals, public works, and so on), the single largest distributor of income (through transfers of income maintenance programs), and the single largest borrower of money (to finance capital investment projects and pay for deficits between spending and revenue). Given this presence, it would be difficult for any government to deny responsibility for what is happening in its national economy.

A second reason for the similarity in basic frameworks of economic management concerns ideas. Since its early, scattered beginnings over two centuries ago, the study of economics has evolved in the twentieth century into a professional speciality with its own language and sophisticated models. By and large the basic concepts of economics have been developed in informal dialogue among international networks of economists.

A critical turning point in this dialogue occurred amid the Depression of the 1930s and wartime planning of the 1940s. These events, which struck with stunning impact in all the nations, led economists to a new conception of government's role in managing a national economy. The basic idea that held sway for a generation of Keynesian economists following the Depression was that, left to its own devices, a modern market economy would *not* automatically reach equilibrium at a level of activity assuring full utilization of a country's capital and labor; government could and should help fill this gap so as to attain full and stable levels of employment. From this basic idea and from a general desire to avoid any repetition of Depression-style unemployment, methods were developed to measure national income and GNP (both new concepts in the 1940s), to quantify the impact of government taxing and spending on aggregate economic demand, and to refine indicators of full employment. These ideas and methods of accounting for economic activity took hold among economists throughout the Western democracies and today constitute the basis for most of the day-to-day work in the central economic apparatus of every nation. These ideas come from a way of thinking that, almost by definition, *presumes* general government responsibility for the economy.

During the 1950s and 1960s, another school of economic thought drew attention to monetary factors (rather than aggregate demand) and the role of central banking institutions in fueling or controlling inflation

(Meltzer). Refinements in monetary theories and in the measurement of money supply added to the common store of economic thinking, and in the 1970s one nation after another began setting explicit targets for managing the amounts of money circulating in the economy.

In the 1970s some economists began emphasizing the role of government in restricting the available supplies of investment capital and remunerative labor. At present, such "supply-side" theories have aroused political attention in some nations, but they have not as yet had the impact of Keynesian or monetarist theories.

None of these approaches has drawn unanimous agreement among economists, and different governments have given different priority to Keynesian, monetarist, and supply-side theories. But seen as a whole, the ideas of economists have everywhere helped create the presumption that government, by acting in a strategic manner, can decisively affect the course of economic activity. Such a presumption holds whether emphasis is on Keynesian demand management, on a monetarist control of the money supply, or on a supply-side strategy of cutting back on taxes and regulations.

One final factor helps explain the universal blurring of public and private sector boundaries. This factor involves the political constraints on the size of the public sector. Governments can and do use a variety of instruments to achieve their policy purposes. But all of the Western democracies are basically market-oriented, private-property based economies, not centrally planned, socialist systems. Thus there are not many economic objectives that democratic governments can accomplish without relying on private or semi-private groups outside their direct control. In accepting responsibility for economic management, governments are pulled into a web of relationships—consultations, financial inducements, and so on—with the ostensibly independent private sector. Reinforcing this relationship is the political incentive everywhere for blurring public and private boundaries. With public budgets looming so large, governments must look for strategies of intervention that do not show up on the budgetary books. Such strategies include the use of quasi-governmental corporations, special credit facilities, various contractual arrangements with private suppliers, and so on. These approaches in effect create a complex set of interdependencies between government and the private economy, so that it becomes very difficult to ascertain where any threshold between the two sectors may lie.

Differences in the Will to Intervene

So far our discussion has focussed on overarching similarities in governmental responsibility for economic management. Yet there are also substantial differences in the willingness of national governments to intervene in economic affairs. Some countries appear to have accepted responsibility unhesitatingly, and indeed show a predisposition in that direction, while other nations seem to act much less deliberately and willingly.

Consider how various countries have responded to common economic problems, such as the OPEC oil embargo and quadrupling of oil prices in 1973 and 1974. In effect these events imposed a large tax on the entire economic product of each oil-importing nation, with the revenues from this oil "tax" going to foreign sources. Every country followed its own course in coping with the resulting loss of national income and in the process evinced its will to intervene in economic affairs.

West Germany. The oil price shock came at a particularly bad time for Germany (Hardach). The government had been trying for a year to hold back growth in an economy that showed signs of growing inflation. Wage settlements were reaching historically high levels, adding further to inflation and the likelihood of a profit squeeze on industry. In late 1973 and 1974, Germany was therefore poised on the edge of a major recession (given the huge oil "tax" on top of the government's already restrictive policies) and a major inflationary spiral (given already high wage contracts that could be expected to escalate to catch up with the cost-of-living increases produced by higher oil prices).

The policy debate was short and decisive (Joint Economic Committee, pp. 131–134). Earlier in 1973 the government had begun deploying its economic powers under the 1967 Act to Promote Economic Stabilization and Growth so as to moderate the anticipated recession (see page 146 for details). Investment taxes on private industry were abolished and special tax credits to foster business growth were introduced. At the same time, the powerful Bundesbank, the government's central bank, decisively restricted credit, thereby curtailing the power of firms to pass through the inflationary price increases that had been caused by the high wage settlements and oil price increases. As it developed, the German recession of 1974 and 1975 was mild by international standards, and inflation (though high by German standards at 7 percent in 1975) was substantially held in check, and then reduced in 1976.

France. The oil crisis dramatized problems that had been emerging gradually for years in France. The French economy was becoming increasingly dependent on international trade, yet there were strong signs that industry was weakening in competition with its foreign counterparts (Joint Economic Committee, pp. 6–35). Moreover, government protection of marginal firms and industries, through price controls, subsidies, and other means, was straining resources and doing little to earn the export revenues that the country needed to pay for imports. Adding to the difficulties of international competitiveness and government subsidization was the fact that French interest rates had traditionally been kept low to aid business investment. Sharp swings in foreign deposits or withdrawals of funds from France—encouraged by a weak export-import ratio—could greatly strain this policy of low interest rates, the value of French currency, and French finances in general. Thus the oil shock of 1973 and 1974 left the country vulnerable to a massive trade deficit through higher import costs, to more demands for subsidizing marginal firms, and to outflows of capital in search of higher interest rates and a stable currency.

French policy makers reacted in 1974 by embarking on a major economic "restructuring" effort. A massive program of accelerated investment in nuclear power was initiated, partly to replace dependence on foreign oil and partly to earn foreign exchange through nuclear industry exports. State investment in the aerospace, armaments, and telecommunications industries increased immensely. A joint public-private sector export drive was launched to reverse the trade deficit. In less than two years, the Bank of France almost doubled interest rates, helping to attract foreign capital and stabilize the currency. The higher interest rates, together with cuts in government subsidization, drove some marginal firms under, while favored areas of production thrived on state investment funds and special credit facilities.

Sweden. Sweden demonstrated even greater dependence on international trade, yet in late 1973 it appeared to be in a far better position to ride out the oil price shock than were most other countries. During the worldwide inflationary boom of the early 1970s, the government had deliberately pursued a policy of restricting growth in the Swedish economy. This meant that at the time of the oil embargo, prices and labor costs were rising more slowly in Sweden than among its major trading partners, and a large balance of payments surplus had been accumulated.

Policy makers tried to take advantage of their fortunate position. In 1974 the Social Democratic government quickly launched a "bridging" strategy to protect its economy from the coming recession that the oil "tax" was expected to impose on the Western world. Government job training programs helped to prop up employment, and spending and taxing devices encouraged industry to maintain levels of production, despite the weakening international market. If the German approach was to accept but moderate the combined recession and inflation, and if the French used the 1973–1974 crisis as an opportunity for a major economic restructuring, Sweden elected to use government policy to maintain a fully employed economy pending the next upswing in the international business cycle. Eventually, the worldwide recession was much longer and deeper than expected, and the Swedish government's aggressive strategy proved, as we shall see, somewhat counterproductive.

Great Britain. As extensive media commentary on the "British Disease" might suggest, economic management in Britain has been plagued with difficulties: a growth rate that has lagged behind that of other developed countries, meager increases in productivity, recurring balance of payments crises, and very high inflation rates. The oil crisis could scarcely have occurred at a worse time (Steward; Shanks). By the end of 1973, the British economy was undergoing a major inflationary expansion. Responding to a 1971 increase in unemployment, the government continued to expand its own spending and ease monetary policy throughout 1972 and 1973. Private consumption was rising rapidly as well, creating an excess of imports over exports and a growing trade deficit. Inflation, which had been comparable to that in other nations until 1971, was racing ahead, further weakening Britain's international competitiveness. In addition, the Conservative government was, by the winter of 1973 and 1974, engaged in an ill-tempered confrontation with the trade union movement over demands for large wage increases and a governmental proposal to regulate strike activity. Meanwhile, domestic investment languished.

In February 1974 the Conservatives were turned out of office on the issue of controlling the unions, and the new Labour government faced a severe economic crisis. One portion of its response was to continue accelerating public spending. Another was to dismantle the compulsory restraint on wages, which had been widely disregarded, and to urge voluntary wage restraint through an informal "social contract" between government and unions. At the same time, the money supply was allowed to expand rapidly, with interest rates actually set below the rapidly rising level of inflation.

On the surface, the British response in 1974 resembled Sweden's "bridging" operation to hold up demand during the impending recession. In fact, only the public budget was encouraged to grow, and there was little intervention to shore up industrial production or restrain wage bargaining. Neither did the government undertake any direct measures to bolster employment or prevent the passing through of cost increases to prices. By mid-1975, inflation in Britain was approaching 25 percent, public spending was widely regarded as out of control, the excess of imports over exports had mushroomed, and the international value of the currency was in a nose dive. The government then shifted its stance to restrain public spending and money supply growth. Even stricter deflationary measures were imposed in 1976 as the condition for obtaining desperately needed loans from the International Monetary Fund. These measures, together with the extremely high wage settlements, produced sharp increases in unemployment during 1975 and 1976. The 1974 policies had been a bridge to nowhere.

The United States. Less dependent on foreign oil than any of the other advanced democracies, the United States might have appeared well able to cope with the oil shock. But appearances can be deceiving. Following a large inflationary boom in 1971 and 1972, the U.S. economy was flattening out in 1973. In response to growing inflation, monetary policy turned sharply restrictive in 1973. From 1972 to 1973, food price increases tripled, in response to agriculture shortages; consumer food prices increased 4.3 percent in 1972 and 14.4 percent in 1973. Federal spending and taxing policy had begun to reverse the economic stimulation of 1971 and 1972, though the rapidly increasing interest rates and food prices were by far the biggest factors in slowing down the economy. Even without the OPEC oil "tax," the U.S. economy in 1974 was clearly headed for a recession (Eckstein).

Complicating the picture was the fact that in 1973 the United States was engaged in an erratic retreat from a system of wage and price controls (Congressional Budget Office; Goodwin). In 1971 President Nixon had imposed a ninety-day freeze on wages and prices; this was followed in 1972 by a second phase of loosely enforced wage-price standards. In January 1973, a third phase instituted a system of voluntary restraints; but, after five months, galloping inflation led President Nixon to reject the unanimous opinion of his economic advisers and to impose a sixty-day price freeze. This in turn created a number of unpopular shortages, and by year's end the whole program was being rapidly dismantled on an industry-by-industry basis.

Thus the oil crisis produced a major transfer of resources from an economy that was already approaching recession, as well as a further boost in price levels that were already rising alongside a disorderly retreat from controls. The American government's response was uncertain and somewhat contradictory during 1974 and 1975. In January 1974 the Nixon administration at first sought extension of authority to use wage and price controls, but quietly dropped the request in the face of conservative Congressional resistance. The program to dismantle wage and price controls was completed in April as inflation reached double digits. As the economy slowed down and went into reverse, monetary policies were tightened further in the first half of 1974 and only gradually relaxed as the recession deepened still more. Government spending, in contrast, was allowed to increase sharply in the first half of 1974 but then held at a constant growth rate and reversed in mid-1975. A public relations campaign to "whip inflation now" was launched to urge voluntary price restraint—to no effect. In September 1974 the new President, Gerald Ford, recommended a tax increase, but later reversed himself and in the spring of 1975 accepted a major tax reduction passed by Congress. Administration proposals for an immediate decontrol of oil prices were rejected, and efforts to frame a comprehensive energy policy remained on the drawing board. That the U.S. economy did not continue along the road to depression could be attributed more to automatic stabilizers (such as countercyclical unemployment benefits) operating in the economy than to any governmental policy decisions enacted during this period (Eckstein).

An Overview of the Differences

Thus, Germany, France, and Sweden all responded to the oil crisis of 1973 and 1974 with decisive programs that showed little hesitation in bringing government pressure to bear on ostensibly private economic arenas. The German credit constraint on the power of business to pass through cost and price increases, the French attempt at economic restructuring, and the Swedish "bridging" operation to protect the labor market all reflect high government self-confidence in handling any presumed division between the public and private sectors.

In contrast are Britain and the United States. The British response to high union wage demands oscillated between compulsory restraint and an appeal to voluntary self-restraint. More indicative is the fact that the primary British response to the crisis was an effort to manage the economic adjustment solely by manipulating the public budget, with a consequently massive increase in deficit spending. Compared to that of the other nations, Britain's effort had little connection with decision making for private investment, labor markets, and financial markets.

In the United States, uncertainty about the justification for continued wage and price controls, the cross-cutting mix of monetary contraction and budgetary expansion in early 1974 and the exact reversal of each after the middle of that year, the directive to Americans to "whip inflation," the attempt at a solution first through a tax increase, then a tax cut—these were signs of a political system deeply ambivalent not simply about the right policy, but even about government's rightful role in the economy. Government policy was defined almost exclusively in terms of moving the "big levers" of the public sector—public spending, taxation, and monetary aggregates—and not as intervention in private investment, labor markets, or finance decisions.

Faced with a fourfold increase in oil prices in 1973 and 1974, policy makers in every country pursued policies based on the attitudinal premises, group pressures, and institutional capabilities at hand. These were not, however, a random collection of factors but instead fell into fairly intelligible patterns reflecting national predispositions regarding the boundary between public and private sectors of the economy.

Of course there is more to economic policy than implicit choices regarding these boundaries. The nations separate themselves more clearly by their selection of policy instruments for managing the economy. By discussing these instruments we can obtain better feeling for the texture of relationships between governments and their economies.

MACRO- AND MICRO-POLICY INTERVENTIONS

INSTRUMENTS

The leading issue for economic policy instruments was once thought to involve a choice between government ownership and reliance on free markets (Corti; King). In socialist and labor parties throughout Europe, nationalization of basic industries was the key priority. Apart from the United States, whole or partial government ownership has occurred, as Table 5.1 indicates. Generally, however, the question of government taking over business enterprises has now receded from the forefront of economic policy debate. The leading exceptions are the French Socialist government of François Mitterand, whose election program promised extensions of government ownership among private financial institutions, and the British Labour party, which has reaffirmed its traditional commitment to nationalization. But even in these cases there is considerable

TABLE 5.1 Government Ownership by Economic Sector*

	France	Sweden	West Germany	Britain	United States
Transportation					
highways	1	1	1	1	1
railroads	1	¾	1	1	¼
airlines	¾	¾	¼	¾	0
car production	½	0	¼	¼	0
Communications					
postal services	1	1	1	1	¾
telephone	1	1	1	1	0
radio/tv	1	½	1	¾	0
Energy Production					
gas	1	½	1	1	0
electricity	1	½	¾	1	¼
coal	¾	¼	0	1	0
oil	½	½	¼	¼	0
Other					
steel	¼	¾	¼	1	0
banking	¾	¼	¼	¼	0
Total Public Ownership	10½	7¾	8	10¼	2¼

SOURCE Adapted from Charles F. Andrain, *Politics and Economic Policy in Western Democracies* (North Scituate, MA: Duxbury, 1980), Table 2.5, p. 23.

*Numbers in the table are rough symbols of the extent of government ownership in each sector, ranging from 1 for complete government control to 0 for complete private ownership. Figures are general approximations rather than exact measures. Thus, ¼ is best interpreted as "mixed ownership, with private predominating," ½ refers to a basically equal balance between public and private sectors, and ¾ means mixed ownership with government predominating.

doubt as to the efficacy of government ownership in economic management. The Mitterand government began by pursuing a number of nationalization plans, but after a year in office was forced to de-emphasize government ownership as an economic cure and to rely on familiar austerity measures (higher taxes, lower spending, and wage-price freezes) to try to halt declines in the value of the franc and bring the 14 percent inflation rate under control. In Britain the Labour party split in 1981, with more moderate members breaking off to form a social democratic party that gave little credence to the tradition of government ownership.

Nationalization appears to have lost ground as an instrument of economic policy in Europe, even among socialist parties. The basic reason is that government ownership in practice has proven a blunt instrument; changing title to ownership seems largely irrelevant to managing the never ending adjustments occurring in modern economies. Employees in nationalized industries are no more likely to moderate wage demands than are their private counterparts; and public-enterprise managers may be even less open to the price competition that restrains inflation and promotes efficiency.

The more telling differences among nations relate not to government ownership, nor to the basic ideas of fiscal and monetary policy, but rather to specific policy instruments at the level of paricular industries and even firms. Known as *industrial policies,* these comprise government activities designed to influence economic adjustments within and among the various industrial sectors (Diebold; OECD 1975). Certain industrial policies predominate in each country and distinguish one country's policy choices from another's. Closer examination of a few national comparisons will make the meaning of industrial policy clearer.

Policy Instruments in France and Britain

Looking again at Table 5.1, we see that both France and Britain rank high in public ownership. We might be tempted to conclude that both countries have chosen similar instruments and in doing so have vigorously extended the boundaries of direct public control over the economy. In fact we have already described the difference between France and Britain in their willingness to intervene in the economy. The difference is carried further when we consider industrial policies in the two nations.

Industrial policy in France builds on a long tradition of centralized state administration and highly articulated forms of government intervention (Zysman 1978; McArthur and Scott). Many important business decisions are made in small group settings where administrative officials of the central government, industrial representatives, and representatives of a few financial institutions negotiate the terms of economic growth and adjustment. These relationships are formed not simply for the purpose of ad hoc bargaining to deal with particular problems when they arise, but exist as a more or less permanent system of negotiation—a customary way of doing business.

Government involvement in business decisions concerning credit, investment, employment, and production is a tradition that goes back many years in France. It has been facilitated by a central administrative elite with close personal, social, and educational ties to leaders in industrial and financial circles. For policy-making purposes, what exists is not separate competing institutions, but a common body of personnel trying to agree upon courses of action. This situation helps explain the success of economic plans in France after World War II. The early plans drawn up by the government's Planning Commission (*Commissariat Général du Plan*) set out relatively simple goals for vastly increasing the capacity of basic industries, such as steel and electricity, and indicated the coordinate factors—investment funds, demand, manpower, and so on—needed for such goals to be met. More important than the final numbers published in the various multi-year plans was the negotiation process by which government bureaucrats, business representatives, and suppliers of credit formulated expectations about one anothers' economic behavior. These expectations guided the distribution of government subsidies to particular industries and firms as well as spending for the nationalized industries. A series of semi-public credit institutions was created to guarantee the availability of low-cost loans to priority industries. Also a comprehensive program of price controls was initiated and remained in effect until 1976. But price controls were not instituted to reduce inflation during this period; rather, they served as fine tuning that government could use (or, more often, hint at using) to influence particular companies' profits, investment, and other business decisions.

Industrial subsidies, credit facilities, and price controls are only three of the important instruments of French industrial policy. Their importance has been vastly increased by their part in a common process for settling economic priorities, symbolized in but not confined to the widely publicized French economic planning process. Yet, as suggested earlier in this chapter, detailed central intervention in the economy has become increasingly troublesome in recent years, as the relatively simple postwar goals of reconstructing basic industries have been superseded by more complex adjustments throughout the French economy. Since the mid-1970s, the formal economic plans have become mainly devices for long-term speculation about economic problems rather than a means of influencing day-to-day decisions. But if planning as a tool of management has decayed, then its place has been filled by other devices. Developments since the mid-1970s provide a fascinating glimpse at how the French tradition of economic intervention has been maintained in a period of ostensible government decontrol.

On the one hand, the government of Valéry Giscard d'Estaing dismantled a number of cumbersome economic controls from the mid-1970s until it lost office in May 1981. Under this program of "liberalization," as it was termed, price controls were ended in 1976, thereby reducing some of the protection of profit margins that less competitive firms and industries had enjoyed. Efforts were made to encourage more competitive conditions in stock and bond markets. A policy of raising interest rates and increasing the international value of the franc was used to put more competitive pressure on less modern, labor-intensive sectors. In 1976 the government also seemed to act on the free market theories of monetarists such as Milton Friedman by instituting a simple yearly target for growth in the aggregate money supply, ostensibly leaving market mechanisms to adjust to the available money supply.

On the other hand, French officialdom continues and has even extended its involvement in industrial adjustment. Government subsidies and other advantages are concentrated on favored exporting industries such as telecommunications, armaments, nuclear power, and steel. But the socialist government of Mitterand is also committed to helping traditional sectors, such as textiles and agriculture, that were hard hit by the earlier government's stress on competitive rationalization.

The continuity of government intervention in a period of decontrol and liberalization is especially well illustrated by the way monetary targeting has worked in practice. To achieve its annual target for aggregate changes in the money supply, the French government has relied on many customary interventionist instruments for directing the flow of money and credit. One such device is the *encadrement de crédit,* a system of rules by which the aggregate monetary target is broken down into specific targets for each lending institution; penalties in the form of much higher reserve requirements are imposed on financial institutions that exceed or fall below their targets, which are expressed as a rate of increase in the institution's net assets. By exempting or giving different weights to certain types of lending, the government influences the flow of credit to favored purposes; for example, loans for energy-saving or export investment may count less toward the target. Likewise, different banking institutions are given different targets, so that those specializing in automobile investment can be favored over those with larger portfolios of personal consumer loans. In essence, the *encadrement* serves as a government instrument to ration and allocate credit within an agreed total.

Another recently evolving instrument of French policy is a system of intermediary financial institutions designed to provide further selective credit intervention. The details of the system are complex; but its most important characteristics are worth noting. First, rather than providing finance directly, these public and semi-public institutions orchestrate packages of financial and other resources from public and private sources for economically favored causes, particularly export-promoting industries. Second, these intermediary institutions are tied in various ways to the government Treasury, particularly in that they are heavily manned by the same administrative elite that circulates in the higher reaches of French government, industry, and finance. After surveying French industrial policy, one analyst concluded:

> . . . decisions, generally, can be made in small group negotiations involving only the Treasury, a few outside financial institutions and the industrial group immediately concerned. Expertise is provided by the permanent and continuing specialization of such para-public institutions as the CNCA [National Agricultural Bank], the Crédit National, and other specialized intermediaries. . . . Once a decision is taken, finance follows easily. The system does not guarantee that every decision will prove a commercial success. But it does make possible a flexible, selective, highly articulated industrial policy oriented toward the future development of French exports. (Joint Economic Committee, p. 35)

Despite the similar levels of government ownership, the contrast with Britain could not be more pronounced. After a period of austerity under the postwar Labour government, wartime controls and economic planning mechanisms were rapidly dismantled in the early 1950s. Instead of detailed intervention in economic processes, both Conservative and Labour governments of the 1950s and 1960s relied mainly on the general public spending and taxation levels of fiscal policy to manage variations in aggregate demand and cope with recurring balance of payments crises (Steward). Periods of general fiscal stimulus to maintain high employment levels alternated with periods of sharp restraint, as expansion produced an excess of imports over exports and lessened confidence in the value of the pound—the so-called "stop-go cycle". This dilemma was in turn related to the economic interests of Britain's internationally oriented financial institutions, which sought to maintain the pound as a major international reserve currency and to the political interests of party leaders, who rushed to defend the pound as a symbol of national pride (Blank).

By the 1960s Britain's poor economic performance led many to propose imitating France's apparently successful planning effort; and in 1965 the new Labour government produced a national plan for greatly increasing economic growth over the next five years. But the plan was largely a paper exercise: There was little mutual understanding among government officials, industry, and financial circles as to what should be done to raise the growth rate. In 1966 the plan was effectively abandoned under the familiar pressures of a balance of payments crisis and a swing to the contractionary phase of "stop-go" management so as to restore confidence in the pound.

As noted in the preceding section, the 1970s brought more severe problems to the British economy. Fiscal tools were heavily relied on, during the crisis years 1976 and 1977 in an attempt to restrain growth in the public deficit and allow some room for domestic investment expansion. In addition, the Labour government during this period convinced unions to exercise wage restraint in the face of a widely perceived inflationary crisis. Restrictions on aggregate economic demand were relaxed somewhat during 1978 and 1979 with a program of reduced taxes and increased public spending; but lost at the same time was the union commitment to wage restraint, and a series of disruptive industrial conflicts in the winter of 1978 and 1979 eroded the government's standing in the country. In the election of May 1979, voters turned sharply in favor of Margaret Thatcher and the Conservative party, bringing in a radically new set of policy instruments.

It would be wrong to think that during this entire postwar period, British policy was devoid of industrial subsidies, credit controls, and other forms of detailed intervention. Special tax relief to encourage investment was begun in 1945; direct investment grants to the private sector were instituted in 1966; in 1967, government premiums were introduced to subsidize wages in firms located in economically lagging regions. Also, throughout the 1950s and 1960s the Bank of England employed selective credit measures to encourage loans for exports and shipbuilding and to restrict consumer borrowing. In the 1970s the pace of government subsidization quickened in an effort to modernize British industry and so try to achieve high rates of economic growth.

In a formal sense, many of these measures were analagous to French industrial policy. However, the British experience differs in three important respects. First, the British approach to industrial policy has been characterized by an arms-length relationship between government officials and the industrial and financial representatives, who are expected mainly to respond to the economic incentives provided by government. No integrated administrative elite of the French type exists to bring together bureaucratic, industrial, and financial circles. Indeed, British administrators advance in their careers with little experience in the problems of industry or finance. Despite experiments with joint committees and working groups, the general approach has remained basically "us and them," with an officialdom of self-contained careers that offers investment and other incentives to the "them" who work on the outside with everyday problems of industry and finance.

Second, British programs have been subject to continual chopping and changing to meet the political needs of alternating Conservative and Labour governments. Conservative governments have tended to rely on tax allowances to assist business; Labour governments have typically supplanted these allowances with direct cash grants and special subsidies for employment. In 1972 the Conservative government's Industry Act provided various forms of financial assistance to modernize plants and equipment. These "schemes," as they were known, covered virtually every sector of the economy while Conservatives were in power, but they fell into the background with the succeeding Labour government's Industrial

Strategy of 1975. This latter effort involved the creation of three dozen joint working parties of business, labor, and government, charged with setting medium-term objectives for their respective sectors and identifying problems in meeting those objectives. A new government-controlled National Enterprise Board was created to finance key industries in exchange for partial ownership; but the Board soon became the center of a conflict over whether it was simply a means for financially bailing out important firms facing bankruptcy (such as the Rolls Royce and British Leyland companies) or a device for implementing the socialist agenda of government ownership throughout industry (as the left wing of the Labour party wanted). In 1979 the new Conservative government quickly dismantled most of these programs.

Thus, compared to the French, the British government's short-term responsiveness to the demands of partisan competition made industrial policies less predictable, a fact that further encouraged government administrators' natural inclination to avoid close and enduring relationships with private economic decision makers. These factors are related to a third difference between Britain and France in their choice of tools. Unlike French policy makers, British officials have found it difficult to operate industrial assistance in ways that give strategic priority to some economic activities over others. Industrial subsidies and tax allowances, although called selective, have in practice been very widely distributed, partly because of short-term political advantages and partly because of administrative "fairness" standards that oppose unequal treatment of firms, sectors, and regions.

For all of these reasons, industrial policy as an instrument of economic management is different in Britain and France (Green). In Britain it is less predictable, more distant from central decision-making processes, and less integrated with the strategies of industrial and financial leadership. Since industrial policy came as something of an afterthought to the British emphasis on aggregate demand management and is far more open to democratic political pressures than in France, it might be considered vulnerable to sudden political change. This is precisely what has happened since 1979.

The Thatcher government in 1979 brought a radical shift in the instruments of British economic policy, although it is doubtful if many people voting for the Conservative party at that time realized the extent of the change entailed by their electoral choice. The essence of this change was to abandon fiscal management of aggregate demand in favor of a wholehearted commitment to controlling the aggregate money supply. With this change, most interest in detailed programs of industrial policy was cast to the winds (Joint Economic Committee, pp. 55–72).

It seems remarkable that British policy making could accomodate such an abrupt shift in the tools of economic management. After all, the British

Treasury had functioned for decades as the bastion of Keynesian demand management. But, considered closely, it is easy to see how singleminded monetarism competed with an almost equally singleminded Keynesianism. Both approaches place total emphasis on government control over key economic aggregates—general levels of total demand in the former, and particular measures of money supply in the latter. Concentrating on these "big levers" excused British officialdom from any deep involvement in the details of industrial production and finance. Thus, whereas in France establishment of a growth rate for the money supply became an opportunity for more extensive *involvement* in the allocation of credit and economic consultation in government, business, and financial circles, in Britain it provided the rationale for government *disengagement* from other economic problems. In France the "liberalization" policy of decontrol went hand in hand with sectoral planning, particularly for export promotion; in Britain decontrol policy was much more singleminded and tended to favor market mechanisms freed of government intervention.

Of course, all of British industrial policy has not been changed overnight, but differences in emphasis are substantial. In 1979 government assistance to especially deprived industrial areas covered 40 percent of the employed population; the new Conservative government sought to cut the percentage to 25 percent in three years. Various industrial aid programs were cut by over one third in the first years of the Thatcher government. The use of high interest rates to control the growth of the money supply added hardships to many industries, with little evidence that the British government—unlike the French—was prepared to fine tune such rates and allocations of credit to achieve particular industrial effects.

Three Variations: West Germany, Sweden, and the United States

Having considered the choice of economic policy instruments in France and Britain, we now turn our attention to Germany, Sweden, and the United States, which offer still other variations. The French/British contrast in industrial policies can serve as a background for drawing out particular themes expressed in the other countries.

The situation in the United States is comparatively straightforward. Only in wartime has the national government been equipped with tools for detailed economic intervention, and the mechanisms, such as wage-price controls and credit allocations, have for the most part been quickly dismantled at the conclusion of hostilities (Wilson; Goldstein). As parts of American industry have faced financial crises (Lockheed during the Nixon administration, Chrysler during the Ford and Carter years), some government assistance has been occasionally forthcoming, but these have been isolated decisions made in response to particular political forces in play at the time and not as part of anything that could be characterized as central planning. Likewise, in the first year of the Reagan administration, savings and loan associations, which had lent long term at low interest rates and could not attract short-term deposits without paying high interest rates, pressed their case for special government assistance; the result was a new system of government subsidy in the form of tax-free savings certificates. Again, however, this represented an expedient worked out between the administration and the Senate; it was not part of an overall government strategy to influence the workings of the private financial sector.

Occasionally in comparative policy analysis there is no comparison that can profitably be made. U.S. industrial policy certainly cannot be compared with the involvement of French officialdom. It is even difficult to draw parallels with Britain, since there has been little policy to change with alternations in party control of the government. The closest comparison that can be made is with various U.S. programs designed to assist economically hard-pressed regions and cities. Even more so than in Britain, multiple arenas of independent power in the United States impose a political imperative to spread such "selective" assistance very widely. Aid supposedly targeted in the form of grants, special lines of credit, and loan guarantees tends to develop so that most Congressmen, governors, and many mayors find a place at the table of federal assistance (Wachter).

Rather than straining for analogies, it is well to recognize that the U.S. national government has little capacity to pursue coherent courses of action below the most aggregate levels of economic management. Experience with wage and price controls during the 1970s provides one outstanding example, but there are others. As economic problems mounted later in that decade, some effort was made to use the President's Council of Economic Advisers and the newly created Council on Wage and Price Stability to analyze industrial sectors and their particular problems. But these efforts produced little enduring policy, and by the end of the Carter administration the latter council was abandoned with hardly a murmur of dissent. Likewise, proposals by the Carter White House to fine tune tax rates so as to moderate inflationary wage settlements (with so-called "real wage insurance" to maintain take-home pay by reducing taxes for workers and companies who struck below-average wage settlements) was stillborn and quickly forgotten.

Like Britain, therefore, the United States relies on aggregate demand management and/or aggregate money supply management as its preferred instruments of economic policy. But unlike its British counterpart, the U.S. executive branch must share extensive powers with an independent legislature. And unlike Britain or any of the continental European nations, the United States lacks a senior class of permanent officials with an enduring stake in policy development. Hence consistent and predictable demand management policies have proven especially difficult to achieve in Washington; Congress can easily overwhelm a President's taxing and spending plans, and such plans themselves frequently change as the temporary officials of the Presidential staff and the departments come and go.

The situation is different with regard to instruments of monetary policy. The Federal Reserve Board enjoys substantial independence from both President and Congress. Board members serve long, relatively fixed terms of office and are assisted by a high-level staff of professional economists. In theory this central financial institution can pursue an independent course of monetary policy, but in practice the "Fed" often has little choice but to accommodate the various swings of fiscal policy determined by President and Congress. For example, in 1966 and 1967 President Johnson first hesitated to ask for higher taxes to pay for increased military spending in Vietnam and then faced further delays in adjusting fiscal policy when Congress debated the proposed tax increase for over a year. The result was a major inflationary movement, which monetary authorities felt forced to counteract by restricting the supplies of money and credit, yielding in turn an unexpected and disruptive credit crunch. Similarly, in 1981 and 1982 the new Reagan administration succeeded against most expectations in gaining not only major federal spending cuts from Congress but also a multi-year program of significant tax reductions. However, increased military outlays and automatic budget increases produced by an unexpected recession had the effect of undermining spending constraints, while the economic downturn reduced revenues even further than foreseen when the commitments for three years of tax reductions were made. The result in this instance was a huge increase in the federal deficit and a severely constrained choice for the Federal Reserve Board: either to abandon the high interest rate policy that had been established to fight inflation, or to keep money tight with the likelihood of forestalling the deficit-produced inflation but also of dampening any of the administration's promised gains in economic growth. Interest rates remained high, though they did so not as part of a long-term financial strategy for the U.S. economy, but as a byproduct of circumstances and unforeseen swings in fiscal policy.

Thus, unlike Britain, the United States has found it difficult to use its aggregate economic management tools decisively. This may or may not be seen as a disadvantage, depending upon one's confidence in government's ability to recognize the "right" policy and to pursue it consistently. If the U.S. government lacks the French capacity for micro-economic interventions, it also lacks the singlemindedness that would allow anything like the Thatcher government's total commitment to the management of money supply. Certainly the conservative agendas of the Reagan and Thatcher governments have much in common: to reduce government spending, taxation, and regulation; to increase military power; and to rely on private market mechanisms. As actually implemented, however, the Reagan policy has not utilized one particular instrument (a money supply target, or balanced budget under fiscal policy, or the like) and applied it with steadfastness. Navigating its first year's program, the Reagan administration had to make many compromises, retaining ad hoc subsidies (for example, to tobacco farmers) and adding ad hoc interventions into the private markets (for example, tax aids to the savings industry). As unemployment and deficits grew in 1981 and 1982, the same public opinion that the President had mobilized to pass his original economic program through Congress now filtered into the highly permeable policy-making process of America's divided institutions to demand changes in the original package (for example, new taxes to help reduce the deficit, more help for the unemployed, and so on). By comparison, in the relatively closed environment of British economic policy making, the Thatcher government could and did march grimly onward along its chosen path.

Germany is also strongly committed to private market mechanisms and has little explicit industrial policy promulgated by the national government. Yet one would be wrong to conclude that Germany resembles the comparatively hands-off approach of the United States in its instruments of economic management. To be sure, experience with the Nazi-controlled economy lessened the attractiveness of centralized government intervention in the economy. But the massive disruptions of the 1920s and 1930s and of World War II also reinforced an already well-developed German commitment to economic stability. The widespread yearning for security led to a policy approach with much more systematic predictability than could be provided by any simple reliance on private market adjustments (which could create great instability and competitive political bargaining).

Like all Western democracies, the German government is involved in many aspects of the economy. It is distinguished by its reliance on a centrally guided banking system to provide the desired stability amid free markets. Direct government aid to industry is generally limited to tax allowances and research grants at the federal level and loan guarantees at the state and local levels. But government aid is distinctly subordinate to the key instruments of economic management: banking institutions and their links upward to central management of economic aggregates and downward to individual industries and firms.

It is important to understand the extremely close and long-standing relationship between local commercial banks and private companies. Banks possess direct power by owning company stock and sitting on the executive boards of many large firms. In addition, banks exert considerable indirect power as the major source of investment funds and financial information for day-to-day decision making in private companies. These functions occur to some extent among banks in every nation; but the interpenetration of banking and the industrial community is much deeper and more enduring here than almost anywhere else. At the end of World War II, the Allied occupying powers attempted to break up the heavily concentrated banking and industrial sectors; but the leading firms only regrouped in even larger structures as the postwar economy grew. Thus industrial and economic policy began to be interrelated because of overlapping industrial and financial structures (performing something of the same function as that of the interconnected elites of French bureaucratic, industrial, and financial circles). The three dominant German banks sit on no fewer than seventy of the supervisory boards of the top one hundred companies.

However, these features would be more a hindrance than an aid to coherent public policy without a link to the central processes of government economic policy making. That link is provided by the single most influential instrument of German economic policy, the *Deutsche Bundesbank* (central bank). The Bundesbank is independent of the government, and its regulatory power extends over virtually every organization capable of supplying credit. Each state of the federal system has its own central bank with direct ties to the Bundesbank. These state units are further subdivided into branches and offices in almost every town of significant size. In all developed countries, central bankers are powerful economic actors; public commitment to a forceful Bundesbank as a stabilizer of German domestic economic policy is, however, more deep-seated than comparable situations in other countries.

However, the central Bundesbank does not intervene directly in details of industrial finance or decision making. That task is left to local units of the banking system. The task of the central bank is to guide monetary policy and indirectly influence industrial policy by regulating the availability of credit and controlling the stock of money in circulation. In addition, the Bundesbank is depended on to maintain stability in the economy. Within general terms set by the Bundesbank, industries are free to innovate and invest, workers to bargain for benefits, financial institutions to supply credit—in response to signals from market mechanisms. Likewise, politicians are allowed to spend and tax as democratic competition may require. But it is with the Bundesbank's policy framework firmly in mind that they have to undertake their ostensibly free negotiations.

Not surprisingly, the power of the central banking authority has occasionally put it in sharp conflict with governmental, industrial, and labor leaders. So far, the Bundesbank has always prevailed. In 1969 and 1970, for example, inflationary pressures were building in the German economy. Despite urging and quiet pressure from the Bundesbank, first the Christian Democratic government and then a newly elected Social Democratic coalition government resisted pursuing a restrictive fiscal policy, a resistance supported by business and labor. In the end, the Bundesbank imposed stringent constraints on the supply of money and credit, arguing that a fiscal package of spending restraint and tax increases would be much less disruptive to the economy. The government gave way, and as the new fiscal package was passed by the parliament, the Bundesbank announced a phased reduction in monetary restraints.

In 1970 the government had to give way; in 1974 it was business and labor. We have noted the German response to the 1973 oil price shock. The Bundesbank was determined to prevent the higher oil costs from causing a surge of inflation. This challenge was intensified when in 1974 business and labor agreed on extremely high wage settlements averaging almost 14 percent that year. The Bundesbank responded by greatly tightening the availability of money and credit, thus making it much more difficult for businesses simply to pass on the higher labor and oil costs in higher prices. Moreover, bank officials made it clear that this policy would be continued for some time regardless of its effects on business profits and employment. The strategy worked. Profits which had been rising at an annual 7 percent rate grew scarcely at all in 1974. Realizing that high wage settlements would inevitably restrict profits further, leading to plant closings and more unemployment, labor agreed to moderate its wage demands; and 1975 wage settlements fell back to the 7 percent range, or roughly to the general rate of inflation.

The Bundesbank and banking system can operate in this way because there is general agreement on the importance of stability in German economic development. The Bundesbank is such a powerful instrument of economic policy not simply because of its independence, but because that independence is supported by a consensus against extreme and unpredictable fluctuations in the economy. Without this supporting context, no financial authority could sustain its position in periodic clashes with the short-term pressures of government, business, and labor.

Stability is symbolized by the Bundesbank's relatively autonomous control over monetary policy and its responsibility for preserving the value of the German currency. But its influence extends further; for banking authorities have not acted to try to preserve price stability at all costs if doing so would seriously destabilize other dimensions of the economy, such as employment, investment, and trade. Thus, while Germany was the first major Western nation to announce targets for aggregate growth in the money supply (in 1974), the Bundesbank has never argued for controlling inflation at all costs. It has not, like the French government, used monetary targets as a lever for detailed industrial intervention; nor has it, as in Britain, singlemindedly pursued such targets as the exclusive means of reducing inflation. At times, as in 1978, the Bundesbank has abandoned its monetary targets in favor of achieving stability in other areas of the economy. But it has done so in the name of stable management, not of hitting arbitrary monetary targets. It is an image of predictable management that the Bundesbank adeptly cultivates in its quiet public relations and in its constant interaction with all the major economic interests of the nation.

Swedish methods of economic management share some characteristics of several nations' approaches. As Table 5.1 suggests, Sweden ranks with Germany in the moderate degree of direct government ownership in its economy. Like Britain, Sweden has traditionally relied on the management of aggregate demand. Sweden, in fact, was among the earliest nations fully to embrace Keynesian-type concepts of fiscal policy, as the Social Democratic party in power in the 1930s abandoned most of its nationalization promises in favor of countercyclical spending and taxation. As economic problems mounted during the 1970s, the Swedish government was led to copy some elements of French-style detailed intervention in order to cope with troubled industries such as steel and shipbuilding.

However, the more distinctive quality of Swedish economic management lies elsewhere. The familiar tools of fiscal and monetary policy are in place; but the most characteristic aspect of Swedish policy is its heavy reliance on unions as the key element in economic management. Labor unions, particularly the huge central confederation of trade unions, *Landsorganization* (LO), have evolved into the most important instrumentality for determining the success or failure of economic policy. This situation is due in part to the high degree of union organization (covering approximately three fourths of the labor force—more than in any other country) and in part to LO's long-standing alliance with the Social Democratic party, which held power for over forty years, until the election of 1976. No less important, however, is the fact that two generations of union leadership have made it their business to advance their interests with bold proposals that could be shown to improve the economy as a whole. In the 1940s and 1950s, for example, the unions advanced a so-called "pro-mobility" policy. Through a complex series of government programs and industrial agreements, this policy sought to ensure a rapid adaptability of labor and capital to changes in international competition while maintaining economic security for workers. In the 1960s a union-led campaign was advanced to reduce inequality of living conditions and to rationalize low-paying, low-productivity sectors of the economy.

We might say that the labor union structure in Sweden performs roughly the same instrumental function that the banking system performs in Germany—namely, to provide a fairly coherent link between microeconomic decision making (at the level of firm and industry) and macroeconomic decision making (at the national level). In Sweden, an informal general division of labor developed in the postwar period whereby government maintained a high level of demand, so as to ensure full employment, in return for which trade unions sought to maintain industrial peace and exercise restraint in making wage and other demands on industry.

Of course actual operations have been more complex. As economic problems multiplied in the 1970s, Sweden's much praised system of management encountered severe difficulties. Union-led adjustment processes that had once produced negotiated settlements now yielded a succession of stalemates. Despite some functional similarities, unions and banks are different instruments of economic policy management. An emphasis on stability is fully consistent with conventional banking preferences for maintaining confidence, predictability, and the status quo. The Swedish trade union movement, however, has evolved its own agenda emphasizing redistributions of wealth and power rather than stabilizing the status quo distribution of shares. While the economy grew rapidly, conflict could be avoided by allowing differential gains for everyone. But slower growth meant that gains for some would occur at the expense of others. Such distributive conflicts occurred more often in all nations as postwar growth slowed down after the late 1960s. Swedish dependence on unions as the chosen instrument of economic management made the issues that much more prominent there. Since Swedish developments of the 1970s increasingly revolved around the distribution of scarcities, rather than of affluence, it is to that category of choices that we should now turn.

COSTS AND BENEFITS OF ECONOMIC MANAGEMENT

DISTRIBUTION

No one can accurately calculate the final distribution of welfare resulting from economic policies. Nor does the policy-making process in any nation actually try to make these calculations. What matters for policy making are the *perceived* costs and benefits around which groups become politically mobilized.

The salient factors in recent years have been the perceived costs and benefits of unemployment and inflation. Perhaps the greatest problem facing economic advisers and their ideas in the 1970s and 1980s has been simultaneous high unemployment and inflation (sometimes dubbed "stagflation") throughout the Western democracies. According to intellectual orthodoxy before the 1970s, high unemployment should have reduced inflation or high inflation should have diminished unemployment. The unwillingness of events to correspond to theory created confusion in traditional approaches to fiscal policy and provided the opportunity for monetary theories to become prominent. This in turn facilitated the introduction of publicly set monetary targets among the Western nations (Germany in 1974, the United States in 1975, France in 1976, and Britain in 1977), although it should now be clear that the same idea meant quite different things in the different nations.

Political Cycles and Redistributive Tradeoffs

Among other things, economic policy is shaped by choices concerning the distribution of economic costs and benefits. The question is, shaped how? As economic performance has deteriorated in the 1970s and 1980s, two major explanations—both with heavy political overtones—have gained prominence among analysts critical of large-scale government spending and taxing programs (Brittan; Buchanan and Wagner).

One explanation links economic management to a so-called "political business cycle" produced by democratic politics. According to this explanation, policy makers' sensitivity to the costs and benefits of economic management is asymmetrical. Policy makers in democratic systems are said to compete for favor by enacting benefits for the population; at the same time, they seek to avoid disfavor by deferring any explicit imposition of costs. In practical terms, this means that economic managers are strongly tempted to institute programs of fiscal stimulus, with major increases in spending for government benefits, while refusing to enact the tax increases necessary to pay for them. Deficits grow, producing higher rates of inflation. Protest against inflation rates also increases, but any bitter medicine to contract the economy will at worst be withheld or, at best, delayed until after the elections that engendered the spending for increased benefits in the first place. Such, in broad outline, is the political business cycle in modern democratic governments charged with economic management.

How applicable is this interpretation? Various methods of measuring economic policy in relation to swings in the political fortunes of democratic politicians have been used to evaluate this model, and the results give cause for skepticism. Although isolated instances of the presumed behavior can be found in most countries, any general patterns are lacking (Cameron 1981).

One recent careful study of developments in the seventeen advanced democracies since the 1960s shows no consistent tendency for governments to increase spending for benefits and avoid tax increases in correlation with the electoral cycle. In fact, more frequently, the effect of economic policy has been to reduce, rather than to augment, increases in disposable income during election years.

Second, if one considers not simply the effects on disposable income (government benefits minus any increases in taxes and social insurance contributions) but the total stimulative impact of all government spending and taxation, there is even less evidence of political business cycles. Table 5.2 summarizes the information on the net fiscal stimulus of government in election years over an eighteen-year period. The odds of having a net fiscal stimulus in any election year were only about fifty-fifty.

TABLE 5.2 The Net Fiscal Stimulus of Governments in Election Years in Sixteen Nations, 1960–1978

	Total Number of Elections	Number of Elections in which Net Fiscal Stimulus > 0
United States		
Presidential (1960–76)	5	1 (1964)
Congressional (1962–78)	5	3 (1966, *1970*, 1974)
Canada (1962–74)	6	0
Britain (1964–74)	5	3 (1966, *1974[1]*, 1974[2])
Ireland (1961–73)	4	4 (1961, 1965, 1969, *1973*)
West Germany (1961–76)	5	3 (1961, *1965*, 1972)
France		
Presidential (1965–74)	3	1 (1974)
Legislative (1962–73)	4	3 (*1962*, 1967, 1968)
Italy (1963–76)	4	3 (1963, 1968, *1972*)
Austria (1962–75)	5	1 (*1975*)
Netherlands (1963–77)	5	3 (1963, 1967, 1971)
Belgium (1977)	1	0
Sweden (1964–76)	5	1 (1973)
Norway (1961–77)	5	1 (*1977*)
Denmark (1964–77)	7	3 (1964, *1968*, *1975*)
Finland (1962–75)	5	3 (*1962*, 1966, *1975*)
Japan (1972–76)	2	2 (*1972*, 1976)
Australia (1961–77)	8	5 (*1961*, 1966, *1974*, 1975, 1977)
	84	40 (15 in which NFS > 1)

SOURCE David Cameron, 1981.
NOTE Net Fiscal Impact is defined as the sum of the change in all government expenditures as a percent of Gross Domestic Product (GDP) and the change in all government revenues as a percent of GDP from the year prior to an election to the year of an election. The italicized dates indicate that the Net Fiscal Stimulus exceeded 1 percent of GDP.

Third, there appears to be little systematic linkage among fiscal stimulus, government deficits, and rising levels of inflation. Countries with above-average government spending have not regularly experienced large deficits; nor have countries with large deficits necessarily experienced above-average rates of inflation. Countries with particularly high inflation have not necessarily experienced significant deficits or electorally timed policies of fiscal stimulation. Inflation may be a way of concealing costs that would otherwise arise from a more explicit conflict over income shares; but that is different from inflation occurring as the result of some inherent electoral dynamic in economic management (Cameron 1982).

Finally, unemployment shows a similar lack of correlation with electoral cycles. In some countries at some times, the level of joblessness does follow the prescribed pattern, *viz* falling as politicians bid for electoral favor, then rising when the bitter post-election medicine of restraint is applied. But there are at least as many observations of inverse movements—that is, with unemployment rising before elections and falling afterwards.

In sum, the political business cycle theory is important because it alerts us to calculations of costs and benefits as democratic policy makers grapple with the ups and downs of modern economies. But it also presumes a degree of consistency, predictability, and control that is very difficult to achieve in practice. Many politicians probably wish they could obtain the kind of strategic control with which abstract theory credits them. But the actual play of political forces in economic management seems too complex for any such fine tuning to occur.

The second basic explanation for economic mismanagement gives less importance to political cycles and more to the general trend of government redistribution. According to this view, the political impulse to compensate people for the costs of economic change has led to a distortion of market incentives. Government transfer payments, public consumption, heavy tax burdens, and other redistributive efforts have combined to break the link between individual efforts and rewards. The result has been declining work effort, reductions in entrepreneurial risk-taking, and less willingness to defer consumption for future investment. Market efficiency and production has been traded off in favor of greater redistribution and income transfers (Gilder; Anderson and Hill).

Many issues raised by this interpretation depend on philosophical premises and causal relationships that can never be conclusively proven or disproven. However, a comparative view of public policy can show that the extent of government intervention and redistributive effort in different nations does not appear to be closely related to overall economic performance. If we rank nations according to the real economic growth rate that they have achieved, there is no noticeable correlation between that ranking and the relative magnitude of government transfers, government consumption, or government redistribution through taxes. In Table 5.3 countries near the bottom of the growth chart rank lowest in government transfers and certainly do not seem to make unusually large efforts at redistribution through taxation. Government consumption does seem higher in countries in the bottom half, but closer inspection shows that government consumption of goods and services has been pushed to these heights by military, not social, expenditures. In general, both high and low economic growth countries vary considerably in their redistribution efforts. This is not surprising in view of the fact that national economic growth rates depend on a highly complex set of socioeconomic and cultural factors, many of which appear unmeasurable.

TABLE 5.3 Economic Performance and Redistributional Effort in Percent

	Real per capita GDP growth 1960–1977	Income Distribution		Government final consumption (percent of GDP)	Income maintenance spending (percent of GDP)
		Pre-tax	Post-tax		
		(Income top 20%/ income bottom 20%)			
Japan	7.5*	5.6	5.2	10	3
Spain	5.0	—	7.1	10	—
France	4.1	12.4	10.9	15	12
Norway	4.0	8.3	5.9	19	10
Italy	3.8*	—	9.1	14	10
Canada	3.4	10.1	8.2	20	7
Netherlands	3.4	7.8	6.6	18	19
West Germany	3.1	7.9	7.1	20	12
Sweden	2.7	6.8	5.6	28	9
Australia	2.6*	5.9	5.9	16	4
United States	2.5	11.8	9.5	18	7
Britain	1.9	7.5	6.1	21	8

SOURCE OECD, *The Welfare State in Crisis* (Paris: OECD), 1981, p. 138.
*1960–1976

The Inflation-unemployment Tradeoff

Distributive choices have been most important in relation to the problems of unemployment and inflation. In the same country at different times, and among different countries at the same time, we can discern varying paterns of sensitivity to the relative cost of fighting inflation or unemployment.

We begin by recalling the two-phase nature of economic developments in the postwar period. Until roughly the end of the 1960s, economic growth was generally rapid, with substantial price stability. In this setting, economic management brought what might be regarded as political good news. A steadily growing economy with minimal price distortion meant that economic policy decisions were mainly concerned with distributing differential gains, perhaps a little more for wages than profits or a little more for public than private consumption. Nevertheless, it was a situation of gain for all with little apparent imposition of costs on any. Even in Britain, where dissatisfaction with economic performance was stronger than elsewhere in the late 1950s and early 1960s, complaints focussed on the low rate of growth compared to other countries, such as France and Germany; however, real gains in living standards were at least as great in Britain at this time as at the height of its Industrial Revolution. In short, there was little perception of economic policy as a zero-sum struggle between labor and capital or private and public consumption, in which a gain for one side entails a corresponding loss for the other side. Economic growth meant more for everybody.

The second phase, since the end of the 1960s, has been a different story. A comparison of the period from 1973 to 1978 with the period of 1960 to 1973 for the ten largest Western economies shows a halving of output and real wage growth and a doubling of inflation. Slower growth, deeper recessions, and unpredictable inflation significantly changed the setting for political management of the economy. New perceptions of scarcity and "tradeoffs" among mutually incompatible economic goals grew throughout Western Europe and the United States. If sustained growth was to be revived, funds for new investment would have to increase; and a tough choice would have to be made between continuing the gains in benefits and wages for workers and shifting resources to private and/or public capital formation. An equally difficult choice was seen between policies for fighting inflation and those for maintaining employment. Both fiscal and monetary policies yielded the same immediate result: Inflation could be countered by slowing down the economy and increasing unemployment. In short, economic management in the 1970s and 1980s has brought the bad news commonly associated with a zero-sum situation.

As inflation rates grew throughout the Western nations in the 1970s, there was a decided shift everywhere toward policies that fought inflation at the expense of full employment. Rarely was this shift explicitly stated as government policy; but, in each country, there was, in the name of fighting inflation, a willingness to live with unemployment rates that would have been declared intolerable in the non-inflationary 1950s and early 1960s. The number of unemployed youth doubled between 1965 and 1975 in the OECD nations, and by 1982 unemployment rates in the United States and Europe were approaching postwar highs (OECD 1978 and 1982).

The willingness of each nation to make this priority shift was so widespread that it must be explained by general, not nation-specific, factors. The most plausible explanation involves the different constituencies affected by anti-inflationary and anti-unemployment policies. Rapid and erratic price increases are distributed widely across a nation's population and in every income level, and they are distributed in an arbitrary manner, even within the thinking of each individual. Few persons doubt that they deserve the higher prices as sellers of goods and services, but not many people feel they deserve the higher prices they must pay as buyers of goods and services.

Sensitivity to the pain of inflation is heightened by a certain "money illusion." In an inflationary period income may rise very quickly while purchasing power does not. Although *real* incomes (that is, incomes in constant prices) may grow, many people feel a loss when they consider how much better off they *should* be with so much money. For example, in the United States, real per capita income increased 28 percent in the "dismal" 1970s, compared to 30 percent in the "golden" 1960s and only 20 percent in the 1950s. But it would have been very difficult to convince Americans that they were doing as well in 1980 as they did in 1950. In the non-inflationary 1950s, money income measured real improvements; in 1980 Americans were more prone to feel dissatisfied: To achieve their 28 percent income growth after inflation, they had experienced a 134 percent increase in money income during the 1970s. Somehow, one should have felt much richer than he did in going from, say, $10,000 to $23,400, even if they were inflated dollars.

In contrast to inflation, the costs of unemployment have tended to be concentrated and predictable. Unemployment tends to fall disproportionately on especially vulnerable groups, such as the young, the unskilled, minorities, and persons in marginal industries. Whereas inflation tends to manifest its costs through widespread disappointment over what inflated incomes will buy, the costs of unemployment are often internalized in various kinds of personal problems—self-reproach for not being able to find a job, mental stress, illness, and sometimes suicide. Thus, for the majority, who have little experience with or likelihood of facing unemployment, retreat on the goal of full employment has often seemed a small price to pay for controlling inflation. If unemployment moves upward into white-collar or other occupations unfamiliar with unemployment, of course, this tolerance may change.

The differential costs and benefits of fighting inflation and unemployment help explain the general shift in distributional priorities that have occurred in the Western democracies in the 1970s and early 1980s. However, nations have displayed varying tolerances for the employment costs of fighting inflation. These differences relate to the political role of organized labor; but the relationship is not simple.

Political scientists in recent years have devoted considerable effort to analyzing the relationship between economic performance and the nature of the reigning political regime, especially in terms of sensitivity to unemployment and inflation. While not conclusive, the results do show some interesting general tendencies. One early and influential study concluded that during the 1960s social democratic governments placed far greater emphasis on fighting unemployment, even at the expense of higher inflation, while non-social democratic governments (or bourgeois governments, in the Europeans' terminology) generally sought price stability even at the expense of unemployment (Hibbs). More recent studies, however, have shown that when one takes account of a broader range of Western nations and the experiences of the 1970s, no such linkage between policy and politics can be found (Payne; Schmidt). A glance back to Figure 5.1 will show that during the economically troubled 1970s both unemployment and inflation increased, but that some countries managed to maintain relatively low inflation without high levels of unemployment while others suffered much higher unemployment without in return obtaining price stability. Closer analysis indicates that economic performance is more complicated than can be accounted for simply by the nature of the political party in office or by clear-cut decisions as to how much unemployment to trade off for how much inflation. The important political factors seem to concern the more general societal distribution and organization of power, although this will of course often be reflected in the electoral success of particular parties. In general, the results to date suggest that, at least during the widespread economic troubles of the 1970s, more effective control of unemployment and inflationary tendencies tended to be associated with political environments having a strong social democratic/organized labor presence as well as a collaborative rather than adversarial relationship between unions, employers' associations, and government (Schmidt). Table 5.4 shows some of these results and also makes clear that there are enough exceptions (Switzerland and Denmark, for example) to remind us that these are no more than general tendencies—not iron-clad laws. Nor should one forget that there are also varying economic conditions, such as a country's position in world markets and inherited inflation and unemployment rates from the 1960s, that are also important in accounting for political and economic performance in the 1970s.

One Swedish social scientist has attempted to explore this politics-unemployment relationship more closely, and some of his results are shown in Table 5.5. This table lists several Western democracies according to the political power of their organized labor. Countries are ranked by the extent to which workers are mobilized (determined by the degree of unionization and the proportion of the electorate supporting political parties associated with labor) and able to exert control over the instruments of government (determined by the proportion of top government posts held by parties associated with labor and the length of time control has been exercised). Clearly one cannot explain each variation in unemployment rates simply in terms of labor's political power; like economic growth rates, unemployment rates depend on a number of complicated factors in each country. But the broadest variation evident in the table—that between the higher rates in the United States and the generally lower rates in Europe—does say something about the differences in political tolerance of unemployment in the two areas. Careful study of unemployment rates has shown that even after taking account of methods of counting unemployed persons, the higher American unemployment rates reflect the absence of many practices encouraging job security and continuity that are common in Europe (Kaufman). Some of these practices—requirements for consulting with worker representatives before layoffs can occur, or mandatory sever-

TABLE 5.4 Inflation, Unemployment, and the Political Complexion of Regimes, 1974–1978

	Government Tendency*	Left Wing Vote	Collaborative Policy Making**	Average Unemployment Rate***	Average Annual Inflation Rate
Austria	S.D. hegemony	51.5%	strong	low	6.9
Norway	S.D. hegemony	47.5	strong	low	9.5
Denmark	S.D. dominance	42.1	medium	high	11.0
West Germany	S.D. dominance	44.5	medium	medium	4.8
Britain	S.D. dominance	40.0	weak	medium	16.1
Australia	Balance	45.0	medium	high	12.8
Finland	Balance	43.3	medium	medium	13.8
Luxembourg	Balance	48.3	medium	low	7.9
Sweden	Balance	48.2	strong	low	10.3
Belgium	Bourgeois dominance	29.6	medium	high	9.2
Iceland	Bourgeois dominance	32.6	medium	low	39.8
Ireland	Bourgeois dominance	14.1	weak	high	15.3
Italy	Bourgeois dominance	41.9	weak	medium	17.0
Netherlands	Bourgeois dominance	36.8	medium	medium	7.8
Switzerland	Bourgeois dominance	26.4	strong	low	4.1
Canada	Bourgeois hegemony	16.6	weak	high	11.0
France	Bourgeois hegemony	42.5	weak	medium	10.7
Japan	Bourgeois hegemony	38.4	strong	low	11.3
United States	Bourgeois hegemony	0.0	weak	high	8.0

SOURCE: Schmidt, 1982, Table 5, p. 135.

*Refers to the political composition of governments during this time, with 100 percent control of cabinet seats counted as "hegemony," one third to two thirds of cabinet seats counted as "balance," and from two thirds to 100 percent counted as "dominance."

**An admittedly judgmental term: "Strong" refers to situations where employers and unions are found espousing a social partnership ideology, strike volume is low, cooperation on some economic policy areas is common, and no mandatory incomes policy was imposed by the government during this period. "Weak" indicates countries where unions and employers customarily approach each other as adversaries and incomes policies were usually imposed. (See Schmidt 1982, footnote 6, p. 165–166.)

***National average unemployment rates above 5 percent are counted as "high"; from 2 to 5 percent as "medium"; and from 0 to 2 percent as "low".

ance benefits paid by the employer, for example—depend on public policies supported by organized labor. Other practices, such as shortening working hours rather than laying off workers, depend more on deep-seated industrial traditions in various nations.

Public expenditures for dealing with unemployment are under somewhat more direct political control than are layoff procedures or industrial traditions. Here too one cannot expect to predict policy outcomes simply in terms of labor's political power in each nation; variations in such spending will also depend on the particular economic conditions prevailing in different nations. What can be said from information such as that in Table 5.5 is that countries such as Sweden and Germany have tended to experience somewhat lower unemployment rates and have spent significantly more on employment programs than have countries such as the United States, Britain, and, to a lesser extent, France. National differences in the economic policies provide some useful clues for understanding these differences.

In Sweden, where unions are extensive, strong, and central to the processes of economic management, tolerance for unemployment has been very low. As noted earlier, Sweden put considerable effort into maintaining employment during the recession of 1974 and 1975. Its employment policies—in the form of training and public employment programs, assistance to declining industries, job security schemes, and the like—have been no less vigorous in other years. But the Swedish policy debate has recently gone beyond the issue of full employment. The union movement has continued to play its traditional aggressive role by pressing new proposals for more fundamental change. Accepting the need to curtail both private and public consumption in favor of investment, in order to revive Swedish competitiveness in world markets, LO in the mid-1970s developed a program calling for the accumulation of huge investment funds under some form of workers' control. By 1982 the Social Democratic party had become fully committed to the union's proposal. In essence, the Swedish labor movement is attempting to sidestep the conventional distributive choice between profits for business investment, and jobs and wages for workers' consumption. In labor's view, the price of restraining consumption in favor of investment cannot be paid with unemployment or unilateral wage restraint by the unions; rather, it must be paid by spreading the ownership of investment capital to the workers themselves. Thus the union launched a major debate in the 1980s on the most fundamental distribution choice of economic management: that between worker and capitalist ownership of the means of production.

Although they are less centrally involved in economic policy making than their Swedish counterparts, German unions are also well organized and extensive in industry. Their power and the overall consensus in favor of stability have also led to considerable efforts to keep unemployment low. In 1974 and 1975 the Bundesbank stood firm against inflationary pressures in ways that avoided major unemployment (which peaked at 5 percent in 1975). Its message was conveyed through a vast increase in short-time work, with almost a million workers on reduced hours in one month of 1975 compared to 44,000 workers on short time in 1973. At the same time, Germany has usually been able to shift some employment costs of fighting inflation onto non-German "guest workers," who return home or otherwise fall out of the labor force during economic contractions.

TABLE 5.5 Political Rule, Unemployment, and Public Spending in Selected Countries

Political Pattern	Country	Average Annual Unemployment Rate 1959–1978	Public Spending for Employment Programs 1975–1978 as Percent of GNP	Total Public Spending as Percent of GNP	
				1950	1975
High Mobilization	Sweden	1.8	1.61	37.5	51.0
and Stable Control	Austria	1.7	0.02	25.0	40.3
	Norway	2.0	0.55	25.5	46.5
High Mobilization and	Denmark	3.9	n.a.	19.4	47.5
Occasional Control	Britain	3.3	0.36	30.4	46.1
	Belgium	2.6	n.a.	26.3	44.9
Medium to High	Finland	2.1	0.22	26.9	37.2
Mobilization and	France	2.5	n.a.	28.4	42.4
Low Control	Italy	3.8	n.a.	27.8	43.1
Low to Medium	West Germany	1.2	0.60	30.8	45.6
Mobilization and	Netherlands	1.8	n.a.	27.0	54.3
Partial Participation	Switzerland	0.1	n.a.	20.8	27.4
Low Mobilization	Ireland	5.7	0.17	n.a.	n.a.
and Exclusion	Canada	5.6	0.26	26.8	41.2
	United States	5.4	0.33	27.4	36.2

SOURCE Walter Korpi, 1980, Table 4, p. 312.

German policies and industrial practices are in fact strongly committed to job security for organized German workers while at the same time tolerant of the necessary economic adjustments. To take a recent example, scarcely a year after it had acquired a multi-million-dollar German steel company in danger of closing, the United States Steel Company sold the plant for exactly one dollar because of the payments, training, and placement services that would be due the employees if the plant were closed (Joint Economic Committee).

France has usually appeared more tolerant of unemployment. By and large, the voice of labor is not heard within the closed circles of negotiation among bureaucracy, industry, and finance. This is not to say that training and other manpower policies are absent from France; but there is a tendency in French policy to insulate decision making from direct labor pressures when government restructuring and other strategies of economic change impose costs. This seems to create the potential for more extreme dissent when dissatisfaction builds up too far (for example, the immense and largely unexpected outburst in May 1968), and many observers have concluded that the same pent-up resentments played a large part in the election of the first Socialist government in 1981. Whether French economic policy making will now be more sensitive to accomodating workers' interests remains to be seen.

Britain and the United States present interesting mixed cases in the politics of distributive choice. For many years after World War II, aggregate demand management in Britain had as its major priority the maintenance of full employment, often at the expense of industrial adaptation and competitiveness in world markets. This priority seems to have had less to do with union participation in economic policy making than with a political interest of both major parties in convincing voters that the severe unemployment and class division of the 1920s and 1930s would not be repeated. Compared to their continental counterparts, British unions have been relatively decentralized and much more involved in plant-level bargaining over wages and working conditions. This fragmentation, plus the traditionally closed process of executive economic policy making, means that unions are in a powerful position to disrupt government economic strategies (by insisting on wage and other compensations at the local bargaining level) but in a weak position to make any positive contribution to overall economic policy management. The distributive struggle surrounding inflation and unemployment policies came to a head in the late 1970s, when the Labour government was unable to sustain its "social contract" for wage restraint once the economic crisis of 1975 and 1976 had passed. The result was the arrival of a Conservative government committed to economic policies abrogating the long-standing commitment to maintaining full employment at all costs. In the name of creating long-term benefits for all by reestablishing market disciplines, the new government of Margaret Thatcher presided over the greatest increases in unemployment and plant closings since the Great Depression of the 1930s. In the face of this harsh economic medicine, decentralized union power was largely ineffective. Whereas unions had been able to protect themselves against inflationary conditions by winning compensatory wage increases (thus further accelerating the inflationary conditions), they could not protect themselves against unemployment. They could not do so unless they accepted lower real wages (like some U.S. and German unions) or (like the Swedish unions), they sought to extend their control over wages to control over the capital that employed them. And that—given the very different structure of union power in economic policy making—has seemed impossible.

At first glance, the United States' economic policy might appear to have even greater immunity from the pressures of unemployment costs. With weakly centralized and small unions (relative to the size of the labor force), U.S. policy makers have little to contend with compared to their European counterparts, with their strong union movements that are closely tied to avowedly worker-oriented social democratic parties. To be sure, the United States has throughout the 1970s and early 1980s exhibited an extremely high tolerance for periodic bouts of severe unemployment. Yet we must also recall the relative fragmentation of the U.S. policy process compared to Britain's. Although government economic policy may at times impose heavy unemployment costs in the name of fighting inflation (as it did in 1974–1975, 1979–1980, and 1981–1982), it is very difficult to fight inflation in ways that avoid pressures for off-setting compensations. The result is a relatively inconsistent set of accommodations (to tobacco farmers but not to dairy producers, to CETA employment programs with private but not with public organizations, and so on) designed to give aid particularly to those who are best organized to penetrate and exert pressure on the government apparatus (savings and loan associations, but not migrant workers). At present, we cannot say to what degree the same tendencies will reappear to affect the Reagan economic program, but the general direction is clear. Faced with an independent legislature and a multitude of other independent power centers in the bureaucracy, the Federal Reserve Board, and the state and local governments, the Reagan administration could not pursue its economic strategy in anything like the singleminded way that the Thatcher government pursued its strategy.

Generalizations from these complex patterns are difficult. Some observers see the political result of the second phase of postwar economic development as a turn to the right. The U.S. election of 1980, the Thatcher government's victory in Britain, the Swedish Social Democrats' loss of office in 1976 all seem to confirm that tendency. But the historic Socialist victory in France, the continuing success of Helmut Schmidt's

Social Democratic party, and the Congressional opposition to the Reagan program in 1982 all suggest a different tendency. What actually emerged from the economic turmoil of the late 1970s seemed to be a public reaction against whatever political group happened to be in office at the time that economic bad news accumulated. What these governments of the 1970s and their successors of the 1980s—either of the Right or Left—could not claim was that economic events were outside their control. Public perceptions of the costs and benefits of economic policy making had evolved too far since World War II. The consequences of economic policy were everywhere regarded as matters of choice, not as the natural or unavoidable results of uncontrollable forces. In that perception lay the great burden and the great opportunity for political management of economic choices in the 1980s.

COLLABORATORS OR ADVERSARIES IN ECONOMIC MANAGEMENT?

RESTRAINTS AND INNOVATION

Management of the economy is a relatively recent development. Events of the 1970s undercut much of the earlier confidence that the rules of economic management were understood and readily translatable into sustained, non-inflationary economic growth. By the early 1980s it had to be admitted that the old sense of mastery over economic developments was gone in policy-making circles in the United States and Europe.

In some quarters, progress in economic management was seen to depend on the arrival of a "new Keynes" to identify a better set of rules for attaining non-inflationary growth with full employment (Drucker). Forgotten in this vision was how much of postwar Keynesian policy was actually a process of trial and error taking place within each nation's particular tradition of policy making. In any event, bold new ideas have not appeared on the horizon, and, pending their arrival, economic policy making must still proceed.

The essential problem for every government in the 1980s has been this: Given weak economic growth and a momentum of inflationary expectations, how can the economy (and thus employment) be revived without creating inflationary pressures? Whatever the theoretical puzzles of economic doctrine, political management of the economy in the 1980s has centered on convincing key economic actors to forego immediate gratification in favor of a longer-term, collective good. To some this has meant holding back government consumption; others have emphasized private consumption and wage restraint; still others have stressed restraining business from passing through price increases, pursuing only short-term profits, and engaging in speculative rather than productive investment to produce more jobs. Typically, policy debate throughout the Western countries has been a mix of all these views. But the essential political problem remains the same—to redirect powerful groups, whose self-interest produces inflation, toward joint action that can produce stable growth.

Such problems of collective action are hardly new in political affairs. Current economic policy, however, poses the problem in particularly dramatic and inescapable terms. Lacking the surpluses produced by high growth in the 1950s and 1960s, economic policy makers in every nation face the difficult task of imposing short-term costs in order to achieve uncertain longer-term gains. Perhaps the most severe restraint in every country lies in the widespread expectations of painless choice built up among consumers, businessmen, unions, and bureaucrats during the postwar period of high economic growth. To overcome this inertia of short-term self-interest, political innovations, no less than innovations in economic theory, seem necessary.

The most widely discussed such political development has been *corporatism* (Heisler; Schmitter and Lehmbruch). Rather than depending on competition among political parties or intermittent pressures of a large number of interest groups, policy making is seen to be (or to be in the process of becoming) a system of high-level bargaining and consultation between government officials and leading actors in the private economy. In essence, corporatist policy making is a process of continuing negotiation among a small number of highly organized and centralized interest groups (especially workers, employers, and professional associations) and an equally well-organized government apparatus that is obliged by law or informal agreement to consider the advice of such groups.

Corporatist theorists generally argue that this system is becoming most noticeable and dominant in the field of economic policy. Political power that once depended on territorial representation now tends to pass to functional representatives of capital and labor. Interests that once were expressed through a large number of separate groups are now more coherently organized into a few peak associations. Collaboration with the government, which once was erratic and ad hoc, is now more continuous and institutionalized, typically with more formal advisory machinery to carry on the bargaining (Berger).

It is easy to understand the attractiveness of the corporatist model for some observers, as economic management has become more difficult. Corporatism suggests a political mechanism for disciplining powerful economic interests by making them jointly responsible for the longer-term results of their actions. Short-term costs of economic adjustment may be more readily accepted in exchange for a continuing part in vital government decisions affecting these groups' interests.

Despite the difficulty of making precise measurements, it is possible to classify countries according to the extent to which they embrace the corporatist end of the policy-making spectrum. One attempt to classify nations is based on such indicators as the extent of interest group organization, the degree of centralization in employers' and workers' associations, and the presence of national-level bargaining machinery (Wilensky 1976). Ranked by these criteria, from the more to the less corporatist systems, the developed nations do show a tendency for corporatism to be associated with more successful economic performance. Success is, of course, a matter of judgment; but many people would probably argue that it has to do with achieving growing prosperity without severe fluctuations in unemployment or continuous inflation. Corporatist bargaining may contribute to this outcome by creating understanding among potential antagonists as to the choices that must be made to reconcile social equity and economic efficiency. As one author said, "labor, interested in wages, working conditions, social security, and, to a lesser extent, participatory democracy, is forced to take account of inflation, productivity, and the need for investment; employers, interested in profit, productivity, and investment, are forced to take account of social policy" (Wilensky 1981, p. 190). This is not to say that corporatist countries will be spared the effects of economic events—such as oil price shocks, more intense foreign competition, and the like. But corporatist nations may be able to deal with such situations in a more coordinated, less ad hoc manner than could adversary, non-consultative systems. If we recall the lack of correlation between economic performance and redistributional effort cited earlier, this association of economic performance with political management is indeed noteworthy.

However, the advantage of corporatist innovations in economic management should not be overdrawn. Tripartite settlements among government, organized business, and labor have proven very difficult to sustain, particularly in the key area of incomes policy (Panitch).

As economic growth slowed down and inflation increased in the late 1960s and 1970s, a major problem of economic management was restraining wage increases that would validate the increases in the cost of living and decrease competitiveness in international markets. The result was a series of attempts to bargain through the terms of such wage restraint—to create some form of "social contract"—along roughly corporatist lines. This was particularly true in Britain, Germany, and Sweden, which are highly dependent on international trade and thus vulnerable to competition from countries with lower labor costs.

Considering the results, one realizes the uncertain prospects for corporatist innovations. In Britain, the new Labour government in 1974 hailed its social contract with the union leadership which was intended to compensate workers' wage restraint with better welfare state benefits (the so-called "social wage"). The government did spend more, but the wage restraint was not forthcoming; and only under the pressure of economic crisis two years later was a disciplined incomes policy actually implemented. But even that policy could not be sustained past 1978. In effect, no amount of corporatist bargaining could compensate for the fragmented, locally independent nature of British unions that made peak-level agreements extremely unreliable as a guide to economic management.

In Germany and Sweden the experience with social contracts was somewhat different, but the implications for corporatism were almost as dismal. Significant instances of sustained wage restraint did occur in Germany. We can also find abundant evidence of continuous collaboration among the well-organized private sector interests themselves and between them and government policy makers in the 1970s. But it is also true that this process has focussed on the wage bargaining process, not on other areas of economic management, such as investment and regulation of competition. Even the concerted action that has resulted on wages has been largely a response to other, particularly monetary, decisions falling outside the realm of corporatist bargaining. In other words, in Germany, as in every other Western democracy, it is difficult to find evidence of true corporatist-style policy making when it comes to monetary policy.

Given its highly organized interest group structure, Sweden should be a prime testing ground for corporatist policy making. On the central question of incomes policy, the recent record has been mixed. Government, business, and labor representatives have made persistent attempts to deal with the problem systematically, considering wages in relation to other economic choices for investment, trade balances, and not least of all the tax rates that determine the real value of any wage increases. But the outcome of these efforts has been problematic.

Agreements on wage restraint tended to have a destabilizing effect on economic management when company profits remained unexpectedly strong in 1974 and 1975. Earlier efforts by LO's leadership had failed to convince the Social Democratic government and central bank to experiment with more flexible exchange rates to stabilize foreign earnings, and by 1975 and 1976 rank and file union members were insisting on compensation for their earlier restraint. A series of high wage settlements then coincided with an unexpectedly long recession in international markets. This in turn stiffened employer resistance to further compromise and encouraged the non-Social Democratic government (elected in 1976 and reelected in 1979) to strike a hard posture on allowable wage increases. The result in 1980 was the first general strike in Sweden in over seventy years and an embittered process of tripartite consultation.

The most appropriate general conclusion seems to be that recent economic difficulties have encouraged certain corporatist tendencies in economic policy making, in terms of greater reliance on functional representation, regular and continuous bargaining among organized economic actors and government policy makers. But such corporatist tendencies may not go far. They apply less well to some areas of economic management, such as monetary policy, than to others, such as incomes policy. Particularly given the differences in organizational cohesion and power among the key participants (government, business, and labor), corporatist tendencies are much less apparent in some countries (such as the United States, where all three potential partners are comparatively fragmented) than in others (such as Sweden or Germany or, with a much diminished role for organized labor, France). Further, even within the same country and the same field of economic management, as in Swedish wage bargaining, corporatist processes cannot exist apart from the larger political context of economic policy making.

In short, corporatist tendencies add a potential new element to the politics of economic management, but they must take their place alongside other more familiar factors. Dependence on international trade and growing vulnerability to unexpected shocks in international markets are a strong incentive for the major organized economic interests in each nation to collaborate in dealing with the common threats; so much the better for corporatism. But the same factors, precisely because they increase the complexity and unpredictability of each group's calculations, can also become a means of undercutting collaborative policy making.

In addition to external economic realities, attempts at political innovation are constrained by the inherited structure of each nation's policy-making system—the extent to which various interests are effectively mobilized and empowered as well as the nature of the official machinery for pulling together policy decisions. One need simply reflect, for example, on the role of organized labor in the economic policy processes of different nations. It is as unlikely that a conservative government could impose Thatcher- or Reagan-like policies on the powerful union movement in Sweden, as that Continental-style union demands for economic democracy would exert a major influence on the fragmented Democratic party and union movement in the United States.

Behind international forces and domestic structures lies perhaps the ultimate constraint on and opportunity for political innovation in economic management: the mass of public attitudes, expectations, and behavior that forms the background for economic decision making. Certainly there is no lack of predictions in policy-making circles about what the public will not stand for and judgments about what the people want or should want. But the scattered empirical information suggests that the role of public opinion is more complicated than commonly assumed. People's relative preferences for, say, unemployment versus inflation can and do change, particularly in light of their recent experiences. Expectations about economic performance and the ability of governments to bring about improvements fall as well as rise; some might interpret a fall as a loss of confidence, others as growing realism on the part of the public. People often appear to be capable of distinguishing between their own personal economic circumstances and the state of management in the economy as a whole (Alt).

What model of democratic pressure on economic management all this implies is uncertain, but it certainly does not imply a simple view of unidirectional, shortsighted, all-or-nothing public pressure on economic policy making. These matters are important, because corporatist theory generally de-emphasizes the problem of how elite bargaining among peak associations can win acceptance among the nonelite and unorganized participants in the economic and political system. Even if corporatist innovations did prosper at the level of national economic policy making, we would still face the problem of how such decisions were to be legitimized and thus rendered acceptable to the larger political community. Dumb acquiescence can hardly be a source of such legitimation.

There is no deterministic answer as to whether economic policy management processes will be used to search out new forms of cooperation or more intensified forms of conflict. As we have seen, the United States appears more inclined to define the terms of debate in a strictly adversarial manner, but does so in ways that prevent adversaries from coalescing into coherent structures of opposition. In France, the sharp ideological conflict on economics at the level of political rhetoric is offset by a dense system of technocratic policy management; it is difficult to say which impulse will prevail, even under a socialist government such as Mitterand's. Britain's traditions of civility and cooperation during crises coexist with a policy system that does coalesce adversaries into confrontations between the governing party and the opposition party, between business and labor. Thatcher policies, much more than similar Reagan policies in the United States, have added greatly to the sense of confrontation and class conflict. So the point and counterpoint could be drawn for any number of countries and policies.

The political problem of choice between cooperation and conflict goes deeper than the question of whether or not economic policy has become a zero-sum conflict. Even if a new sense of economic scarcity does mean that what one side wins the other loses, the issue of political choice remains. Zero-sum conflicts can be fought out by the law of the jungle, but they can also be handled in more cooperative, collaborative ways. Economic contestants might agree that if one side wins this year, the other side can win the next; the penalties for losing can be lessened by offsetting compensations; a sense of fair play can be preserved by limiting the rewards of winning; various sides can agree to search for ways to redefine the game itself; and so on. Given everything that can be said about restraints, scarcity, and limited economic options, people still do help create their own future.

* * * * *

Economic policy is, therefore, a field rich in both intellectual and practical political challenges. Compared with other policy areas, it is a subject with a widely shared language and measures of success, even if theories compete with each other and economic success proves elusive. Events of the past decade and a half have posed a number of common problems for the advanced industrial democracies, and whatever the nature of the political regime, there has been no escaping the harsh economic facts of life. Problems of reconciling high employment with price stability, of meeting increased international competitiveness while restructuring aging industrial sectors, of managing an omnipresent public sector while promoting private market incentives—these are some of the inescapable constraints that reality imposes on today's governments, whether these be governments of the new right or the social democratic left. At the same time, however, nations have their own distinctive forms of political management that grow out of institutional traditions and the play of political power. Any realistic appraisal of economic policy making requires an appreciation of both the inherent constraints and the capacities for choice that exist.

6
TAXATION POLICY

A government's power to tax undergirds to a large degree the scope of the country's activities in the other domestic policy areas. Governments must raise revenue to pay for the services they provide, but they can also finance these by going into debt. These options in turn are related to the state's general economic management, since the relative reliance on taxation and borrowing may affect employment and inflation rates. Taxation policies have come to be powerful instruments of macro-economic policy; but they are also a means of achieving social policy goals and micro-economic objectives. Taxation policy is thus characterized by a complex interaction between revenue-raising functions on the one hand, and other economic and social policy functions on the other.

Many forces in and out of government try to manipulate taxation policy toward diverse and often conflicting ends. Situations in which one "school" achieves sweeping changes—such as the Reagan tax-cut legislation of 1981—are relatively unusual. Normally, taxation policy is hammered out among tax experts, with the result that the "essence of a tax question moves swiftly from general principles to excruciating legal details. . . ." Even members of the U.S. Senate Finance Committee are expected to follow their staff specialists: When questioning became too prolonged in one session, the committee chairman was said to have remarked in frustration that "if the members insist on knowing what's in this bill we'll never get it passed!" (Shultz and Dam, pp. 44, 63).

CHOICES IN TAXATION POLICY

Scope and Thresholds

The flexibility that legislators enjoy with regard to matching revenues and expenditures may be limited by the nation's constitution. Certain restrictions may forbid a government from engaging in deficit finance or may place limits on certain kinds of taxes. Governments may then choose to accept such constraints or alter them, either by amending the constitution or by encouraging change at the sub-national level. The long-term trend has been toward eliminating such constraints, but there have also been some recent tendencies in the opposite direction.

Clearly, the scope of tax extraction is partly determined by how governments perceive taxpayer resistance—are there thresholds beyond which taxation levels should not rise? Governments can regularly increase the ratios of taxation to national incomes, or they can avoid crossing taxation levels of 30 percent, 40 percent, or 50 percent of Gross National Product (GNP). During the period from 1950 to 1975, all Western governments increased these ratios, but they varied in the degree to which they did so.

The per capita amount of taxation rose in all countries, partly because of increased government activity, partly because of inflation. In the United States the $1000 mark was passed in 1967, the $2000 mark in 1975, and the $3000 mark in 1979. But in Europe, Denmark passed the $3000 level in 1975, and Sweden in 1977 passed the $5000 level, which Denmark then passed in 1979.

Cross-national comparisons can illuminate both institutional and behavioral constraints on taxation policy alternatives. Thus it has been pointed out that European and other countries have successfully administered taxation practices held to be infeasible in the United States. "This suggests that a number of administrative or political constraints, often accepted as data for the purposes of reform discussion in the U.S., are not, in fact, operative" (Whalley, p. 212).

Instruments

National governments can choose either to monopolize the tax-collecting function, or to allow regional and local governments to collect certain kinds of taxes. The Netherlands follows the first pattern; the second is found in all federal systems, and in many unitary systems as well.

In some federal systems, such as West Germany's, national, regional, and local governments share the proceeds from one jointly administered tax. Elsewhere, national governments may get priority in the use of direct taxes such as income taxes, while state governments must rely mainly on indirect taxes such as sales taxes. Within the overall taxation system, governments differ in their reliance on direct taxes and on indirect taxes.

The more kinds of taxes that a government can rely on—the broader the tax base—the more marginal tax rates can be kept down. If a taxpayer has to yield to the state $70 of each additional $100 earned, he may decide to substitute leisure for work. If such "substitution effects" are considered undesirable, the government can minimize them by adjusting its reliance on different taxation instruments.

Administrative feasibility is an important factor in a government's selection of instruments. Most European nations, for example, have adopted a value-added sales tax, which is levied at each stage of production and collected disproportionately from larger firms, because it is easier to implement than a retail sales tax. It has been claimed that this must be looked at as tax. It has been claimed that this must be looked at as a European argument that does not fit in the North a European argument that does not fit in the North American context, however, since those states with retail sales taxes encounter no major difficulty in tax collection (Whalley, 223). Of course, if U.S. state governments choose to increase the sales tax levels from the 5 to 8 percent range to the 15 to 25 percent range found in Europe, they might also encounter greater collection difficulties.

Distribution

In selecting taxation instruments and directing them at the various income groups, governments attempt to act with regard to concepts of fairness. Thus the principles of *vertical* equity pose choices as to whether the rich should pay smaller, equal, or larger shares of their income than should the average income earners and the poor. If emphasis is placed on across-the-board sales taxes, the taxation system may increase income inequality; if emphasis is placed on progressive income taxes, the system may decrease after-tax income inequality.

If the social goals of taxation policy have higher priority than revenue-producing and other economic goals, taxation systems tend to have greater redistributive effects. In Sweden, the linking of social, revenue-producing, and macro-economic goals led to a taxation system that altered the incomes of the top 20 percent of households in relation to the bottom 20 percent from about 7:1 to 6:1 in 1972. In the United States taxes had a much smaller effect in reducing the 9:1 advantage of the well-to-do. And in France it had no effect on an 11:1 advantage of the rich over the poor, mainly because the French taxation system is largely based on sales taxes (Sawyer, p. 14).

When tax legislators choose to apply different instruments or rules to income derived from different sources, they engender problems of *hori-*

zontal inequity. That is, taxpayers who earn the same income may be taxed at very different rates, depending on whether they pay taxes on the gain on appreciated property or wait to pay only after they sell their property. The favored treatment accorded to so-called "capital gains" in the United States has drawn charges of inconsistency, since it allows the investor in antiques to defer taxes while the savings account depositor must pay.

Restraints and Innovation

Prior to the mid-1970s, governments could avoid many tough choices because economic growth and modest inflation levels produced automatic revenue increases—often to the point where revenue-producing was not even perceived as a major problem of taxation. But the "stagflation" of the 1970s, which combined low growth with high inflation, led to a situation where tax extractions rose more quickly than real incomes. As a result, the disposable income of an average family of four in most countries grew more slowly than its gross earnings. Such families suffered a 15.6 percent relative loss in Britain, a 6.4 percent relative loss in France, a 3.5 percent relative loss in Sweden, and a 2.3 percent relative loss in the United States between 1972 and 1976 (OECD 1978).

Governments could pursue several policy options in response. One option was to apply corporatist instruments to distribute the costs of belt-tightening in an equitable manner. Another option was to shift emphasis among taxation instruments, perhaps from the more visible to the less visible. Another option was to increase tax extraction by tightening up on existing tax collection. Attempts at increasing restraints on tax avoidance and tax evasion had varying effects, among them encouragement to various tax protest movements and parties. Thus came about the Danish tax protest party of 1973 and the California Proposition 13 victory of 1978, which in turn led to further constraints on those who devised tax and revenue policies.

Treasury and finance ministry bureaucrats, who in most countries dominate the discussion of taxation policy alternatives, were thus challenged to produce innovations. It was mainly others, however, who produced and pushed to passage proposals to "index" tax levels. Indexation ties tax levels inversely to price levels, thus mitigating the automatic rise inflation causes in money incomes and tax extractions, and hence the automatic fall in real after-tax incomes. Indexation was opposed by many because of the additional limits it would place on policy makers, but as they proved unable to manipulate taxation and other fiscal instruments to manage the economy, more were willing to accept such a limitation. Consequently, Canada, the Netherlands, and later also Sweden and the United States, became committed to indexing their income tax systems.

THE BOUNDARIES OF TAXATION

SCOPE AND THRESHOLDS

In recent years the per capita amount of taxation has risen in all nations, partly because of increased government activity and partly because of inflation. In all countries, the scope of taxation is at least partially defined by taxpayers, whose resistance (or potential resistance) determines thresholds tax levels should not pass. In this section we will discuss the scope and thresholds of taxation policy, focussing on the evolution of tax systems, the differences in various national tax levels, and particular factors affecting tax limits.

The Evolution of Tax Systems

The ancient world and medieval Europe relied on direct taxation of subject classes and territories, and of products of the agricultural economy. Indirect taxes became a major revenue source only when commerce and industry became more important. Customs tariffs and levies on luxury and other consumption goods then augmented property taxes and other traditional tax forms. In an absolute monarchy, the aristocracy and other privileged groups were often exempt from taxation; but with the broadening of political representation, high-income groups became less immune. As middle-class groups won political influence, some countries, such as Britain (in 1842) and Austria (in 1849), introduced proportional (or flat-rate) income taxes on a permanent basis.

In nineteenth-century Europe, possession of the franchise was linked to the payment of property taxes, so that the lower classes who owned little real property had no legislative representatives who could effectively protest the governments' reliance on regressive indirect taxes. When the lower classes won the right to vote, the parties that represented them pressed for greater reliance on direct taxes, as well as on an "ability to pay" doctrine (Ardent): This implied changing income tax structures from the principle of *proportionality,* according to which all taxpayers paid equal proportions of their incomes, to the principle of *progressivity*, according to which the larger income earners paid at higher tax rates. A taxation system is defined as progressive if the average tax rate rises as income rises. It is regarded as *regressive* if the tax burden on lower incomes is greater than that on higher incomes. In 1909, when he sought to finance new welfare programs, Britain's Lloyd George made the tax more progressive by introducing rising marginal tax rates (Sabine).

How National Tax Levels Vary

As welfare, education, and other public sector programs have grown, so the proportion of GNP collected as tax revenues has risen. In the mid-1950s this proportion approached 25 percent in some "low tax" countries and 33 percent in some "high tax" countries. By the late 1970s all the developed Western European countries had tax ratios ranging from 34 to 50 percent of the Gross Domestic Product (GDP). The tax percentage has increased in all countries, in some more rapidly than in others. As Table 6.1 shows, the United States has increased its tax ratio, but more slowly than the other countries. In the mid-1950s the United States had the lowest tax percentage, 24.6; in 1980 it still had the lowest, 30.7. Only Germany had slower tax growth in the period from 1955 to 1980. The tax growth of the European Community (EC) countries was twice that of the United States, and Sweden's was three times as fast.

In the decade up to 1976, the ratio of taxes to GDP increased in all twenty advanced industrial countries. This suggests that the high tax countries were able to help change the perception of what taxation levels were acceptable in order for popular social policy goals to be realized. However, there was no such convergence pattern. Countries that had comparatively high tax to GDP ratios in the 1960s tended to increase them disproportionately in the 1970s, while those with low ratios experienced below-average increases. Sweden, Denmark, and the Netherlands levied more taxes, while the United States and Britain held down tax ratio increases.

Differences existed also in the average levels and starting points of income taxes. In 1976 the average tax rate for a family of four with average earnings ranged from zero in France to 35 percent in Sweden. However, the French family paid much more in social security contributions than did the Swedish one. In Belgium, Sweden, and Britain, the income level at which a citizen started paying income tax was quite low. In both Canada and the United States, it was more than twice as high as in Britain. When Margaret Thatcher's Conservative government took over

TABLE 6.1 Tax Revenue as a Percentage of Gross Domestic Product, 1955–1980

	Percentage			
	1955	*1965*	*1980*	*1955–1980 increase*
Britain	29.8	30.8	35.9	6.1
France	32.9	35.0	41.2	8.3
Netherlands	26.3	35.5	46.2	19.9
Sweden	25.5	35.6	49.9	24.4
United States	24.6	26.5	30.7	6.1
West Germany	30.8	31.6	37.2	6.4

SOURCES *Revenue Statistics of OECD Countries 1965–1980* (Paris: OECD, 1981).
Long-Term Trends in Tax Revenues of OECD Member Countries, 1955–1980 (Paris: OECD, 1981).

in 1979, it raised the minimum threshold and lowered the basic income-tax rate. But to compensate for lost revenue, the government significantly raised an indirect tax, the value-added tax, from 8 percent to 15 percent.

Table 6.2 compares countries in 1977 on the progressivity of the main direct taxes. The table illustrates how income and social security taxation rates varied for families whose incomes were equivalent to the average production worker's gross earnings, as against those who earned one third more, two thirds more, twice as much, or four times as much. The Scandinavian countries show high progressivity; families with twice the income of the average worker paid tax at rates which were half again as high (for example, Norway: 40.3 percent v. 26.9 percent). By contrast, France and the United States exhibited low progressivity (for example, France: 12.5 percent v. 10 percent for one-earner families).

Table 6.2 also illustrates an aspect of tax legislation which has become more relevant as more wives have entered the labor force. In the past such work was often discouraged, especially for middle-class women whose husbands were already earning high incomes, because the after-tax earnings were often low—especially after babysitting or nursery school costs. The question is whether the earnings of a second income-earner should be taxed at a different rate. In Sweden, Norway, and Canada, double-average income families are taxed at a considerably lower rate if both husband and wife work than if only the husband works. In the

TABLE 6.2 The Progressivity of Income and Social Security Taxation Rates by Income Level and Marital Status for a Two-child Family, 1977

*Family Earnings**	100		133	166	200		400
*Husband's Earnings**	50	100	100	100	100	200	200
*Wife's Earnings**	50	0	33	66	100	0	200
	Taxation as a Proportion of Income						
Britain	16.2	25.4	22.7	25.6	27.5	31.6	34.1
Canada	10.0	16.0	16.0	18.0	19.0	26.0	28.0
Denmark	29.0	32.5	33.4	34.9	37.6	47.0	49.5
France	10.0	10.0	11.8	13.4	14.7	12.5	19.0
Italy	10.8	13.3	12.9	13.7	14.5	19.8	20.1
Japan	7.9	8.0	9.0	10.6	11.5	14.8	17.6
Netherlands	29.3	31.8	32.1	32.9	34.0	35.2	37.2
Norway	21.6	26.9	27.4	28.8	30.9	40.3	45.6
Sweden	23.0	35.0	33.2	33.5	37.2	53.0	54.0
United States	16.0	17.0	19.0	21.0	21.0	22.0	29.0
West Germany	26.1	27.0	28.1	29.7	32.2	28.7	38.5

SOURCE *The Tax/Benefit Position of Selected Income Groups in OECD Member Countries* (Paris: OECD, 1978), pp. 112–113.

*Expressed as a percentage of an average production worker's gross earnings.

United States and the Netherlands, tax rates did not exhibit such significant differentials; but the position of two-earner families has improved in the United States since 1982.

Factors Affecting Tax Limits

Economists have argued fiercely over whether there are limits beyond which tax extractions can have destructive economic consequences. Some hold that such limits may vary over time and between countries, and they have tried to identify the factors that cause this variation.

Historically, tax legislators have tended to defy the pronouncements of theorists. In the late nineteenth century, it was argued that taxes amounting to 15 percent of national income were generally excessive. At the conclusion of World War II, when tax rates were rising in all countries, the British economist Colin Clark urged that tax ratios be held to peacetime levels of below 25 percent lest inflation and other harmful economic consequences ensue. Nonetheless, by 1980 the tax ratio in some countries had exceeded 50 percent.

Certainly tax escalation has been accompanied by both inflation and taxpayer resistance. But there has been no clear cause-and-effect relationship. Countries with the highest tax ratios, such as Sweden and the Netherlands, have not suffered from either excessive inflation or inordinate tax protest. So the political limits on tax extraction have seemed to depend on how people fared individually. If purchasing power declines, people have tended to become more sensitive to high marginal tax rates. Thus the *avoidance of steep progressivity* has recently become a principal concern in taxation policy.

In the early 1980s most Western nations faced policy consequences by lowering the tax rates applicable to the upper income brackets. They differed considerably, however, in how they implemented this plan.

Sweden provides an example of how this was done in a system with strong social corporate infrastructure, where highly unionized workers could demand wage increases that would more than offset tax increases. There the non-Socialist government sought to gradually reduce the top marginal rate in the national income tax schedule to 50 percent by 1986. Rather than attempt to pass this rate change with their slim parliamentary majority, they sought to engage the opposition Social Democrats in a compromise, which was accepted on the condition that the effects, when taken together with outcomes of wage bargaining, would not be allowed to worsen the position in after-tax incomes of blue-collar workers in relation to middle-class groups. Thus, this compromise encouraged a linkage between taxation and incomes policies. It also shielded most social services, since these were largely financed from sub-national income taxes whose rates were not reduced.

In the United States, the Reagan administration passed its massive tax reduction bill of August 1981 without a compromise with the Democratic leadership, but instead with the support of right-wing Democratic Congressmen ("Bollweevils") who supplied the necessary votes in the House. Both backers and opponents of the bill agreed that it would strongly change the after-tax position of lower- and higher-income recipients in favor of the latter. While the Democrats oratorically attacked this trend, they put greater actual effort into attempting to recapture control of the tax policy agenda, a deciding element of Reagan's 1980 victory. Toward this end some Democrats introduced a variety of alternative income tax schemes, including one for a flat-rate tax system which would eliminate rather than merely weaken the system's progressive features. The wily Democrats sought to cover all the policy options in the Statement on Issues adopted by the Democratic National Party Conference in June 1982, declaring: "The Democratic party must be the party to call for the overhaul of the existing federal tax system. . . . Therefore our party will lead the national debate over the four major reform alternatives: the progressive expenditure tax, the simplified progressive tax, the value-added tax, and the flat-rate tax" (*New York Times* 28 June 1982).

VARIATIONS IN REVENUE RAISING INSTRUMENTS

There are several rough categories of national taxation: redistributively oriented systems; broad tax base systems; traditional, non-centralized systems; and systems that minimize direct taxation. Within any taxation system, governments differ in their reliance on direct and indirect taxes. Whereas some countries consider it advantageous to rely more heavily on the less visible indirect taxes, others choose to diversify their revenue sources by relying on a variety of both direct and indirect taxes. In this section we will discuss the different tax systems and their reliance on direct and indirect taxes as well as their use of another important instrument, revenue sharing.

Direct and Indirect Taxes

Governments employ both direct and indirect taxes. They differ, however, in the extent to which they rely on direct rather than indirect taxes, in how they develop, then eliminate, various taxation instruments, and in the extent to which national governments monopolize tax extraction or share that power with local and state governments.

Table 6.3 illustrates the pattern of similarities and differences among our six nations. France differs significantly in its lower degree of direct taxation; but its lower income tax receipts are made up for by higher sales and excise taxes and social insurance taxes paid by employers. Another

TABLE 6.3 Tax Sources as Percentages of Total Revenues

	Britain	France	Netherlands	Sweden	United States	West Germany	OECD average	Lowest OECD country	Highest OECD country
Direct Taxes									
Personal Income	31.3	12.5	26.6	42.4	36.5	28.9	32.6	11.9 Greece	50.3 Denmark
Corporate Income	7.6	4.7	5.8	3.1	11.1	6.0	7.4	3.1 Sweden	18.4 Luxembourg
Employees Social Security	6.6	10.6	16.2	0.0	9.6	15.2	7.3	0 Norway Sweden	16.7 Switzerland
Indirect Taxes									
Sales and Consumption	26.9	31.3	25.2	23.9	16.5	26.9	29.4	16.5 United States	45.1 Greece
Property	12.2	3.4	4.1	0.9	10.5	2.7	5.6	0.9 Sweden	12.2 Britain
Employers Social Security	10.4	29.4	17.3	26.0	15.0	18.3	15.8	0.5 Denmark	40.0 Spain
Other Taxes	5.0	8.0	4.9	3.7	0.8	2.0	1.9		
Total	100	100	100	100	100	100	100		

SOURCE *Revenue Statistics of OECD Member Countries, 1965–1980* (Paris: OECD, 1981).

apparent difference is that Britain and the United States rely more on property taxes than do the Continental countries. France, Germany, and the Netherlands derive more of their tax income from social security contributions. What are the reasons for these differences?

In France, the oldest centralized bureaucratic system in Europe, citizens have developed legendary wiles for avoiding direct taxes (for example, deliberately maintaining a dilapidated facade on their houses). Consequently, the state has developed sophisticated indirect taxes, particularly the value-added tax (VAT), through which a tax is collected at each stage of production and distribution. In this way businessmen are forced to monitor one another on how they forward taxes to the state. In order to equalize conditions in the emerging Common Market, other members of the European Community have adapted their sales tax systems to the VAT model; sales taxes are now levied at fairly similar rates by all EC member states.

In Britain and the United States, property taxes are more important because of local government taxation powers. Other countries gradually reduced or eliminated these local taxes as their national systems became more uniform. But where local government prerogative remains strong, property taxes remain in force, even though they are more difficult to assess fairly and collect. Local politicians in the United States hate to give up the favors which property assessment power allows them to distribute. In a centralized system such as the Dutch one, where even city mayors are appointed by the national government, local party machines do not demand such lubrication.

Political factors also help explain why income taxes are such prominent tax sources in Britain, the United States, and the Scandinavian countries. During much of the past half century, the governments of these countries have been controlled by left-of-center parties, which have tended to prefer income taxes because of the possibility of imbuing them with progressive components. Thus the tax rates of the highest brackets reached 90 percent in the 1960s. In the 1970s they were 80 percent in Britain and 70 percent in the United States, before they were sharply lowered in the early 1980s. By the 1960s in Sweden, however, Social Democrats shifted from a preference for the income tax to increased reliance on sales taxes. As skilled workers moved into higher tax brackets, "the distributive impact of the income tax . . . [differed] much less from that of a sales tax than it did in the earlier phases of its modern history. The income tax share has thus lost much of its attraction as a redistributive device and bids to become the major object of taxpayer resistance" (Musgrave 1969, p. 141).

By contrast, countries which have had more center and right-wing governments have tended to rely more on social security contributions (which tend to be levied at flat, or proportional, rates) and on sales taxes than on progressive income taxes. U.S. federal income tax rates rise consistently for each income class, but right-wing administrations have tended to flatten the tax curves. In 1977, a four-member family with a $100,000 income paid federal income taxes at three times the rate (30.8 percent) that a $10,000-income family paid (10.2 percent). But the Reagan tax cuts scheduled for 1982 through 1984 propose to reduce this progressivity considerably: The tax rate for the higher-income family in 1984 will be only twice as high (30.6 percent) as that of the lower-income family (13.6 percent) (*National Journal* 18 August 1981).

Political reasons also explain why countries do not always distribute taxation efforts among a greater variety of instruments. For example, let us consider why the United States has not adopted a value-added tax. Various administrations and Congressmen have supported such a measure, but strong local interests have made it difficult to get such a bill through Congress. State politicians oppose it because of the competition it would create for sales tax proceeds. In Europe, the VAT is levied at different rates for different kinds of luxuries or essential goods; in the United States, these differentials would be difficult to achieve again because legislative party cohesion would probably give way to the pressures of special interests.

On the other hand, *corporate income taxes* are more prominent in the United States. U.S. stockholders must pay a "double tax" on dividend income; that is, the corporation pays as well as the individual stockholders. In Europe, tax harmonization trends are to give stockholders tax credits for the corporate taxes paid by their companies (Bracewell-Milnes, Ch. 8). Thus the lower personal income taxes paid by high-income Americans has sometimes been partly offset by the higher corporate income tax rates. It must be noted, however, that vastly accelerated depreciation allowances together with the "leasing" of capital investment deductions and tax credits in effect since 1981 may lead to a back-door elimination of the American corporate income tax in the course of the 1980s.

Sales and Excise Taxes

Excise taxes apply to specific categories of consumer goods (for example, liquor and tobacco); *sales taxes* apply to all unexempted categories. Their merits depend largely on how one evaluates the substitution effects they engender. Welfare economists view excise taxes with disfavor, because, without raising any more revenue than a direct tax, they reduce the consumer's freedom by pushing him from a taxed to a non-taxed commodity. However, some groups want governments to use taxation powers precisely in this way to induce consumers not to purchase items that are "bad" for them, such as alcohol and tobacco. In Scandinavia, tobacco taxes are much higher than in the United States, in good part because tax rates have been deliberately increased to discourage use.

Historically, general sales taxes have tended to replace excise taxes on specific goods. The reason for this shift lies principally in the ease of administration. Numerous excise taxes are difficult to administer, because of the diversity of products and the many retail outlets involved. Most value-added sales taxes, however, can be collected more systematically from larger manufacturers and wholesalers.

Sales taxes can levy higher rates on less essential or luxury goods; thus they can be progressive, in the sense that they can extract more from the higher-income groups. This potential progressivity diminishes in the developed industrial countries, however, where there are fewer consumption pattern differences between the rich and the poor, and where there is a higher degree of commercial integration. Where the lower middle class buys cheaper replicas of the same goods enjoyed by the upper class, it is difficult to design sales taxes which will extract more money from the rich purchasers. Automotive taxes were mildly progressive as long as it was part of upper-middle-class social style to drive expensive Cadillacs and Mercedes-Benzes, but since smallness has become fashionable that no longer holds.

If sales taxes have a tendency to be regressive, so, somewhat surprisingly, do social security taxes. The rates at which they are levied are usually proportional, not progressive. The U.S. social security tax, which was at one time proportional and collected only up to a moderate cut-off point (incomes up to $14,000 in 1975), was strongly regressive. Millions of low-income workers below the income tax level were paying nearly a 6 percent flat rate social security tax. This regressivity has since been somewhat diluted as Congress has sharply lifted the income levels at which social security taxes must be paid (to $29,700 in 1981 and $39,000 in 1984). The adoption of earned income credits for low-income households has also helped retain progressivity.

The panorama of choices which governments have include numerous trade-offs and compensatory relationships among the various components of their taxation systems. For instance, social security systems and consumption taxes are more interrelated than is apparent at first glance:

> The income redistribution role of consumption based taxes may probably be related to the scope of a country's social security system. If that scope is limited, then the attempt might be made to achieve as much progressivity in tax design as possible, basically through the exemption of necessities and the higher taxation of luxuries. If a country has a highly developed income transfer system, however, it might be argued that even necessities should attract the standard rate of sales tax, because

the transfer system can adequately compensate for the relatively greater degree of regressivity which this may entail (Cnossen, p. 115).

Grouping National Taxation Systems

How, then, can we classify the countries of Western Europe and North America according to their taxation instruments? Table 6.3 shows some comparisons. Adapting one political scientist's statistical analysis (Peters), we can distinguish four tendencies:

Redistributively Oriented Systems. Sweden and Norway, characteristic of this group, evince high reliance on progressive income taxes and low reliance on flat-rate workers' social security taxes. But high sales and other consumption taxes are also employed to help meet large revenue needs in these developed welfare states. Denmark and Finland, the other two Scandinavian nations, differ somewhat in their heavier continuing reliance on property taxes and lesser use of employers' social security taxes.

Broad Tax Base Systems. Austria, Belgium, Germany, and the Netherlands fall into this category, with Ireland a marginal member. They tend to make significant use of most taxation instruments to create a suitable balance for their mixed but less conspicuously egalitarian political economies. They rely somewhat more on sales and consumption taxes than on either individual or corporate income taxes.

Traditional, Non-centralized Systems. Three federal systems—Canada, Switzerland, and the United States—and Britain constitute this group. They are distinguished by the retention of high property tax components especially among local governments, and by greater reliance on corporate income taxes.

Systems that Minimize Direct Taxation. France and Italy avoid direct taxation as much as possible, rely strongly on consumption and social security taxes, and augment tax revenue with user charges for publicly operated services.

Revenue Sharing

In addition to choosing which kinds of taxes to levy, national governments choose how to share revenue-raising powers with their own states, counties, and local governments. The choice depends on whether state and local governments are entitled by the constitution to raise their own taxes, as is the case in federal systems, and on the degree to which traditions of local self-government reinforce their own taxing powers. If they do have such powers, mechanisms may exist to prevent the disparity of resources among local and state governments that results in regional divergences in the quality of public service, which may diminish the guarantees of "equality of access" with which the constitution endows national citizenship.

The proportion of the total taxation which is raised by state and local governments is higher in federal systems, between one third and one half in Canada, Germany, Switzerland, and the United States. Among unitary systems the variation is greater, from almost nothing to around 30 percent, as Table 6.4 illustrates. In the Netherlands and Italy, sub-national taxation amounts to only a small percentage of the total.

The composition of state and local taxes differs from the all-levels-of-government composition, though in various ways among groups of countries. Sales taxes are disproportionately utilized in the federal systems, as are property taxes, especially in the English-speaking countries with stronger traditions of local government. The degree to which income taxes are levied varies more sharply. They are utilized less in the United States and Canada, but bear almost the total burden of local and county revenue raising in Scandinavia. (See Chapter Nine for more detail.)

All governments have programs of intergovernmental revenue cooperation to assist poorer sections, but they vary in the techniques that they emphasize. The U.S. federal government relies heavily on complicated programs of grants-in-aid and some revenue sharing, but each level of government maintains distinct tax-raising powers and machinery. Germany offers a contrasting model, where two thirds of the total tax revenue directly raised by the national and *Land* (state) governments is derived from taxes whose proceeds are directly shared by two or all three levels of government.

In the United States the federal government, most states, and some cities collect income taxes, but they are levied separately. Under the German system the income taxes collected from individuals and corporations are shared among the federal government (43 percent), Land govern-

TABLE 6.4 Proportion of Taxes Collected by Various Government Levels, Mid-1970s

<table>
<tr><th></th><th colspan="3">Percentage of Total Tax Revenue Collected</th></tr>
<tr><th></th><th>National Governments</th><th>State or Provincial Governments</th><th>Local Governments</th></tr>
<tr><td>Britain</td><td>87.3</td><td>—</td><td>12.7</td></tr>
<tr><td>France</td><td>93.5</td><td>—</td><td>6.5</td></tr>
<tr><td>Netherlands</td><td>97.6</td><td>—</td><td>2.4</td></tr>
<tr><td>Sweden</td><td>70.4</td><td colspan="2">29.6</td></tr>
<tr><td>United States</td><td>54.4</td><td>22.7</td><td>18.9</td></tr>
<tr><td>West Germany</td><td>53.1</td><td>33.7</td><td>13.2</td></tr>
</table>

SOURCE R.J. Bennett, *The Geography of Public Finance* (London: Methuen, 1980), p. 274.

ments (43 percent), and local governments (14 percent). Proceeds from the value-added sales tax are divided 30–70 between the federal and Land governments. Administration of these taxes is integrated, with the Land finance ministries collecting on behalf of the other levels of government.

In Germany as elsewhere, wealth and income levels differ considerably. A poor Land such as the Saar can expect only about three fifths the revenue from the same tax rate applied in a rich Land such as Baden-Württemberg. According to the American model of federalism, the poorer Länder (states) might be expected to pay lower teachers' salaries and to maintain schools of lower quality than those of the richer Länder. In 1974, school expenditures in the United States did indeed vary between $700 and $1,800 per student, with noticeable differences in the quality of school and university education. The Germans consider differentials of this range intolerable in view of their interpretation of constitutional "equality guarantees."

The near equality of per capita revenues of Länder is maintained through various equalization techniques, which operate in a much more fundamental and sustained manner in Germany than in the United States. Through the *vertical equalization* program, a portion of the jointly collected revenues is earmarked to help bring the tax income of the poorer states close to the average. Another important instrument for equalizing financial capability among the Länder governments is the program of *horizontal equalization,* which requires the richer Länder to subsidize the poorer ones. Because their economies are less developed, the normal income tax receipts per capita of Länder such as the Saar and Lower Saxony would be 20 to 30 percent lower than that of the average of all Länder. But through a combination of horizontal equalization and other programs, their tax income is brought up to at least 95 percent of the Länder average. With some 25 percent of the population, the four poorer Länder have been receiving about 24 percent of total final Länder tax revenues (Bennett).

TAX EXTRACTION AND TAX BASE EROSION

DISTRIBUTION

The complex sets of rules, organizations, and enforcement techniques through which governments extract tax revenue from their citizens exemplify national differences in administrative style, political culture, and enforcement strategy. For example, in the United States income taxes are self-assessed, whereas in Europe for the most part citizens report their income sources and officials then assess the taxes due. If one calculates the cost of the income tax collection as a percentage of the total tax revenue, then a vigilant and intrusive taxation bureaucracy such as the German one is relatively expensive, with costs of about 4 percent.

The British, who also use official assessment, employ 4 times as many officials as the United States does, and spend about 2 percent on collection expenditures. In the mid-1970s there were 30 U.S. federal tax officials per 100,000 population, compared to 70 in Canada. On both national and regional levels, there were 100 in Sweden, 130 in Britain, and 175 in Germany (Barr *et al.*, p. 150; Mennel, p. 68). The U.S. collection costs were only one half percent of income tax revenue, whereas those of Sweden and Canada were about 1 percent.

In the European systems which do not practice self-assessment, the tax bureaucracies tend to distribute their personnel to achieve wide coverage at the examination level. The U.S. authorities, in contrast, concentrate on a more intensive review of a relatively small sample of returns. Only 2 to 3 percent of returns are examined in the United States, and only about 1 percent are subject to internal review.

Income Tax Assessment

Under the self-assessment system in the United States, 97 percent of the income tax returns lead to an adjustment at the end of the year, usually in favor of the taxpayer. In Britain this occurs in only about one seventh of the cases, since withholding is adjusted during the tax year. Because they want year-end refunds, most American taxpayers resist lowering their payroll deductions, even though the interest foregone in overpayment actually raises their tax rates. The same prospect of a refund motivates a timely completion of returns. Proposals to introduce self-assessment in Britain have had to contend with the problems of educating the taxpayer and adjusting the taxation system. As Table 6.5 makes clear, British citizens do not at present practice self-assessment in any way. The table shows how Britain compares with the United States and other countries in the degree to which taxpayers, or those hired to prepare

TABLE 6.5 Degrees of Self-assessment in Income Tax Administration for Wage and Salary Earners

Standard Practice of the Taxpayer	Britain	France	Sweden	Canada	USA	West Germany
Adds own income sources	No	No	Yes	Yes	Yes	No
Computes deductions	No	No	Yes	Yes	Yes	Yes
Calculates tax payable	No	No	No	Yes	Yes	No
Sends tax due with return	No	No	No	Yes	Yes	Yes
Sample checks by administration	No	No	Yes	Yes	Yes	Yes

SOURCE Nicholas A. Barr, *et al.*, *Self-Assessment for Income Tax* (London: Heinemann, 1977), p. 153. Supplemented by additional data provided by Dr. Annemarie Mennel.

their taxes, carry out practices which elsewhere are carried out by state tax officials.

Although self-assessment may allow the taxpayer to cheat marginally, from the government's point of view, it has the compensating advantage of "shifting a lot of the cost of tax collection from the civil service to the individual citizen." One economist argued in 1971 that "the American system seems to be effective in inducing the vast bulk of middle-class taxpayers to pay their taxes promptly . . . and fairly cheerfully," whereas self-assessment might be offensive to Europeans accustomed to more emphasis on "individual equity and the policing of individual cases." He described the period prior to April 15 in the United States "as a sort of rueful national festival and collective penitential experience justified by the subsequent sense of relief and accomplishment" (Johnson, pp. 79–84).

Compared to their European equivalents, U.S. tax authorities present the public with quite elaborate tax rules. In 1964, the U.S. tax code's substantive income tax provisions ran 754 pages, nineteen times as long as the equivalent sections of the Dutch tax code (40 pages). The Dutch code was briefer because it was far more abstract, mainly because it was intended for trained personnel rather than for the general public. The same was true for the German (50 pages), Belgian (100 pages), and French (120 pages) codes (Wright, p. 342). However, while the U.S. Treasury must foot a larger printing bill, it supports fewer tax-collecting agents and gets by with less elaborate examining and auditing procedures for most taxpayers.

In France, where citizens generally manifest low civic consciousness in their income-reporting behavior, the state feels obliged to monitor taxpayers at the grass roots level. In Paris, for example, this means that each of the twenty *arrondissements* is divided into four quarters, with sixty-seven tax offices covering the various sectors of the city. An inspector conducts an annual building-by-building census of his sector, is personally in charge of some 400 corporate and 300 individual taxpayers, and is generally familiar with the wealth, income, and tax status of *each* of these taxpayers.

In some European systems certain categories of taxpayers are subject to periodic scrutiny. In Germany all small businesses can expect to be audited every third year. In Sweden tax authorities used to select a different professional group every year for a thorough review of the tax returns of all its members. In 1970 such a check on physicians located many small-town bank accounts in which Stockholm doctors had deposited unreported payments from patients, and large amounts of additional taxes were extracted. U.S. district tax directors can also use some staff for "prowl time," but they have not yet attempted such a large-scale "dragnet" action.

Tax Extraction Intensity

According to cross-national studies of the processes and norms of tax collection, the intensity of bureaucratic scrutiny is directly proportionate to success in tax extraction. The costs of confrontation between taxpayers and collectors, manifested in control, inspection, and appeal processes, were assessed in terms of the resources they absorbed and in terms of the negative feedback leading to increased tax resistance. The British system was found to be less than fully effective but relatively inexpensive, the German one very effective and also very expensive, and those of France, Italy, and Spain were found to be expensive—and ineffective (Schmoelders).

The researchers found that the success of the German system is characterized by more frequent visits from the tax inspector and more time spent in checking tax declarations. Thoroughness is deemed necessary because an official assessment notice becomes final within one month. Among small businessmen in Germany the more frequent confrontations with tax officials have fed an undercurrent of hostility, with the officials themselves complaining about the difficulty of enforcing overly detailed regulations (Struempel, p. 74). Moreover, prosecutions there are relentless. In Britain prosecution through the courts leads annually to about 100 convictions for tax evasion, compared to about 6,000 in Germany.

In Germany, tax officials are somewhat feared and taxpayers are thus timid in dealing with them. For one thing, German taxpayers greatly overestimate the infallibility of tax offices. Indeed, the vast majority think it impossible to file a misleading return without being caught. Moreover, only 14 percent of taxpayers have ever utilized the opportunity to appeal tax office decisions (naturally, the more educated predominate among this group). Perhaps this might be partially attributed to the behavior of tax officials, who do not believe that "ability to deal with the public" counts strongly as promotion criteria. Hence social scientists who observed contacts in a tax office concluded that the German tax administration failed to make real efforts to reduce the social distance between itself and the taxpayers (Grunow *et al.,* pp. 204–211).

By contrast, the British system has been found to treat "businessmen and professionals with great caution," dispensing with most administrative auditing, offering a wide variety of loopholes, and imposing fewer obligatory accounting procedures than are required in Germany. The British Inland Revenue Office was once chided by a Royal Commission for having been "led by a laudable anxiety to protect the subject from any needless official imposition to overestimate the extent to which certain simple requirements for the filing of returns could fairly be resented by the general public." Noting that total penalties had scarcely increased while the tax volume had tripled, economists observed: "The informal penalties employed in Britain may provide a more gentlemanly method of encouraging compliance than methods used abroad, but the greater use of more formal penalties might be more effective" (Shoup, p. 196; Barr *et al.*, p. 41).

The French system of tax collection, on the other hand, assumes that several of the most important non-salaried groups subject to income tax—the well-to-do, small businessmen, and professionals—will not declare their real incomes no matter what the law says. Small businessmen and professionals whose annual turnover is less than 500,000 francs ($100,000) are entitled to use the "agreed income," or *forfait,* system, under which taxes are individually negotiated on the basis of sales and expenditure estimates. Those who use this option (approximately one million taxpayers, 80 percent of those eligible) do not even have to keep records of their sales. Because tax level is bargained out with the tax inspector according to the flimsiest evidence, this system allows great potential for personal influence. It is not surprising that the vast majority of workers and employees, who *are* taxed on their real incomes, believe that the French tax system is unjust.

In the United States tax officials are subject to relatively substantial public scrutiny. Rulings by U.S. tax authorities have in recent years become more accessible, and now any taxpayer is entitled to see any written Internal Revenue Service (IRS) determination, as well as file documents relating to it. Earlier one of Ralph Nader's groups submitted twenty-two identical tax reports to as many IRS offices across the country and received tax determinations varying from a refund of $812 to a tax due figure of $52. Another review of IRS procedures found that the higher the tax deficiency the IRS initially claimed, the lower the percentage it finally accepted in settlement. The Federal Administrative Conference suggested that this was due to the ability of rich taxpayers to hire lawyers, who then negotiated more favorable settlements. This group also raised questions as to why the IRS Appellate Division had over the preceding two decades reached settlements at regularly smaller percentages, coming down to a level of only about 30 percent. "Such a continuing low rate of sustension obviously raised questions concerning the validity and accuracy of either the officer's proposed assessments, or the settlements accorded by the Appellate Division, or both" (U.S. Congress 1975, p. 118).

National tax systems differ enormously both in the number of tax loopholes based upon permitted deductions and exemptions of categories of income or expenditure and in the prevalence of illegal but tolerated forms of tax evasion. Both of these factors contribute to massive erosion of the income tax base. France incurs tremendous erosion prior to the income-reporting stage by accepting massive legal and quasi-legal non-reporting of certain kinds of income. Britain and the United States achieve a fairly high income disclosure rate, but then permit taxpayers to take advantage of numerous deduction possibilities. Consequently, the proportion of personal income which is finally subject to tax is usually about half the total reported in national income accounts. Table 6.6 makes evident how much some nations "lose" the capacity to tax large portions of personal income.

Tax Avoidance

Since American legislators have allowed a variety of loopholes, exemptions, and "write-off" privileges, most clever or well-to-do taxpayers have no need for clearly illegal forms of tax evasion. Instead, they can hire specialized assistance to help them avoid taxes legally. Ingrained libertarians can vent their hostility to the tax system by spending their free time in finding loopholes with which they can outsmart the tax officials. Concessions to special interests, if written into the lengthy tax codes, permit administrators to accept enormous tax erosion while claiming a high compliance level. One German writer commented sarcastically about American tax erosion figures, "If it really is the intention of Congress to use the steep progressiveness of the tax rates merely as a political display slogan, then the figures show that it has realized its intentions" (Bellstedt, p. 286). By the 1980s some Congressmen had come to accept the validity of this criticism.

As concern for economic growth has become more predominant among economists and politicians, equity of tax distribution has often had to take second place. The instrument which most easily permits the wealthy to hold their tax rates down is the special treatment of capital gains. Until 1970, gains on assets held more than six months were taxable at a maximum rate of only 25 percent. Then the rate for individuals was raised to 35 percent, only to be lowered again in 1978 to 28 percent. This provision currently allows upper-income American taxpayers to avoid

TABLE 6.6 Erosion of the Income Tax Base*

	Reported Income as Percentage of Total Personal Income	Taxable Income as Percentage of Total Personal Income
Britain	75.1	43.2
France	23.8	23.8
United States	79.3	45.0
West Germany	92.3**	79.0

SOURCE Vito Tanzi, *The Individual Income Tax and Economic Growth: An International Comparison* (Baltimore: Johns Hopkins Press, 1969), pp. 78–80.

*Personal income figures were derived from national accounts statistics, and the other data from tax reporting figures.

**This figure for West Germany applies only to income from wages and salaries. The figure for all income is probably somewhat lower.

half or more of the income taxes they would otherwise have to pay. In fact, the effective rate of taxation on the rich and the upper-middle classes declined in the years between 1952 and 1967, and has again dropped considerably in the 1980s.

The prevailing undertaxation of capital gains constitutes the most important inequality in the treatment of various income sources. Although France and Canada have recently begun to levy this tax, most Western countries tax realized gains only lightly, and unrealized gains not at all. In Germany gains from assets held for more than six months escape taxation altogether, a practice which contributed significantly to the concentration of ownership in the postwar German economy and to the unusually high rate of capital investment. Sweden taxes declining proportions of capital gains as the holding period lengthens, but adjusts for inflation in a way the United States does not.

As more taxpayers have become liable to more taxes, and at the same time have been able to take advantage of many complicated loopholes, a private "tax minimizing industry" has expanded at a rapid rate—much faster, in fact, than the public tax bureaucracy. This industry has long been prevalent in the United States. As early as the 1950s one observer noted that "The minimizing art in the United States has been carried to a degree of perfection," and that "tax avoidance in Britain is rapidly approaching the degree of refinement now common in the United States" (Shoup, p. 195). In the United States an expert on public finance also lamented the "social waste" constituted by the "immense amount of effort that has gone into tax avoidance." If the tax system were simpler, with lower rates and fewer loopholes, the "keen intellectual qualities of the accountant and lawyer members of the tax industry could be devoted to other purposes" (Eckstein, p. 83).

Thus there exists a certain lopsided adversarial relationship between the "tax minimizing industry" and the public tax bureaucracy. This is shown in the distribution of financial rewards among private and public tax experts. Thus one can compare the gross compensation of the chairman of the largest U.S. accounting firm, Peat, Marwick, Mitchell & Co.—$804,000 in 1977—with that of the IRS Commissioner—$52,500. It is also relevant to remember the storm of criticism that arose in the late 1970s when it became known that many accounting firms had not critically noted that some corporate clients had made illegal payoffs to win contracts both at home and abroad. Another controversy concerned tax shelters. When the IRS Commissioner called upon accountants and tax lawyers to report cases where they had led their clients to "take positions in their tax returns that were 'knowingly inconsistent' with the Internal Revenue Code," the accounting and legal professions resisted, claiming that it would "destroy the independent relationship between them and their clients."

Tax Evasion

How much national income evades taxation altogether, because it is blatantly unreported, is politically a hot issue that concerns both tax administrators and policy makers. One aspect of this issue concerns how much income derived from perfectly legal activity is lumped with profits from illegal criminal activity under the unbrella of the "underground economy." This label has come to be applied to all income which evades taxation because it is non-reported. The examples range from a carpenter who does a small private job for cash payment, which he never declares on his income form, to a drug dealer who might hide vast sums.

In a report on both the legal and illegal components of income in the United States in 1976, the IRS listed their quantitative significance as a proportion of all unreported income:

Self-employment (legal)	30–33 percent
Wages and salaries (legal)	20 percent
Drug traffic (illegal)	16 percent
Gambling and prostitution (illegal)	8–9 percent
Dividends and interest (legal)	7–10 percent

The total estimated unreported income was between $100 billion and $135 billion, which corresponded to between 6 and 8 percent of GNP. Estimates of similar magnitudes were published by authorities in Britain, Italy, Sweden, and other countries.

Some economists have made indirect calculations suggesting that the magnitude of the "underground economy" might be even larger, constituting as much as a quarter or even a third of GNP in the United States and other Western economies. This analysis for the most part blames high marginal income tax rates, which are assumed to drive some perfectly legal activity into the barter or moonlighting corners of what has come to be called the "underground" or "informal" economy.

Those who claim a large underground economy make much of such indicators as the amount of cash in circulation, which by 1980 had risen to $2,500 per American family of four. Yet suggestions that this necessarily implies an expansion of large hidden transactions has been countered by claims that an increasing proportion of the American currency may be held abroad, especially in countries where the inflation rate has been higher than in the United States (Tanzi, in Tanzi 1982, Chapter Six).

Other estimates of the hidden economy are based on discrepancies between income and expenditures data at the national level. Studies in France and Belgium showed unexplained differences of about 20 percent of GNP, while recent ones in Scandinavia have produced estimates more in the 4 to 6 percent range. In comparative studies some relatively low-tax countries, like Italy, the United States, and Spain, have been to shown to have larger underground sectors than the Scandinavian countries, leading to the conclusion that "it is quite implausible that the tax rate is the only determinant of the size of the hidden economy" (Frey and Pommerehne, in Tanzi 1982, p. 18). Rather, they point to the structure of labor markets and to attitudes toward tax morality and the public sector as other crucial factors in explaining cross-national variations in the magnitude of the underground economy.

Distributive Justice

The viability of a taxation system lies ultimately in its administrative implementation. What matters is not how many more or less progressive taxes are legislated, but how toughly, cunningly, and thoroughly the extractions are carried out. Tax evasion is a common problem, and the question is how well civic values, political ideology, and administrative ingenuity can serve to contain its corrosive effects on revenue receipts. We have seen how much national political culture and citizen-bureaucracy relations differ in these respects. Tax burdens of similar magnitude may elicit very different reactions depending on how deprived some taxpayer groups feel in relation to others. Indeed the visibility of different tax avoidance techniques may rank with the visibility of taxes themselves in determining the attitudes of voters-cum-taxpayers.

COPING WITH TAX BACKLASH AND INFLATION

RESTRAINTS AND INNOVATION

Resistance to taxation has occurred at many points throughout history, including present times. Though violent tax revolts are more rare today than they were in the sixteenth and seventeenth centuries, when they actually caused serious insurrections in Europe, political initiatives based on tax grievances have recently become more common, in both Europe and the United States. Thus have policy makers, in attempts to defuse potential taxpayer revolt, been called upon to find ways of insulating tax levels against the effects of taxation and of making more visible exactly *who* benefits from such tax provisions as deductions and credits.

Taxpayer Resistance

Perceived inequities in the tax system or hostility toward tax increases do not often become the central issues in an election campaign; but when they do, they can generate massive voter shifts. In the United States such shifts have recently occurred at the state and local levels through referenda initiatives, as in the case of California's Proposition 13 in 1978. In

Europe, where sub-national government has fewer tax-setting responsibilities, taxpayer protest has sometimes led to the sensational rise of national "flash parties" led by colorful antitax crusaders. In the early 1970s a Danish tax lawyer, Mogens Glistrup, generated an astonishing protest vote with an antitax platform that drew half a million voters away from the established parties, permitting him to emerge the leader of the second-largest party in the Danish parliament.

Attacking the expansion of the public bureaucracy, Glistrup's Progress party won twenty-eight seats in the December 1973 national elections, while both the Social Democrats and the established bourgeois parties lost more than a third of their seats. As the *Economist* commented, "When 16 percent of the voters in a mature and non-volatile country like Denmark can be brought, in the period of a few months, to switch their allegiance to an untried party created and led by a man whose ingenuity in baffling the tax collectors is being investigated by whole squads of police experts, something is indeed rotten in the state" (8 December, 1973).

With an average per capita revenue of $1,297 in 1970, Denmark was third behind Sweden with $1,656 and the United States with $1,404. Considering developments in the 1970s, we might ask: Why were the highly taxed Swedes more reluctant to form tax protest parties? Was the subsequent defeat of the Swedish Social Democrats due to dynamics similar to those operating in Denmark in 1973? How should one compare the American tax protest movements, such as the Proposition 13 movement in California, with the European examples? Can one draw any generalizations about which negative effects of the tax policy-inflation-low growth syndrome are most likely to lead to voter retaliation?

The fact that tax protest varied can be partly explained through a comparison of the *rate* of tax expansion in the two Scandinavian countries. Average tax levels from 1965 to 1971 were higher in Sweden than in Denmark, both absolutely and in relation to GNP. But the Swedish buildup had been gradual since the early 1950s, whereas the revision of Danish income taxes led to a sudden 22.1 percent increase in 1970. An increase of one third in tax extraction over a three-year period prepared the ground for Glistrup. During these years, no less than three quarters of the GNP gain was being soaked up by increased taxes.

Also, potential for a tax revolt was especially great among groups such as small shopkeepers, who were more than twice as prevalent in Denmark as in Sweden. Indeed, Glistrup received much larger support from the urban petit bourgeoisie than any other group (Esping-Anderson, pp. 157, 422).

Compared to the United States, where self-assessment and tax preparers have allowed taxpayers to use loopholes, Danish taxpayers' high tax morality had assumed that an honest administration treated all taxpayers with equal severity. Therefore, when Glistrup boasted on Danish television that he had exploited loopholes in the new tax legislation to avoid paying any income tax at all on his large income, he caused much more of a sensation than he would have in the United States.

Although the Glistrup success triggered something of a European "wave," tax backlash parties elsewhere clearly were not able to replicate Glistrup's initial success. A similar party in Norway made a modest splash in the early 1970s, then weakened but returned to parliament in 1981. In Germany the antitax Citizens party was founded in 1978 by none other than the former chairman of the Tax Officials Association (Fredersdorf). But it also disintegrated before it could mount a serious challenge to established parties who combatted it vigorously.

In California, by contrast, the tax reduction movement met with little strong party resistance. Surprisingly, Democrats were equally willing to support Proposition 13 and to join in bringing a 2 to 1 victory for the measure. The Democratic governor, Jerry Brown, even reversed his position to endorse radical tax cutting, which weakened all liberal resistance. The immediate impact was startling. Within a few years California dropped from third-ranking state in per capita tax burdens to twenty-third. Other states which relied on progressive state income taxes and had above-average state tax burdens also experienced moves to set tax limits, usually by initiative. Of the ten states with the most redistributive tax systems, all but three (Wisconsin, Minnesota, and Alaska) adopted tax or expenditure limitations in the period between 1976 and 1980 (Hansen 1981).

Often the object of tax resistance has been the local property tax, which, according to surveys in the 1970s, was the most unpopular American tax. Dissatisfaction with the unfairness of this and other taxes and increased distrust of government, as in Denmark, provide ideological support for the tax protest movement. When Ronald Reagan and other conservatives then traded on this sentiment at the national level, more of the ire came to be directed at the federal income tax, which in 1980 replaced the property tax as the one regarded as "worst and least fair" (Advisory Commission). How does our understanding of the factors causing recent electoral changes clarify the causes of tax backlash mobilization?

Decline in Real Income. Prior to the 1976 Swedish election, in which the Social Democrats were defeated, the real after-tax income had declined by 2 percent annually for several years, though it is not evident that resentment against this or the tax issue in general caused the defeat of the Social Democrats. But in contrast to Denmark tax resistance did seem to benefit one of the established parties, the Conservatives, and thus attracted less working-class support (Hibbs, p. 421). Much of the difference in the two cases can be attributed to differences in the legitimacy of existing non-socialist parties as proponents of tax resistance as well as to differences in the strength of the Left in general. In the United States

FIGURE 6.1 TOTAL TAXATION AS A PERCENTAGE OF GROSS DOMESTIC PRODUCT (1965–1977)

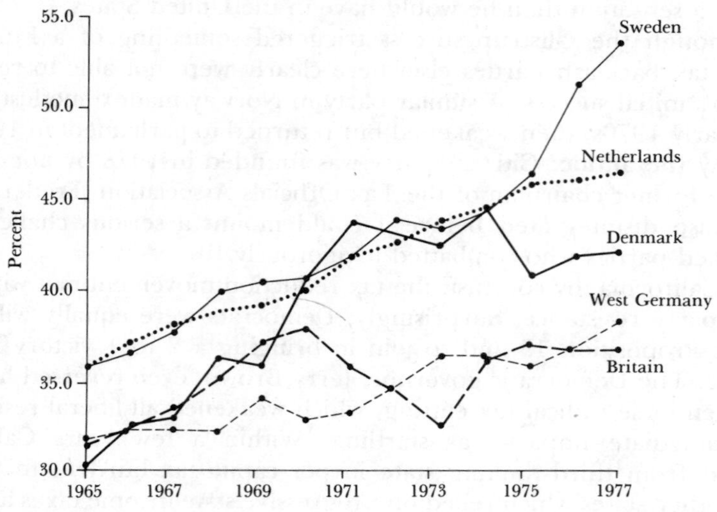

DIRECT TAXATION ON HOUSEHOLD INCOME AS A PERCENTAGE OF TOTAL TAXATION (1965–1977)

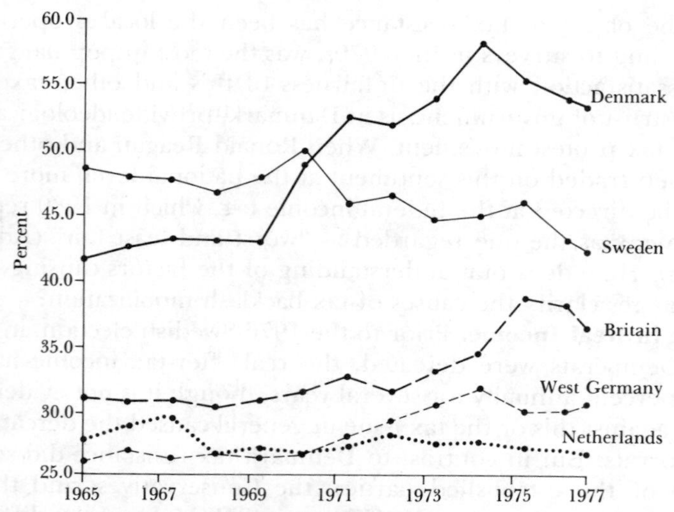

SOURCE OECD, *Revenue Statistics of OECD Member Countries* (Paris: OECD, 1979), Tables 1, 3.

too, middle-class dissatisfaction with declining incomes was a powerful factor, fueling both local and national mobilizations.

Tax Visibility. One reason Germany and the Netherlands have not experienced strong tax protest is that although their tax ratios are high, they rely more on less visible indirect taxes. As Figure 6.1 illustrates, in the mid-1970s the Dutch were taking only a quarter of household income in the form of direct taxes, whereas the Danes were taking about half. Students of tax politics tend to conclude that governments can foster tax illusions by clothing extractions as social security contributions or less direct sales taxes (Wilensky 1975). Many governments have moved in this direction, among them the Thatcher government in Britain, which decreased income taxes and increased sales taxes soon after taking office in 1979.

Poor Value for Public Services. Important components of the backlash are the quality of public service and the differences in income between public servants and private-sector workers. A key target of Glistrup's attack in Denmark was the fact that civil servants' incomes had been increasing while private-sector earnings had been decreasing (Hibbs, p. 428). Governments elsewhere were wise enough not to let this happen. Jealousy of public officials generally has not caused backlash provided voters were satisfied with the quality of services being offered. Conservative politicians in Germany and the Netherlands have shied away from proposing cutbacks in public services to the extent proposed by Reagan and others in the United States.

Tax Indexation

Tax protests in Denmark and elsewhere taught governments a lesson about the political costs of allowing inflation to increase tax ratios automatically. Policy attention was thus turned to devising techniques which would relieve reductions in real incomes caused by the simultaneous impact of consumer price increases and escalating tax withholding from take-home pay. Countries with low economic growth and above-average inflation were identified as prime settings for voter retribution against incumbent governments. The possibility that national governments could go "bankrupt"—not in a literal sense, since they could always print more money, but in the sense of losing credibility with their voters—was raised dramatically by some social scientists (Rose and Peters).

The more farsighted leaders of some of the smaller welfare states anticipated and developed techniques to cope with some of these problems. One such technique, implemented in Sweden from the early 1970s, was the adaptation of wage and salary bargaining from a pre-tax to an after-tax basis. Thus, the government bargained about its tax changes just as employers and unions bargained about wages and, to some extent, prices.

Another innovation was tax rate indexation, through which tax levels come to vary with levels of prices or wages. Tax indexation keeps real levels of taxation from rising with inflation, just as indexing social security benefits keeps real levels of pensions from falling as prices rise. The Netherlands introduced such a scheme in 1971. Denmark followed, and then Canada introduced the most complete and automatic indexation program in 1974. Previously, the Netherlands had made three major adjustments of tax rates between 1956 and 1971; since 1971 it has made annual adjustments. Using an indexation formula reduces the government's decision-making powers, but it also allows the finance minister to cancel, or disregard, up to 20 percent of the tax adjustment. Denmark also did not tie taxes automatically to inflation, but tied the tax rates to wage rather than to price levels. It worked this way: In 1975, the national income tax yielded 22.2 billion kroner. Without indexation it would have risen to 28.1 billion in 1976; through index limitations the rise was held to 25.3 billion (OECD 1976).

According to American tax legislation in 1981, income tax indexation will also be introduced in the United States by January 1985. After annual tax reductions are implemented through 1984, tax levels will be insulated against inflation so that future rates will apply to real incomes. This model follows the Canadian practice of introducing price escalators and calling for full, automatic, annual adjustments. To bring this about, tax brackets, exemptions, and deduction figures will be increased annually at a rate equal to the inflation rate, as measured by the Consumer Price Index.

It is not clear that European experience is a good basis for predicting the consequences of American indexation. Neither the Danish nor the Dutch case provides full, automatic indexing, and in France indexation only operates when inflation passes a given threshold. The Canadian case seems more relevant. In Canada income tax revenues inched up from 10 to over 15 percent of GDP in the nine years before indexation. Since 1974 income tax receipts have stabilized in the 14 to 15 percent range. But in Canada (as well as in Australia), the reduction of revenue produced fiscal problems which caused strong calls for eliminating the indexation experiment.

The adoption of indexation by a 57–40 vote in the U.S. Senate (moved without hearings and without a separate roll call in the House) surprised some observers who had not believed that Congress would surrender its power to legislate semi-annual "tax reduction" adjustments, which will henceforth come automatically. The voting lineup was not wholly in line with ideology. Some liberals were opposed, because indexation potentially limits expenditures on social programs, but others were in favor, because it gives protection to lower-income groups that have tended to be hit hardest by "tax bracket creep." However, such protection may be undercut if there is a simultaneous shift to unindexed indirect taxes, which are generally more regressive. One of the costs of indexation is that it deprives policy makers of the ability to target tax cuts for micro- or macro-policy purposes.

Another argument against indexation is that it may undermine resistance to inflation by cushioning some of its impact. In some heavily indexed economies, inflation-fighters have sometimes had difficulty lining up public support, because many people were protected against some of the effects of inflation. Somewhat characteristically, these ramifications had scarcely been explored when Congress acted precipitately in 1981—even though its own legislative research machinery had suggested that "although indexation makes it easier to live with inflation, evidence is conflicting as to whether or not it is effective in lowering the rate of inflation" (U.S. Congress, 1980).

Tax Expenditures

In recent years some national governments have begun more systematically to organize information about revenue losses due to the panoply of exemptions, deductions, and tax credits written into tax codes in general and the income tax codes in particular. These have come to be seen as "tax expenditures," which ought to be scrutinized as closely as normal budget expenditures. As Table 6.7 makes evident, the U.S. Congress has over time added many diverse expenditures since passing the first income tax law in 1913. Exemption and deduction levels have often been raised. The federal government used approximately 150 kinds of tax expenditures amounting to about $124 billion in 1980 to subsidize a multitude of activities.

Many of the most costly tax expenditures were introduced during the first several decades. Tax subsidies were considered simpler and more efficient than government spending programs, a belief that was often linked to a preference for private initiatives which might be spurred by tax incentives. Thus the exclusion of tax payments for pension plans and medical insurance was initiated at a time when no public programs existed. Later, in the 1930s, benefits from the social security programs were also excluded from taxation.

Since the 1950s, the income tax has become even more a "social workhorse," providing indirect subsidies for a variety of special activities which some lobbies or reformers persuaded Congress to further. This form of promotion was often chosen because tax expenditures came to enjoy the support of "a peculiar alliance among conservatives, who find attractive the alleged reduction in the role of government that would follow from the extensive use of tax credits, and liberals anxious to solve social and economic problems" (Aaron, p. 5).

TABLE 6.7 How the U.S. Tax Expenditure List Lengthened, 1913–1980

Date of Introduction	Some Tax Expenditures	1980 Fiscal Year Estimated Costs in Million Dollars	
1913 Income Tax Law	Deductibility of consumer credit interest	12,235	37,600
	Deductibility of state and local taxes	17,655	
1914 to 1930	Capital gains preferences	22,270	56,490
	Deductibility of charitable contributions	7,955	
	Exclusion of employer contributions to pension plans, medical and life insurance	24,435	
1931 to 1950	Deductibility of medical expenses	3,120	16,885
	Social security benefit exclusion	8,105	
	Public assistance benefit exclusion	395	
1951 to 1980	Residential energy credits	435	11,950
	Investment tax credits	3,090	
	Exclusion of scholarship income	365	
	Credit for child-care expenses	705	
	Credit for employing AFDC* recipients	40	
	Credits and deductions for political contributions	100	
			ca. $124 billion

*Aid to Families with Dependent Children.

Who benefits from tax expenditures? People in all income groups pay lower taxes because of them, with even those in the lowest group able to claim deductions like those for such things as interest on consumer credit. Thus in 1977 and 1978 families with incomes of less than $10,000 had 54 percent of their taxes discounted through tax expenditures. At the other end of the income scale, those with incomes over $50,000 escaped 41.6 percent of taxes they would have had to pay were there no tax expenditures. However, the middle income groups were less fortunate, experiencing below average savings on their tax bills due to the effects of tax expenditures.

* * * * *

Tax policy, then, is a product of contending political forces interacting with contending economic paradigms. While the Keynesian paradigm and economic growth prevailed, all Western governments increased their tax ratios. But since the mid-1970s, manifestations of tax resistance have combined with monetarist and supply-side paradigms to exert pressure for policy reversals. Income tax systems have lost much of their progressivity as top rates have been lowered, especially in Britain and the United States, promising stimulation of investment that was slow to arrive. Quickly visible, however, were the cutbacks in government social programs which the budget deficits created by the tax reductions were intended to facilitate. Thus did the ascendancy of fiscal conservatism lead to "the distributional goals of horizontal and vertical equity. . . being relegated to a secondary position behind the stabilization objective (Herbers, in Roskamp and Forte, p. 68). And as middle-income groups realized that they were benefitting less from tax expenditures than either the lower- or higher-income groups, politicians responded by once again seeking new tax models which would be both simpler and fairer.

7
INCOME MAINTENANCE POLICY

The origins of the welfare state in the nineteenth century were accompanied by expectations—fears among conservatives and hopes among socialists—that a government-led expropriation of private property was about to occur. In the past one hundred years, however, events have taken a different turn. Instead of a "nationalization of the means of production," in the socialist style, the trend has been what might be termed a "nationalization of the means of consumption," as national governments throughout the West have become a major factor in determining the distribution of disposable income. Contemporary welfare states perform this distributive function through the combined impact of two activities: taxation policies that distribute extractions from people's income, and income maintenance policies that distribute cash payments to augment people's income.

This reshuffling of income in national treasuries (often called the *fisc,* from the French word for "money basket") is much more complicated than simple payment of taxes and receipt of government transfers. Any ledger sheet of the income flow between private households and the public sector would begin with private employment income, add any public employment income, deduct income taxes and social security contributions, add back into household income social security benefits and other government transfers, subtract indirect taxes on the family's consumption expenditures, then add back into household income the value of any special subsidies or services from the public sector.

For present purposes, a partial picture of this interaction can be gained by looking at Table 7.1, which shows the changing relationship of social insurance transfers and total government revenue for a number of Western democracies since World War II. Several points are worth noting. First, major increases in transfers and taxes have occurred in every nation (though less so for taxes in West Germany and France). Second, social insurance transfers everywhere have risen faster in relation to the economy than have total taxes. Finally, within this general pattern of growth, certain national variations remain intact. Britain and the United States, which rank low in social insurance spending at the beginning of the period, remain low at the end of the period, although each country today stands at much higher levels of spending than it did thirty years ago.

Given the joint impact of taxes and transfer payments, and increasing awareness among the general public of this impact, we should recognize that taxation policy and income maintenance policy are closely linked. The overall distribution of income depends on both together. Yet, income maintenance programs are also important in their own right, and in fact are generally the largest items of government spending today. Through such programs, spending power is transferred from the employed to the unemployed, from the healthy to the ill, from the middle-aged to the very young and the old, from the affluent to the poor—and also from the poor to the affluent. Thus, even under the stringent budgets of the Reagan administration in the United States and the Thatcher government in Britain, income maintenance programs remained the largest single component of government spending between 1980 and 1983.

Income maintenance programs are also important because of the growing economic and political problems associated with this policy area. Generous provisions adopted in the Western nations during the periods of high economic growth of the 1950s and 1960s have proven difficult to finance as the economic pie has grown more slowly in the 1970s and 1980s. Complicating this short-term problem has been the longer-term forecast of future financial difficulty as the European and American "Baby Boom" generation born at the end of World War II approaches retirement at the end of this century, while the smaller working-age population must strain to pay for social security benefits. Fears of a possible crisis in social insurance have grown on both sides of the Atlantic, although the results have been somewhat different.

Thus, income maintenance policy—relatively uncontroversial in a period of affluence—has grown politically troublesome in recent, more difficult years. In this chapter we will examine the general characteristics and the politics of income maintenance policies among the Western nations as a whole. In the course of our discussion, we will also refer to the particular experiences of the United States, Britain, France, West Germany, and

TABLE 7.1 SOCIAL INSURANCE EXPENDITURE AND TOTAL GOVERNMENT REVENUE AS A PERCENT OF GNP/GDP

	1953–55	1959–61	1965–67	1971–73	1975–77	1979
Austria						
Social Security	13.7	14.9	18.2	18.4	20.8	n.a.
Tax	31.1	31.8	35.3	37.2	38.8	41.4
Britain						
Social Security	9.6	11.0	12.9	14.6	17.2	n.a.
Tax	30.7	30.2	32.2	34.1	35.7	34.0
Denmark						
Social Security	9.9	11.2	14.3	20.8	24.4	n.a.
Tax	24.9	27.3	31.8	42.9	41.4	44.1
France						
Social Security	13.3	13.4	15.4	18.8	24.8	n.a.
Tax	33.5	34.7	35.0	35.3	38.8	41.2
Netherlands						
Social Security	7.8	11.1	16.8	22.1	27.1	n.a.
Tax	30.8	33.7	36.8	42.6	45.8	47.4
Norway						
Social Security	7.8	9.9	11.2	17.3	19.0	n.a.
Tax	30.9	34.9	34.9	44.2	46.1	46.1
Sweden						
Social Security	10.1	11.5	15.1	20.9	28.0	n.a.
Tax	30.7	34.1	36.5	42.9	47.8	50.3
United States						
Social Security	4.6	6.4	7.8	12.3	13.6	n.a.
Tax	25.0	27.1	27.1	29.4	29.9	31.3
West Germany						
Social Security	14.7	16.0	17.4	18.1	23.4	n.a.
Tax	35.4	36.0	32.0	34.7	36.8	37.3

SOURCES Social Security Expenditure: Total social security expenditure from International Labour Office, *The Cost of Social Security* (Geneva: International Labour Office, 1958, 1964, 1967, 1972, 1981).

Gross National or Gross Domestic Product: ibid., OECD, *National Accounts of OECD Countries,* Volume I (Paris: OECD, 1981). In a few cases it was necessary to make a linear interpolation to make the national accounts data conformable with the fiscal year of the respective countries. For countries other than the United States this was done on the basis of the OECD publication. For the United States, quarterly national accounts data were employed from U.S. Department of Commerce, Bureau of Economic Analysis, *The National Income and Product Accounts of the United States 1928–1974.*

Total Revenue as A Percentage of GDP: OECD, *National Accounts of OECD Countries 1950–1968* (Paris: OECD, 1970) was used for the periods 1953 to 1955 and 1959 to 1961. For later periods OECD, *Revenue Statistics of OECD Member Countries 1965–1980* (Paris: OECD, 1981).

Sweden. From this survey we will try to gain a sense of the reasons for similar and different national approaches to satisfying the common human need for economic security.

CHOICES IN INCOME MAINTENANCE POLICY

Scope and Thresholds

In theory, one could imagine a society with no government involvement in income maintenance whatsoever. The flow of income to individuals would be strictly private—earnings from work, returns from renting one's property or loaning one's capital, gifts from a family member or friend to another, charity, and many other personal arrangements. Government might still be important in the distribution of income (for example, by building highways in one area and not another, by setting minimum wages, or by hiring more soldiers and fewer doctors and nurses, or vice versa), but without income maintenance programs any government income transfers would be more or less accidental byproducts of its other activities (Reynolds and Smolensky, Chapter 1).

The society we have just described, with its private and largely unplanned income flows, was approximated in the nineteenth century in most countries. Table 7.2 shows the large role now played by government transfers in the advanced democracies. In most nations the amount of money distributed through government has risen to levels equaling one third or more of all income earned through wages and salaries. In the United States and Britain the proportion is closer to one fifth, but this is a vast increase in each nation compared to its situation in the early 1950s.

In thinking about the trend evident in Table 7.2, one can imagine a society in which the income flow is entirely determined by income maintenance policies: In effect, all earnings and income sources would be replaced by a collectively arranged system of transfer payments.

Clearly, modern income maintenance policy falls somewhere between these two theoretical extremes. In effect, though not necessarily with any such intention, modern welfare states have crossed an important threshold in the past one hundred years, going beyond privately determined and often inadvertent flows of income. But they have also stopped well short of trying to substitute public transfers for all private economic transactions. How have these choices of public versus private boundaries been made in different nations?

Instruments

Comparison reveals much cross-national similarity in income maintenance policy, with every country using the same basic program instruments. The first and most dominant instrument, in terms of its costs and the number of people benefiting from it, is *social insurance*. Through the payment of specially earmarked taxes (sometimes called "national insurance" or "social security contributions"), an entitlement to certain cash benefits is acquired. Commonly, such programs cover risks of income loss due to old age or retirement, sickness, industrial accidents, widowhood, and unemployment.

The second basic instrument of income maintenance policy is *public assistance*. Such programs characteristically rely on some form of income test to determine need and usually entail a good deal of administrative discretion in dealing with individual clients. Benefits are given not only in cash, but also "in-kind," for example, food stamps, medical services, day care for mothers on welfare, and so on. Unlike social insurance entitlements, public assistance benefits typically place a considerable stigma on the recipients in the eyes of the general public.

These widely shared tools of income maintenance are arranged in quite different ways. Social insurance in Germany, for example, has traditionally emphasized matching benefits to differences in individuals'

TABLE 7.2 GOVERNMENT TRANSFERS AS A PERCENTAGE OF WAGES AND SALARIES OF TOTAL LABOR FORCE

	1953–55	1959–61	1965–67	1971–73	1977–79
Austria	24.2	25.8	29.5	26.6	25.7
Britain	9.9	11.2	12.9	15.2	19.6
Denmark	13.8	15.8	18.1	23.6	30.6–32.6*
France	40.4	39.8	41.2	41.4	50.9
Netherlands	20.4	26.3	34.9	40.4	53.5
Norway	13.9	18.4	22.2	28.9	30.9
Sweden	12.5	15.0	17.0	21.8	33.7
United States	6.8	9.8	10.3	15.0	18.7
West Germany	28.5	30.3	25.2	23.5	30.8

SOURCES For the periods 1953–1955 and 1959–1961 (for the Netherlands also the period 1965–1967), OECD, *National Accounts of OECD Countries 1950–1968* (Paris: OECD, 1970).

For the remaining periods, OECD, *National Accounts of OECD Countries 1962–1979* Volume II (Paris: OECD, 1981) for France, West Germany, the Netherlands, Sweden, Britain, and the United States.

The series for 'wages and salaries' covering the periods 1971–1973 and 1977–1979 in Denmark, Norway, and Austria was conducted by applying the growth rates of 'compensation of employees' to the earlier series. For the transfer payments in those cases, *OECD Economic Survey: Austria* (OECD: Paris, 1982), *OECD Economic Surveys: Denmark* (OECD: Paris, 1982) and *OECD Economic Surveys: Norway* (OECD: Paris, 1981).

*A range rather than single number has been provided since transfers during this three-year period include payments to households and recipients residing outside Denmark.

earnings; in Britain the same social insurance technique has generated a basic uniformity of transfer payments. Different mixes of insurance and assistance programs are also discernible. In Sweden entitlement programs loom very large, whereas in the United States public assistance programs play a more important role.

Distribution

The thresholds and instruments of income maintenance policy clearly have important distributive consequences. The general trend in the past fifty years has been away from the assumptions of individual equity in strictly insurance-type programs—that is, one's benefits correspond to one's contributions—and toward emphasis on the social adequacy of benefits—benefits should meet basic income needs. Entitlement to income security has become less individually earned and more a social right of citizenship (Marshall).

However, one should not exaggerate this commitment to redistribution in the name of social citizenship. Tables 7.1 and 7.2 give some indication of the extent to which countries vary, even as they apply the same overall techniques of social insurance and public assistance. Moreover, the harsher economic climate of recent years has tended to raise new questions about the limits of social citizenship—even in countries such as Sweden and Britain, which have given greater emphasis to redistributive goals than have other countries.

Restraints and Innovation

Social insurance was a historic social innovation, offering an ingenious means of pooling risks to economic security across the population while recognizing individual circumstances and doing so without the stigmatizing effect of traditional public assistance. As the social and economic dislocations of modernization increased, social insurance provided a timely political compromise between the respective demands of collectivism and individualism (although, as we shall see, the timing varied considerably among nations).

Economic and social dislocations of the 1970s and early 1980s were certainly less severe than those at the beginning of this century; nevertheless, recent economic troubles have generated debate in many countries about the need to make tough choices in income maintenance policy. Indeed, the difficulties of policy innovation may be even greater today than they were during the origins of the welfare state, if only because current expectations of what public policy can do are so much higher and the momentum of existing social programs is so much greater and thus more difficult to arrest.

The emerging policy debate suspends income maintenance programs between two perspectives. One, a strictly economic perspective, stresses the smaller margin of resources, produced by slower economic growth, left to pay for transfer programs. Questions are also asked about the effects of public income maintenance on private savings, investment, and work effort, thus raising the specter of a downward spiral to even lower growth.

The second perspective is social. Recent economic troubles are seen to have increased insecurity among workers and their dependents, producing a need for additional income maintenance. Some observers would go further: Since the immense spending on transfers has had only marginal impact on overall economic inequality, some social democratic reformers would, rather than refine transfer payments, intervene more strongly in the original, pre-transfer distribution of income.

Whatever the intellectual arguments, the debate on income maintenance policy must also be carried on within a political environment that is extremely sensitive to the popular outrage that can be created by any intimation of cutting government benefits. What taxpayer resistance is to taxation policy, anticipated beneficiary backlash is to income maintenance policy—namely, a profound constraint on policy innovation.

GROWTH OF THE TRANSFER SOCIETY

SCOPE AND THRESHOLDS

Students of comparative public policy have devoted considerable energy to trying to unravel the effects of economic and political variables on public policy. Nowhere is this more true than in income maintenance policy, which many consider the quintessential policy feature of developed welfare states. Enough evidence has now accumulated so that we may draw some fairly reliable conclusions regarding the complex interaction of the various factors. The conclusions are far from simple.

The most common way of specifying the boundaries of income maintenance policy is to consider spending for such transfer policies in relation either to the size of national income or to total public spending. The first general conclusion is that for many countries economic development determines the extent of government involvement in income maintenance programs. Nations at a high level of economic development have with very few exceptions extended the boundaries of government transfer payments much further than have poorer nations, regardless of the type of political regime in power (Wilensky).

In a way this is surprising. Of course rich nations have more money to spend than do poor nations. But why should rich nations of all political persuasions spend a higher proportion of national income on welfare policies for poor people than do poor nations? Part of the answer is that income support programs in the modern welfare state are not just for poor people. They are programs in which citizens at many income levels take part. Thus even in the United States, where the boundaries of income maintenance policy are narrowly drawn compared to other nations, no less than one third of all households received some form of federal assistance in 1980, and most of the households receiving benefits in 1979 were *above* the official poverty level (Havemann, *National Journal,* 21 March 1981, pp. 492–493).

The nature of economic development itself also helps explain why rich nations spend proportionately more than poor nations do on income maintenance. As economies develop, real incomes increase, but so, too, do people's economic vulnerability and perceived deprivation. Having more to lose, people in richer nations are inclined to spend more through government to protect what they have. Economic development also typically entails reductions in the economic security offered by large extended families at the same time that personal income is increasingly drawn from non-agricultural pursuits. Reaping the benefits of economic growth depends on having purchasing power in a market place of other increasingly specialized producers; purchasing power depends in turn on the sale of labor in return for wages and salaries. More than ever, social security in developed nations depends on earning wages or salaries and on earning them *without serious interruption.* Whatever their political arrangements, industrial populations feel a common need for programs counteracting the major forms of interruption in wages and salaries: injury at work, old age, illness, death of the breadwinner, and unemployment. And as economic development continues, structural shifts from manufacturing to service sectors impose further strains on marginal workers who are less adept at white-collar work.

At the same time that economic development attenuates traditional forms of social and economic support and heightens vulnerability to the insecurity of earnings, it raises general income standards and definitions of what is acceptable as a standard of minimum economic need. Absolute definitions of poverty—minimum resources needed for basic physical survival—tend to be replaced with relative definitions based on prevailing higher standards. According to the best available estimates, in the United States at the beginning of this century, roughly half of all Americans fell below a minimum, absolute poverty level; by 1929, the proportion was in the range of 20 to 30 percent; and by 1950, almost no one could be counted as poor by turn-of-the-century standards (Patterson, pp. 11–13, 78–80). But the effective realities on which policy choices were made were not affected by the fact that many of those unemployed in the Depression and most of those targeted in antipoverty programs of the 1960s were not poor by earlier standards. In the course of economic development, deprivation had become a relative concept.

Extensions of programs to the non-poor as well as the poor, heightened vulnerability to income insecurity, and the operation of relative standards of deprivation together provide a plausible explanation for the higher incidence of income transfers in richer nations—regardless of the left/right complexion of the governing regime.

Yet if level of economic development explained everything about income maintenance policy, then the boundary choices would look alike in all countries at the same economic level. But they do not. Nations such as Sweden, Germany, Canada, and the United States rank high in economic development (that is, GNP per capita), while among developed nations Britain, Italy, and Ireland rank low (with per capita income calculated in standard monetary units less than half that of the richest nations). However, the extent of government transfers in these countries in no way corresponds with their economic development. Rich nations and less rich nations alike spend varying amounts on government transfers. The variation between the most and least affluent countries is as great as the variation in the scope of income maintenance spending, but the two sets of variation do not at all correspond with each other.

Thus a second general conclusion is that level of economic development *per se* is not the most important factor in determining the boundaries of government transfers. Instead, according to the most plausible conclusion that can be drawn from the host of aggregate statistical studies, economic conditions and relatively enduring configurations of political power together determine how welfare state boundaries are drawn. This general conclusion is illustrated by several specific research results.

Age of Program and Bureaucratic Momentum

Transfer payments are particularly significant in nations where programs have been in effect for many years (Wilensky; Pryor). There are many non-economic factors at work: The longer a program has been in operation, the more people may earn an insurance benefit entitlement or demand one; as programs age, administrators running them seek successive piecemeal expansions; once in place, programs become part of a status quo and thus more difficult to cut than to extend.

Why, then, have some nations crossed the threshold earlier from a distribution of income determined more or less through private economic relationships to one heavily infiltrated by government transfer payments? One approach to this question is to examine the conditions associated with the first introduction of major national government intervention in the form of social insurance programs. Such an examination does not suggest that social insurance programs were initiated as various countries attained certain levels of economic development; Austria, Sweden, and Norway initiated programs at relatively low levels of development (measured in terms of degrees of industrialization and urbanization), whereas Britain did so only at a very high level of economic modernization. Nor is there much evidence to support the idea that modern income maintenance programs were introduced as nations reached high levels of political mobilization among the working classes, even though early social insurance legislation was concentrated on industrial workers. Depending on the country and the program, legislation was initiated when working-class parties received as little as 0 percent and as much as 50 percent of total votes (Flora and Alber, in Flora and Heidenheimer, pp. 65–68).

However, perhaps a trade-off occurred between political structure and economic structure that would help explain the age of income maintenance programs we see today. That is, programs may have been initiated early in the economic development of a country if there was strong working-class mobilization to push the issues; on the other hand, weak working-class mobilization may be compensated for by socioeconomic problems associated with a high level of industrialization and urbanization. This interaction of economic and political variables is a sound theory, but we must draw distinctions. First, we must use as the unit of observation, not simply the particular year in which a social insurance program was introduced, but a period of years during which a sequence of initiatives may have been applied. Second, we must distinguish among groups of nations at different times. For example, under these restrictions it is possible to say that in the period from 1900 to 1920, some European states (such as Britain) traded off higher economic development and lower working-class mobilization in the introduction of major social insurance programs.

Still, there is a period—1880 to 1900—and group of countries—Germany, Sweden, Norway, Denmark, and France—for which other explanations must be found. The oldest, and thus often most extensive, income maintenance programs are found in nations that originated their programs at comparatively low levels of both economic development and political mobilization. At early stages of industrialization and with weak signs of democratic mobilization (for example, limited suffrage rights and/or a powerful executive bureaucracy), these countries were the first to cross the threshold from private distribution to public income maintenance. Again, an explanation lies in the interaction of economic and political variables. Compared with nations at a comparable level of economic development, such non-parliamentary regimes often faced a greater need to legitimize their power at early stages of economic change when a growing industrial working class was still politically weak. Moreover, these regimes already had strong paternalistic bureaucracies in place to create and carry out social insurance innovations, as we will see in the subsequent section on policy instruments.

Economic Dependence and Left or Right Dominance

In economic policy, a strong relationship exists in many countries between the rapid expansion of the public sector since 1960 and dependence on international trade. There is some evidence that a similar relationship has developed recently with regard to the boundaries of income maintenance policy. Table 7.3 indicates that whereas in 1962 dependence on imports and exports had little to do with the extent of income maintenance spending, by 1972 the relationship was much stronger. This probably reflects a tendency in recent years for countries that are dependent on the fluctuations of an increasingly unstable international economy to use income transfer programs to cushion the effects of these fluctuations.

At the same time, little relation seems to exist between the growth of transfer payments and the presence of socialist governments. Table 7.3 suggests that for international dependence to affect public income support, it is not necessary that a leftist government be constantly in power; it is more important that rightist parties should *not* be firmly entrenched in power. Table 7.3 combines information from Tables 7.1 and 7.2 to show social security spending as a percentage of GNP for selected years. Countries are arrayed into five groups, depending on (1) how extensively the working class is politically mobilized (that is, degree of unionization and average votes for social democratic parties or other parties of the left) and (2) how often working-class parties have participated in minority or majority control of the government (proportions of cabinet and parliamentary seats held by parties of the left and duration of such participation in government). Also shown is the extent of popular electoral support for parties of the right. Thus we can identify nations where mobilization has been high and control generally stable (such as Sweden and Norway) and nations where mobilization has been high but control sporadic or low (such as Britain or France). The table indicates that there is at best an unreliable and fairly weak relationship between leftist dominance and extensive income transfers relative to the economy. More striking is the fact that where socialist parties and strong labor movements are more or less absent, government transfers are consistently smaller in the aggregate. In the middle range—where power is more evenly balanced—the reliance on government transfers appears little different from that in countries where the political left has been dominant.

It would, therefore, be wrong to think that the growth of government redistribution is simply a function of leftist power, although rightist power may be significant in retarding major innovations or dramatic policy expansions. Yet even these results are ambiguous. One cannot simply punch into a computer what one knows about the political power of the right or left in a country and obtain a reading of high or low public income transfers. A much more refined understanding is required. Using

TABLE 7.3 INTERNATIONAL DEPENDENCE, LEFT OR RIGHT DOMINANCE, AND SOCIAL SECURITY SPENDING FOR SELECTED YEARS

	Imports and Exports as Percentage of GDP 1975	Average Vote for Major Party of the Right 1958–72	Social Security Expenditures as Percentage of GNP/GDP		
			1960	1970	1977
*High mobilization, Stable control**					
Austria	67	45	15	19	21
Norway	91	19	9	16	20
Sweden	59	15	11	19	31
High mobilization, Unstable control					
Britain	55	45	11	14	17
Belgium	93	16	15	18	26
Denmark	69	19	11	16	24
New Zealand	55	n.a.	13	12	18
Medium-high Mobilization, Low control					
Australia	30	45	8	8	14
Finland	57	16	9	13	19
France	39	35	13	15	26
Italy	50	40	12	16	23
Low mobilization, Partial control					
Netherlands	101	12	11	20	28
Switzerland	60	22	8	10	16
West Germany	47	46	15	17	23
Low mobilization, Political left Excluded					
Canada	48	37	9	12	15
Japan	26	52	5	5	10
United States	16	48	7	10	14

SOURCES Korpi, Table 4, p. 312; Castles 1981, p. 130, note 3; Castles and McKinlay, Table 1, p. 158. International Labour Office, *The Cost of Social Security* (Geneva: ILO, 1981), Table 2, pp 58–60.

*Political 'mobilization' here is determined by the degree of unionization and average votes for social democratic parties or other parties of the Left. Indications of 'control' reflect the proportions of cabinet and parliamentary seats held by parties of the Left as well as the duration of such government participation.

the available aggregate statistical studies and a number of historical case studies, we can make the following generalizations. When a country must choose when to cross the line between public and private income distribution, the power of the political right probably is important in delaying, circumscribing, and otherwise restraining the vigor with which public policy goals are allowed to interfere with private arrangements (Derthick, Heclo, Castles and McKinlay). This generalization may not hold if the political right, supported by a strong national bureaucracy, chooses to try to defuse the pressures for change by itself introducing new public policy commitments (Flora and Heidenheimer). (Examples of such "defensive innovation" will be given throughout this chapter.) Once an important boundary is crossed and the dust of political controversy has settled somewhat, all sides of the political spectrum tend to accept the inherited structure of income maintenance policy and to busy themselves with what are regarded as incremental improvements in existing policy. But because this step-by-step approach can produce a cumulative outcome that no one intended, a subtle potential exists for radical change within incrementalism. Once the cumulative impact of many small changes is felt and questioned, the stage may be set for a new period of more fundamental debate about boundary issues and policy realignment.

Such, in general terms, is an outline of income maintenance policy development for many nations during this century. However, having said all this, we should note that important exceptions to any rule can be found. Moreover, even if there were a perfect fit among the various measures we have used, we should not suppose that the results prove causation. One author whose data we have used in Table 7.3 concludes that "A large party of the right will tend to impede welfare state provisions. . . ." (Castles 1981, p. 168). But it is just as plausible that the same public attitudes that render a party of the right popular will "cause" any party—right, center, or left—to limit its ambitions for income redistribution.

In addition to the problems of ambiguous statistical relationships and uncertain lines of causation, we face the difficulty of determining what we mean by "income maintenance policy." Most analyses equate the policy variable with expenditure figures, and spending totals can be a very superficial indicator of the content of such policies. One painstaking study of old age pensions compares the adequacy of minimum pensions in a number of nations. The results show that while level of economic development seems important to some measures of benefit adequacy (for example, measured as the ratio of minimum pension to average earnings), the differences among rich nations cannot easily be explained by one or two simple factors. "One lesson I learned from this study," the author reported, "was to respect the uniqueness of each program in the light of its historical antecedents, social policy, and economic and political constraints" (Fisher, p. 298).

The most reasonable approach, therefore, is to recognize that political and economic variables are not in competition with one another as the real cause of welfare state expansion. Public policies are complex phenomena, and humility is desirable in those who seek to discover enduring relationships. A good way to gain a deeper appreciation of the interaction between political and economic factors is to examine the actual experiences of particular nations. This is the approach we shall take to examine the choices of instruments in income maintenance policy.

VARIETIES OF PUBLIC SUPPORT

INSTRUMENTS

It is important to begin by recognizing the similar underlying significance in the basic idea of social insurance. In one Western nation after another, the invention and diffusion of this income maintenance technique in the late nineteenth and early twentieth centuries eventually freed large sections of the population from dependence on charity, local poor laws, and the ubiquitous stigma surrounding means-tested assistance. In practice, a test of means typically entailed a degrading examination of all one's personal circumstances so as to prove to some local official that there were no viable means of support from work, family, or friends. The advantages of the new insurance technique were immense. Decisions regarding eligibility were now automatic, since they were based on nationally standardized rules rather than on the discretion of local poor-law officials or private charity workers. Degrading investigations into a family's means were unnecessary in a system in which beneficiaries had earned the right to support by virtue of past contributions. Focussing insurance on certain contingencies or accidents (industrial disability, widowhood, unemployment, loss of earning power with old age, and so on) also meant that administrative decision making could concentrate on whether or not a particular contingency had actually occurred and not on the moral character of the claimant. Moreover, the political costs were less apparent, inasmuch as this new system could be paid for by "contributions," rather than by more visible taxes on the population. After centuries of reliance on medieval poor laws, the advent of social insurance was a great watershed in the history of income maintenance policy.

Despite this underlying similarity in the conceptual significance of social insurance, nations have, in using the technique, varied considerably in rationale and emphasis. Current policies reflect their histories; and this is certainly true with regard to the slow-changing contours of income maintenance policy. Tably 7.4 maps a few overall differences by breaking down income maintenance spending into component parts. Some countries, such as Germany and Austria, appear to emphasize pensions (although old age and invalidity insurance is the biggest share of the total in all countries).

Others, such as New Zealand and Belgium, give a large share to child allowances; and still others, such as Britain, the United States, and the Netherlands, devote more resources to means-tested public assistance. Of course there are other similarities and differences that might be discussed, but the important point to recognize is that behind these numbers (and accounting practices differ among the nations, so the numbers should be treated with caution) lie different historical experiences.

The Legacies of Past Choice

Among the sixty independent countries choosing to introduce national social insurance over the past one hundred years, only one—Albania—did so as a self-declared socialist nation (Collier and Messick, p. 1314). In most countries the basic social insurance concept has been shaped through a complex, three-cornered interplay among employers, workers, and the state itself (including both politicians and administrators) in mixed capitalist economies. In no nation have the choices been made in exactly the same way; and many of the underlying configurations

TABLE 7.4 EXPENDITURES ON MAIN ITEMS OF INCOME MAINTENANCE, 1972*

	Percentage of Total Income Maintenance Spending					
	Old Age and Invalidity Pensions	Child Allowances	Sickness Cash Benefits	Unemployment and Related	Means-tested Public Assistance	Other
Australia	63	15	2	2	0	19
Austria	80	11	4	2	0	4
Belgium	52	22	15	5	2	3
Britain	63	7	12	9	9	0
Denmark	65	16	11	6	3	1
Finland	70	7	12	4	3	4
France	56	20	11	2	4	7
Italy	67	11	11	3	1	7
Japan	65	3	15	8	6	2
Netherlands	54	15	14	5	12	0
New Zealand	56	28	2	0	6	0
Norway	68	16	10	2	2	3
Sweden	62	14	18	4	3	0
West Germany	72	3	8	3	4	10
United States	73	0	4	7	12	4

SOURCE OECD, *Public Expenditure on Income Maintenance Programmes,* Table 2, p. 20.

*Data given are for 1972 for all countries except Austria, Japan, and West Germany, which are for 1973.

of policy and politics that developed have had remarkable enduring power. Let us examine Germany, Sweden, Britain, France, and the United States.

Although it lagged behind Britain in economic development, Germany in the last quarter of the nineteenth century experienced all the social problems of rapid industrialization. National social insurance programs (for industrial accidents, sickness, and old age pensions) were introduced in the 1880s as a defensive innovation designed to counteract the growing socialist movement and to ensure the loyalty of the new industrial working class. In making this effort, the prime movers behind German social insurance—certain elements of the government bureaucracy, large-scale industrialists, some academics, and Chancellor Bismarck himself—drew on a long tradition of state paternalism for artisans, craftsmen, coal miners, and other workers that had developed during the preindustrial period of German development. The resulting social insurance programs of the 1880s and 1890s established a curious mixture of state centralization (with a new Imperial Insurance Office compelling membership and compliance with rules) and intermediary organizations (accident insurance associations, sickness insurance funds, and the like), which were co-opted into, but also highly influential within, the state social insurance structure. The German approach focussed on particularly important sections of the industrial work force and made no pretense of creating a comprehensive social policy for all workers and their families. Even so, these programs—with rigidly bureaucratic mechanisms for deciding claims, compulsory contributions from wages, and benefits little higher than those in poor-law public assistance—were not particularly popular with the workers themselves (Tampke and Ullmann in Mommsen; Saul).

In view of the vast upheavals in twentieth-century Germany, it is remarkable how much of the basic social insurance structure has remained intact. The Nazi government reshaped many intermediary insurance organizations (particularly those with a trade union, Jewish, or socialist presence) and never created its promised uniform system of social insurance for all citizens. At the end of World War II, the Allied occupational forces in cooperation with some West German reformers proposed the creation of a single, comprehensive program of national insurance modeled along the lines of the Beveridge system that had been instituted in Britain in the 1940s (see p. 218). This proposal came to little in the face of intense opposition from bureaucrats and insurance fund officials, who had helped their programs survive the political turmoil of previous decades, from self-employed and higher-paid workers, who insisted on a separate identity for their social insurance funds, and from leading politicians of the new Federal Republic, who discounted any need to rely on foreign models of a policy technique that the Germans themselves had invented. Postwar policy, despite the much higher benefits and wider coverage, would have looked familiar to a citizen of Bismarck's Second Reich: a complicated system of funds for accident insurance, paid for entirely by employers; an even more complicated arrangement of sickness insurance funds, paid for jointly by workers and employers; and a system of state-subsidized public pensions, differentiated among categories of workers and closely attuned to differences in workers' earnings.

Sweden at the end of the nineteenth century was among the poorest nations in Europe and still predominantly an agrarian economy. Swedish reformers during this time were heavily influenced by the new social insurance ideas in Germany and, like the Germans, could rely on a strong central bureaucracy to create and implement new policies. However, in spite of distinctly Bismarckian overtones of paternalism and social control that accompanied the introduction of social insurance in Sweden, Stockholm's elite administrators and politicians presided over a more open policy process than did their German counterparts. In Sweden, social insurance developed in a freer political climate, with party competition, liberal reform, and independence for interest groups and the parliament. Consequently, much time was lost between the first proposals by liberal parliamentarians at the end of the 1880s and the final enactment of social insurance for the aged in 1913. But, for the purposes of building a broad-based political consensus, the time was well spent. It is easy to forget that at this time Sweden was wracked by intense social divisions and economic conflict. Powerful agrarian interests, national administrators, academics, businessmen, unions, socialists, and laissez-faire liberals all disputed the advantages and disadvantages of social insurance. However, two important features must be pointed out: that Sweden's political process drew these disparate groups into active and continuous participation in the policy-making system, and that it did so early, before the participants became too firmly locked into opposing positions. Gradually, a series of official investigations, commissions, legislative proposals, defeats, renegotiations, false starts, and reinvestigations moved the participants toward agreement.

After two decades of debate, the final plans were worked out in an investigative commission led by national civil servants but also composed of representatives from the major political parties, business interests, and labor interests. In the end, the workers' and employers' representatives were in substantial agreement. With strong national administrative capabilities and a pre-industrial tradition of royal concern for equal protection of all citizens, Sweden enacted its 1913 pension law, becoming the first country in the world to adopt a contributory social insurance scheme covering virtually the entire population. In subsequent years, this system became the model for other social insurance programs. The long tenure of the Social Democratic party (from 1932 to 1976) helped greatly to expand social insurance as a comprehensive tool of income support organized for the entire population. The concept of individually earned insurance was gradually laid to rest in favor of more uniform basic benefits with major financing from general revenues.

Compared to either Germany or Sweden, Britain was economically a much more developed nation at the end of the nineteenth century. Its administrative resources were relatively weak, whereas organized labor, competitive political parties, and the parliament were relatively powerful. During the last quarter of the nineteenth century many proposals for contributory social insurance were made by middle-class reformers but they all ran up against three major obstacles. First, many key participants, including civil servants themselves, were doubtful of the administrative capacities to run a contributory program, and were committed instead to advancing administration of the British poor law (which was more centrally controlled than that of any other nation at this time). Second, liberal and conservative politicians as well as the popular media generally objected that social insurance of the German type would involve a state regimentation that would be "un-British." But by far the major practical obstacle was the entrenched power of the workers' own organizations, the Friendly Societies, which already collected workers' contributions for death benefits; these societies feared state competition. Employers, some of whom pointed out the advantages of social insurance as a disciplining device and aid to industrial peace, were far too fragmented to assume any coherent position pro or con the new initiatives.

Given this situation, the first pensions in Britain (1908) were simple grants to the poorest of the aged, and constituted a largely improvised administrative response to continued agitation from labor groups for an alternative to the degrading poor law. But with the difficulty of paying for pensions without worker contributions, and with labor opposition to further means tests to restrict the number of people eligible, these pensions were not a policy tool capable of sustained development. Instead, reform-minded liberal ministers and their civil service advisers worked out plans for contributory social insurance largely outside the domain of public debate. In 1911, against labor opposition to contributions and with rather passive acquiescence from other parties and interest groups, the liberal government introduced the world's first national unemployment insurance program. At the same time a limited scheme for workers' health insurance was instituted, giving the Friendly Societies the responsibilities and financial rewards of the program's administration. Thus, by the interwar period, the British policy process had produced one false start (non-contributory pensions) and an ad hoc mixture of two other insurance programs, one run by the state for particular categories of workers and one heavily influenced by the private-sector societies.

In general, Britain's pragmatic arrangement lacked the coherence and authoritarian rationale found in Germany and the positive consensus for contributory state insurance found among the interested parties in Sweden. Only with World War II and the accompanying sense of national solidarity was a more thorough reform of social insurance accomplished. The basis for a postwar consensus on income support policy was laid by William Beveridge, who as a civil servant had helped create the 1911 unemployment insurance plan, and a committee of government civil servants. Now there was close consultation with trade union leaders who were essential to the war effort. Having experienced the degradation of the "dole" that followed the financial collapse of unemployment insurance during the late 1920s and 1930s, labor leaders were now much more receptive to the value of insurance contributions as a means of establishing a right to benefits and providing a sound financial basis for income support. Developed as the war-weary nation sought a symbol of postwar hope, the Beveridge plan was eventually accepted by all parties by the end of World War II. In essence, all social insurance programs were integrated into a comprehensive national insurance applicable to all citizens. Separate contributions remained, not as a means of earning individually differentiated benefits, but as a demonstration of the citizen's right to claim support. Since virtually the same cash benefits would be paid to everyone for all types of income loss, uniform contributions were deemed essential, which had the added advantage of keeping administration simple. A separate but limited subsidy from general revenues was used to help keep the level of contributions low, since all earners, from the lowest- to the highest-paid, had to contribute exactly the same amount for their national insurance. These ideas—comprehensive coverage, uniform treatment, and minimum income levels to avoid destitution—were Britain's essential policy legacy in the postwar period.

Developments in France followed a rather different course. Although it did not industrialize nearly as rapidly as Britain, Germany, or (after 1900) Sweden, France embarked early on a policy of publicly subsidized voluntary insurance plans. This approach owed much to the presence of strongly organized, regionally (and often religiously) distinct groups of workers in semi-industrial handicraft occupations who resisted assimilation into a German-type national insurance program. Adding to the inertia of this approach were a succession of politically weak governments with no inclination to antagonize workers by demanding compulsory contributions and a closed administrative elite little interested in social reform.

Table 7.5 gives some indication of the French position *vis-à-vis* the three other countries we have discussed. Percentages exceeding 100 percent indicate coverage extending beyond the work force to non-economically-active segments of the population, a condition found early in Swedish pensions as well as in British health insurance after the creation of the National Health Service in the late 1940s. Social insurance in France, on the other hand, covered only small portions of the work force and this

TABLE 7.5 SOCIAL INSURANCE COVERAGE, BY PROGRAM AND COUNTRY FOR SELECTED YEARS

	Membership in Program as Percentage of Economically Active Population															
	Britain				Germany				Sweden				France			
	I	H	P	U	I	H	P	U	I	H	P	U	I	H	P	U
1880	—	—	—	—	—	—	—	—	—	—	—	—	—	—	—	—
1885	—	—	—	—	18	26	—	—	—	—	—	—	—	(5)	(6)	—
1890	—	—	—	—	70	36	—	—	—	—	—	—	—	(5)	(6)	—
1895	—	—	—	—	81	39	53	—	—	(4)	—	—	—	(8)	(8)	—
1900	—	—	—	—	75	44	51	—	—	(13)	—	—	(10)	(9)	(8)	—
1905	(76)	—	—	—	72	46	49	—	(17)	(21)	—	—	(13)	(13)	(8)	—
1910	(76)	—	[55]	—	87	51	52	—	(20)	(27)	—	—	(20)	(17)	(8)	—
1915	(76)	75	[55]	11	78	50	58	—	(22)	(24)	136	—	(20)	(15)	9	—
1920	(77)	79	[55]	22	75	56	58	—	56	(28)	132	—	(20)	(17)	14	(1)
1925	(77)	83	[55]	59	72	57	61	—	51	(29)	132	—	(50)	(21)	14	(1)
1930	(77)	89	90	59	75	59	64	44	55	(35)	131	—	(50)	(33)	15	(1)
1935	(77)	89	91	65	77	53	64	36	57	(32)	135	(2)	(55)	35	37	(1)
1940	(78)	105	104	70	88	58	68	45	62	(49)	136	(7)	(55)	46	47	—
1945	(75)	111	109	62	90	60	65	45	70	(84)	143	(27)	(55)	52	52	—
1950	90	160	101	85	91	77	69	53	73	(99)	138	(35)	55	75	70	—
1955	89	155	100	81	100	91	78	53	79	162	140	(37)	58	79	89	—
1960	92	155	99	79	92	87	82	59	76	158	140	(37)	65	92	93	50
1965	92	155	99	77	96	85	79	62	76	161	140	(42)	70	124	100	50
1970	93	160	98	74	98	97	81	72	74	160	135	(55)	80	120	100	50

I Occupational Injury Insurance H Public Health Insurance P Pension Insurance U Unemployment Insurance

NOTE Parentheses indicate publicly subsidized voluntary schemes or employers' liability programs in the case of occupational injury insurance.
Brackets indicate non-contributory pensions.

SOURCE Flora and Heidenheimer, Tables 2.7–2.10, pp. 74–77.

mainly through government grants to workers' own insurance schemes. As late as the 1930s, less than a fifth of the economically active population was covered by the one compulsory social insurance program that existed. Only in the post-World War II period did the figures among the nations begin to converge.

However, the apparent convergence in numbers should not obscure the differences in the ways the same policy tools were used. Despite government efforts in the immediate postwar period to create a single state pension scheme for the entire work force, the tradition of separate funds proved too difficult to overcome. Existing occupational funds and newly established schemes for the self-employed, supervisory, and technical personnel successfully exerted pressure to remain outside the basic minimum pension system (*le régime général*); the effect was to limit severely the base of financial contributions to the basic pensions and to provide a continuing rationale for not upgrading the benefits of the régime général beyond basic minimum levels. On the contrary, finances from the basic pension fund have typically been used to subsidize financially weak occupation-specific funds and to pay for other services, such as medical research and training grants. Moreover, the whole complex French system of social insurance funds and financial transfers among them is not counted as part of the official government budget, and (under the Fifth Republic) most social security issues are not voted on in the French parliament. As several observers have noted, this allows the government to gain credit by responding to social demands concerning income transfers, while maintaining the appearance of fiscal soundness in its own budget and imposing financial strains within the social security budget. This, in turn, contributes to a political climate of austerity for income maintenance policy and helps undercut any popular consensus behind the general scheme of basic pensions (Freeman, pp. 21–23; Cohen and Goldfinger, pp. 75–77).

The United States has had a longer tradition of mass suffrage, interest group activity, and democratic politics than any of the other nations we have discussed. Ostensibly, this situation should have been favorable to the early extension of welfare programs, especially in the rapid industrialization that began after the Civil War. Many forces were at work in the opposite direction, however. The United States lacked the more centralized administrative institutions of Europe—a reflection of a deep popular distrust of government power. The pluralistic sharing of powers among separate branches of the central government and the federal division of powers among national, state, and local authorities meant that veto of new proposals was possible and—except under extraordinary circumstances—probable from many places. News of social insurance experiments in Europe reached a United States where the counterpoint to a weak, fragmented labor movement was a strong, self-assertive business community that had succeeded in identifying the business ethic with the tradition of American individualism.

In this setting, social insurance programs of national scope were not only relatively late to arrive, but came imbued with an individualistic rationale, and—paradoxically—were less adaptable through open political processes. So rarely did any general program pass through the many screens of particular interests and the unease about government power that there was great incentive to leave policy guidelines alone rather than risk further political debate. Once the basic concept of social insurance was accepted, incremental improvements, often of profound significance, passed largely into the hands of program bureaucrats and other policy experts (Derthick).

The movement for social insurance in the United States was represented by the American Association for Labor Legislation, a private pressure group organized in the beginning of this century and led by academicians, social workers, and some civic and labor leaders. Workman's compensation could be clearly shown to be favorable to industrial efficiency, and laws soon were instituted in most states. But this was not viewed by business as social insurance, and reformers seeking more far-reaching sickness, old age, and unemployment insurance did not find similar support from either business or labor. Leaders of unions were particularly opposed to sickness and unemployment insurance, largely for fear of weakening union influence over workers and increasing workers' dependence on the government. Lacking any political or mass backing, the association found its educational activities frustrated throughout the first third of the twentieth century. The fragmented American system did offer an opportunity for the social insurance lobby to gain a foothold at the state level, and by the end of the 1920s eight states had old age pension programs, typically with strict eligibility conditions to direct aid only to the neediest. But the competitive subunits of American federalism hindered income support policy more than they advanced it. Unemployment insurance, for example, aroused very little state action because of fears that the insurance contributions would drive businesses into other states without such costs.

Only the Depression and the arrival of the Roosevelt administration created those exceptional circumstances necessary to overcome the inertia. By then unions had reversed their opposition to pensions and unemployment insurance, and mass agitation for free pensions (the Townsend movement) threatened politicians as never before. Roosevelt had already, as governor of New York, become convinced that social insurance offered the necessary alternative to degrading poor-law relief. The important role of administrators in policy formulation was again shown when the essentials of the 1935 Social Security Act were worked out by experts under the auspices of the Department of Labor. The Labor Department planners showed that social insurance could be interpreted within the American liberal tradition of individual self-help. Typical European distinctions between manual and other employees had no place in their perspective, but neither did coherent nationwide standards. Only in the contributory old age pensions were uniform national standards established; conditions and benefits of unemployment insurance and public assistance were largely left to the vagaries of state discretion. Administration policy makers judged health insurance to be politically too controversial for action. As for contributory pensions, emphasis was clearly on the individual's contractual right to an earned benefit. Thus there were no government contributions from general revenue, a low ceiling on the wages from which an individual's contributions could be deducted, a large spread (depending on earnings records) in monthly benefits, and no national floor on minimum benefits. Absence of a national administrative structure had hindered the drawing up of social insurance plans, but the very newness of the enterprise meant that framers of the policy could set up a new administrative apparatus that would be firmly committed to the new insurance doctrine and would insulate the basic policy approach against future interference from pluralistic politics. The doctrine of individually earned insurance became firmly imbedded in both the 1935 Social Security Act and the new Social Security Administration.

While maintaining doctrinal adherence to individually earned benefits and no support from general government revenues, American social insurance in practice nevertheless has changed substantially. In 1939, for example, "unearned" benefits for dependents were introduced, the large fund of individually contributed accounts was abandoned, and pension payments were begun far earlier than could be justified by recipients' contribution records. Yet this major change occasioned little public debate. It was supported by business interests fearful of a large public insurance fund and program bureaucrats and liberals eager to provide more adequate pensions. Major liberalizations occurred in subsequent years, usually with the agreement of both parties and little public controversy, as rapid postwar growth provided seemingly endless financial resources. In practice, the insurance concept has been characterized not by individuals earning their own benefits with their own contributions but by an intergenerational contract in which today's pension benefits are financed entirely by payroll taxes paid by today's workers. Paying the growing social security bill has been politically easier with these less visible taxes than with higher income taxes. Moreover, avoiding subsidies from general revenues has helped maintain the impression of "getting what you paid for" in social security. This doctrine can be found in the history of social insurance in many countries, but it has persisted with particular strength in the United States.

Our brief survey of the introduction of social insurance suggests how the meaning of a policy instrument may vary. Consider, for example, the relation between social insurance and union movements. In some cases, union leaders in different countries have held quite divergent views of the same policy instrument, whereas in other cases these views have themselves changed over time in the same country. In Germany, weak unions opposed the new social insurance technique as a further aggrandizement of an already strong central state power. In Sweden, unions were also rudimentary, but they were led by men who foresaw the advantage of social insurance for workers and who were allowed to participate to some degree in the formulation of national policy. In Britain, unions were much more powerfully organized, but they were also concerned with protecting their own independent prerogatives, not least of which was the right to collect workers' contributions for union benefits. For the first forty years of this century, Britain's labor movement resisted contributory social insurance (preferring uniform benefits paid from general revenues) and played little positive part in policy development. In the United States, unions were relatively weak as a political force, but, like some of their foreign counterparts, they were fearful of anti-union governmental power. Above all, however, U.S. labor leaders decried social insurance as contrary to American traditions of self-help and volunteerism. The economic pressures of the Depression eventually modified these hostile views of social insurance; but it is difficult to describe the American labor movement as a major force behind the diffusion of social insurance techniques.

It is, therefore, rather unproductive to debate whether general patterns or national subpatterns are ultimately more important for understanding the choice of income maintenance tools. From a general perspective we can see that social insurance grew in importance everywhere during this century; and we can see a pervasive tendency to shift from a strictly insurance-based relationship between contributions and benefits to more generous attention to benefit adequacy. But within these common trends are different national features. Both the general patterns and the national subpatterns are essential to the full picture of structured variation that exists.

Contemporary Patterns

Many of the policy differences visible today are related to historical trends. To live in Germany or Sweden, which committed themselves early to contributory social insurance, is to be part of a comprehensive system of public transfers that may seem almost as routine as a paycheck. In countries that embraced income entitlements more hesitantly, such as Britain and the United States, the distinctions between those who have and who have not earned their benefits are sharper, and one's feelings as a recipient might be rather different. Here, as in other policy areas, the choice of instruments is not simply a technical, value-neutral problem of finding the most efficient means to accomplish given ends. Means shape ends.

Table 7.6 distinguishes the techniques of income maintenance for several of the countries. The first section of the table illustrates the wide differences in the percentage of families with incomes from various sources. Reliance on means-tested public assistance transfers does not differ greatly among the nations. But in other transfer entitlements, Sweden's more comprehensive coverage differs significantly from Britain's and even more so from the United States'. The second section breaks down participation rates in public transfer programs by income level, from the lowest to the highest income earners.

The table indicates important differences among the nations. In Sweden, non-means-tested income security programs cover all of the citizenry, blurring distinctions between economically "dependent" recipients and "independent" non-recipients, and between persons of high and low income. Britain has moved in the same direction, without going as far. In

TABLE 7.6 PARTICIPATION IN GOVERNMENT TRANSFER PROGRAMS BY TYPE OF PROGRAM AND INCOME LEVEL

	Britain 1972–73	Sweden 1968	United States 1970
Percentage of all non-aged families who receive:*			
Private pensions	2.6	2.5	5.2
Private transfers (alimony, gifts from relatives, etc.)	3.6	1.2	2.4
Public child allowance	40.5	61.6	0
Social insurance benefits	24.6	46.0	11.4
Means-tested transfers	7.9	9.5	7.0
*Percentage of families** in each sextile of earned income who receive government transfer payments*			
Top sixth	64.2	93.7	3.4
Fifth sextile	60.7	92.1	6.0
Fourth sextile	72.0	98.5	8.0
Third sextile	77.4	98.3	13.6
Second sextile	74.5	98.8	27.2
Bottom sixth	77.7	94.6	51.4

*Families where at least one spouse is between the ages of 25 and 54.

**Refers to non-aged families with children.

SOURCE Lee Rainwater, Martin Rein, and Joseph Schwartz, *Family Well-Being in the Welfare State: A Comparative Study* (Forthcoming, 1983).

the United States, the distinctions are much clearer: The majority of the lowest income earners receive government transfers, with participation dropping sharply beyond that. Notice, too, that these figures apply to families headed by persons aged 25 to 54, in other words, persons in prime working years who pay most of the taxes to support government transfers. It is reasonable to think that the spread of entitlement-type benefits among many persons, almost as a right of citizenship, creates a much smaller constituency for an anti-welfare backlash, especially compared to the "us-them" patterns that develop in nations where means-tested benefits are concentrated on a small and distinctively poor fraction of the population.

WHO PAYS, WHO BENEFITS?

DISTRIBUTION

It would be simplistic to think that there is any single clear egalitarian goal associated with income maintenance policy. Some income support programs do pay particular attention to the needs of the poor and, in that sense, are devoted to an egalitarian ideal. But many programs, particularly in the area of social insurance, are intended to meet the income security problems of people who may not fall below any given poverty line. Furthermore, it is never easy to determine who pays for the costs of income transfers. Financing transfers through general revenues is considered by some to be more egalitarian than the use of payroll taxes earmarked for social security, but this conclusion rests on at least two assumptions that are difficult to prove: (1) that general revenues, especially income taxes, are actually distributed according to the ability to pay—that is, they are progressive; and (2) that income support programs detached from their own special revenues, such as social security contributions, could compete successfully with all the other spending programs that bid for shares of general revenues.

Thus, although clearly government income transfers are redistributing immense sums of money (see tables 7.1 and 7.2), it would be wrong to think that this redistribution necessarily results in, or was ever intended to be, a thoroughly *egalitarian* redistribution of income. There are, however, important distributive differences among nations, which seem related to the political role of organized labor and social democratic parties.

A variety of measures have been used to gain some understanding of the extent of egalitarian redistribution. Though these measures are admittedly imperfect, and the data far from complete, the overall pattern is noteworthy. One measure is the percentage of national populations falling below a given poverty line (standardized at two thirds of the average disposable income in each nation). Another indicator is the redistributive profile of the government budget; this is expressed as the share of public spending going to social security times the share of total revenue raised through direct taxation (again, on the assumption that direct taxes and social security spending are more redistributive than indirect taxes or other public spending). A third measure is the difference in public support for families with children. Such support may be given through special tax allowances or direct cash grants or some combination of the two; since tax allowances are usually of the greatest benefit to those with the highest tax liabilities, and cash allowances are of equal benefit to all, the ratio of the value of cash allowances to tax allowances for children gives some indication of redistributive effort.

These measurements are shown in Table 7.7, with countries ranked according to the political role of organized labor in each country. It would be easy to overinterpret this information, and one should be aware of the anomalies that exist. For example, France appears to have an unusually large poverty population, but this is due primarily to a large agrarian population for which cash incomes traditionally have been low, poorly measured, and offset by non-cash forms of income. Britain and the United States again seem to have more in common with each other than with the Continental nations. Moreover, the measurement of labor's political role is probably too refined and formal when applied to distinguishing countries such as Germany and the Netherlands from other countries with higher levels of social democratic mobilization and control. The most reasonable interpretation is that generally egalitarian redistribution is stronger in nations with a powerful working-class political presence and weaker where this presence is lacking. Levels of economic development and democratic political forms as such (that is, with or without a strong social democratic presence) do not appear to explain these differences (Korpi, Hewitt).

Obviously these aggregate data can suggest only a rough approximation of the situations that prevail in each country. A closer comparison of redistributive effects requires a careful compilation of individual household statistics, and such information is available for only a few countries. The small amount of data available does, however, tend to confirm the patterns identified earlier. In Table 7.8 we return to the three-nation comparison made in Table 7.6 and ask about the effects of government transfers on various types of families. Female-headed families with children are perhaps economically the most vulnerable of all non-aged household types. In Britain, Sweden, and the United States, they comprise a similar percentage (9 to 12 percent) of all families. And, as the table indicates, they are quite likely to fall below a standardized poverty line in all three nations prior to government transfer payments. Apart from these common features, however, the three nations diverge considerably. The more comprehensive coverage of income security programs for all family types operates in Sweden and to a lesser extent in Britain. In

TABLE 7.7 REDISTRIBUTION AND WORKING-CLASS POWER

Pattern*	Percentage of Total Population Who Are Poor**	Redistributive Profile of Government Budget†	Ratio of Value of Cash to Tax Allowances for Children††
HIGH-TO-MEDIUM MOBILIZATION			
Stable Control			
Austria	n.a.	9.3	1.9
Norway	5.0	6.9	6.0
Sweden	3.5	9.5	7.3
Periodic Control			
Britain	7.5	6.0	0.4
Denmark	n.a.	6.5	5.5
Low Control			
Finland	n.a.	5.2	1.6
France	16.0	4.2	4.9
LOW-TO-MEDIUM MOBILIZATION			
Partial Participation			
Netherlands	n.a.	8.8	5.6
West Germany	3.0	8.3	0
General Exclusion			
Canada	11.0	3.6	0.9
Ireland	n.a.	2.2	0.2
United States	13.0	4.5	0

*Political 'mobilization' here is determined by the degree of unionization and average votes for social democratic parties or other parties of the Left. Indications of 'control' reflect the proportions of cabinet and parliamentary seats held by parties of the Left as well as the duration of such government participation.

**Defined by OECD as proportion of population, disaggregated by family size, falling below two thirds of average disposable income in each nation. Data for early 1970s.

†Ratio of social security spending to total government spending times ratio of direct taxes to total revenue, data for 1962 to 1964.

††Ratio of value of cash allowances to tax allowances for two children. Tax allowances represent the difference between the income tax liability of a couple without children and the liability of a couple with two children. Values of cash and tax allowances are expressed as a percentage of gross earnings for an average production worker in each nation. Data for 1972.

SOURCES Korpi, p. 311; Hewitt, p. 454; OECD, *Public Expenditures for Income Maintenance Policies,* 1976, p. 27.

contrast, resources in the United States are much more concentrated on single women with children. Even so, U.S. government transfers are much *less* effective in lifting female-headed families above the poverty level. The same holds true for raising the other two family types above the poverty line.

In the United States, the greater targeting of income maintenance resources on particular categories of people does not necessarily imply more adequate income support for those who are assisted. In fact, the opposite seems to be the case. Countries with more comprehensive programs of income security also seem to do the most to raise those at the lower income levels.

Consistent with the preceding generalization is the fact that the one comprehensive income maintenance program in the United States turns out to have the greatest impact on reducing poverty: the social security program. Probably few Americans are aware that their insurance contributions pay for the nation's largest anti-poverty program. In 1976, 27 percent of all American families would have ranked as poor before the payment of social security and other transfers; social security reduced this proportion to 15.7 percent, whereas all other assistance programs (including means-tested cash aid, food stamps, and so on, but excluding medical benefits) reduced the proportion only slightly further to 11.3 percent (Congressional Budget Office 1977). Even among non-aged families, social security had as great an impact in reducing poverty level incomes (from 18.6 to 14.2 percent) as did all other income maintenance programs combined (which further reduced the proportion to 10.6 percent). Among the founders of social security, who wanted broad coverage of the population, there was a saying that "programs for poor people only will be poor programs." It is not a misleading generalization.

TABLE 7.8 POVERTY AND GOVERNMENT TRANSFERS BY FAMILY TYPE* IN THREE NATIONS

	Britain			Sweden			United States		
	I	II	III	I	II	III	I	II	III
Percentage of each family type receiving government transfers	22	71	89	47	96	98	11	15	56
Percentage poor** on the basis of private income	5	6	59	5	5	40	5	12	61
Percentage moved beyond poverty level by government transfers	75	63	40	45	68	77	26	18	26

*Family type I is a married couple without children, II is a married couple with children, III is a single woman with children.

**In this case poverty is defined in terms of standardized family size and income levels less than 50 percent of the median income in each nation.

SOURCE Lee Rainwater, Martin Rein, and Joseph Schwartz, *Family Well-Being in the Welfare State: A Comparative Study* (Forthcoming, 1983).

Lacking better methods of measurement, it is very difficult to speak with precision about the distribution of benefits and costs of income maintenance policy. In a way, however, the difficulty of constructing any net balance sheet of who pays and who receives is the most interesting fact of all. Political rhetoric is full of allusions to a basic distinction between taxpayers and others, who presumably are dependent on taxpayers. And income maintenance policy, unlike other policy areas, is distinguished by a common unit of measure—cash—that should facilitate identification of distributive issues. Against this is the fact that the programs interact with one another and with the true incidence of taxation in complex ways. In addition, it is unclear that a taxpayer, even if he receives no government transfer benefit in return for his or her taxes, is a net loser, considering the costs he or she might otherwise incur to support aged parents, or, more profoundly, to live with—and bequeath to his or her children—the social dislocations created by the economic want of others.

Taking a broad historical view, there appears to be little doubt that absolute poverty—the want of economic means for basic physical survival—has been all but eliminated in the countries covered in this volume (Kelley). This is due mainly to the high levels of economic growth in the Western nations during the twentieth century, but it is not unreasonable to think that expanding public transfers have helped ensure that the dividends of such growth have been more widely shared than they might otherwise have been. Yet, there is also general agreement among in-depth studies in several nations that since the end of World War II, the overall shape of income distribution has not changed greatly, nor has progress against relative poverty (low income defined according to rising standards of general affluence) been great (Roberti; Reynolds and Smolensky). This is a paradoxical result. Although immense sums are transferred in any one year and do raise many low-income families above poverty levels, the overall shape of the distribution of final incomes (after taxes and transfers) does not appear to have changed significantly during the postwar years in the countries for which reliable information is available.

Three reasons for this paradox lie close at hand. First, income maintenance policies—and, indeed, the entire tax-transfer shuffle of disposable income—are only partly aimed at producing a greater equality in income distribution, however that term is defined. Providing income security frequently means securing differences in living standards acquired throughout the course of peoples' lives. Hence, insuring against economic insecurity often means insuring for inequality. Second, government transfer payments, large as they are in every country, are still small and relatively inflexible compared to the immense scale and adaptations of a national economy. In a sense, income maintenance policies are always in the position of playing "catch-up" against the power of national economies to generate inequalities. Finally, the redistributive effect of income maintenance policies has been subject to a law of diminishing returns as coverage has become more comprehensive. At the early stages of welfare statism—when few people benefit and the resources of those better-off are largely untapped by taxes—a small amount of transfers may have rather large effects on the shape of income distribution. At later stages—when huge numbers of people are receiving benefits—taxes typically must be spread lower into the income distribution to pay for the benefits, thereby diluting the redistributive effect of each transfer dollar spent (Klein 1980).

INNOVATION IN A PERIOD OF SCARCITY

RESTRAINTS AND INNOVATION

After a long postwar period of economic growth and relative calm in the expansion of income maintenance policies, the policies again became a focus of major controversy in the 1970s. The specific arguments are complicated, but the general reason for growing controversy is not: new perceptions of economic scarcity in relation to the growing cost of government transfers. Those charged with economic management worried about "disincentive effects," social insurance officials projected the higher costs of supporting an aging population, union officials became sensitive to the effects of social security taxes on their members' take-home pay—and all formed a new constituency for questioning the momentum of income maintenance policy. It is a constituency that scarcely existed in the more confident and economically buoyant 1950s and 1960s; now it can be found in every developed nation (Rosa).

Harmonizing Economic and Social Policy

The central issues are encompassed by the term *harmonization*. Harmonization refers to the reconciliation of income maintenance policy with the perceived needs of economic management in ways that do not incur disastrous political costs.

Prominent harmonization problems of the past ten years can be broken down into three basic categories, although the emphasis may differ in the various nations. First is the need to integrate overall income maintenance policy with the requirements of economic adaptation. Early in the adoption of Keynesian economics, there was considerable discussion of using government transfers countercyclically to help stabilize economic fluctuations. Forms of income maintenance such as unemployment insurance have an automatic stabilizing effect by increasing during recessions (thus adding to aggregate demand) and receding during economic upturns. But the largest categories of income maintenance policy—pensions, health insurance, and so on—are not so automatic. No economic managers have seriously considered reducing pension checks or health insurance payments in order to stabilize the economy. Increasing transfer entitlements may be economically justified and politically easy in bad times (as long as higher taxes can be deferred), but decreasing entitlements in good times is everywhere regarded as politically impossible.

The main problem facing economic managers in recent years has been not how to cut current benefits but how to prevent the inbuilt momentum toward higher benefits from sustaining or adding to inflationary impulses arising elsewhere in the economy. During the 1950s and 1960s, one nation after another adopted some formula for indexing social insurance benefits to price changes, wage changes, or a combination of the two. Whatever the formula, the general result was to strain social insurance financing in the stagflation of the 1970s: Benefits pegged to prices rose sharply in this inflationary period, but the wage base to pay for them often stagnated. Adding to the problem has been the need to maintain international competitiveness. If income maintenance taxes raise the cost of doing business above the costs faced by employers in other countries, the economic competitiveness of a country dependent on foreign markets may be damaged (Geiger).

A second area of harmonization involves *disincentive effects,* which some analysts claim are associated with government transfers on their present scale. Economists, particularly in the United States, have pushed this theme on several fronts. Supply-side economists have argued that transfers and taxes impose a disincentive to work, as with public assistance clients whose benefits are reduced by some fraction of outside earnings, or with the elderly who must retire before receiving a government pension (Boskin 1977; Munnell; Judge). A variant on the same theme identifies a reduction in private savings and capital formation caused by government pensions that are not funded by the accumulation of a large fund of contributions (Feldstein in Boskin 1977). Yet another argument is that large social security taxes imposed on employers discourage the employment of workers and encourage the substitution of machines for labor (Freeman and Adams).

The evidence on these points is inconclusive (Danziger 1981). If one believes that such disincentive effects outweigh beneficial effects of the same programs, it is fairly easy—in theory—to design remedies. Disincentives for work can be reduced by avoiding large benefit cuts for outside earnings and by strengthening the work requirements for public assistance recipients. Such "work incentive" measures have been prominent in the United States in recent years, often over the objections of welfare clients. The retirement and earnings test for social security pensions could be eliminated, but this would be very expensive to do. To deal with savings disincentives, a large social security fund could be accumulated and invested to pay for future pensions. But this implies a political will to, in effect, impose forced savings on the population; moreover, conservative financial interests in every country worry about the impact of a huge investment fund left in government hands. Only in Sweden, under strong labor pressure, has there been any major experiment with such state funds. The problem of high labor costs associated with social insurance payroll taxes suggests the advantage of making greater use of general revenues and indirect taxes for financing social security. Such a shift is underway in several countries, although it is never administratively or politically easy to switch among different forms of taxation.

A final harmonization problem involves national bargaining over the *distribution of income.* Inflation and higher social security costs have pushed more workers everywhere into higher tax brackets. In a situation of high inflation and high marginal taxes, and with public benefits dependent on income, even large wage increases can lead to little improvement in take-home pay. This, in turn, can cause union demands for ever more inflationary wage increases. For example, the average Swedish blue-collar worker seeking a net 5 percent income increase (after taxes and inflation) in 1974 would have had to win an increase in money wages of 32 percent. With social security taxes rising in most countries faster than general revenues or earnings, it would be difficult for any government to gain labor's cooperation in wage restraint without some quid pro quo in tax restraint. In addition to wages and taxes, a third element is social transfer benefits distributed by government. In theory, these income supplements (or "social wages" as they came to be called in Britain in the 1970s) are an offsetting factor that makes large wage increases unnecessary. What complicates the picture, however, is that governments, in the name of conserving economic resources, are under pressure to target social benefits according to economic need and income tests. Thus, without some coordination, the contradictions among wage increases, the social benefits that are won or lost, and the taxes that are incurred can produce dissatisfaction on all sides.

In effect, these elements combine to produce a system of national bargaining over the distribution of disposable income for the succeeding year or two. More corporatist political systems, such as those in Scandinavia, have tended to pursue such bargaining in explicit terms, whereas others, such as the United States', have relied on separate skirmishes over tax reduction, social security reform, and various other issues. Yet, even if there is no system of national bargaining on take-home pay and social wages, another kind of distribution must be faced within the national budget itself. Income maintenance programs have become so prominent in every national budget that it is very difficult to make fiscal adjustments without dealing in some way with this sector of spending. Politically, it is unwise to alter existing entitlements to transfer payments; economically, it is difficult to find any maneuvering room in national budgets without changing them. Thus, the need for harmonizing economic and social policy is reinforced and its realization rendered more difficult.

These three areas of needed coordination pose a serious challenge for policy makers in democratic political systems. To some observers, the problems constitute an international crisis in the welfare state (OECD 1981). Are they, as advertised, a crisis? Or are they another instance of pressures toward a new round of piecemeal adjustments? For some clues, we should compare the actual responses of the various countries.

The Crisis in Practice

The generic problem of the welfare state may be stated as follows: First, government must be created that is capable of disciplining private market forces; then, the government must be capable of disciplining itself. Since the mid-1970s, self-discipline has become the abiding theme in many countries—without leading to the dismantling of major income maintenance programs. The trend has been one of "tinkering" with the gears of income maintenance policy without overhauling the basic machinery.

The tinkering involves avoiding extensions in coverage or introductions of costly new programs, adjusting the indices by which transfer benefits are increased, and expanding the revenue base for future benefits (Simanis, Copeland).

In Britain, the failure of the Labour government's income supplement, or social wage, strategy of the mid-1970s has been followed by a more far-reaching strategy of restraint under the Thatcher government. In 1975 the Labour government took a bold step in tying social insurance benefits to changing levels of wages and prices, requiring automatic benefit increases depending on which of the two indices was rising faster. The Thatcher government has sought to limit this pension indexing to prices only, and has raised certain short-term benefits (for unemployment, disability, and maternity) by 5 percent less than would be required to match price increases. The Thatcher government also reduced and then in 1982 abolished earnings-related supplements to basic unemployment and sickness benefits under national insurance.

In Sweden, the non-Social Democratic governments first elected in 1976 and reelected in 1979 proceeded more cautiously, but by the early 1980s they too had begun to tinker with the gears of automatic growth in the nation's elaborate system of income transfers. In 1981 the government instituted an adjustment to the basic index for calculating almost all transfer payments; the effect was to withhold increases in benefits due to higher prices insofar as such price increases were caused by higher energy costs or indirect taxation.

In France, the government in 1978 experimented with a temporary and selective abatement of employers' portions of social security contributions. To ease the financial strains, it has extended compulsory contributions for health insurance to retired persons. Most important in holding down the growth of income maintenance transfers, France has continued the practice of forcing social security finances to pay for a variety of subsidies to separate pension funds and non-insurance-based social programs (including some educational and medical research and construction programs).

West Germany has displayed perhaps the greatest initiative in holding back the growth of income support programs, even during a period of Social Democratic rule. After a controversial attempt to delay pension increases following the 1976 election, the government succeeded in "uncoupling" automatic pension increases from changes in prevailing wage rates. This, together with new efforts to control health costs (see Chapter Three), has contributed to a substantial slow-down in the growth of social spending. Total social expenditures, which had grown at a substantially faster rate than the economy as a whole in the early 1970s, actually fell as a proportion of GNP during the last half of the 1970s (Alber).

Recent developments in the United States are in some ways the most interesting of all. We have seen the tendency for major social policy initiatives to occur later, and subsequent expansions to occur more hesitantly, in the United States than in other developed democracies. Yet, in the past ten years, American policy makers have found it particularly difficult to restrain income maintenance policy in the light of changing economic conditions. Attempts by Presidents Ford, Carter, and Reagan to trim even small portions of the social security program encountered floods of political opposition and were quickly abandoned. (Among the proposals were a 5 percent ceiling on cost-of-living adjustments for social security benefits under Ford, a cutback in some dependents' benefits under Carter, and a reduction in future benefits for early retirees under Reagan.) To date, no European-style changes in the indices for calculating social security benefit increases or any other cost-trimming maneuvers have proven possible in Washington. At the same time, however, the Reagan administration during its first two years was stunningly successful in cutting back spending for those income maintenance programs that lay outside the social security system, particularly public assistance payments, food stamps, and related programs.

This peculiar combination of political stalemate and flexibility stems largely from the inherited presumptions underlying income maintenance policy in the United States and the historically clear demarcation between social insurance and welfare programs. So thoroughly has the concept of contributory "insurance" benefits permeated the politics of social security that any alterations in the program in the name of economic policy—even alterations involving cutbacks to generous benefits not payable until the next century—arouse severe complaints about tampering with individually earned rights to income. By contrast, public assistance programs enjoy no such legitimacy based on claims of individual equity and rights, and this small portion of income maintenance spending has proven much more vulnerable to demands for cuts. In effect, the nation's largest anti-poverty program—social security—has remained politically untouchable even in a more conservative, budget-balancing era; others in the poverty population who are not aged have not been so well protected and have had to bear a disproportionately large share of the economizing pressures.

Given the immense political constraints on any changes in social insurance programs in the United States, policy makers have frequently felt compelled to resort to the rhetoric of "crisis" as a device to force change. Since the mid-1970s, in the United States perhaps more than in any other nation, the policy debate has tended to revolve around a series of impending crises in social security financing. This appears to relate less to the actual state of social insurance accounts in the United States vis-à-vis other countries than to the political imperatives facing anyone attempting to tamper with social security spending amidst a policy psychology of individually earned rights. However, the sharp reaction to such rhetorical flourishes early in the Reagan administration also showed that popularizing the idea of the social security crisis could easily raise political anxieties that thwarted rather than facilitated a more open and informed discussion of policy alternatives. Debate quickly shifted to who would do the most to protect beneficiaries from the crisis and away from a reasoned discussion of the income maintenance choices that lay ahead.

In fact, the basic financing problems in social insurance are not greatly different in any of the developed Western nations. With the unexpected stagflation of the 1970s, every country faced short-term problems paying for benefits that were geared to keep pace with higher prices but having to do so with revenues from wages and other economic resources that were not rising nearly as fast as expected. In the long term, every country also faces a problem of matching social insurance systems to the demographics of an aging population, as the number of workers drops in relation to the large "Baby Boom" generation reaching retirement in the early twenty-first century. In every country it has proven difficult to find the political will to deal with these long- and short-term policy problems; and controversy around social insurance has grown apace. The politics of crisis that was most peculiar to the United States had as its main effect the general confusion of these separate long- and short-term problems.

Taking a broader view, the general tendency in recent years has been an attempt to adjust or fine tune the inherited structures of income maintenance policy to the new perceptions of economic scarcity. Nowhere in the Western democracies is it possible to find evidence of any major dismantling of these structures. To advocates of the welfare state, that may be a hopeful sign. To critics, it is a confirmation of the political infirmities that prevent major policy adjustments corresponding with economic rationality. Whatever one's judgment, several things seem certain. The gradual growth of income maintenance policies has redistributed significant amounts of economic resources without posing a stark or ultimate political choice as to what is the "right" amount or purpose of the redistribution. Such a bald confrontation on the issue of redistribution would only have the most unsettling political consequences in any nation. Critics of welfare state transfers must recognize that income maintenance policies have themselves become part of the prevailing distribution of income. Any effort at major change will now be widely regarded as a fundamental venture into income redistribution.

* * * * *

Income maintenance policy is a good example of structured variation on comparative public policy. Each nation has clearly crossed the border between public and private distributions of income, some more hesitantly, some more decisively, but no country has tried entirely to replace market-determined distributions of purchasing power. Common policy tools in social insurance and means-tested assistance are used, but in different combinations and with different emphases. The shift in insurance concepts from individual equity to social adequacy has been a long-term trend in every Western democracy in this century. But the United States has maintained a stronger belief in individually earned benefits than have other nations, and countries with the strongest base of working-class politics seem to make the greatest efforts at conscious redistribution. Still, no government transfer system is committed to thoroughgoing egalitarianism so as to produce enduring shifts in the overall structure of income inequality. This is because the normal course of democratic politics in advanced capitalist nations permits no easy or final choices between those who claim a right to differential rewards and those who claim a need for fairer distribution, between economic and social conceptions of rational policy. Thus income maintenance policy, broadly understood, endorses neither equality nor inequality as the supreme principle of social organization. The result is an ongoing series of ambiguous compromises between competing values. Today's policy compromises, no less than those accompanying the introduction of social insurance decades ago, involve a complex interplay of economic and political forces.

8
URBAN PLANNING

During the last hundred years, growing governmental responsibility for education, health, housing, income maintenance, and a host of other public programs was inextricably tied to the expansion of cities as the centers of economic growth in Western Europe and the United States. Industrial growth pulled migrants to the city, separating them from their traditional networks of kinship and community support, and forcing public authorities to step in to assist those who were unable to take care of themselves. Of course, industrial growth also generated the wealth that governments taxed in order to finance public services and benefits. With advancing metropolitan growth throughout Europe and the United States in the twentieth century, public authorities have been increasingly challenged to exert some control over the urban physical environment, which for most people plays as important a role in determining the quality of life as do social services and benefits. In this chapter our subject is the choices available to governments to influence urban development.

CHOICES IN URBAN PLANNING

Scope and Thresholds

How much responsibility should government assume for the physical development of cities? This question highlights, as clearly as any policy question posed in this volume, the conflict between public welfare and private interests.

There can be little doubt that the quality of life in urban areas constitutes what economists call an "indivisible good." That is, a safe, well-ordered, and unpolluted environment is a benefit enjoyed, not just by a few, but by virtually all of a city's inhabitants. Nor can there be any doubt about the important link between the physical environment of cities and their ability to generate economic growth. Given these facts, it is not surprising that the physical development of urban environments has become a concern of governments. Inevitably, governmental intervention in urban development brings public authorities into conflict with private interests. When they exercise their constitutional right to purchase land owned by private parties (the right of *eminent domain*), or restrict the ways in which a private owner may use his own property, governments are asserting the primacy of the collective welfare over the rights of individuals. They are, in short, using the coercive power of the state to promote the public interest.

In most cities of Europe and the United States, this power is largely in the hands of appointed, rather than elected, public officials. Typically, city planning commissions and planning departments are staffed by professionals whose vision of the city has been shaped in schools of architecture and engineering, rather than in political party caucuses. But their ability to translate that vision into concrete reality depends heavily on their relationships to local politicians and interest groups. As we will see, urban planners in Europe have been both more ambitious in their vision and more aggressive in confronting private interests than have their American counterparts.

Instruments

Urban growth is shaped by thousands of individual decisions made by developers, builders, home owners, renters, and commuters. How far planners can go in influencing these private decisions depends on the instruments at their disposal, which may be broadly classified as either subsidies to promote growth in desired directions ("carrots"), or regulatory measures to prevent undesirable development ("sticks"). For example, public authorities may offer low-interest loans or tax concessions to encourage developers to build in neglected areas, while forbidding development in other areas to be preserved as open space. Similarly, transportation planners who want to reduce downtown traffic congestion may opt to subsidize fares in order to make mass transit a desirable option for commuters, or they may prefer to institute sufficiently strict controls on driving and parking to discourage motorists. Obviously, the balance among these instruments depends on the resources available to planners to offer as carrots, and the political costs incurred by encroaching on the rights of property owners and motorists.

One important determinant of the leverage enjoyed by planners is the pattern of intergovernmental relationships, particularly the degree of coordination among local governments. Many of the problems addressed by urban planners involve entire metropolitan regions, containing dozens of local jurisdictions whose actions must be reconciled. Land-use patterns, transportation systems, water supplies, and air pollution are examples of planning issues which cross jurisdictional boundaries and are therefore tackled most effectively at the regional level. How is regional planning to be achieved? One way is through voluntary cooperation among the various jurisdictions; another is through coordination imposed by a higher level of government. As we will see, policy makers in Europe and the United States have differed significantly in the extent to which they acknowledge a *national* responsibility for urban planning.

Distribution

In 1970 a British urbanist wrote a book whose title perfectly expresses the distributive choices facing urban planners: *Whose City?* (Pahl). The question is how government actions influence the distribution of urban space among the many groups and activities competing for a place in the city. Public policy in both Europe and the United States since World War II has contributed to decentralizing manufacturing jobs—and many workers along with the jobs. At the same time, planners have promoted many alternative land uses, including office buildings, hotels, shopping complexes, expressways, and residential developments of various kinds. Not until the late 1960s did public interest begin to focus on the distributive consequences of this postwar trend, particularly on the effects of the construction boom on the low-income residents whose neighborhoods were often damaged by the new development. By the mid-1970s, the growing incidence of one- and two-person households, the accelerating costs of new suburban construction, and the sharp rises in energy prices had increased the appeal of central cities as residential areas, thereby intensifying the conflict for space. In many European and American cities, planners must balance the city's need to develop land in ways that generate tax revenues against its commitment to housing an increasing share of society's elderly and poor.

Restraints and Innovation

To a great extent, cities are shaped by forces beyond their control. The way that space is used in a city is strongly influenced by trends in national and even international economic markets—for example, the types and cost of energy available for production, transportation, and housing; the decisions by industrial capitalists about where to locate their investments; and the fluctuations in global demand for the goods and services produced in the city. During periods of high growth, policy choices generally involve the degree to which the private market is to be regulated, and its impact on the city mitigated. As we have already observed, European planners have shown a much greater willingness than their American counterparts to take measures which restrain the private market.

Not surprisingly, the current era of economic stagnation has led American policy makers to talk about reducing what is already a comparatively limited effort at regulating private market forces in the cities. More noteworthy, perhaps, is the fact that this trend is being seen in Europe as well. The new economic conservatism in Britain has prompted a similar impulse toward easing land-use and environmental regulations in cities, and using public power to adapt the city to the requirements of business, rather than forcing business to adapt to planners' requirements. It remains to be seen whether the Continental cities, with their long tradition of strong planning, will demonstrate a similar response to slowed growth.

PLANNING TRADITIONS IN WESTERN EUROPE AND THE UNITED STATES

SCOPE AND THRESHOLDS

The use of public power to regulate urban growth was common in Western Europe much earlier than in the United States, and so the scope of public intervention in land-use, transportation, and housing is today considerably wider in European cities. Although the need for some form of government regulation in urbanization is presently acknowledged on both sides of the Atlantic, Europe's longer experience with such regulation, as well as the existence there of certain cultural and governmental patterns especially conducive to planning, has given European city officials greater power.

The Planning Tradition in Europe

Many European cities still bear signs of the town planning carried on in medieval times. The winding streets that connect churches, marketplaces, and homes may give the impression of spontaneous, unplanned growth, but urban historians tell us that impression is false: "The esthetic unity of the medieval town was not achieved any more than its other institutions without effort, struggle, supervision, and control" (Mumford, p. 311). Later, in the Baroque period, monarchs undertook monumental building projects in many capitals to reflect their power and tastes. But perhaps the greatest spur to public planning in Europe was industrialization, whose advance in the nineteenth century brought pollution, crowding, and general deterioration to city life. In response, municipal socialists of the late nineteenth century carved out public parks, upgraded water and sewer systems, took over private transportation companies, and built workers' housing projects. By the early twentieth century, many cities had adopted "master plans" to guide such activities.

Moreover, some European planners looked beyond the overgrown industrial centers, to advocate the creation of healthier and more efficient new towns. These brand new "garden cities" would contain all necessary basic services, along with industrial plants to employ residents, but would be designed on a small town scale. The first such garden city was Letchworth, England; established in 1903, it became the model for new towns developed a half century later in Britain, France, Sweden, and several other European countries.

Both in preserving their aging urban centers and in creating brand new towns, European governments have benefited from a much older planning tradition than exists in the United States. Land is considered a resource which is subject to strong government regulation, a view that can be traced all the way to feudal times, when all land tenure was enmeshed in a hierarchy of rights and obligations descending from the sovereign to the peasants. This tradition has bred a degree of public acceptance of government intervention in and regulation of land use that is far greater in Europe than in the United States. It is hardly surprising that Europe's planners have taken advantage of this hospitable climate to launch planning ventures that are bold by American standards.

To an American observer, the most striking characteristic of European urban planning is the scale at which it has been undertaken since World War II. In most of Europe's big cities, planning initiatives have been focussed on the entire metropolitan region rather than confined within the boundaries of individual municipalities. In postwar Britain, for example, the response of policy makers to rising traffic congestion and deteriorating living conditions in London was to place a limit on the size of the city. They did so by creating the "Green Belt," a permanent girdle of open space about five miles wide around London's built-up center, to prevent indefinite sprawl. Recognizing, however, that setting up the Green Belt would not halt population growth in the southeast region of England, Parliament also provided for construction of complete new communities of moderate size beyond the open space. From 1946 to 1949, eight new towns were established within a radius of thirty-five miles from central London. To minimize commuting across the Green Belt, planners designed the communities to be reasonably self-sufficient, with services, shops, and even a large number of industrial jobs. In the late 1960s, three more new towns were created in the Greater London region, fifty to eighty miles from central London, the greater distances an effort to guarantee that they would not become commuter towns. Together, the new towns and the Green Belt comprised a comprehensive regional plan for the decentralization of people and jobs from London.

In Paris, as in London, postwar planners drew up a master design for the entire metropolitan region. Adopted in 1965, the plan designated open space, projected a series of new towns to be built from scratch, and selected several older suburbs for development into higher-density nodes. The new towns program was undertaken in 1966, and by 1975 five new towns were functioning within twenty miles of Paris. In addition, three major nodes of development have been built up closer to central Paris, at La Défense, Créteil, and Bobigny, in an effort to siphon some office development away from the central city (see Figure 8.1). The long-term goal of the plan was to redress the growing regional imbalance between employment, which was concentrated in central Paris, and new housing, which increasingly was being built in the suburbs. Besides causing a tremendous strain on the region's transportation network, this imbalance threatened eventually to make Paris unlivable.

FIGURE 8.1. REGIONAL PLAN FOR PARIS, SHOWING TWIN AXES PROPOSED FOR FUTURE GROWTH

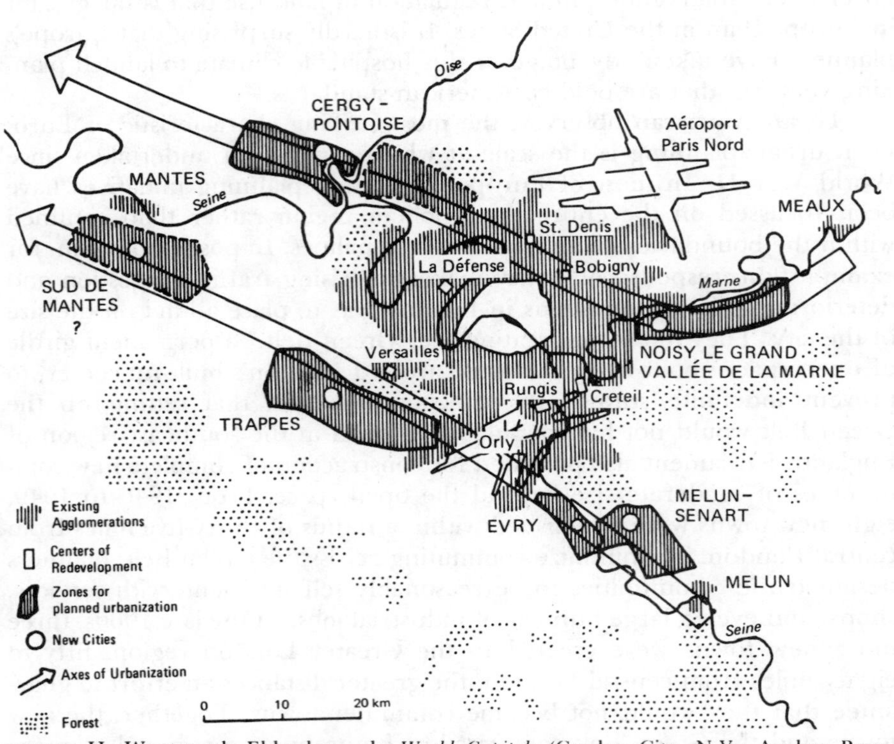

SOURCE H. Wentworth Eldredge, ed., *World Capitals* (Garden City, N.Y.: Anchor Press, 1975), p. 84.

Among professionals, one of the best-known examples of comprehensive planning for a metropolitan region is Stockholm. Although occasionally criticized on social and esthetic grounds, the well-ordered suburban communities that ring Stockholm are widely acknowledged to be among the best-planned in the world. The 1952 General Plan for Stockholm proposed an entire system of these communities, and by 1970 twenty-seven of them had been completed. While economically dependent on the central city, each of these suburban centers (called "satellite cities") has its own shopping, recreational, and cultural facilities, as well as basic social services and health care. Unlike new towns in Britain, Stockholm's satellites are not expected to be self-sufficient; instead, the central city is assumed to continue as the major employment center of the region. Figure 8.2 shows the plan for the city center of one such town.

One final example will suffice to illustrate the ambitious scale at which European urban planners have operated since 1945. This is the case of the *Randstad,* or "ring city," in the western Netherlands. A metropolitan region in the shape of a horseshoe, about thirty miles long and thirty miles wide, the Randstad connects Rotterdam, The Hague, Amsterdam, Utrecht, and a number of smaller cities (see Figure 8.3). Dutch planners after World War II saw that these growing cities might actually sprawl outward to meet one another, eventually swallowing up the open space in the center of the horseshoe. Starting in 1949, Dutch authorities began charting a regional plan which evolved through several stages (Hall 1966, p. 111), finally to encompass both the preservation of an existing "green heart" as open space, and the channeling of future growth along a few transportation arteries extending outward from the horseshoe. As in Stockholm, much of the land between the arteries was to be preserved as open space.

The Randstad planning scheme exemplifies the principle that ambitious plans on paper do not always produce proportional results on the ground. Beginning in the late 1960s, the plan ran into serious opposition. The targets for limiting growth in the green heart had not been achieved; still more damaging was the widespread belief that the government had acceded to pressure from the Shell Oil Company to add a new town not included in the original plan. By the 1970s, expectations that the entire green heart could be saved from development had waned. Nevertheless, the fact that planners were unable to implement the plan *in toto* should not detract from the essential point here: that planners in the Netherlands, as in most of Europe, work at a much more ambitious scale than do their American counterparts.

The Tradition of Privatism in the United States

In his historical study of Philadelphia's growth, Sam Bass Warner identifies "privatism" as the single quality which best characterizes America's urban inheritance. In Warner's view, it has been private institutions and individuals that have been responsible for guaranteeing the productivity and social order of American cities (Warner, p. 214). The emphasis on private interests in urban development reflects the commitment to individualism and limited government that have characterized so much of America's political tradition.

The physical shape of American cities provides a highly visible example of the consequences of privatism. The townscape is determined by the "speculative ground plan," which treats urban land as a commodity whose worth is expressed strictly in terms of market value (Mumford, p.

FIGURE 8.2. PLAN FOR THE CENTER OF VALLINGBY, A NEW TOWN IN SUBURBAN STOCKHOLM

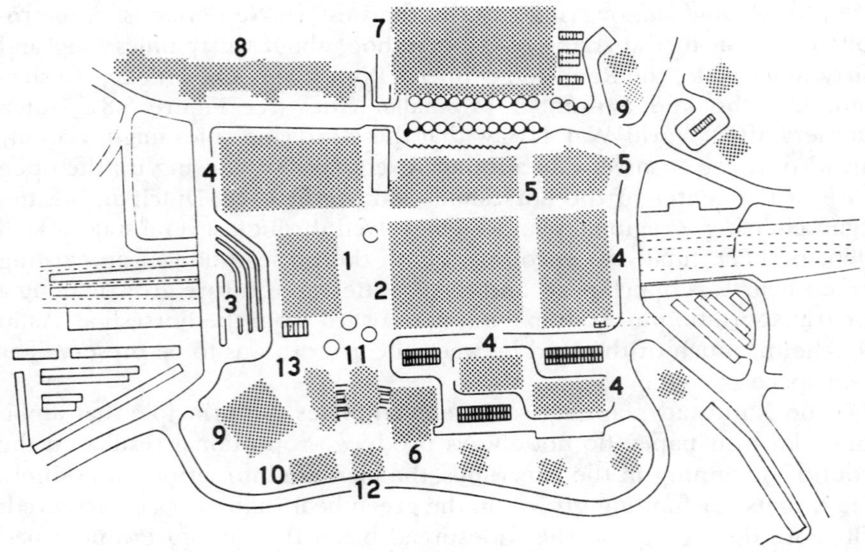

1 transit station
2 commercial building
3 bus platforms and taxi stands
4 commercial buildings
5 stores
6 residence hotel
7 600 stall parking garage
8 apartment building
9 churches
10 library
11 cinema
12 youth center
13 community hall

Transit station, department stores, and shops are incorporated into a system of pedestrian streets with the transit line beneath. Parking facilities are at approaches to the center and in a parking garage on the northern side. Multistory housing development is on both long sides of the center.

SOURCE David Pass, *Vallingby and Farsta: From Idea to Reality* (Cambridge: MIT Press, 1973), p. 100.

FIGURE 8.3. RANDSTAD ("RING CITY") OF THE NETHERLANDS WITH GREEN HEART AT THE CENTER

SOURCE Peter Hall, *The World Cities* (New York: McGraw-Hill, 1966) p. 98.

421). This type of ground plan dates from the seventeenth century, when capitalists began to engage in land development and sale as commercial ventures. This form of capitalism has had profound effects on the physical organization of cities. Because the rectangular building lot is the unit most conveniently handled by surveyors, speculators, builders, and lawyers, it formed the basis of the gridiron plan that was promoted by the complex of real estate interests: "On strictly commercial principles, the gridiron plan answered, as no other plans did, the shifting values, the accelerated expansion, the multiplying population, required by the capitalist regime" (Mumford, p. 424).

No collective commitments such as those that the medieval city had spawned in Europe restrained the private pursuit of wealth in the newer, faster-growing American cities. In the expanding capitalist economy of the nineteenth century, liquid assets were at a premium, and profits from real estate speculation depended primarily on frequent turnover. The pursuit of profits therefore encouraged the continual destruction of older urban structures and their replacement with new ones yielding higher rents.

Even today American public authorities remain relatively powerless to intervene in the cycle of decay, clearance, and reconstruction that proceeds in the nation's cities. That process is dominated by market forces. In fact, the federal urban renewal program actually perpetuates the cycle, by its reliance on private capital for construction on renewal sites. Redevelopment projects, whether they are undertaken by individual investors or by large firms such as Alcoa and Reynolds Aluminum, may generate favorable publicity for investors, but such benefits are of secondary importance, compared with the primary objective of such undertakings: to provide shareholders with a reasonable return on their investment. Thus the choice of sites to be cleared and redeveloped must be made to suit the investors who supply the money to build on them. In 1981, when General Motors agreed to consider building a new Cadillac plant in Detroit, the city's redevelopment officials had to find an acceptable location. Determined to secure the plant, Detroit offered GM a 456-acre site that included a Polish neighborhood of 3500 people. Ignoring protests and even fighting a lawsuit, the city argued that this massive urban renewal project involving $320 million in government subsidies would serve a public purpose by providing jobs for Detroit's ailing economy. It was necessary therefore to demolish the aging neighborhood in order to accommodate the corporation's requirements for space.

The nature of urban renewal projects, like their location, is market-determined. No clearer example exists than New York State's Urban Development Corporation, created in 1968 as the most powerful renewal agency in the nation. A decade later its mission had shifted dramatically from building housing for low- and moderate-income families to building high-priced apartments, luxury hotels, and a convention center, and supporting industrial expansion. The reason for the shift was simply that the development corporation could not attract sufficient investment to carry out its socially desirable but financially risky projects. Its director admitted, "The projects we now select to do are ones which the private sector can almost do without government participation" (*New York Times* 15 July 1979).

The governmental role in planning American suburbs has been even more marginal than in the redevelopment of inner cities. Granted, federal housing and transportation policies after World War II were instrumental in facilitating suburban growth; but the United States has no parallels to the regional planning efforts mounted in Europe's metropolitan centers in the 1950s. On the contrary, suburban growth in the United States is the result of private planning by commercial developers. And while the minimum standards for constructing houses and even entire subdivisions are established by local building codes and subdivision regulations, public authorities have almost no control over the timing and the scale of new development within their boundaries.

Nor is there any parallel in the United States to the systematic creation of new towns in the metropolitan regions of Europe. After a half-hearted eight-year experiment with a program to encourage new towns, the U.S. Department of Housing and Urban Development (HUD) in 1978 gave up the effort. At its close, one commentator called the program "a disaster whose magnitude surprised even the program's harshest critics" (Evans and Rodwin, p. 90). Never did this experiment put the kind of public power or public money behind the new communities that European governments have committed to their new towns. Instead, like the urban renewal program, it relied on private developers. Federal support for the program was limited to backing the bonds that builders sold to raise the money they needed.

Launched in 1970, when the housing market was still booming, the new towns program ran into problems that are typified by the example of Newfields, one of the federally assisted new towns started near Dayton, Ohio, by a millionaire housing developer. He assembled the 4000-acre tract and secured federal backing for his borrowing in late 1973. The next year construction started, but it quickly became clear that the developer's sales revenue simply could not keep pace with expenses. Because it was built from scratch, Newfields tied up vast amounts of money and a large tract of land for a long time before it could begin to generate revenues. Prospective buyers were not eager to invest before they actually saw the community taking shape. Moreover, the housing boom slowed down in the mid-1970s as interest rates rose, and federal housing subsidies were curtailed by the Nixon administration. By the time the developer abandoned the project in late 1975, he had borrowed $18 million—

loans for which HUD was ultimately responsible. The government had no choice but to take the project into receivership, scale it down, and look for another developer to buy it.

Public Ownership of Land

Surveying the historical contrasts between European and American city planning, we must note the tremendous importance of the different attitudes toward public land ownership on the two continents. Owning large tracts of land enables public officials not only to decide how specific parcels should be developed, but also to time development so that it fits with the provision of public services. European municipalities have vigorously pursued this course of action in order to control urban growth; American cities have not.

Stockholm has the largest land bank of any metropolitan area in Western Europe. At the turn of the century, the Stockholm city council embarked on a program to purchase outlying land for future expansion. Ironically, the impetus for the initial decision came not from the Social Democratic party, but from a Conservative party banker and financier on the city council. In 1904 the council began buying large areas of farm and forest area on the open market. Gradually, the city's holdings grew, with the greatest period of acquisitions in the 1960s. The city's acquisitions, totaling 138,000 acres since 1904 (Strong, p. 43), now range over the entire metropolitan area, with two thirds of the land lying outside Stockholm's city limits, within suburban jurisdictions. Once acquired by the city, these lands are almost never resold; rather, private parties who wish to develop the tracts must negotiate long-term leases with the municipal government. In negotiating the leases, the city requires that any development conform to the town plan. The extent of municipal ownership in the region thus provides city officials with significant control over new development. Furthermore, Stockholm's leasing system is a money-making proposition; the city earns more than enough from its leases to pay off the debts it has incurred in buying the land (Ratzka).

Dutch municipalities began land banking even before the Swedes, with Amsterdam's first purchase in 1896. In the Dutch case, as in the Swedish, initial support for land banking came from the business community. The completion of the North Sea Canal in 1874 brought rapid growth in shipping and industry to the major cities of the Randstad, and the merchants who dominated the powerful Liberal party viewed public land acquisition as the only way to build housing fast enough to accommodate the migrants flooding into the cities (Strong, p. 103). Traditionally, it has been relatively easy for Dutch cities to acquire surrounding agricultural land for planned urban expansion; municipalities could do so at a price only slightly above the existing use value.

Within cities, however, authorities have had more restricted powers of expropriation. In city centers expropriation could at first be used only to condemn "unfit" housing or to make room for public projects, not to gain land for resale to private developers. However, the war damage suffered in several Dutch cities brought modifications of this rule. In the years immediately following World War II, cities were given exceptional emergency powers to acquire large tracts of war-damaged land within their boundaries in order to rebuild. This special authorization was granted to several municipalities, some of which (Rotterdam, for example) opted to sell the land back to private entrepreneurs once it had been cleared. Amsterdam, on the other hand, acquired land, prepared it for rebuilding, and then leased most of it out on long-term contracts. This policy may be accounted for, at least in part, by the fact that the Amsterdam city council in the late 1940s and early 1950s, having Labor and Communist party components, leaned further to the left than other Dutch city councils.

The success of the postwar programs, along with a growing sense of urgency regarding urban renewal, led the national government in the Physical Planning Law of 1965 to ease restrictions on municipal expropriations. The 1965 legislation provided that a municipality could expropriate any land in the city center with the approval of the crown, so long as the site was included in an approved development plan. Thus, local governments are no longer prevented from acquiring any city tract, although they are restrained by a cumbersome appeal process, generous compensation provisions, and the problem of relocating displaced tenants. By the early 1970s the scope of the Dutch cities' acquisitions was so great that in one year 83 percent of new development was on land bought or leased from municipalities (Strong, p. 106).

Although only a small proportion of public purchases in the Netherlands is by eminent domain, the issue of land expropriation is politically sensitive. In fact, a dispute over expropriation procedures actually toppled the national government of Prime Minister Joop Den Uyl in March 1977. The five-party coalition, which had been in power since 1973, fell apart over the issue of how much money local governments should have to pay owners whose land they expropriated. The leftist Labor party argued that the more centrist Catholic People's party wanted to give too much protection to landowners, while the centrists accused the leftists of seeking to give local governments too much power over compensation.

From the American perspective, one of the most interesting European cases is the French adoption of land banking policies in 1958. France came to land banking much later than its neighbors, largely because its political tradition places a strong value on private property ownership. In the words of Albin Chalandon, Gaullist minister of public construction,

> The principal enemy of urbanism is the Frenchman's attachment to ownership of land. . . . A "municipalization" or, more precisely, a "collectivization" of land of a progressive and rational sort, which is the only definitive solution of the problem, is too utopian to wish tc realize instantaneously (Strong, p. 140).

As a compromise that would be acceptable within the framework of French political culture, the Gaullists devised an intriguing system based not on large-scale public purchase of land, but rather on a limited amount of public acquisition supplemented by a public *option* to purchase. According to this system, a local government anticipating new development in a particular area can designate a specific tract of land as a zone for priority urbanization (or "ZUP") and establish a detailed plan for its development. The locality may then acquire a small portion of the zone through eminent domain. But, rather than buy all of the land outright, the local government reserves for a period of four years its option to buy any of the land within the zone that might henceforth be offered for sale. Thus, if an owner declares an intent to sell his land for development that violates the municipal plan for the zone, the municipality can buy him out first in order to prevent that development. Since the price to be paid by the municipality is fixed on the date when the zone is first designated, the landowner is likely to get less from the municipality than from a private buyer. This circumstance gives authorities considerable leverage over development, even though the bulk of land transactions remains in private hands.

In 1968 the French government authorized a second type of development zone, this time giving local governments the power to designate zones and then turn the responsibility for planning and development over to a private developer (this second type of zone is known as a "ZAC"). The private developer may invoke the power of eminent domain to buy land, but does not enjoy the option-to-buy that local governments may exercise in the ZUPs. All of the new towns established in the Paris metropolitan region from 1966 to 1975 were built as either ZUPs or ZACs.

How widespread is the use of land banking by American municipalities? Despite a lively interest in the idea among planning professionals, its use is extremely limited. Public landownership in the United States is heavily concentrated in remote areas; very little public land lies within major metropolitan areas. With the exception of New York State's short-lived effort to use its statewide Urban Development Corporation to build new communities from scratch, there has been virtually no suburban land banking by public authorities that could seriously influence development patterns. Within cities, municipal governments have often used their power of eminent domain for urban redevelopment, but only to assemble individual project sites which are then sold to private developers as quickly as possible. Typically, a city expropriates land not to restrain or control development, but rather at the behest of a private developer who has selected a specific site for investment. In return for the much needed investment, the city acts as the developer's agent, assembling the site for him by using its power of expropriation. Normally, the only land parcels remaining in municipal ownership are those for which no private buyer can be found.

GUIDING URBAN GROWTH

INSTRUMENTS

What are the instruments wielded by European planners in exercising their formidable influence over urban growth and development? In this section we will examine the main regulatory devices available to them, and contrast these with the weaker planning controls in the United States. Probably the most important characteristic of Europe's more successful planning efforts is its combination of land-use planning with transportation planning. Government actions in one sector reinforce those in the other.

Most local governments in Europe are responsible for drawing up plans that project land-use patterns in their communities, and for monitoring all construction to see that it conforms to such plans. Residential neighborhoods, industrial plants, recreational areas, and all public infrastructure are subject to municipal control, and the linkages among the various types of land use are considered in issuing building permits. Local government regulates both the density and height of new development, as well as the particular use to which the land is devoted.

So far, this description of European cities sounds very similar to municipal responsibilities in the United States. Most American communities, especially large ones, have developed land-use plans which are expected to guide public decisions on building new infrastructure and issuing permits for private construction. However, because they lack the advantages of land banking, public planners in the United States have had to rely on the *zoning ordinance,* a device that has very limited utility either for planning new development or for controlling development that is already underway. The zoning ordinance, a statute which restricts the types of construction that are acceptable on a particular parcel of land, is a classic example of a reactive instrument. Clearly, the aim of the zoning ordinance is to encourage conformity with already existing use patterns; though zoning may prevent unacceptable structures, it cannot provide an adequate framework for planning new developments.

Moreover, it would be difficult to argue convincingly that zoning really constitutes an expression of "public purpose" in American cities. Although the zoning ordinance is adopted and enforced by public officials, the nature of the device is such that it operates on the urban fringe to enforce conformity to a set of private decisions made by commercial developers. Large-scale builders frequently plan a development which violates existing zoning codes. Then they launch a campaign to persuade the local zoning board to permit the development, chalking up the legal fees involved in obtaining the variance to their development costs. A recent study of the massive land-use planning apparatus operating in suburban Suffolk County on New York's Long Island concluded that it had practically no impact at all on the county's growth: "The over-all land use pattern resulting from this process is one that would occur if there were practically no zoning at all" (Gottdiener, p. 104).

Controls on Land Speculation

Land speculation is a permanent feature of the urban real estate market in the United States. Land is a commodity which, if offered for sale at the right time and price, brings profits. One of the main factors in any kind of new development—public or private—is the cost of the land, which normally inflates as soon as news of the impending development is made public. A long-time property owner may thus reap tremendous profits, not because he has improved his property, but simply because the land he happens to occupy is desired for some new development. This phenomenon of massive price inflation preceding development is an accepted feature of the land market in the United States. Even when government expropriates land in the American system, it must pay the owner a "fair market value" which takes into account the land's development potential.

European governments, in contrast, have intervened actively in urban land markets to reduce the potential profits of speculation. They have had two primary purposes for doing so: (1) to capture for the public treasury some of the inflation in land values that occurs in improving areas, and (2) to ensure that when local governments buy land for public purposes, they do not have to pay prices that have been inflated by speculation. We will examine in turn the instruments most commonly used to pursue each of these goals.

The device used to accomplish the first purpose is a "betterment tax" levied on the difference between the value of a property in its present use and its value if it is used in a more profitable way. For example, West Germany's 1971 Urban Development Law stipulated that when local governments completed urban renewal projects, the property owners in the renewal district would have to pay a betterment tax equal to the difference between the original site value and the new site value. This is known as a 100 percent levy, because it amounts to the entire profit that the owner would otherwise realize from the inflation of his property. Compared to some other European betterment taxes, Germany's is quite limited in scope, as it applies only to urban renewal districts where it is reasonably certain that government investments caused the inflation to occur.

In 1975 the Social Democratic party (SPD) actually moved to extend the betterment tax to *all* unearned increments in land value, not just those occurring in renewal districts. The SPD's intitial proposal was for a 100 percent levy, but opposition arose from the Free Democratic party (FDP), the socialists' coalition partner in the government. Not only did the FDP balk at the 100 percent figure, but also the government anticipated strong resistance from the *Bundesrat,* the conservative upper house in Germany's parliamentary system. As a compromise, the proposal was changed to a 50 percent levy, but even this diluted version met resistance. Ultimately, the government withdrew the proposal altogether.

The most determined proponent of the betterment levy in Europe is undoubtedly Britain's Labour party. Three times since World War II, Labour governments have experimented with mechanisms to obtain some of the profits of land development for the public treasury. Under the 1947 Town and Country Planning Act, the Labour party levied a 100 percent tax on unearned increments in land value. Obviously, this tax eliminated the incentive for land speculation by private real estate developers. The Conservative government which took office in 1951 declared that the Labour party's policy placed far too great a restraint on private capital, with the result that the activities of private developers were severely hampered. In 1953 the Conservatives abolished the betterment tax, and by 1959 they had lifted *all* restrictions on development, leaving land to trade at its full market value even in transactions involving the government.

After Labour returned to power in 1964, the government reinstituted restrictions, this time in the form of a Land Commission, a national corporation that began in 1967 to buy up land which was intended for development. The commission paid the owner the existing use price, plus a *percentage* of the value increase that was expected to result from development. The new policy differed from the earlier betterment tax in that the government captured only 40 percent of the increase in value instead of the entire increase. Then, once again, the incoming Conservative government of 1970 scrapped the Labour policy.

Returning to power in 1974, Labour tried a somewhat different strategy to capture development values. The Community Land Act of 1975 sought to move Britain toward a system in which *all* land scheduled for development or redevelopment by any party would first have to pass through the hands of the local government. This "municipalization" would allow governments either to retain land for public projects or to resell it to private developers who agreed to abide by the local authority's land-use plan. Since the authority would buy the land from the seller at its existing use value and then resell it at the higher market value, it would capture for the community all of the value increase. However, Britain's economic problems in the late 1970s prevented this scheme from taking off. In the first two years of operation, less than four square miles of land was acquired by local authorities under the plan (Department of Environment), which in any case was repealed by Conservatives when they regained office in 1979.

The second purpose of European government intervention in land markets has been to relieve governments themselves of the necessity to pay inflated prices for land. The most imaginative approach to this problem is that of the French "zones for deferred development," or "ZADs." This device was created by the French parliament in 1962 to complement the already existing ZUPs. Under the law, a municipality, a regional prefect, or a national ministry can designate a tract of land lying in the path of development as a ZAD. Having created the zone, public authorities then enjoy a fourteen-year option to buy any land within its boundaries that is offered for sale. The cost to the public authority is usually fixed at the value of the land one year *before* the creation of the ZAD. So appealing to public authorities was this anti-inflationary instrument that as of 1974 about 1 percent of the nation's land area had been placed in ZADs, about a third of it in the Paris region (Strong, p. 243). No one expects that all of this territory, or even most of it, will be government-owned, but the option to buy gives French municipalities and other public authorities extraordinary power over the land market, while at the same time assuring them that they will be able to buy land for public projects at uninflated prices.

Transportation Planning

The single most important influence on urban form in the twentieth century has been the automobile. At the edge of growing cities, the automobile has facilitated low-density suburban sprawl, because it has freed residents of the necessity to live near mass transit lines. Within the central city, the growing dependence on the automobile since World War II has enlarged the amount of space devoted to automobiles—for roadways, parking garages, service stations, automobile dealerships, and so on—and has increased congestion in central business districts.

The first of these two effects—suburban sprawl—is much less advanced in Europe than in the United States, where car ownership rates surpass those in Europe (see Table 8.1). The second effect—central city congestion—is more pronounced in Europe, despite lower car ownership rates. That is because the shape of many European cities even today reflects medieval configurations. The spatial limitations imposed by early fortress walls resulted in densely built-up areas with narrow streets radiating from a central market district. Consequently, many European cities

TABLE 8.1 OWNERSHIP OF PASSENGER CARS, 1968 AND 1978

	Cars/1000 people		Percentage change
	1968	1978	
United States	414	540	30%
Sweden	262	346	32
France	230	328	43
West Germany	195	345	77
Britain	198	256	29
Netherlands	145	290	100

SOURCE Calculated from United Nations, *Statistical Yearbook 1969, 1979/80* (New York: United Nations, 1970, 1981).

have even worse traffic problems at their centers than those which plague American cities. Furthermore, European town centers frequently contain historical sites considered worthy of preservation, so that planners are reluctant to bulldoze through the central city to develop expressway networks that would speed auto traffic.

We have seen that several national governments in Europe have intervened to guide suburban growth in their major metropolitan regions. Recognizing that any movement of people and economic activities outward from the center increases the demand for transportation, planners in some nations have tried to coordinate transportation investments with land-use planning. The leading example is Sweden, where Stockholm's expansion program has been integrated with transportation planning since the 1940s. In fact, the initial impetus to suburban planning came when the transit company began developing plans to extend the subway into the suburbs. The so-called "finger development" that resulted from spacing suburban communities along the public transportation lines was intended not only to promote high-density development and preserve the open spaces between the lines; an equally important goal was to ensure that the transit lines, once constructed, would have a ready market to serve—a market of commuters living at sufficient densities to make it financially feasible to offer high-quality rail service.

In addition to helping guide suburban growth, mass transit is of course an important tool in minimizing auto traffic in central cities. If commuters can be persuaded to leave their automobiles at home and travel to work by train, subway, or bus, central cities will have less congestion and less need to devote space to roadways, garages, and other facilities.

In an effort to influence the cost-benefit calculations made by motorists, most European governments had begun imposing heavy costs on private driving even before the fuel crisis of 1973 and 1974, usually in the form of high taxes on gasoline, automobiles, and auto accessories. And while the costs of motoring multiplied in the 1970s, these governments took steps to provide an attractive alternative—cheap mass transit. In 1971 Stockholm introduced a bargain monthly card for use on all buses and subways in the region. In addition to this card, which costs about $17, the region's transit authority issues 175 different special fare cards to students, soldiers, senior citizens, mail carriers, airport personnel, and others. In 1975 Paris began issuing a monthly Orange Card, which, for about $14, allows the holder to ride on all buses, subways, and rail lines. By comparison, London Transport has traditionally maintained rather high fares on subways and buses, recovering over 70 percent of its cost from the fare box—compared to only 33 percent recovered in Paris (Public Technology, Inc., p. 51). In June 1981, however, the new Labour majority on the Greater London Council (GLC) announced a 25 percent reduction in subway and bus fares, thereby fulfilling a campaign pledge.

Another approach to influencing motorists' calculations is to inhibit the use of cars in cities. The British and Dutch governments since World War II have increasingly moved toward restricting auto use, with the British government meeting far stronger opposition from pro-auto interests.

Conflict over urban transportation problems emerged in Britain in the early 1960s, centering on the question of how far public authorities should go in limiting the use of the private automobile in towns. Neither Labour nor the Conservatives wanted to appear an enemy of the motor car. To Conservatives, measures to restrict motoring appeared to place intolerable restraints on individual freedoms. Labour politicians feared that increased restrictions on owning and driving cars would tend to freeze existing ownership patterns; such an outcome would clearly violate the party's concern with an equal distribution of goods in British society. The "restrictionists" therefore found no strong support in either of the major political camps.

In 1963 a national commission appointed to review the growing problem of auto traffic in towns concluded that British motorists would not tolerate serious restrictions on their driving, and that urban congestion could be tackled only by building road networks that would accommodate increased traffic while segregating high speed traffic from secondary traffic by the use of tunnels, bridges, and barriers. The report, in short, advised massive reconstruction of British cities to accommodate automobiles, warning against trying to curtail motorists' freedom:

> A car-owning electorate will not stand for a severe restriction. And even if a severe restriction could be got on to the statute book, it would be almost impossible to enforce. It is a difficult and dangerous thing in a democracy to try to prevent a substantial part of the population from doing things that they do not regard as wrong; black markets and corruption are the invariable fruit of such attempts at prohibition (Buchanan et al, p. 3).

When planners in London tried to apply the policies outlined in the commission's report, however, they discovered that adapting the city to the automobile in this way entailed costs, both financial and political, that were too high. In line with the commission's conclusions, both Labour and Conservative majorities in the GLC supported the construction of a massive system of four ring roads successively farther from the center of the city, combined with a series of radial arteries to bring traffic from the ring down into the city. Yet the strong opposition from community groups against the enormous construction projects, coupled with the tremendous cost of the enterprise, finally led to the plan's abandonment. Instead, the GLC settled for the much less ambitious—though far less expensive—alternative of increased parking restrictions to discourage motorists from driving into town.

The Dutch have been especially sensitive to the problems presented by the automobile. Given that the Netherlands is the most densely populated nation in Western Europe, it is not surprising that the Dutch were among the first to recognize the devastating consequences that the automobile could have on city centers (Valderpoort), and to take measures to restrict auto traffic. In 1972 the national government cut highway expenditures by over $20 million, in spite of the politically damaging 15 percent reduction in road construction employment. Then, in 1973, the government introduced legislation to require a deposit of about $90 on each new car sold in the Netherlands. The deposit, which was to be refunded upon receipt of proof that the car had been scrapped, was obviously intended to discourage people from abandoning old cars; in addition, however, it was expected to inhibit the growth of automobile ownership. The government evinced determination to withstand the political pressure generated by the scheme, then pushed the measure through despite official protest from the Association of Dutch Municipalities that the idea was unworkable and posed too great an administrative burden.

No Dutch city has yet banned cars entirely, but more than a dozen have set up large pedestrian zones within which automobiles are prohibited. Most of these zones are in commercial districts; the most celebrated example is probably the Lijnbaan, a shopping mall in central Rotterdam. Dutch cities have also pioneered an innovation in urban design known as the *woonerf*—a residential area where autos are not banned, but their movement is severely restricted, while the street is converted into an extension of living and play space for residents. The streets within the *woonerven* are modified in ways that limit the speed of motorists—for example, by humps in the roadway, sharp bends and narrow sections, and street furniture.

In the United States, the greater reluctance of local governments to impose restrictions on motorists must be understood in the context of the more limited systems of mass transit. In most American cities, motorists simply do not have the option of public transit that is convenient and reasonably priced. Like their European counterparts, some of the older cities on the east coast of the United States (for instance, Boston, New York, Philadelphia), which had assumed their urban character before the advent of the internal combustion engine, do possess functioning rapid-rail transit systems. In New York, which has by far the most extensive subway system of any American city, over half of all persons entering and leaving the downtown area for work each day travel by mass transportation. New York, however, is the exception rather than the rule in American urban transportation; it is one of only six American cities now operating rail transport networks. The more common pattern has been the degeneration and finally the phasing out in the 1930s and 1940s of once viable street railway and rapid transit systems. In fact, collective transportation in American cities was at its peak at the turn of the century, when most major cities had several competing transit companies. Numerous factors—including increased operating expenditures, massive indebtedness incurred in mergers, and legal constraints requiring fixed fare schedules—contributed to the financial squeeze on street railway companies that began about 1910. One of the most important factors was the emergence of transit holding companies. These private businesses, which virtually determined the direction that urban transportation would take for decades in many American cities, offer an excellent illustration of the impact of private decisions on American urban society.

One such company was National City Lines, which in a ten-year period (1938 to 1947) managed to acquire control over forty-six transit systems in forty-five cities. The investment capital for these acquisitions was supplied by a group of motor interests that included General Motors, Firestone, and Standard Oil of California. In return for the capital, the holding company negotiated ten-year contracts specifying that its transit lines would purchase vehicles and supplies only from the companies furnishing the money. The agreement between the parties was "to further the sale of and create an additional market for the products of suppliers . . . to the exclusion of products competitive therewith" (Smerk, p. 50). In other words, the holding companies bought out streetcar lines with the intention of replacing them with passenger buses. Many cities lost their street railway networks through such private business agreements in the 1930s and 1940s.

Even in cities where mass transit systems survived, they faced increasing competition from the automobile, encouraged by massive highway construction in and around cities after World War II. Between 1950 and 1970 the annual vehicle miles of service provided by buses and trolleys dropped by over 30 percent nationally. By 1970 almost three quarters of all mass transit passengers in the United States were concentrated in only the twelve largest metropolitan areas (Gorham and Glazer, pp. 283 and 293), and residents of the vast majority of American cities did not even have a realistic alternative to the automobile.

Having lost much of their mass transit network between the 1940s and 1960s, American cities now have difficulty reviving them, because land-use patterns have changed in ways that make mass transit less viable. Residential development and business activity have dispersed into low density suburbs around the major cities. To be financially viable, mass transit, as its name implies, requires a large number of people living along the route to patronize the service regularly. But daily trip patterns are now so widely dispersed in most American metropolitan areas that it is impossible to consider superimposing mass transit lines on these regions. Traffic densities simply do not justify the expense. In short, land-use patterns based on the automobile, once in place, discourage the development of mass transit.

The Role of National Governments in City Planning

Compared to American public authorities, European governments have more numerous and more powerful instruments at their command to influence urban development. In particular, we have noted their ability to discourage speculation in urban land and their methods of discouraging automobile traffic in towns. But how is it that European planners have been able to use tools which are so seldom used by their American counterparts? Are European local officials simply more aggressive and more enlightened in pursuing the public interest?

Of course, the answer is no. In Europe, as in the United States, local officials tend to view problems from a local perspective, which is strongly colored by the views of their local constituents. Because their first concern is with the welfare of their own community, issues of regional and national balance remain secondary. They are as little disposed to contain development or to restrain automobile use as are American city officials.

The great difference lies in the much stronger role in urban planning played by the national governments in Europe. In most European nations, the responsibility for urban planning is shared by authorities at the national and local levels. Typically, city officials devise a comprehensive land-use scheme for which they must seek the approval of the appropriate national ministry. Obviously, European cities obtain significant financial and political support for this comprehensive planning effort from the national governments, many of which have formulated national urbanization policies. In Europe the national governments have recognized that they have a stake in controlling the location, the pace, and the character of city growth within their borders. In the United States, it is true, many federal and state programs have influenced urban development—some quite dramatically (for example, tax and transfer policies, and the FHA mortgage guarantee). Yet their impact on cities has been largely unplanned; any conscious efforts to guide development in metropolitan regions have been made by local authorities.

Compared to national officials in the United States, European national policy makers have the obvious advantage of operating within political cultures which are much more conducive to public planning than is the American milieu:

> Hierarchical social and political systems, where the governing class is accustomed to govern, where other classes are accustomed to acquiesce, and where private interests have relatively less power, can more readily evolve urban and regional growth policies at the national level than systems under the sway of the market, local political jurisdictions, or egalitarian political processes (Berry 1973, p. 180).

How is this national interest in urban development reflected in European policy? First, national governments have intervened to try to restrain competition among cities and regions, and to redress some of the imbalance created by that competition. The well-known cases of regional planning for Europe's metropolitan areas (for example, London, Stockholm, Paris) have typically been stimulated by *national* initiatives. Some national governments have gone so far as to pass legislation discouraging localities from competing with one another for business by offering tax concessions to firms to relocate their plants; Germany is an example (Boesler, p. 218). The greater leverage which European governments exercise in promoting cooperation among localities has much to do with the larger national subsidies to local governments.

Money is also the key to national influence on the land-use and transportation decisions made by local governments. Obviously, the ability of local governments to acquire large tracts of land depends on having the necessary funds. France's extensive land banking program relies heavily on national funding. While municipalities select the sites for ZUPs, the finances for most zones are handled by public/private companies (*sociétés d'économie mixte*) whose loans come primarily from France's Central Savings Bank. Typically, 65 percent of the capital invested in these public/private development companies comes from government sources (Underhill, p. 32), and control over the companies tends to be exercised by national officials in collaboration with private lenders.

National governments may influence local land acquisitions not only by direct lending, but also by their authority to control local borrowing. In the Netherlands, for example, municipalities in theory have the responsibility for managing growth, including the acquisition of land. But since localities cannot borrow money for such purchases without provincial and national approval, their plans must take account of national planning objectives.

National initiatives have been crucial to building and preserving mass transit systems as well. Stockholm's metropolitan transportation authority would never have been established without national intervention in 1965. It was the national government's pledge to furnish 60 percent of the funds for the new subway extensions that persuaded the city and suburban governments to cooperate in transportation planning (Anton, p. 109).

The contributions which the national governments in Europe have made toward solving the burdensome problems of local traffic congestion have not been confined to handing out subsidies to city administrators. National administrators have also played more active roles at the local level. At a minimum, they have acted as mediators in deadlocked local disputes. On other occasions, however, they have promoted schemes that, because of political implications, could not reasonably have been promoted by local officials. An illustration of active national concern for local traffic problems is found in Paris. Even though it is one of the most intensively used subway systems in the world, the Paris métro still suffers from financial problems. Studies of both the bus and subway systems in Paris showed that during the 1960s mass modes were constantly losing ground to the private automobile. By 1970, passenger fares were covering only about half the cost of maintaining public transportation, the deficit being made up by government funds, with a full 70 percent of that operating deficit being shouldered by the French national government. National concern was heightened by the observation that Paris's elected city council was showing reluctance to take unpopular steps against private car owners, even in the face of what is perhaps the worst traffic congestion in the world. For example, the first parking meters appeared in Paris only in 1971, and many city streets still have no parking meters.

Parisian city officials not only appeared to lack the political will to confront their car-driving constituents; they were also making little visible progress toward improving subway facilities, despite periodic public declarations about future plans. Finally, in February 1970, the national transport minister seized the initiative on the question of mass transit by supporting the controversial *taxe d'équipement.* This was a proposal which had initially surfaced in the National Assembly several months earlier under Communist sponsorship. The premise was a simple one: Collective modes of transportation provided benefits for Parisian businesses by enlarging both the labor and consumer markets on which they could draw; therefore, businesses ought to contribute to financing mass transit. Transport Minister Raymond Mondon was uncertain as to the best method of imposing the obligation on business—whether to base the assessment on the amount paid in salaries by an employer, the volume of business, or the number of employees. Nevertheless, Mondon saw the *taxe* as "simple and at the same time productive." The proposal was immediately denounced by Paris merchants and manufacturers, but the national government continued to pursue the idea under its new transport minister, Jean Chamant, and in July 1971 Parisian businesses employing nine or more people began paying a tax that was equivalent to 1.7 percent of their firm's payroll to help put mass transit back on its feet. In June 1973 the law was extended to cover eight provincial cities with populations of 500,000 or more. The *taxe d'équipement* was a controversial measure whose promotion depended on national political "muscle"; in all likelihood the tax would never have been introduced by the city council on its own. Thus it illustrates the important role played by national officials in urban transportation decisions.

WHOSE CITY?

DISTRIBUTION

Urban planning is by definition an activity with strong distributive overtones; its purpose is to influence the distribution of people and economic activities across the urban landscape. Stated slightly differently, urban planners are concerned with the allocation of urban space to different socioeconomic groups, different firms, and different land uses. Viewed from this perspective, the activities of European and American planners have had rather different effects.

European planners have concentrated their efforts on shifting population and economic activities away from congested central cities to planned suburban communities, or even to distant regions of the country where development is lagging. If we look at the kinds of economic activities and the kinds of people moving away from central cities in the postwar period, we see that they have been predominantly manufacturing firms and blue-collar workers. Britain's new towns program presents the best example. The jobs provided in new towns have tended to be manufacturing jobs. And since getting a house in a new town is normally tied to getting a job in the community, the residents of Britain's new towns are, disproportionately, skilled industrial workers. Suburban and new town development around Paris has followed the same pattern; the factories located at the edge of the city are surrounded by working-class residential developments. In fact, the industrial suburbs of Paris are sometimes called the city's "red belt," because of the support they deliver to Communist candidates.

It has been much more difficult for public authorities to decentralize office jobs away from the central cities. Powerful forces in the 1960s combined to increase the growth and concentration of corporate management, banking, insurance, finance, marketing, and advertising in central cities. In the late 1960s Paris tried to tighten its restrictions on the construction of office buildings in the city, but proved unable to stem the tide (Sundquist, p. 138). Britain's national government in 1964 tried to impose controls on office development in London and then in Birmingham similar to the controls that had helped decentralize manufacturing from London. Would-be developers were required to obtain a permit from the national government as well as the normal planning permission from the local authority. This permit system proved ineffective, however, because the ministry dispensing the permits had great difficulty distinguishing between offices that needed a central location and those that did not, and so gradually the system was dismantled (Sundquist, p. 76). The Netherlands has had a similar experience—greater success in luring manufacturers to suburban developments than in luring office developers.

It is not surprising, then, that while large numbers of factory workers have moved to the suburbs, central cities in Europe continue to house significant numbers of middle-class office workers. Indeed, central city residential districts are often the most desirable locations in a metropolitan region, and are therefore populated by middle-class and even upper-middle-class professionals who can afford the high rents. The less affluent are relegated to the edge of the city. One outspoken critic of Parisian urban planning labeled the workers who inhabit Parisian suburbs "the victims of commuting and of the dormitory suburbs" (Lojkine in Harloe, p. 152).

The distribution of population and economic activities in American metropolitan areas shows certain similarities with that in Europe, but also some striking contrasts. Central cities in the United States have also lost manufacturing firms to suburban locations, and public policy has contributed to that trend. The interstate highway system has made it cheaper and more convenient for manufacturers to locate their plants outside congested central cities, and federal tax policies favoring new construction over rehabilitation have encouraged manufacturers to move their plants to the metropolitan periphery rather than rebuild them in central locations. A second similarity is that American cities have retained their appeal for corporate headquarters and for the service industries—finance, insurance, real estate, and so on. These activities still require face-to-face contacts and therefore cannot be easily decentralized (Perloff in Leven).

The obvious difference in the postwar development of American and European metropolitan areas is in the allocation of residential space to the middle and lower classes. Suburban communities in the United States have been built primarily for middle- and upper-middle-class residents, while central cities are home to the society's working class and unemployed poor. The contributions made by public policy to this distribution pattern are well known; the FHA program, which exerted a strong influence over postwar housing development, favored middle-income buyers and suburban locations. The federal public housing program, on the other hand, concentrated its low-rent projects almost exclusively in central cities. The Interstate Highway System encouraged movement to the suburbs, by providing cheap transportation between outlying communities and central employment districts. Even the federal tax code increased the appeal of the suburbs to middle-income taxpayers, who could deduct both interest payments and property taxes paid on new suburban homes. As suburbanization continued through the 1960s and 1970s, more working-class Americans migrated to the suburbs, following the outflow of manufacturing jobs. Large residential districts in aging inner cities, especially in the Northeast and Midwest, have become the exclusive preserve of the unemployed poor. Gradually over the postwar period, the central cities have became business districts, dominated by skyscraper office buildings and ringed by decaying neighborhoods populated by those who could not afford to "escape" to the suburbs.

A large proportion of the people left behind were, of course, minorities. The very large concentration of blacks, Hispanics, and other minorities in the inner city has complicated planning issues in the United States compared with Europe. Moreover, there can be no doubt that racism accelerated the flight of many residents and businesses out of the inner cities. As large districts became identified as minority areas, they lost their appeal to white residents. But, having come to dominate these areas of the city, minority communities found that they had gained little except control over deteriorating houses and dying businesses.

Among the European countries, only Britain has experienced similar problems. In the large cities there, growing numbers of immigrants from Britain's former colonies are clustered in inner city neighborhoods, including blacks from Africa and the West Indies and Asians from India and Pakistan. These people began migrating to British cities after World War II to work on subways and buses, in textile mills and hospital laundries, and on sanitation crews; as their numbers increased, they became more visible in urban neighborhoods and aroused growing concern—both from leftists who worried that they were taking jobs from British workers, and from conservatives who worried about law and order and, in the words of Margaret Thatcher, about "being swamped by people with a different culture." Especially during periods of economic hardship in Britain, racial tensions have broken into open street fighting. As in the United States, minorities in Britain tend to live in the most economically depressed parts of the city.

Other European countries have experienced similar difficulties, but on a much smaller scale. In some Dutch cities, for example, Indonesian immigrants have come into conflict with police, and in France many of the Algerians who were granted French citizenship following Algerian independence in 1962 still live in run-down shacks at the edges of the large cities. But in the inner cities of Continental Europe, we see few parallels to the takeover of whole districts by poor minority groups in the United States and, increasingly, in Britain. On the contrary, the central districts of most European cities remain prime residential locations for middle- and upper-middle-class families.

However, one trend which is common to the cities of both Europe and the United States is the increasing share of inner city housing that is occupied by the elderly. Often living alone, they require a high level of services; yet they have disproportionately low incomes, with little to invest in improving their homes. As a result, the urban elderly are often concentrated in deteriorating districts.

Within the past decade, to the surprise of many observers, we have seen signs that some of the inner city neighborhoods that were earlier abandoned by the middle classes are now beginning to attract them again. The persistence of white-collar employment in central business districts, along with soaring fuel and housing costs in the suburbs, has led many middle-class whites to move back to the city, reclaiming areas that had been left to low-income families. Typically, the influx of the new "gentry" into these neighborhoods has been accompanied by large investments in the rehabilitation of houses and in improvements to community facilities. As a consequence, housing values and rent levels in such "gentrified" areas have risen markedly, and the lower-income residents often find themselves displaced by newcomers who are able to pay the inflated prices.

In effect, this process redistributes space in central city neighborhoods, taking it away from long-term residents and allocating it to more affluent newcomers. The trend was observed in the 1970s in both British and American cities (Laska and Spain; Hamnett and Williams), and its critics have charged that in many cases the actions of local government actually contribute to the redistributive process. Public grants to home buyers for rehabilitation and public investments in community improvements both contribute to making such neighborhoods more attractive to the middle class. Criticisms of this kind and appeals to government to intervene to prevent displacement of the poor have provoked very little response from local officials. The reason is obvious. The vitality of the local economy and by extension the vitality of the local tax base are improved by an influx of middle-income residents. Thus, it is simply not in the interest of local officials to discourage such an influx. On the contrary, they have everything to gain by encouraging the trend, if necessary by investing public money to attract middle-income residents.

The gentrification of urban neighborhoods is only one illustration of the undeniable convergence of the interests of city government and those of the city's dominant economic groups. City governments throughout Europe and the United States depend in some measure on tax revenues generated from profitable businesses and from middle-class residents, and city officials must therefore put a high priority on attracting and retaining those groups in the city. But how far should local governments go to accommodate the preferences of key businesses and affluent residents?

One school of political scientists in Europe and the United States—the so-called neo-Marxist school—has portrayed public planners as the agents of the dominant economic classes in cities, and urban public policy as simply an extension of the interests of those classes (Castells; Harloe; Harvey; Walton.). In many ways this case is more easily made for the United States than for Europe. Few observers of urban development policies in American cities would dispute neo-Marxist claims that the key function of local government in the American system has been to influence the distribution of economic growth (Molotch), and that the main impact of land-use planning in American cities has been to adapt land-use patterns to the needs of production and exchange (Mollenkopf). The direct influence of developers and business interests on urban policy is in fact institutionalized in the policy process, for the legal and political frameworks within which American city planners operate require that they constantly consult and accommodate the important private development interests in the city. In fact, American public planning can be seen in large part as a mechanism for facilitating and protecting private development activity (Barnekov and Rich).

The argument that public planners operate simply as tools of the city's dominant economic interests is not so convincing for European cities, mainly because their planning process is somewhat different. Typically in Europe, the activities of public planners have very low visibility in the urban community, and so planners do not experience the same degree of pressure from either powerful private interest groups or from citizen lobbies that American planners must continually confront. And, since conflict over planning issues is often confined to debate within and among administrative bodies, the European city planner is typically less responsive to external pressures. This has been particularly true in Continental Europe, where municipal bureaucrats (as distinct from elected officials) enjoy very high status and play the dominant decision-making role. But even in Britain, where local politics more closely resembles the American scene, the Chamber of Commerce, labor unions, and other organized economic interest groups have much less influence on land-use and development planning than in the United States (Elkin).

The relationship between local governments and local interest groups is strongly influenced by the extent of national intervention in local affairs. Because European national governments supervise many of the activities of the local governments, local officials often take on the additional role of agent for the national government in the community. While it may limit their administrative options, this link to national agencies may also provide a political "backstop" for local officials in their dealings with local pressure groups.

The political economists who employ a neo-Marxist framework do not necessarily presume that there is overt, direct manipulation of local officials by the capitalist class. Their analysis posits instead the existence of an ideology shared by planners with the capitalist class. The ideology, which reinforces class power, need not even be consciously recognized by the public officials who apply it. An example of this analytical perspective is Manuel Castells' criticism of the Parisian urban renewal program for its emphasis on office development as opposed to housing. Castells does not claim that developers exerted direct influence over public planners. Rather, he asserts that the view which public officials held of their own interests coincided almost perfectly with the interests of developers (Castells, p. 317–320).

The neo-Marxists' model of urban politics, in which the interests and priorities of capitalists are translated almost mechanically into public policy, no matter who is in power, is consistent with the findings of much research on local politics done in the 1960s and 1970s. Studies of the factors influencing urban policy have overwhelmingly concluded that the political orientation of the group in power in local government is not an important determinant of policy outputs (Fried).

Given the failure of most researchers in the field to establish linkages between party politics and local policy, should we conclude that local politics is moribund in the cities of Europe and the United States? Such a conclusion would be premature. Instead, we see local political conflicts increasingly fought outside the bounds of traditional party politics. The phenomenon of the single-issue citizens' protest group, unaffiliated with any established party and formed on an ad hoc basis, has long been a feature of American local politics. Such groups have recently become common in Europe as well. Typically, they take the form of territorial coalitions of residents whose space is threatened by government action. In Germany, for example, civic action groups known as *Burgerinitiativen* have sprung up in virtually every big city in response to public redevelopment projects. In Munich such groups have been formed to protest demolitions of housing and to stop the *Land* (state) government from building on the grounds of a city park. In Hamburg groups have protested against the disruptions caused by new highway construction, and against the planned construction of a nuclear power plant north of the city (Sorensen, p. 7). After a celebrated, decade-long struggle in London, citizens' groups finally forced the GLC to abandon its plan for a massive new road network (Hart, Thomson). In Amsterdam the city's urban renewal program has engendered resistance from dozens of campaign committees carrying such determined names as "Stay Out of Our Neighborhood" and "The Strong Arm" (Heinemeyer and Gastelaars). Even in Sweden, where public protests against government actions have been exceedingly rare, there were in the 1970s signs of citizen unrest. In Malmo, for example, a citizens' protest movement forced the abandonment of a plan to build a one hundred-foot-wide road through the center of the old city (Wiedenhoeft 1977).

In the case of the United States, the abundance of such citizen action groups has often been explained as arising from the weakness of local political parties. American political commentators have often expressed envy of European systems, because by comparison local parties in the United States "are neither ideologically oriented nor do they have a sustained social program" (Aiken, p. 111). Consequently, they do not aggregate collective interests in a social program that is sustained by an ideology.

But how do we explain the proliferation of single-issue groups in Europe, where political parties at the local level are directly tied to ideological, programmatic, national parties? Local party competition in most European cities is structured around the same party organizations and ideologies that compete at the national level. Yet the presence of strong local party organizations in Europe does not necessarily help to structure political conflict on *local* issues. Voters tend to select their party identification based on the various parties' stands on national issues rather than on local issues. Consequently, the local party organizations play a weaker role in mediating local conflicts than we might expect. In fact, it may be that these national/local linkages, so envied by Americans, actually contribute to the growing incidence of political activism outside the bounds of party politics. That is the intriguing suggestion made by one recent study of British local politics. Examining the dominance of national parties on the British local scene, the authors noted that voters tend to vote for local candidates on the basis of their party affiliation. Local issues in fact have little influence over electoral outcomes. That being the case, local politicians do not consider their electoral fortunes tied to their decisions on local issues and, as a consequence, may easily become less responsive to constituents' opinions on those issues. The authors' conclusion was that "national partisanship impedes responsive governance at the local level" (Peterson and Kantor, p. 198).

The rising tide of citizen activism in European cities can be read not only as a show of dissatisfaction with local party politics; perhaps even more significant is the implication that citizens are dissatisfied with the planners and technicians who make the important decisions. With increasing frequency, citizens' groups are asserting that the decisions made by the planning bureaucracy represent more than technical solutions to problems—they represent distributional choices about whose property is expropriated, whose street is widened for heavier traffic, and whose neighborhood is changed. These questions must ultimately lead to challenges to the political authority that planners have historically wielded.

LIMITS TO PUBLIC POWER

RESTRAINTS AND INNOVATION

One of the major policy concerns of urban planners throughout Europe and the United States in the 1980s is the extent to which they can and should influence the distribution of people and economic activities across metropolitan regions and among the various regions of the country. With increasing frequency in the United States and Britain, doubts have been voiced about the wisdom of trying to combat or even restrain the operation of market forces in urban areas. The political tide in both countries has turned in favor of giving private enterprise a freer hand to shape the economy of the nation, of cities, and, by extension, of the urban physical environment.

There are two major explanations for this free-market bias in urban public policy. One is that the fundamental trends in urban growth and development are not only universal throughout the post-industrial world, but are based on underlying economic trends that cannot easily be reversed. For example, consider the shift in the fortunes of older American cities since the 1950s, a situation that is too well known to require elaboration here. Not only have central cities lost population and jobs in the decades since 1950; since 1970 metropolitan areas as a whole have been losing growth to small towns. The United States, in short, has been witnessing a "counterurbanization" (Berry 1976). Britain shows much the same profile for the 1960s and 1970s. The dominant trend in the two most recent decades was accelerating decentralization out of central cities and even out of metropolitan areas. Central cities during this period experienced not simply slower growth than the suburbs but an absolute loss of population (Drewett in Berry 1976, p. 51).

Continental European countries have experienced this decentralization process to a lesser extent, yet signs of similar trends do exist. By the 1960s, the residential population of metropolitan areas was dispersing out of central cities to the suburban rim, and since 1970 this process has only accelerated. Thus far, however, the Continental nations have not witnessed the same shift away from metropolitan areas that both the United States and Britain have experienced. Demographers and economists explain that most of Continental Europe is at an earlier stage of industrial and urban evolution than the United States or Britain; but it can be expected to proceed in much the same direction as its economies mature (Hall and Hay; Leven in Leven; Glickman and White).

Even for Sweden, the least likely case, recent research has demonstrated that contrary to the impression of Swedish policy makers in the 1960s and 1970s, the cities were undergoing much the same process, albeit at a much more gradual rate. Population within the metropolitan regions was dispersing to the periphery; and over the country as a whole, population was growing faster in many small towns than in the metropolitan centers. Furthermore, Swedish research concludes that since regional development policy was not enacted early enough to have had a real impact on these trends, "an explanation of interregional shifts of the population must ultimately be based on an explanation of the structural changes in the economy as a whole" (Falk, p. 75). Thus the apparent breadth and depth of these trends throughout the post-industrial economies raise doubts about how much influence public planners can hope to exert over urban development.

The second reason for the emerging free-market bias is increased awareness in the late 1970s of the competition that Western countries are facing in the world market, and the consequent emphasis on productivity. The pressure on the Western economies to compete with Third World economies, where goods can be produced more cheaply, has brought the issue of economic productivity to the forefront. This trend is crucial for urban policy because it weakens the case for policies aimed at containing and redistributing growth to achieve an optimal distribution of population and economic activities within the national land area. Planning for balance and containment of urban growth is perceived by many policy makers as incompatible with an all-out effort to maximize productivity. Advocates of pro-growth policies are likely to want to give private entrepreneurs free rein to make locational decisions that maximize their productivity, regardless of whether those decisions conform to government planners' notions of the optimal distribution of people and firms. Considerations of this kind have already led the United States and Britain to shift their urban policy emphases.

In reality, this shift requires no dramatic change in U.S. policies, for American urban planning has always operated essentially to support rather than to control private market forces. The "public planning" done by city renewal authorities in the United States consists largely of furnishing support services for private real estate interests: selecting sites which the authority believes will be attractive to private capital, acquiring the sites through condemnation or purchase, and clearing them in order to resell to private developers. Local public authorities have not only provided a service to private developers in assembling redevelopment sites, but the national government has subsidized the purchase of the land by private enterprise, through the device of the "write-down." Under the 1949 Urban Renewal Act the local authority, after purchasing and clearing a site, can resell it at a price far below what they paid for it; the national government then pays the city between two thirds and three fourths of the difference between the city's expenditures (in buying, clearing, and developing the tract) and the price charged to the private developer. Frequently, this provision has allowed private developers to purchase prime city lots with several million dollars worth of federal subsidies. This subsidy system operates on the premise that the urban renewal program must compete with other forms of investment for the developers' interest and that renewal opportunities must therefore be made particularly attractive to private capital. As one federal official observed in 1960, urban renewal in the United States is "in essence private real estate development with a brief interval of government intervention" (Brownfield, p. 737).

In the 1970s the role of public planning as a complement to, and support for, private capital began to receive increased emphasis. The 1974 Housing and Community Development Act and subsequent legislation in the community development field (such as the Urban Development Action Grants, or UDAGs) emphasized the obligation of city officials to use public development funds to "leverage" private investments in cities. If this "leveraging" is to occur, then private investors must be given a central decision-making role in virtually all housing, commercial, and industrial development planning for cities. In the late 1970s, the Carter administration reinforced this trend by basing its urban policy on the premise that urban decay results from a decline in the over-all economic position of central cities in the national and world economy. Programs to aid cities therefore must focus primarily on encouraging economic growth in cities. Only weeks before he left office in 1981, President Carter received the report of his blue ribbon Commission for a National Agenda for the Eighties. Its controversial recommendations on urban policy went even further than the administration itself had gone in stressing economic growth: "The federal government's concern for national economic vitality should take precedence over the competition for advantage among communities and regions" (*Report of the President's Commission*). At a time when successes are so few and public resources so meager, the commission argued, it is futile to try to restrain the flow of private capital from the inner cities of the Northeast and Midwest to newer suburban centers and to the Sunbelt. Instead of wasting government resources trying to prop up deteriorating cities, public policy should subsidize the migration of unemployed people to locations where jobs are available. The priorities and preferences of private capital, in short, should be given free rein, regardless of the cost to the nation's aging industrial centers.

Even some of the most outspoken free marketeers in Congress, such as Republican Representative Jack Kemp of New York, balked at the harsh recommendations of the Carter commission, preferring to see local governments make an all-out effort to attract private investors through a device known as the "free enterprise zone." Cities would designate these zones in certain distressed sections, and would offer to potential business investors a package of financial incentives in exchange for their locating in the zone and hiring local workers. The incentives would include a variety of federal tax breaks—a cut in capital gains taxes, a reduction in business taxes, a huge reduction in Social Security payroll taxes, and accelerated depreciation allowances on plant and equipment. In addition, the businesses would be exempt from a range of government regulations ranging from health, safety, and environmental regulations to the minimum wage. Local governments would be expected to follow the federal example by reducing local taxes and regulations in the zone. The hope was that dramatic reduction of the burdens imposed by government taxes and regulations would lure wary investors back to the urban core. Originally put forward by conservative Republicans, the idea has been endorsed by President Reagan, but also by liberal groups including the NAACP and the Urban Coalition.

American conservatives did not invent the enterprise zone idea; they borrowed it from British Conservatives. In 1978, while still in opposition, Conservatives formulated a proposal which was later implemented when the Thatcher government came to power in 1979. Although the version ultimately inserted in the March 1980 budget fell short of the original proposal, it maintained the basic principle that areas would be designated in British cities where businesses would benefit from fifteen years' exemption from corporation tax, complete freedom from Britain's development land tax, and increased capital allowances. At the same time, the Thatcher government has moved to reduce the government's role in urban land-use planning. In distinct contrast to Labour policies, the Thatcher Conservatives are "striving to limit the state's role to providing basic unremunerative infrastructure and the facilitation of private development" (Cox, p. 276). The Thatcher government has also imposed significant cutbacks in the regional programs which had been accepted by both parties since 1945. Throughout the 1970s the national government attempted to redistribute economic activity in the nation by giving blanket aid to lagging regions and discouraging expansion in already congested regions. The Conservatives under Thatcher have abolished the Regional Economic Planning Councils, dramatically reduced the amount of aid to lagging regions, and cut back on the scope of industrial location controls.

As in the United States, the shift away from urban policies designed to constrain private market forces toward policies which support and stimulate the private market is supported by a broad spectrum of political groups. The perception is widely shared in Britain that the cities are in trouble because of the country's declining economic fortunes, and that to rebuild them one must first address the larger economic question. Even the prestigious Town and Country Planning Association, long an advocate of government control over land development, has come to the conclusion that trying to prevent the forces of decentralization at work in Britain's metropolitan areas is futile and costly. Instead, the government should support private enterprise in its move to decentralize (TCPA; see also Lawless, pp. 224–225).

So far; the Continental countries have not followed the Anglo-American lead. Even in the face of economic stagnation, European conservatives on the Continent are more reluctant to shift to a pure free-market approach than are American conservatives. This is because most conservative parties in Europe contain not only "neo-liberals" who advocate laissez-faire policies to give business interests a free hand, but also statists who see the need for firm government guidance in the economy and society. The French Gaullists provide the classic example. Even in Britain, Thatcher's neo-liberal wing of the Conservative party had to make concessions to the party's more traditional conservative elements in drawing up its urban policy (Cox, p. 289). Hence, we might expect to see considerable resistance from Continental conservatives to the notion of giving free rein to private interests in the city.

In fact, Continental European nations, whose cities have not experienced comparable levels of out-migration and urban deterioration, are pursuing containment strategies rather than the pro-growth strategies adopted by the United States and Britain. Many Continental cities have actually retreated from their expansionist policies of the 1960s, when an economic boom brought massive new construction projects in the form of offices, commercial complexes, and urban expressways. In the 1970s, growing public opposition to the "Americanization" of European cities led many city officials to give greater emphasis to preserving city centers and controlling private market trends rather than adjusting urban spaces to their requirements (Appleyard, p. 11; see also Lottman). It remains to be seen whether these policies can be maintained in the face of slowed economic growth.

* * * * *

Urban planning, then, is one of the most visible activities of government, both because it affects the physical circumstances in which people live and because it frequently brings government into direct conflict with the rights of citizens. When conflicts have arisen between private property and the interest of the community as articulated by public authorities, European planners have prevailed more regularly than American planners. Blessed with a cultural tradition that accepts public regulation and ownership of land in the city, and backed by national subsidies, local planners in Europe have not been limited to projects that generate immediate pay-offs. Hence, they have been better able to balance economic gains with other considerations such as the architectural value of historic districts and the equitable distribution of the benefits of development. Their latitude of choice may well narrow, however, if the current economic slowdown threatens the vitality of Continental cities as it has already threatened American and British cities.

9
THE CAPACITY OF LOCAL GOVERNMENTS

Throughout this volume, we have focussed on the collective choices among competing values that are reflected in public policy. This chapter will be concerned with two sets of choices—those arrived at by national governments and those arrived at by local governments. Even in nations with relatively homogeneous political cultures, we observe constant tension in intergovernmental relations between the autonomy of local governments and the power of national governments to impose their choices on localities. In all of the countries included in our study, local governments are established as separate, democratically elected units of government. Yet the growing economic interdependence among communities in the post-industrial era has created an increasingly complex set of relationships, whose primary axis is the link between national government and sub-national units.

We will explore these complex relationships by focussing on the role of local governments, whose obligations have grown dramatically in recent decades. Unfortunately, their capacity to fulfill their increased obligations has not grown proportionately; in fact, the disparity in some nations seems to be widening. In any discussion of local government's capacity to meet the demands placed on it, the main factors to be considered are financial and structural. Accordingly, we will concentrate on how local governments get their revenues and how a local government's structure influences its capacity to deliver services.

CHOICES REGARDING THE ROLE OF LOCAL GOVERNMENT

Scope and Thresholds

The most fundamental choice involving the role of local government concerns the range of services and goods to be provided locally. While that range varies substantially from nation to nation, the trend in all post-industrial societies is toward a broader range of responsibilities being assumed by local governments. Some of the growth can be attributed to the demands by local electorates for more services, but another major stimulus has been the action of national governments both in mandating more and better services throughout nations and in providing subsidies to help pay for them.

The current distress experienced by many cities in Western Europe and the United States can be attributed to local governments expanding their functions dramatically, without a corresponding increase in control over resources. Their ability to raise revenues depends on several elements that are beyond their control. By their very nature, they remain vulnerable to trends in national politics and in the national economy. At the same time, national governments have picked up an increasing share of the costs of local functions, through the device of intergovernmental transfer payments to state and local authorities.

Many observers have commented on the growing importance of national subsidies in bolstering local government budgets, concluding that local officials are losing authority over their own budgets and programs. This reasoning is consistent with predictions that have been advanced for at least thirty years about the inevitable centralization of politics in welfare states. Indeed, this centralization has even been seen by some social scientists (for example, Parsons, Deutsch) as synonymous with political development. The explanations commonly offered for this inevitable centralization include: (1) the increasing integration of national territories through advances in communication and transportation technology, (2) the accelerating concentration of private economic power into large corporations which can only be balanced by national economic policies, and (3) the relentless popular demand for more welfare programs which can only be initiated and funded on a national basis (Sharpe in Sharpe 1979, pp. 9–17). These forces and others, it is argued, have gradually and inevitably led to a decline in the importance of local jurisdictions, whose functions have been usurped by higher levels of government. In this chapter we will challenge this general line of reasoning as being too simple and mechanical an interpretation of an extremely complex set of relationships and trends.

Instruments

Increases in national transfer payments to cities and towns have not relieved localities of the need to search constantly for ways to bolster local revenues. Facing a steady increase in demand for services, local officials have only limited options for enhancing local revenues on their own. Normally, local officials are not entirely free to choose which kinds of taxes they levy or even to set tax rates. There appears, moreover, to be a universal tendency for central governments to "hog" the growth taxes, while delegating to localities the forms of taxation that are least likely to expand with an expanding economy (Sharpe in Sharpe 1981, pp. 6–14). Hence cities are caught in a squeeze between a rapid growth in the cost of supplying public services and a slower growth in the tax base. For both political and economic reasons, local tax rates cannot simply be raised indefinitely. Mayors and councils must therefore look to other revenue sources.

One source is the credit market. More and more, local governments in post-industrial nations are borrowing money from banks and other credit institutions, especially to finance capital investments. Like any other borrower, a local government must eventually pay back loans, but the constant inflation of the last decade has at least guaranteed that the debts can be repaid over time with cheaper and cheaper currency. Moreover, most national governments have taken steps to assure local governments special access to credit, either by setting up governmental lending agencies to serve local governments, or by granting tax concessions to private lenders who are willing to make loans to local governments.

Yet another approach to the problem is to improve the capacity of local government by restructuring it, typically by consolidating a group of smaller jurisdictions into a single large one. Again, this is an alternative which is really beyond the control of officials in any one community; it cannot be undertaken unilaterally and in fact has usually been initiated not by local officials, but by policy makers at higher levels of government who exert enough leverage over local governments to force cooperation.

Distribution

How have the costs and benefits of local government expansion been distributed? The answer to this question depends as much on the methods used to raise local renevues as it does on the allocation of goods and services produced by local government. Broadly speaking, local governments are not very good vehicles for promoting a redistribution of resources from more affluent to less affluent segments of the population. That particular goal of public policy is better accomplished by national programs whose impact is spread across the entire population. When local governments initiate such redistributive policies, they risk losing a portion of their tax base; firms and individuals can always move out to escape the costs of such policies.

National governments, as we will see, may choose to respond in at least two different ways to the unequal distribution of taxable wealth among local jurisdictions. The first way is to equalize local government revenues by transferring resources from the national treasury. Since national taxes are generally of a more progressive nature than local taxes, this option may have a significant redistributive impact. The other way is to try to channel economic growth into geographical areas with weaker tax bases, so that the taxable resources available to local jurisdictions are more evenly distributed.

Restraints and Innovation

At first glance, the generosity of national governments in channeling subsidies to their cities is something for which local officials and citizens should be grateful. How then do we explain the complaints so often voiced by local politicians against their benefactors? What local officials dislike about national subsidies are the accompanying "strings" which restrict the use of the money at the local level. Local policy makers may be constrained to spend transfers in ways they would avoid if granted full discretion. The degree of restraint placed on local decision makers is obviously greatest when the money comes as a conditional transfer whose use is carefully limited by law to specific projects or services. But, as we will see, national governments can also exercise significant influence over local budgets even when their grants are of an unrestricted nature. The block grant, though a recent innovation in the United States, has a longer history in Europe, though its use there has not necessarily broadened the powers of local governments.

THE GROWTH OF LOCAL GOVERNMENT IN WELFARE STATES

SCOPE AND THRESHOLDS

During the past fifty years local governments in welfare states have been assigned increasing responsibilities, which have required corresponding increases in their capacity to deliver services. The reasons for this increased reliance on local governments are rather obvious. First, national goverments have most often preferred to use local government as the vehicle for delivering the vast number of personal social services which they subsidize. Health services; special care for children, the elderly, and the handicapped; manpower training; and other human services that require face-to-face contact between clients and service-providers are most often delivered in communities by local, county, or state agencies, even when they are financially supported by national agencies. Because such services must be tailored to the characteristics and needs of specific populations, it makes sense to put them under the supervision of local authorities who know the conditions best.

Second, as governments have taken increasing responsibility for the growth and stability of the national economy, they have invested more tax dollars in the development of economic infrastructure—roads, bridges, water and sewer systems, ports, airports, and other public works projects that support and encourage economic development. Typically, these projects too are planned and executed locally. While national funding frequently depends upon national approval of local, county, or state plans, nevertheless the projects are most often initiated by local officials, who then bear the responsibility for implementation.

Third, as governments have introduced national minimum standards for the delivery of various social services, the trend has been one of "leveling up." That is, the establishment of uniform standards has tended to push the poorer, less active jurisdictions toward the standards set by the more active ones (Newton, p. 89, Sharpe in Sharpe 1981, p. 16). Naturally, this generalization applies more directly to some countries than others. By and large, the unitary governments of Europe have been more active than the U.S. government in setting uniform standards for local services and monitoring local performance. By contrast, the U.S. government has traditionally acknowledged enormous differences in the operations of local and state governments across the country—differences as fundamental as those of taxation systems and police powers. Given these wide geographical variations, federal programs have been subject to quite different eligibility requirements and benefit levels in different parts of the country. One way to interpret the rapid rise in federal aid to state and local governments in the United States from 1965 to 1973 is to see it as a temporary push on the part of federal authorities to equalize services in cities and states, especially services to residents of older industrial cities. By 1974 the price tag for this campaign to standardize services was seen by Congress and the administration as too high, and since then federal aid to state and local governments has grown much more slowly.

The range of services provided by local governments differs widely from nation to nation. Britain's local governments, for example, have assumed an extremely broad range of responsibilities, from providing the most common local services (police, fire fighters, public schools) to delivering family welfare services, consumer and environmental protection, cultural facilities, and a network of higher educational institutions known as polytechnics. One reason is the absence of any intermediate-level jurisdiction between local and national authorities to share the responsibility for delivering services (jurisdictions such as France's *départements* or Germany's *Länder*). Historically, local government in Britain was not a creation of the national government. In fact, many municipal corporations predated the formation of the central government, but were later integrated into the national system. Municipal corporations early won the right to send their own representatives to Parliament, and have never had any intermediate authorities imposed between them and the national ministries and Parliament. In the absence of any provincial, regional, or state governments, however, British local authorities must shoulder an enormous service burden.

In France local government operates altogether differently, as a hierarchical system in which intermediate units exercise a measure of administrative and financial control over the local *communes.* By the eve of the Revolution in 1789, the independence of *communes* and provinces had already seriously eroded under the determined hand of the monarchs. Napoleon's post-revolutionary regime consolidated this centralizing trend, creating in 1800 the local government system that remains largely in place today. It linked together in a hierarchical chain of command the *départements,* then the *arrondissements,* and finally the smallest level of government, the *communes.* While each of these levels has an elected council, the major administrative office in the provinces has remained the departmental prefect, who is appointed by the national Minister of the Interior.

Despite the greater degree of hierarchical control in France than in Britain, it would be a mistake to attribute the expansion of local services in France entirely to central directives. Some of the larger French cities have historically enjoyed considerable leverage over their own services. The classic example is the Paris municipal council's decision in the early twentieth century to build the *métro* (subway) against the wishes of the national government. Nevertheless, what is different from the British model is that throughout France there is an intermediate level of government, the *département,* which shares with local governments a significant part of the responsibility for local services.

Sweden offers another example of an intergovernmental system like Britain's, in which municipalities operate within a strictly unitary system of government without a strong intermediate-level jurisdiction between the central and local levels. Swedish municipalities, or corporations owned by the municipalities, operate public transportation systems, libraries, schools, hydroelectric plants, airports, harbors, theaters, and a host of health and human services for virtually all age groups. All social services in Sweden are delivered by counties or municipalities, because the national government maintains only a very small bureaucratic apparatus. Yet Sweden's national government maintains a constant, direct interest in local services, reserving for itself the power to approve local policy initiatives in the fields of land-use planning, education, public health, and welfare, as well as the power to approve all local borrowing. By far the largest share of local budgets is spent on programs prescribed by the national government; most estimates approach 80 percent. Indeed, so many local functions are mandated by national legislation that some observers consider Swedish local government merely an arm of the central administration. Ironically, Swedish localities at the same time enjoy complete freedom to determine the rate of taxation levied at the local level, a privilege that is rare among European nations. Having outlined the degree of formal authority exercised by national over local authorities in Sweden, however, we must hasten to add that in a political system marked by consensual decision making, this authority is seldom overtly imposed.

Somewhere between the British and French models of intergovernmental relations lies that of West Germany. German municipalities are among the most active in the world; they provide an even wider range of services than that provided by either British or American local governments. In addition to extensive public transportation and utilities, German cities operate warehouses, markets, slaughterhouses, and banks, and provide cultural facilities such as theaters, opera houses, museums, and conference centers. Many German cities even support orchestras, theaters, and opera companies primarily out of the city budget. The expansion of these services has come about through administrative activism, rather than through the electoral process. Professional administrators have traditionally dominated local affairs in Germany, and despite efforts made in the years immediately after World War II to encourage a more active cadre of elective officials, administrative elites remain extremely powerful.

While the variety of local services provided in Germany is probably as great as in any Western nation, we should recognize that in its federal system of government a great part of the administrative and financial responsibility for these services is shared with the state governments, or Länder. Unlike Britain, German local budgets include only 40 percent of housing expenditures, and only 24 percent of public school costs (see Table 9.1).

In the United States up to the 1930s, local and state governments received only very limited aid from Washington for their public works projects and social services. When the New Deal social programs increased the federal financial commitment to cities, they did so largely by passing funds through state governments. (Only one of the New Deal urban programs, public housing, sent support directly from Washington to the cities.) Coupled with the constitutional powers held by states controlling the types of services provided and the taxes collected by local governments, the states' ability to channel federal funds to localities gave state legislatures significant leverage over local governments. There is, of course, considerable variation in the degree to which different states have granted "home rule" powers to cities, and there is also a great deal more autonomy available to big-city politicians than to small-town officials. For example, some states carry major portions of public school budgets and even support extensive junior college systems, while others delegate those reponsibilities to local governments. Generally, the affluent states delegate more responsibility to localities than do the poor states, especially poorer Southern states.

TABLE 9.1 DISTRIBUTION OF PUBLIC EXPENDITURES BETWEEN LEVELS OF GOVERNMENT FOR SELECTED FUNCTIONS, 1971

	National Government	State Government	Local Goverment*
Environmental Resources and Primary industries			
Britain	81%	—	19%
France	76	—	24
West Germany	40	21	39
United States	78	17	4
Transport and Communication			
Britain	40%	—	60%
France	82	—	18
West Germany	44	26	30
United States	20	57	23
Education			
Britain	18%	—	82%
France	95	—	5
West Germany	12	64	24
United States	13	39	48
Police, Law, Fire, and Prisons			
Britain	20%	—	80%
France	93	—	7
West Germany	6	78	16
United States	6	23	71
Housing Subsidies and Mortgage Support			
Britain	25%	—	75%
France	78	—	22
West Germany	11	49	40
United States	25	—	75

SOURCE Werner Pommerehne, "Quantitative Aspects of Federalism: A Study of Six Countries," in Wallace Oates, ed., *The Political Economy of Fiscal Federalism* (Lexington, MA: Lexington Books, 1977), p. 314.

*For France, includes all sub-national jurisdictions (*départements, arrondissements,* and *communes*).

Gradually, through the 1950s and 1960s, more direct ties were established between the cities and Washington. This trend was emphatically reinforced by the Great Society initiatives of the 1960s, which sought to expand local services to the disadvantaged by a series of subsidy programs, many of which bypassed state governments entirely. New services were created, ranging from early childhood education to legal aid and neighborhood health care centers, while existing services were expanded.

The service burden on local government rose dramatically from the mid-1960s to the mid-1970s, fueled by the expansion of intergovernmental assistance (Peterson in Gorham and Glazer, p. 59).

Given the proliferation of services and the gradual "leveling up" in the quality of local services throughout welfare states, it is hardly surprising that local government expenditures have risen as well. A study by the Council of Europe in the mid-1970s surveyed local finances in thirteen European nations and concluded: "The dominant characteristic is the steady evolution of local authorities. The steady upward trend in the proportion of local expenditure to public expenditure is the most striking feature" (Council of Europe 1975, p. 21). In many nations local spending has been the fastest-growing part of the public sector in recent years. From 1963 to 1973 in the Netherlands, France, and the United States, local spending grew faster than public sector spending as a whole, while in Germany local spending kept pace with public spending as a whole (Ashford 1979, p. 79; Williams and Colijn in Ashford 1980a, p. 181). In Sweden local spending grew almost twice as fast as total spending in the latter half of the 1960s, but then slowed significantly in the early 1970s (Hansen in Sharpe 1981, p. 171). Of the nations examined in this volume, only in Britain did local spending grow more slowly during this period than public spending as a whole (Ashford 1979, p. 79). And in all the nations local advances were more pronounced for current spending (that is, operating budgets) than for capital investments (that is, capital budgets).

Yet, it may be objected, these figures describe trends in the late 1960s and early 1970s, and they apply to local government across the board, rather than simply to the largest cities where service costs are rising most rapidly. As we saw in the previous chapter, many of the big cities in the United States and Europe are no longer experiencing the growth in population and economic activities that characterized earlier decades. Indeed, since 1970 the trend has been toward population stability and even decline in a number of aging industrial centers. Perhaps, then, in these cities we should expect to see a decline in local government spending.

However, several trends work against that possibility. First, the aging industrial cities of Europe and the United States contain a disproportionate share of society's elderly, poor, and others who depend heavily on public services and benefits. Second, the population loss from most of the aging cities had been compensated for by a growth in the *number* of households: While the size of urban households shrinks, the number of households increases (married couples have fewer children, and more youths and elderly people live by themselves). For many types of local services, including garbage pick-up, street cleaning and repair, and police and fire services, cost is a function of the number of households served, rather than the number of persons served. Yet even if it were able to reduce the level of service to households, a city government would be unlikely to realize substantial savings. This is because the city's growth over time has been accompanied by the building of a physical plant that is designed to serve larger and larger numbers. Once built, the city's housing, schools, utility lines, public hospitals, and so on operate most efficiently when running near capacity. Unfortunately, when forced to operate below capacity, these facilities generate far higher unit costs (Peterson in Gorham and Glazer, p. 45; Salathiel). Moreover, research shows that as the capital infrastructure of cities ages, it becomes more expensive to maintain. Old subways, sewer systems, streets, and so on are more costly to operate than new ones. So the post-industrial cities of Europe and the United States can be expected to spend more per capita on capital infrastructure as they age.

We have already noted that relative to national budgets, the budgets of local governments have expanded massively in the past few decades. But if local spending has been growing in relation to spending by other levels of government, an increasing share of local budgets is being supplied by higher levels of government, especially by the national government, through the device of transfer payments. Hence, we might characterize the relationship between levels of government either by stressing national dependence on local units to carry out programs, or by stressing local dependence on national governments as a source of revenue. The difference here is greater than the difference between labeling a water glass either "half full" or "half empty." At the heart of this discrepancy in viewpoints is a major political question for post-industrial societies: How far has the reach of national governments extended into local affairs?

Virtually all studies of public finance in post-industrial nations have commented on the growing interdependence among levels of government. The budgets of nations, municipalities, and all intervening levels (provinces, states, regions, and so on) are so tightly interwoven that they defy simple characterization. (American scholars have long since abandoned the "layer cake" metaphor for American federalism; now even the replacement "marble cake" metaphor appears inadequate to describe the incredibly complex pattern of relations between local, state, and federal levels of government in the United States). How has this growing interdependence affected the political authority of local governments?

It seems that a growth in the size of national transfers would mean a growth in the amount of national control over the recipients of those transfers. If national governments are paying the piper, can we not assume that they are calling the tune? Not necessarily; the connection between money and power in an intergovernmental system is not that simple. Neither the increase in the size of national transfers nor the elaboration of national administrative networks has guaranteed national dominance over local governments, even in the unitary states of Europe. Perhaps the most striking confirmation is furnished by the Netherlands, where national authorities provide the largest percentage of local budgets of any country under study here. (See Table 9.2.) Yet the institutional structure of national/local relations is such that the national government has little direct leverage on policies in individual localities, mainly because the amounts of aid going to cities, individually and as a group, are negotiated between the national government and the *Vereniging van Nederlandse Gemeenten* (VNG), the Dutch association of local governments. Funded by contributions from municipal budgets, this interest group naturally represents municipal interests and has therefore a quasi-public standing. In negotiating for increases in national transfers to localities it plays a pivotal role. And while the fiscal problems experienced by a particular city may provide the impetus for opening the bargaining with the state, the outcome of the VNG's negotiations with the Dutch government invariably extends to all cities. Thus, "the degree of national control over urban government is not a function of the proportion of the local revenue which comes from transfer payments, but rather the proportion plus the form" (Williams and Colijn in Ashford 1980a, p. 201).

Even in France, recent research has challenged the traditional assumptions about the centralization of the unitary state. According to the classic theory of the French state, lower levels of government receive their authority from the nation, which is always empowered to revoke that authority. The national government deploys a vast network of administrators across the national territory to guide the affairs of the *départements* and *communes,* and the preoccupation of Paris officials with the smallest details of local administration is legendary. Yet this classical model has been called into question by studies of specific programs; generally, these have uncovered a greater degree of informal authority exercised by local officials and a smaller degree of central administrative control exercised by national agents than the classical theory would have predicted (Milch; Thoenig).

TABLE 9.2 SOURCES OF LOCAL REVENUE IN SIX NATIONS

	Direct Taxes			Indirect Taxes			Transfers		
	1961	1970	1978	1961	1970	1978	1961	1970	1978
Britain	0%	0%	0%	42%	36%	31%	42%	48%	55%
France	22	21	20	52	24	26	17	48	47
Netherlands	—	0	0	—	4	1	—	81	84
Sweden	56	55	60	3	3	2	27	30	29
United States*	12	15	18	70	61	51	15	20	27
West Germany*	43	40	42	29	31	28	18	18	19

SOURCE Organisation for Economic Cooperation and Development, *National Accounts of OECD Member Countries, 1961–1978,* Vol. II., Paris, 1980.

*For the United States and West Germany, "local revenue" includes state and local revenues.

All of this leads us to the inevitable conclusion that neither the level of local expenditures nor the scope of local responsibilities is likely to diminish in the foreseeable future. Granted, a slower growth rate in the Western economies as a whole may dampen the growth rate of local spending. But the political necessity for local officials to serve their voters, combined with the long-range trend toward standardizing and upgrading public services in the welfare states, will require that local government capacity be even further strengthened. The growing importance of intergovernmental transfers in local budgets has not produced a proportionate decline in local governments' discretion in spending funds, nor in their accountability in the eyes of local voters for solving local problems. On the contrary, as local budgets have grown, so have the expectations of citizens, prompting officials to search for ways to raise yet more revenue at the local level.

MEETING THE DEMAND FOR LOCAL SERVICES

INSTRUMENTS

How have local governments met the increasing demands placed on them by both national governments and local electorates? In this section we will first examine the most common instruments available to local governments to raise revenues for local services—taxes and borrowing. Then we will turn to the efforts of several European governments to enhance the capacity of local governments by reorganizing them into larger jurisdictions.

LOCAL REVENUE INSTRUMENTS

Taxes

Among the nations under consideration here, there are dramatic differences in the levels and types of local taxes, as well as in the extent to which localities support their budgets by local tax revenues. These differences are shown in Table 9.3.

The first column of the table shows that among the European countries, the state and local governments of Germany and local authorities in Sweden make the most substantial tax effort, relative to the tax effort of all levels of government. In these two nations, the local and state tax effort is about equal to that of American state and local governments—that is, they raise about one third of the amount of taxes collected by all levels of government. At a somewhat lower, but still significant level, is the local tax effort in Britain and France. In sharp contrast, local governments in the Netherlands generate only 2 percent of all the tax revenues in that country.

At least as important as the relative tax effort made by local governments is the proportion of their total budgets that they must cover with locally generated revenues. The table shows that in this respect, Sweden and Germany cover the highest proportions among the European systems; this is hardly surprising, since in these nations local tax effort is the highest, relative to other government levels.

It might seem reasonable to conclude that taxpayer resistance would be most pronounced in the countries where local governments depend most heavily on revenues generated from local taxes—that is, Germany, Sweden, the United States, and Britain. But taxpayer resistance depends not only on the level of taxation; it is also influenced by the type of taxation that is imposed.

We can designate local taxes as either direct or indirect. Direct taxes, such as the wage tax, are levied on the incomes of individuals and businesses in the community. Indirect taxes are levied instead on the production, sale, or use of goods and services, and are normally passed on by producers to consumers. The most common indirect taxes levied by local governments are property and sales taxes. Both direct and indirect taxes have their advantages and drawbacks.

Direct taxes on individuals and businesses have the important advantage of being elastic—that is, they quickly respond to upturns and downturns in the local economy, because they are directly tied to incomes. In periods of high inflation the revenues derived from direct taxes tend to reflect rather closely the rise in prices and wages in the local economy, thus giving local government the flexibility to cover the increased costs of delivering services. If a progressive tax on wages or income is levied, then governments reap even greater benefits from

TABLE 9.3 STATE AND LOCAL TAX REVENUES IN SIX NATIONS, 1977

	As Proportion of All Taxes Collected in the Nation	As Proportion of All Revenues Received by State and Local Governments
Netherlands	2%	5%
France	7	47
Britain	10	30
Sweden	29	63
United States	32	67
West Germany	32	68

SOURCES Organisation for Economic Cooperation and Development, *National Accounts of OECD Member Countries, 1961–1978,* Vol. II, (Paris, 1980), and Organisation for Economic Cooperation and Development, *Revenue Statistics of OECD Member Countries, 1965–1979,* (Paris, 1980).

inflation, because taxpayers are pushed upward into higher tax brackets as inflation swells their incomes; taxpayers thus pay progressively larger shares of larger incomes into the public treasury. By comparison, indirect taxes are normally less elastic, responding more slowly to changes in the local economy.

Another important feature of taxes is visibility. Tax experts generally assume that the most visible taxes will provoke the most resistance from taxpayers. By and large, direct taxes are more visible, because they are levied either on the individual's paycheck or in a lump sum at the close of the tax year. In other words, such taxes come right out of the pockets or paychecks of individuals and businesses. On the other hand, an indirect tax such as a sales tax amounts to a small percentage of each individual purchase made by the consumer, and is therefore a relatively painless form of taxation. A tax on the production of goods is even less visible; it is passed from producer to consumer in the form of an increase in the price of the item. There is, however, one glaring exception to the principle that indirect taxes are less visible than direct taxes. That is the property tax, which typically is collected from property owners in a lump sum once or twice a year, and which may be the most unpopular tax of all.

If we return now to the four countries where local governments depend most heavily on locally generated revenues, we must recognize that they do not rely equally on indirect taxes. Table 9.2 shows that Sweden depends hardly at all on indirect taxes, including the property tax. Instead, local governments get over half of their revenue from a direct tax on incomes. This reliance on income taxes is cited as the main reason why Swedish communes (and local governments in other Scandinavian nations as well) face few serious fiscal problems, despite the fact that they have larger and more rapidly expanding budgets than municipalities in other parts of Europe (Hansen 1977, p. 94). Following this logic, we would characterize German cities as being in better fiscal condition than they might appear at first glance, because they get over 40 percent of their revenues from direct taxes and only 28 percent from indirect taxes, chiefly on goods and services rather than on property. In fact, the historic problem of German cities has not been over-reliance on indirect taxes, but rather over-reliance on direct taxes, especially the tax on businesses. Prior to 1969, German cities relied heavily on a tax levied on business assets and profits. The elasticity of this direct tax, usually viewed as an advantage, came to be seen by the national government as a drawback. Its responsiveness to local economic conditions conferred increasing tax advantages on the jurisdictions that were lucky enough to contain large industries. On the other hand, the industry-poor areas were falling further and further behind in their ability to raise revenues. To mute these inequities, the national government in 1969 introduced a tax reform which diverted 40 percent of the revenues collected from the business tax to the state and national treasuries. In exchange for this sacrifice by local governments, the national government began sharing 14 percent of its revenues from the national income tax with localities.

The equalizing effect of Germany's tax-sharing scheme is evident from Table 9.4, which shows the revenues derived from local business taxes in ten cities. The wide variations in per capita revenues flowing from the business tax (column 1) are somewhat offset by the per capita contribution of the income tax (column 2). The result is that the discrepancies in total tax receipts among the localities (column 3) are not as wide as they would have been under the pre-reform system, in which cities relied on the direct tax on businesses for about 70 percent of local tax revenues.

As Table 9.2 shows, local governments in Britain rely on indirect taxes about as heavily as they do in Germany, but a much larger proportion of these indirect tax revenues comes from property taxes. On average, British local authorities must generate 95 percent of local tax revenues through property taxes. Thus they are less likely to see their tax base keep pace with inflation, and more likely to face taxpayer opposition. Such opposition was heard, for example, in 1974 and 1975, when British local governments raised property taxes (known as "the rates") an average of 35 percent in a single year. Organizations of ratepayers at the local level, most of them unaffiliated with political parties, protested so loudly that the national government came up with emergency subsidies to local authorities and then set up a committee of inquiry on local government finance. The Layfield Committee strongly recommended in 1976 that

TABLE 9.4 LOCAL TAX REVENUES DERIVED BY TEN WEST GERMAN CITIES, IN U.S. $ PER CAPITA, 1975

	Local Tax Revenue from Business Taxes	Local Share of National Income Tax Revenues	Total Tax Revenue from All Sources
Frankfurt	$386	$141	$603
Munich	170	131	374
Cologne	190	125	364
Hannover	166	128	356
Essen	134	111	283
Dortmund	125	103	265
Muenster	93	103	231
Saarbrucken	85	97	222
Goettingen	80	96	213
Paderborn	74	79	175

SOURCE Horst Zimmerman, "Cushioning the Fiscal Effects of Economic Changes in Cities," Working Paper No. 0237-01. The Urban Institute, Washington, D.C., 1977.

Britain earmark a portion of the national income tax for local governments (Local Government Finance 1976). So far, that recommendation has been ignored.

It is not surprising that taxpayer resistance is even more vociferous in the United States, since American state and local governments obtain fully half of their total revenues from indirect taxes, of which the property tax accounts for 62 percent and sales taxes another 22 percent. The most visible sign of the taxpayer revolt was the referendum campaign waged in California for a constitutional amendment limiting property tax rates to 1 percent of assessed value. The passage of Proposition 13 in the fall of 1978 was followed by voter approvals in other states of similar constitutional amendments, and by passage in a number of state legislatures of bills to limit taxation. By 1980, half the states had one or more forms of fiscal limitation laws.

Borrowing

Given the bleak picture of the mismatch between increasing service demands and stagnating tax bases, it is hardly surprising that cities in Europe and the United States have resorted to borrowing to help provide local services. Public awareness of this longstanding situation rose suddenly in the United States in 1975, when the nation's largest city approached bankruptcy. After years of deficit financing, in which the city borrowed money each month to pay its expenses (including the interest payments on prior loans), New York finally reached the point of no return. In spring 1975, the banks informed the city government that it was perceived as such a credit risk that no buyers could be found for municipal securities. The state government's subsequent attempt to rescue New York was unsuccessful because the state's own credit rating was contaminated by its entanglement with the bankrupt city. Banks also refused to lend the state money needed to pay for the city's continuing expenses.

The relative indebtedness of the major cities in each of the six countries is portrayed in Table 9.5. Perhaps the most dramatic point is that American cities are not unique in their practice of borrowing heavily to finance local government. In fact, interest payments account for a larger share of the budgets of big cities in Europe than in the United States.

On both sides of the Atlantic, municipal borrowing is most commonly used to finance capital projects, such as streets, hospitals, schools, and airports. Such construction projects invariably require large amounts of money all at once, and therefore cannot be financed out of operating revenues. Borrowing is the main option available to local governments, which have the major responsibility in all nations for building and maintaining urban infrastructure. In recent years French local governments have financed 45 to 60 percent of their capital investments by borrowing; American state and local governments have financed 50 to 75 percent in this fashion; and for British local governments the figure is as high as 90 percent (Sbragia 1979a, p. 214). Some European cities control their own savings banks, which constitute a major source of loans. This is the case, for example, in almost all major German cities. Hamburg's municipal bank was estimated in 1975 to control assets totaling $4 billion, while also controlling several large businesses (*New York Times,* 15 October 1975). Munich and Cologne have only slightly smaller municipal banks from which the local government can borrow.

Given the massive and growing municipal debt that characterizes most post-industrial societies, it is appropriate to examine the scope of national responsibility for this debt. This issue was starkly posed in the United States by New York's near-default in 1975. Having exhausted its credit on the private market, and unable to obtain relief from the state government, New York turned to the national government. The federal administration's initial response was summed up by the New York *Daily News* in its famous headline of October 30, 1975: "Ford to City: Drop Dead."

Eventually, the national government did come to the city's rescue, imposing tight controls over city spending in exchange for a series of short-term loans. But Congress's grudging response to New York's crisis by no means settled the issue of national responsibility for local debts. The emergency loan legislation was tailor-made for New York, and did not reflect general Congressional acceptance of responsibility for the fiscal viability of local governments. Compared to other industrialized nations, the U.S. national government is still distinguished by its lack of responsibility for, or control over, local borrowing (Sbragia 1979b, p. 15).

TABLE 9.5 MUNICIPAL DEBT AND INTEREST PAYMENTS IN SIX NATIONS

	Municipal Debt per Capita	Interest Payments as Percentage of Total Operating Expenses
Britain	$1092	19.7%
France	161	8.5
Netherlands	1521	—
Sweden	1576	13.6
United States	660	7.2
West Germany	725	8.8

SOURCES Robert Fried, "Inequalities Among Cities in Advanced Societies," *European Studies Newsletter,* Vol. VIII, No. 4, January/February 1979, p. 8.
Alberta Sbragia, "Borrowing To Build: Private Money and Public Welfare," *International Journal of Health Services,* Vol. 9, No. 2, p. 219.

The only federal policy that has a significant direct impact on local borrowing is the federal income tax exemption for interest earned on municipal bonds. This exemption encourages both individuals and banking institutions to lend their money to municipalities at relatively low rates of interest. Other than this tax provision, the national government has no direct concern with local borrowing.

By comparison, the nations of Europe assume much greater responsibility for local government finances, both in monitoring local spending and in rescuing cities in trouble. In fact, it is virtually impossible for cities in Europe to go bankrupt by defaulting on loans, for European legal systems make no provision for municipal bankruptcy, as does American law. In the United States, municipalities are treated in law much like private corporations; they can declare bankruptcy and go into receivership, with a court-appointed referee managing their debts.

Since they are ultimately responsible for local debts, European national governments also exercise greater control over local borrowing. A striking example is provided by France, where the primary coordinating point for controlling capital spending has been the *Caisse des Dépôts et Consignations,* which acts as a central dispenser of subsidies and loans to localities for capital programs (Ashford in Ashford 1980b). By law, local governments must deposit their funds in the *Caisse,* which is the largest single lender to local authorities in the nation. Technically, local governments can go instead to private lenders, but the terms offered by the *Caisse* are better than those available in the private market. Furthermore, because of legal ceilings on the interest rates that local governments can pay to private lenders, they find that banks and other lending institutions are seldom eager to extend the loans they need. The relatively generous terms offered by the *Caisse* are accompanied, however, by strong government controls on the level of borrowing. All local government applications to the *Caisse* must be approved by the Finance Ministry, whose decisions are strongly influenced by France's national economic plan. By controlling the level of total borrowing, the *Caisse* strongly influences the level of local capital spending.

In Britain local governments are by comparison less subject to national control. The British case constitutes a middle ground between the American and French patterns. The closest British counterpart to France's *Caisse* is the national Public Works Loan Board (PWLB), which in the mid-1970s was financing about two fifths of all local government debt, while private lenders were financing three fifths. Unlike their French equivalents, local governments in Britain have a real choice between private and public lenders. Most local borrowing, whether it is from public or private sources, must be approved by the national Department of Environment. But national control over local borrowing is less thorough in Britain than in France: Faced with the prospect of national veto power over their capital programs, British local officials have found ways to use their access to private credit as a bargaining chip in dealing with the national Treasury (Sbragia 1979b, p. 29).

Scandinavian cities in the 1970s offer another example of local officials' ability to get around national restrictions. When the national governments tried to stifle local borrowing by cutting back on loans to municipalities, a number of larger cities in Sweden and Norway began to go to banks in other European countries to obtain the loans they needed.

If they offer less direct assistance to localities than do their European counterparts, American federal authorities also exert much less control over local decision making on capital projects. The greatest constraint on local capital spending is exercised instead by the local electorate, for the laws in most states require local officials to submit their plans for issuing general obligation bonds to a popular referendum. In many cases, a two-thirds majority is needed to approve such bond issues; thus, the ability of local governments to incur such debts is highly subject to taxpayer opposition.

LOCAL GOVERNMENT REORGANIZATION

One widespread response to the increasing service demands placed on cities is to redraw the political and administrative boundaries of local jurisdictions so that they reflect more accurately the realities of local and regional economies. Movements in favor of local government consolidation on both sides of the Atlantic have claimed that such reforms would improve the delivery of public services in several ways: (1) by creating larger, more equitable tax bases for local government to tap, (2) by increasing the opportunities for localities to hire professional administrators to manage local services, (3) by improving efficiency in service delivery through economies of scale, and (4) by internalizing the "spillover" costs which neighboring localities impose on one another by their actions. In virtually all Western nations, the number and variety of services have vastly multiplied in the last century; yet, most of these nations entered the post-World War II era with local government structures unchanged from those that had existed a hundred years earlier. It is not surprising, then, that in the last twenty years many European national governments have attempted to reform local structures, invariably by seeking to enlarge the local government units to give them the geographic area and the fiscal resources to address important local problems. Several European nations have achieved dramatic successes in this restructuring, among them Sweden and Britain.

One of the earliest reforms in the post-war period was the reorganization of Sweden's communes, which began in 1952 and was extended by a second reform measure in 1962. The goal of the consolidation was to guarantee a minimum population of 8,000 in the smallest communes, because this was estimated to be the minimum required to maintain basic public services. Boundaries were redrawn to ensure that each of the larger new communes would contain at least one town as a service center, even in rural areas. The cumulative effect of these two legislative actions was to reduce the number of communes by 90 percent, from 2,500 in 1952 to only 274 in the mid-1970s. As revolutionary as this reform may appear, it excited little resistance, even from the locally elected officials whose jobs were eliminated by the reform! In fact, the first stage of the reform was initiated in the 1950s by communal officials themselves, and its extension in 1962 was endorsed by the Swedish association of local governments, the *Kommunförbundet* (Anton 1974, pp. 88–89).

How can we account for the apparent lack of resistance to, even enthusiasm for, consolidation on the part of Swedish local governments? Some explanation is required for such unexpected cooperation among local officials in legislating their own power bases out of existence. For Swedish citizens and officials, local government is regarded primarily as a service provider, rather than a political entity. The justification for the consolidation was precisely that it would allow local governments to respond more efficiently to the growing demand for public services. "Responsiveness" was defined in terms of the availability within local jurisdictions of the resources, including organizational resources, needed to supply services.

Moreover, Swedish cities do not display the same degree of residential stratification by class, and certainly not by race, as do American cities. The absence of differences in incomes and lifestyles means that Swedish localities did not have a strong reason to resist consolidation with their neighbors. Nor does Sweden show the wide variation in service levels that exists among American cities. As we have seen, the largest share of local budgets in Sweden is spent on programs prescribed by the national government. Given the similarity in the mandated services offered by all Swedish localities, individual communes were not likely to resist consolidation in order to preserve their own package of public services.

Finally, we must recognize the potential leverage that was available to the national government in pushing through communal reform. Even if local officials had not held an enlightened view on consolidation, the national government could have put considerable pressure on them. Consider, for example, the Swedish government's willingness to intervene in the consolidation of metropolitan Stockholm, from its 1949 order establishing the Stockholm Regional Planning Commission, to its creation in 1962 of a Royal Commission to study regional cooperation on housing, to its pressure in 1964 to create in Stockholm a regional transportation authority. All of these national actions pushed Stockholm and its surrounding suburbs gradually closer to the eventual agreement of 1966 to create a regional government, the Stockholm Greater County Council (Anton 1975).

Undeniably, the power of the Social Democratic party, both nationally and within many communes, was instrumental in ensuring that the communal reorganization be generally accepted. The Social Democrats supported the reform early on, for they saw the creation of larger units of local government as a way to improve and equalize the levels of service throughout the country. As the main instruments of the welfare state, the communes were critical to the success of the Social Democratic agenda (Brand). Moreover, the socialists' long-term control of the national government between 1952 and 1976 gave them ample opportunity to accomplish the reform they had initiated. The national party's backing was especially important, because there was prior to 1970 enormous overlap in the memberships of local governments and the national parliament, with as many as 70 percent of the legislators in the national Riksdag also holding local office.

Britain undertook its reorganization of local government in the 1970s, carrying out reforms that constituted a dramatic break with the past. Called a "frontal attack of the central government on local government structure" (Ashford in Tarrow et al, 245), the reorganization was initiated when the Labour government in 1966 appointed the Redcliffe-Maud Commission to study local government. Both major parties agreed that the existing structure of local government, unchanged since 1888, was unwieldy. In addition to distinguishing between counties (for rural areas) and county boroughs (for urban areas), the system included separate and overlapping district councils of three different types (non-county boroughs, urban districts, and rural districts), as well as small parish councils. After a detailed three-year study, the Redcliffe-Maud Commission recommended in 1969 that this complicated pattern, which had evolved over centuries, be swept away and replaced with a simple system of fifty-eight "unitary areas" with populations between 250,000 and one million. Each of these new local jurisdictions would be governed by a single authority responsible for all services. Only in the three largest cities would there be a two-tier system of regional authorities alongside smaller units.

The commission's report was mostly accepted by Labour, which argued the case for these massive new authorities on two grounds: administrative efficiency and local democracy. The latter point was expressed in this way in the government's White Paper on the issue:

> Unless local government is organised to meet the needs of the future, and in particular is organised in units large enough to match the techni-

> cal and administrative requirements of the services which it administers, its power must diminish and with it the power of local democracy (Labour Government White Paper 1970, p. 7).

Admittedly, this formulation is entirely consistent with Labour's drive in the postwar period to expand and improve social services. But many observers saw in the Labour proposal an attempt to erode the power of small-town Conservative constituencies, by submerging them in these larger new authorities whose borders were drawn to link country and town.

It was therefore no surprise when in 1970 the new Conservative government altered the unitary approach of the previous government. The Conservatives designed and implemented in 1974 a two-tier system throughout Britain. In the major metropolitan regions, the lower level of government ("district") continued to carry the major operating responsibility for services, while the upper tier ("county") was assigned mostly planning responsibility for capital projects, also sharing certain powers with the lower level (for example, for parks and recreation). In the rest of Britain, the upper tier enjoyed relatively stronger position *vis-à-vis* the lower tier because in these areas the upper tier was responsible for operating educational and social services. Moreover, in these non-metropolitan areas the historic parishes survived the Conservative reform and still operate as the lowest level of local government.

Thus, as eventually implemented by the Conservatives, local government reorganization was less sweeping than the Labour party had envisioned. Nonetheless, it did reduce the number of upper-tier or county governments by 60 percent, while reducing the total number of local government units from about 1,000 to about 400. Perhaps more significant, it eliminated the jobs of about 11,600 local councillors and over 4,000 aldermen (Benjamin, p. 76).

As in the Swedish case, we must ask how such far-reaching changes could be accomplished with minimal opposition from local governments. We find some important parallels in the two cases. Both Sweden and Britain have unitary political systems in which local governments perform basic housekeeping functions, many of which are mandated and regulated by the national government. In the Swedish case the delegation by national government of so many functions to the local governments has led to a "nationalization" of important local issues, with the national government becoming involved in debates over major local controversies. This trend is reinforced by the nationalized party system in which many individuals simultaneously hold local and national public office. In Britain, too, local budgets and services are carefully overseen by national agencies, so that local authorities are in many instances no more than the agents of central departments. But in contrast to the Swedish case, central dominance does not necessarily imply close linkages with local political organizations. In fact, the British national government may have been helped in undertaking so sweeping a change as the 1974 reorganization by its insulation from local political conflicts and interests. If national and local offices had overlapped in Britain as they did in Sweden, then national actions affecting the localities might have been less sweeping and less high-handed, because such actions would have been shaped in part by local forces (Ashford in Tarrow et al, pp. 249–250).

Our Sweden-Britain comparison suggests that the following factors are important in successful local government reorganization:

1. The balance of power within party organizations. In the successful consolidations (Sweden, Britain, Germany), the party hierarchy has been strong enough to overcome potential resistance from local party politicians. The national parties in Sweden and Britain and the state-level parties in Germany represent the locus of party power—both in terms of organization and money. Local party politicians are clearly subordinate to them and rely on their support.
2. The availability of sufficient resources at higher levels of government (in the form of regulatory power and subsidies) to "buy" compliance from local governments.

In short, when higher levels of government dominate political party organizations and contribute a large proportion of local revenues, they can successfully promote reorganization of local governments. The importance of these two factors is highlighted by comparison of our European examples with the United States, where very little has been accomplished in the way of local government consolidation.

As we noted in the preceding chapter, the suburbanization of American cities has been a long-term trend, dating back at least to the 1920s and accelerating rapidly in the 1950s and 1960s. As they left the cities and established new communities at the edges, the new suburbanites founded new local governments. The fragmentation of local government caused by this outward migration is evident in the statistics: From 1957 to 1972, over a thousand new municipalities were formed (Maxwell and Aronson, p. 78). Even more startling than this increase in municipalities is the mushrooming of special districts, formed to provide a narrow range of services, with boundaries overlapping those of the municipalities. They are most commonly established to operate sewage disposal systems, transportation networks, water supply systems, and metropolitan park systems. Some are confined to only one metropolitan area, like the Massachusetts Bay Transportation Authority, created by state legislation to handle mass transit in Boston and twenty-seven neighboring towns. Others join together several major population centers; an example is the Metropolitan Water District of Southern California, which supplies water to Los Angeles, San Diego, and dozens of other cities. Still others overlap state boundaries; the best known of these interstate compacts is the Port Authority of New York and New Jersey, which operates airports, bridges, tunnels, and terminals throughout the New York metropolitan region. Unlike traditional local governments, most of these special districts are prohibited from levying taxes. Typically, they finance their operations by service charges, tolls, and bonds which they must pay back out of operating revenues. So appealing is this solution to regional problems that between 1957 and 1972 their number almost doubled, from 14,405 to 23,883 (Maxwell and Aronson, p. 78). We can attribute this growth in special districts to the fact that they do not threaten the existing local power structure, but are merely added to it.

In addition to planning problems, suburbanization has generated serious fiscal problems in most metropolitan areas, mainly because of an increasing "mismatch" between city and suburban resources. Left with a growing proportion of the poor, central cities have watched their tax base drift into the suburbs. Once begun, this separation has provided further incentive to out-migration from central cities, because it relieves residents of the tax burdens associated with central city government, including the bill for a wide range of non-residential services associated with industries, offices, tourism, and so on (Peterson in Gorham and Glazer, p. 79).

The problems created by governmental fragmentation at the local level stimulated a burst of reform activity in the United States in the 1950s. Study commissions were formed in over a hundred metropolitan areas, and referenda were put before the voters in thirteen of them. The actual record on consolidation in the United States is disappointing, however. Only four consolidations of major significance have been carried through: Miami, Nashville, Jacksonville, and Indianapolis. One reason for this poor record is the reluctance of state legislators to press for consolidation. Clearly, in the American federal system, state governments are the units that would have to pressure local governments toward consolidation. But state budgets, relative to municipal budgets, are too small to permit them to buy compliance in such reforms. And, while state regulatory powers are potentially broad, they cannot be boldly exercised, given the undeniable fact that local parties control the money and organization upon which state politicians rely.

The Costs of Local Government Consolidation

Proponents of local government consolidation have often argued that it can produce savings from economies of scale. Larger units, they assert, are able to purchase equipment and supplies less expensively than smaller units, may enjoy greater flexibility in deploying their work force than do smaller units, and in general may take advantage of more professionalized management, which will increase their efficiency. One of the clearest statements of this argument is found in the Redcliffe-Maud report, which in 1969 recommended the consolidation of Britain's highly fragmented local government system into only sixty-one jurisdictions. One of the assumptions behind their recommendation was that these larger jurisdictions could provide services far more efficiently than the multitude of smaller ones. Yet, even though this argument appears convincing at the theoretical level, the efforts by researchers to test it empirically have produced mixed results (Bennet, p. 122).

On the one hand, some Scandinavian studies have shown that larger units do enjoy economies of scale in delivering certain kinds of services (for example, port authorities in Sweden, sewage systems in Norway, old-age homes and high schools in Sweden) (Lotz, p. 239). Yet other studies show precisely the opposite—that bigness actually generates some *dis*-economies of scale. In Britain, prior to local government reorganization, one study examined housing management, health services, and highway construction, concluding that after a certain threshold, the cost per capita to provide these services actually rises as the population of the authority increases. Another study showed a similar trend for educational authorities—larger authorities spent more per student on textbooks and equipment than smaller authorities (Benjamin, pp. 82–83). While this evidence is by no means conclusive, it is provocative.

To this evidence from Britain, we can add some scattered observations about the impact of consolidation in Germany. One commentator reports that "it has become increasingly apparent that there is a direct relationship between increased size of municipalities and higher personnel and service costs per citizen" (Gunlicks 1977, p. 190). A study in North Rhine-Westphalia demonstrated that personnel costs rose in municipalities of 10,000 or more much faster than in smaller municipalities. Another study of the impact of municipal consolidation in Lower Saxony suggested that rather than saving money, the reforms actually led to higher expenditures. Finally, we can cite a study of public expenditures in French *communes,* as they were related to size, which found that for every 1 percent increase in population, the increase in spending *per inhabitant* was:

2.34 percent in cities of 50,000 to 100,000
3.39 percent in cities of 100,000 to 200,000
4.52 percent in cities over 200,000 (Council of Europe 1968, p. 40).

These fragments from Europe fit into the growing body of research pointing to the disadvantages of consolidating small units into larger, multi-purpose regional governments. A growing number of economists now argue that consolidation increases the cost of local government because it eliminates the government's incentives to economize. Besides increasing the distance between policy makers and their constituents it seems to lower the probability that the individual taxpayer will be able to get what he wants from local officials. In contrast, the fragmentation of local government into many small, overlapping jurisdictions may ensure more efficiency and responsiveness (Benjamin).

At present this debate about the relationship between urban size and efficiency remains largely theoretical. We know of no conclusive empirical research for any of the post-industrial systems we examine in this volume, including the United States. Moreover, there are many possible explanations, apart from size alone, for the higher costs of services in large jurisdictions. Many cities attract a disproportionate share of the needy and therefore must provide more, and more costly, services than smaller communities. Because they act as regional and even national centers, big cities must supply a range of specialized services that are unnecessary in smaller towns. In addition, the higher density of people and economic activities in big cities makes social problems both more visible and more expensive to treat. Moreover, the more professionalized bureaucracies which tend to develop in larger cities are paid higher salaries than those in small towns. We could cite numerous other explanations as well (Newton, p. 164), all bearing out the same point—that the cost of providing services depends not simply on the size of the governmental unit, but also on the character and needs of the population being served.

THE GAP BETWEEN LOCAL NEEDS AND RESOURCES

DISTRIBUTION

As we saw in the area of urban planning, recent research on the political determinants of urban policy has frequently shown that party control over local governments has only a marginal impact on local spending patterns (Fried). When leftist parties have controlled local governments in Western Europe, they have not necessarily outspent conservative parties, nor have they necessarily adopted different spending priorities. This surprising finding may be explained in part by the rise of non-traditional political activity in the cities (that is, political activity organized outside the bounds of traditional parties). Another explanation, however, lies in the nature of local government activity. At the national level, the political influence of leftist parties has been reflected most directly in the expansion of redistributive policies, including progressive tax systems, income maintenance and social security programs, and social services. At the local level, very little government activity involves redistributive programs. Indeed, local government is probably the level of government least suited to initiating such programs. Granted, local jurisdictions often act as the arm of higher governments in administering transfer payments and social services. But when we survey locally initiated and locally funded activities, we find few examples of a redistributive nature.

The reason is simple. Local governments have fixed boundaries that are easily crossed by households and businesses seeking the best location. The technology of transportation and communication has made both individuals and firms highly mobile, multiplying their locational choices. Any actions on the part of local governments that threaten to shift resources away from the "haves" toward the "have nots" can easily provoke the "haves" to move away, taking their resources with them. Naturally, this tendency is most pronounced where there are wide disparities in the levels of services and benefits provided by different localities, as there are in the United States. Conversely, in countries where national standards promote uniform service levels across all localities, as in Britain and Sweden, there are fewer incentives to relocate in order to enjoy better services or lower taxes. Nevertheless, throughout the industrial countries the established pattern is for national governments to initiate and pay for most redistributive programs, while local governments take responsibility for delivering services and promoting economic development. The latter function may in fact lead localities to redistribute wealth away from the moderate-income residents, and toward the more affluent, by subsidizing the "haves" at the expense of the "have nots." One example is the practice of offering incentives, in the form of reduced taxes or subsidies to land and construction costs, to businesses and middle-class households moving into the community.

A widespread practice, this local boosterism often has regressive effects because the concessions granted to businesses and middle-class residents shift the tax burden to the rest of the community. That burden often takes the form of indirect taxes, which tend themselves to be regressive. The best example is the property tax, which takes a larger fraction of the incomes of lower-income owners and renters than of higher-income households. Lower-income households normally have a much larger proportion of their total wealth tied up in their homes than do higher-income households, and therefore they are hit harder by a tax on property. A similar case can be made regarding sales taxes, which constitute a larger proportion of the budgets of low-income consumers than of high-income consumers.

Less often considered is the potentially regressive effect of user fees and charges as a source of local government revenues. User charges assess the cost of a particular service to those who are the consumers of that service. They can vary from special assessments to pay for sidewalks, parks, or other community facilities, to fees for using particular recreational facilities such as swimming pools, public housing, and public libraries. The relative importance of such fees in local budgets varies widely from nation to nation, although in general they have declined as a proportion of local revenues. In Britain, for example, the decline in the contribution made by user charges over the past twenty-five years is due largely to the vigorous opposition to rent increases mounted by tenants in council (public) housing. In Germany, where local governments are required by law to charge cost-covering fees for many of their services, the proportion of local revenues contributed by such charges hardly changed in the inflationary 1970s—from 20.5 percent in 1970 to 22.6 percent in 1977 (Schäfer in Sharpe 1981, p. 264). For Sweden the trend in recent years has been similar but complicated by a marked difference in the behavior of larger and smaller municipalities. For Swedish localities as a whole, fees and user charges have drastically declined as a proportion of local budgets, from 33.5 percent in 1965 to only 18.6 percent in 1975. Yet, at the same time, Sweden's twenty-one largest cities have become *more* dependent on user charges, which rose from 40.8 percent of their budgets in 1965 to 48.4 percent of their budgets in 1974 (Hansen in Sharpe 1981, pp. 190–191). Thus, by the mid-1970s, user fees constituted the largest single source of revenue for Sweden's largest cities and towns. In the absence of deliberate countermeasures, such a shift would have had seriously regressive effects, restricting the use of many city services to those who could pay for them. Such regressive effects have been blunted, however, by the introduction of sliding fee schedules for many social services, so that users pay for day care, health care, and many other public services according to their ability to pay.

Even the practice among local governments of borrowing money to finance capital projects may have regressive impacts on local populations. When they borrow money and assume the obligation to pay it back on a fixed schedule with interest, local governments may be forced to adopt strategies that they would not otherwise use. First and foremost, local officials must be concerned about obtaining a sufficient return on their capital expenditures to permit them to repay with interest. This unavoidable necessity turns the borrower (the local authority) into an investor, in the sense that officials must be assured of an adequate return on the project for which the money was borrowed. This usually means either diverting tax revenues from other public services to service the debt, or imposing user charges (for example, rents in public housing or admission fees for swimming pools, zoos, museums, and so on), that are calculated on the basis of loan repayment requirements. Under such circumstances, a "service" may become a "business," catering to those who can pay for it rather than those in greatest need (Sbragia 1979a, pp. 218–219). In sum, the instrument of borrowing, like indirect taxes and user fees, is a strategy with some potentially regressive effects.

Local government consolidation, in contrast, is an approach to building local capacity that can offer substantial redistributive benefits. In fact, reorganization is frequently justified on the grounds that it can promote a fairer distribution of the costs and benefits of local government, because the resources of wealthier districts and poorer districts are pooled together. At the same time, it is precisely these redistributive overtones of consolidation that excite the most vehement opposition to the idea—especially from the more affluent jurisdictions whose taxes would be channeled into services for less affluent neighbors.

Despite the successes that some European nations have achieved in local government reorganization, the common trend both in Europe and the United States is a widening gap between needs and resources. Typically, central cities throughout the industrialized nations now contain disproportionate shares of elderly, poor, and immigrant people—groups with greater than average needs for public services. At the same time, the economic base of many cities is stagnating, creating a severe budgetary squeeze.

How have national governments responded to the apparent inability of local governments to cope with this growing imbalance between resources and needs? Two logical alternatives are: (1) national governments may assume an increased share of the financial burden of local governments, so that less affluent communities need not rely so heavily on their own tax base to finance public services; and (2) national governments may take steps to try to distribute economic growth more evenly, by discouraging over-concentration in some areas while other areas suffer from depopulation and economic decline.

The first alternative—national assumption of a larger share of local budgets—is accomplished by intergovernmental transfers. Table 9.2 shows that in the six countries considered in this volume intergovernmental transfers constitute substantial and growing revenue sources for localities in the Netherlands, Britain, and France; a smaller but growing proportion in the United States; and fairly stable proportions in Sweden and Germany. The French case in particular requires some explanation to account for the phenomenal increase in national transfers that took place during the 1960s.

In 1966 France introduced a law replacing the *taxe locale,* a local indirect tax, with a system of national subsidies called the VRTS (*versement représentatif de la taxe sur les salaires*). The VRTS furnished French *communes* and *départements* with yearly payments from Paris of a portion of the national tax on salaries. Local shares were based not solely on the tax effort made by individual localities, but also took account of the differing abilities of localities to raise taxes. Though the effort at equalization under the VRTS has not proceeded as far as was originally projected (Mény in Ashford 1980a, p. 149), the French government at least acknowledged its responsibility for helping to close the gap between needs and resources at the local level.

Britain too takes account of differential needs and resources in distributing aid to local governments. One element of the national Rate Support Grant to local authorities is the so-called "resources element," which is designed to equalize the tax bases of local governments. In 1979 and 1980, for example, the resources element was calculated to assure the equivalent of 175 pounds of taxable value per inhabitant to each local authority; those whose tax base fell below this minimum were compensated accordingly. In addition to the resources element, which accounted for 30 percent of the Rate Support Grant in 1979–1980, the government also included a "needs element," which accounted that same year for 61 percent of the Rate Support Grant (Simpson). The needs element is intended to compensate local authorities for their different spending needs; it is calculated on the basis of past spending patterns combined with a number of demographic indicators, such as proportion of children, elderly, and other dependents in the population; proportion of households lacking basic amenities; and extra costs imposed by the dispersal of the population. Some observers have criticized the limited extent to which the Rate Support Grant does in fact redistribute resources among local authorities (Newton in Ashford 1980a, p. 108). Such critics do not question the principle that the national government ought to use its transfers for redistributive purposes; rather, their complaint usually is that the Rate Support Grant does not go far enough in doing so.

Another approach is to redistribute the economic growth which is the basis for local tax revenues. We saw in the preceding chapter that several European governments have moved quite far in this direction, by providing incentives to individuals and firms to locate in stagnating areas and discouraging growth in the most congested centers. Britain and France have since the 1960s engaged in regional development planning at a national scale, building whole new towns from scratch to draw population and businesses away from the largest cities. In the Netherlands the government has concentrated on channeling growth in and around the Randstad, the ring of urban development connecting Rotterdam, Leiden, Amsterdam, Utrecht, and many smaller communities in the western section of the nation. Comparing the achievements of these governments to the much weaker regional planning efforts made by the American and German national governments, we see that the unitary governments, which contribute the largest percentages of local government budgets, are at the same time making the most serious efforts to redistribute economic growth among regions. In the federal systems of the United States and Germany, by contrast, national governments take less responsibility for contributing to local government support and for channeling growth to stagnating regions. In these latter systems, therefore, we expect the financial disparities among local governments to widen most dramatically.

TRENDS IN INTERGOVERNMENTAL TRANSFERS

RESTRAINTS AND INNOVATION

Earlier in this chapter, we noted the almost universal trend in post-industrial societies toward larger transfers of revenue from national treasuries to local governments. According to some, one major consequence has been the subordination of local goals and purposes to national goals and purposes. Their argument is that by means of massive transfer payments, national governments have substituted their priorities for local ones. In the United States this observation is often made by opponents of big government, who doubt the wisdom of federal officials substituting their judgment for that of local officials.

A classic illustration of this displacement phenomenon is New York City's decision to rebuild the West Side Highway after a portion of it collapsed in 1973. This critical artery along the Hudson River, which carried more people to work each day than any other highway in the region, might have been repaired at relatively modest cost. Even its replacement by a mass transit line would have been more cost effective than the project that was finally approved, which entailed construction of a larger new highway at a cost of $300 million per mile, bounded by 243 acres of new land fill for recreation and open space. Opponents of the massive project like urbanist Jane Jacobs complained that it took one more step toward "Los Angelizing" New York by accommodating further to the environmentally-destructive automobile. Why did the city select the most expensive and controversial of the alternatives? The answer is the availability of federal funds. Had they chosen to repair the existing highway, the city and state would have borne the entire cost. And while federal subsidies were available for mass transit, they would have been granted at a less favorable ratio to local dollars than funds for highway construction (Herzlinger). Thus do local governments, in pursuit of subsidies, sometimes abandon their own priorities and adopt those of the funding source.

Yet the strength of such displacement effects in the United States must be weighed against the well-known skills of many local officials who operate in the grant environment more as entrepreneurs promoting their favorite local project than as pawns of state and federal governments. Furthermore, it should be noted that national agencies must navigate a sea of jurisdictional complexities that can seriously dilute the impact of federal programs at the local level. In the first place, most federal grant programs are entirely voluntary, so that states and localities must be persuaded to participate. Once they have agreed to participate, the recipients exercise significant discretion over most grants-in-aid; the guidelines for many such programs fix only very broad parameters within which state and local authorities must operate. In fact, one of the greatest challenges involved in drafting federal legislation dealing with local problems is to design administrative arrangements for implementing the legislation that will maximize the probability of national objectives being met, while minimizing the opportunities for state and local officials to subvert those objectives.

In Europe, where historic patterns have favored a larger national role in local affairs, we might expect a more pronounced displacement effect. Yet recent research cautions against overestimating the influence of national officials over local priorities there too. One study in Germany examined the influence of federal and state grants on local decisions to invest in six types of capital projects (schools, cultural facilities, social facilities, health care, roads and housing, and public installations). The state-by-state analysis did indeed show that, in general, in the states where the highest proportions of these local projects were financed by transfers, there was the closest correlation between the amount of intergovernmental grants and the size of the local investments (Reissert in Ashford 1980b, p. 156). This appears to mean that if they offer enough subsidy, federal and state governments can get local governments to adapt their spending patterns. But the study qualified this generalization in two important respects. First, the control effects were not necessarily higher for those investment sectors in which the most generous subsidies were available. Localities seemed most responsive to the availability of grants in areas of social infrastructure, where the subsidies were *less* generous than for roads, housing, and public installations. This suggests that local officials were exercising some discretion in pursuing subsidies, rather than simply drifting toward the most profitable sectors. Furthermore, the research showed that the influence of grants on local investment decisions was more significant in poor communities than in affluent communities, which can afford to have their priorities diverge more from those of the grant system (Reissert in Ashford 1980b, p. 152).

Can a unitary system like Britain's be assumed to display more pronounced displacement effects than those visible in Germany's federal system? One piece of research on the relative degree of control exercised by central government over current expenditures (as opposed to the capital expenditures examined in the previously mentioned German study) went so far as to assert that "the heavy financial dependence of British local authorities on central government has not produced a demonstrable effect on policy choices in the sub-national system" (Ashford 1974, p. 320). At first glance, this finding may be surprising. After all, national subsidies account for over half of local revenues in Britain. Should we not expect to see such massive transfers influence local spending priorities? The answer depends largely on the form in which the transfers are passed to localities—as conditional grants or as unrestricted block grants.

If national transfers are earmarked for specific uses by the local government, then their availability for some purposes but not for others may influence local spending priorities. This kind of conditional transfer has been the predominant form of federal aid to states and cities in the United States, where national subsidies have been designed primarily to support projects that state and local governments would not have funded on their own. In fact, the "maintenance of effort" provisions incorporated into thirty-seven of the fifty-two largest federal grant programs were specifically intended to prevent local governments from accepting federal subsidies and then cutting back their own spending by an equivalent amount. Hence these provisions require that recipients maintain their level of prior spending in the areas being supported by transfer payments, thereby discouraging localities from using national subsidies to finance core services. But in Europe, national governments have played a larger role in supporting the traditional urban services. City officials are less likely to be faced with the choice between programs most crucial to the city's welfare and the programs for which they can obtain external funds. Thus displacement effects are less visible in European cities.

The transfer of unrestricted funds is a better-established practice in Europe than in the United States. As Table 9.6 shows, in France, the Netherlands, and Britain, unrestricted block grants constituted the vast bulk of national transfers to local governments in the mid-1970s. Interestingly, the percentage of funds transferred to local governments in unrestricted form was higher in these three unitary systems, where the national government furnishes the largest percentage of local support, than in either the United States or Germany, both federal systems in which national transfers play a less significant part in local budgets. One possible interpretation of the apparent association between the size of national transfers and the willingness of national governments to use unrestricted block grants, is that the acceptability of unrestricted transfers is greatest where national officials are most confident that the national administrative apparatus can effectively monitor the use of the funds (Ashford 1978,

TABLE 9.6 INTERGOVERNMENTAL TRANSFERS COMING TO LOCAL GOVERNMENTS AS UNRESTRICTED GRANTS

Britain (1974)	80%
France (1974)	100
Netherlands (1976)	95
Sweden (1976)	24
United States (1973)	13
West Germany (1973)	43

SOURCE Douglas Ashford, "Territorial Politics and Resource Allocation," *European Studies Newsletter*, Vol. VIII, No. 2, November 1978, p. 2.

p. 2). Hence, a higher proportion of transfers is passed in unrestricted form in the systems with elaborate national bureaucracies than in either the federal systems or in Sweden, where national agencies have smaller bureaucracies and depend more heavily on lower-level bureaucracies to administer their programs.

The 13 percent figure shown in Table 9.6 for the United States reflects the American situation of the early 1970s, a situation that has changed significantly with the advent of the "new federalism" of the mid-1970s. Various forms of general and special revenue sharing introduced in the 1970s have since given local officials greater discretion than was available under categorical grants-in-aid. Both general revenue sharing and the block grants in such fields as law enforcement and community development are distributed to states and localities, not in response to applications, but rather on the basis of nationwide formulas incorporating such factors as population size, proportion of population with low incomes, age of housing stock, level of unemployment, and so on. These unrestricted grants were introduced with support from both major political parties as a way of delegating more discretion to local governments in the use of federal funds. The Reagan administration has moved even further in this direction by replacing more categorical programs with block grants: The initial budget proposal for fiscal year 1982 called for consolidating eighty-five categorical grants into seven block grants. In the process of Congressional review, the Reagan proposals were significantly diluted, resulting in the establishment of nine block grants whose actual provisions fell far short of the Reagan proposals, both in the amount of money involved and the conditions associated with the grants. These new block grants did not go nearly as far in consolidating programs as the administration had requested, leaving out some of the largest categorical programs in education and health. Furthermore, Congress insisted on attaching many strings to the grants, restricting their use by a variety of reporting requirements and prohibitions. The only part of the administration request that was honored by Congress was a proposal to cut funding for the programs involved by 25 percent.

Although Reagan's first budget proposal did not achieve all of its objectives, there is no doubt that it continues the shift in the United States toward a greater use of unrestricted transfers from national to state and local governments. While the consequences of this trend in intergovernmental relations are being debated, the longer experience of several European nations makes several points clear. First, unrestricted grants are by definition transferred in lumps whose size is determined by some entitlement formulas. But the fact that such grants are not earmarked for specific purposes does *not* necessarily mean that local governments have complete freedom in spending. The degree of latitude enjoyed by localities depends heavily on the extent to which local governments are mandated by higher governments to provide specified services at specified levels. In Britain, for example, a very large proportion of national funds comes as an unrestricted Rate Support Grant, but close supervision of local services means that local governments do not actually exercise much discretion in spending the funds.

Second, a gradual shift toward unrestricted grants usually means that communities are increasingly reliant on transfers to finance their traditional core services. Once this occurs, local governments become far more dependent on national transfers, not simply to support peripheral projects, but also to support the very heart of the local operating budget. In this sense, the shift to unrestricted grants increases local dependency.

One of the most important implications of the shift toward unrestricted grants is that it appears to become easier for national governments to impose ceilings on the growth of transfers to local governments. A single lump-sum allocation to local governments is more visible and more easily controlled than the sums paid out under a multitude of separate categorical programs. With lump-sum grants, national governments can place a limit on the total allocation to local governments by deciding first what the total funding pool will be and then distributing the pool according to an entitlement formula. With categorical programs, it is much more difficult to establish such spending limits in advance, especially if national subsidies are fixed as a percentage of local expenditures for certain types of services.

In fact, the most cynical commentators on the Reagan administration's enthusiasm for block grants speculated that the federalism issue was merely a smoke screen for budget cutting. This suspicion was fueled by the fact that the so-called block grants created by the Reagan proposals retained many of the strings that had previously been attached to the categorical grants which they replaced. Indeed, their biggest impact was in cutting back the level of federal funding for social programs. Rather than raising state taxes to replace the lost federal funds, most states began almost immediately to reduce or eliminate programs. Some states that could afford to pick up the burden (Texas, Oklahoma, and Louisiana) were not inclined to use state resources in this way, while legislators in other states (Michigan, Massachusetts, and New York) felt the need and the inclination to continue social programs in hard times but lacked the resources to do so.

We can find striking parallels in several European systems. One example is in Britain, where transfers to local government have been declining in proportion to local expenditures since 1976, the result of a deliberate strategy on the part of national government to limit local spending. So severe were the cuts announced by the new Conservative government in November 1979 that they were expected to bring total spending by local governments for 1980–1982 down to the 1977–1978 level, despite the significant inflation that had occurred in the three-year interim. In its 1980 Local Government Planning and Land Bill, the Thatcher government took a further step to curb local spending by changing the formulas for calculating the Rate Support Grant. Previously, those formulas had taken into account both the past expenditure levels and the existing tax rates of individual jurisdictions in such a way that high-taxing and high-spending authorities tended to receive larger Rate Support Grants than low-taxing and low-spending authorities. The system introduced in 1980 bases the Rate Support Grant on a standardized tax rate for the whole country, and on a government-determined "need factor" that does not hinge on previous spending patterns in a jurisdiction. In defending this change, the Conservative Secretary of State for the Environment clearly tied it to the need to curb aggregate spending by local governments:

> So far as overspending is concerned, while a majority of local authorities have shown a willingness to keep in step with the Government's guidelines on public expenditure, a minority of authorities persist in maintaining levels of expenditure which the present economic circumstances simply do not justify (Michael Heseltine, quoted in Burgess and Travers, p. 139).

A similar motive existed for France's elimination in 1966 of the *taxe locale* and the establishment of a system for sharing a portion of the national tax on salaries with localities. In practice, the new system has not kept pace with the growth of local budgets; the national transfers constitute a smaller share of local revenues than was contributed by the old *taxe locale* that they replaced. There is therefore some reason to view the reform of 1966 not simply as a way to equalize local expenditures, but also as a vehicle to increase national control over aggregate local spending (Ashford 1978, p. 3).

We would argue that the widespread interest in unrestricted grants reflects the changing view of national policy makers regarding the economic role played by local governments. One of the distinguishing features of post-industrial politics is the expanding responsibility assumed by national governments for ensuring economic stability through policies that minimize the disruptive effects of booms and slumps in the national and international economy. As local spending constitutes a larger and larger share of GNP, its impact on the national economy becomes more pronounced. In the eyes of national policy makers, local governments are seen increasingly as major consumers whose spending habits influence the economic stability of the nation as a whole. The goal of national policy, then, becomes the dampening of public expenditures in the aggregate, with relatively little regard for the ways in which the money is spent. Precisely because unrestricted grants are awarded in lump sums, they appear to be a more suitable means for manipulating aggregate local spending than are categorical grants. It follows, then, that the accelerated interest shown by national policy makers in aggregate levels of local spending will reinforce the shift toward unrestricted grants. The ceiling imposed on block grants will be particularly troublesome to local governments in the many areas where national or state governments have mandated the minimum standards to be maintained in delivering services. Once seen as a boon by local officials who were eager to upgrade local services, such performance standards may now be viewed by the same officials as an intolerable regulatory burden.

* * * * *

Relationships between local and national government, then, form a complex web of interdependencies in which the choices available to officials at all levels are double-edged. As demands for local services grow, should local authorities seek higher subsidies from the national treasury instead of increasing the burden on local taxpayers? That strategy may be preferable to local taxpayers, but it is likely to restrict the officials' latitude in spending the money. Should localities then lobby for more block grants which they can spend as they wish? Block grants may increase local discretion but, as we have seen, they also increase local dependency. Should national policy makers prefer block grants to categorical programs? While they make it easier to control the total amount transferred to localities, block grants make it more difficult to ensure that the money is spent in ways that are consistent with national priorities—an increasing concern as local governments are now among the biggest spenders in the national economies of the West.

10
POLICY CONTRASTS IN THE WELFARE STATE

The year 1983 marks the 100th anniversary of the founding of the modern welfare state, conventionally identified with the German introduction of compulsory health insurance under Bismarck. Yet we now find social scientists and politicians in disagreement about some crucial questions concerning its development and future: How serious is the "crisis" of the welfare state in the low-growth 1980s? Are we witnessing a movement away from the cross-national convergence patterns of previous decades, and toward more divergent policy paths by Western nations? Why have Britain and the United States tended to cut back social entitlements more than some of the Continental countries?

To discuss these and other questions we call upon four old soldiers of welfare state battles:

DAVID LLOYD GEORGE (1863–1945), the Liberal minister who introduced much of the initial British social security legislation between 1908 and 1911.

KONRAD ADENAUER (1876–1967), West Germany's first Chancellor, who in the 1950s faced problems of how to extend and continue the policy inheritance of previous regimes.

HARRY TRUMAN (1884–1972), U.S. President from 1945 to 1952, who sought to continue the Roosevelt traditions by proposing the Fair Deal social policy program.

TAGE ERLANDER (1901–), the Swedish politician who in the 1950s and

1960s helped shape many of the social and economic policies of the Swedish Social Democrats.

Adenauer: I would like to begin by asking Lloyd George how Britain and the United States compared with Germany in the introduction of welfare state programs, and how their coverage has developed since then.

Lloyd George: Well, if you identify the welfare state with the four basic social security programs, three of which Germany initiated in the 1880s under Bismarck, then you can say that we British initiated them about a quarter century later, around 1910, and the Americans about a half century later, in the 1930s. For a while in the 1940s British programs led other countries in coverage against illness, accident, and unemployment, and in old age protection (see Figure 10.1), but then we were overtaken by the Scandinavian countries. The United States approached our protection levels, but remains significantly behind, mainly because they still don't have a general health insurance program. The British loss of leadership may be related to relative economic decline, but I don't quite understand why the Americans haven't caught up more.

Truman: Well, it may be due to the fact that our lower-income citizens are less organized, and vote less frequently, than do lower-income Europeans. When they have gotten mobilized—in the 1930s and 1960s, for example—we have put through and expanded our basic legislation. However, most of the time our institutions—from the Congressman who disregards party loyalty, to the private T.V. station that allows fat cats to buy political time—favor those who beat the drums against Big Government. They sure hit me for a loss when I treid to introduce public health insurance in the 1940s. And even LBJ had to settle for a partial program in the 1960s. So, relative to the task of moving a whole, diverse continent, not a homogeneous medium-sized country, our policy instruments have somewhat limited capability most of the time. But what about the Germans—have they been able to pursue more consistent social policies?

Adenauer: Not completely, but for the most part yes. In the half century after Bismarck, German politics was marked by rather strong class-based hostilities. That's the reason we didn't introduce unemployment insurance until 1927 . . . and it proved inadequate when the Great Depression hit. People turned to Hitler in search of security, which of course led to the dismemberment of the empire Bismarck had brought together. Yet, let me point out that underneath these traumatic upheavals, the commitment to social security was consistently maintained by all regimes. If you got a pension entitlement under the empire, then you or your heirs could collect under the Nazis, or later under the Federal Republic. I would even say that we consciously gave priority to developing the social security system in the 1950s over, say, education or transportation. Thus, in 1957 we paved a new policy path, guaranteeing the value of old age

FIGURE 10.1 THE GROWTH OF SOCIAL INSURANCE COVERAGE

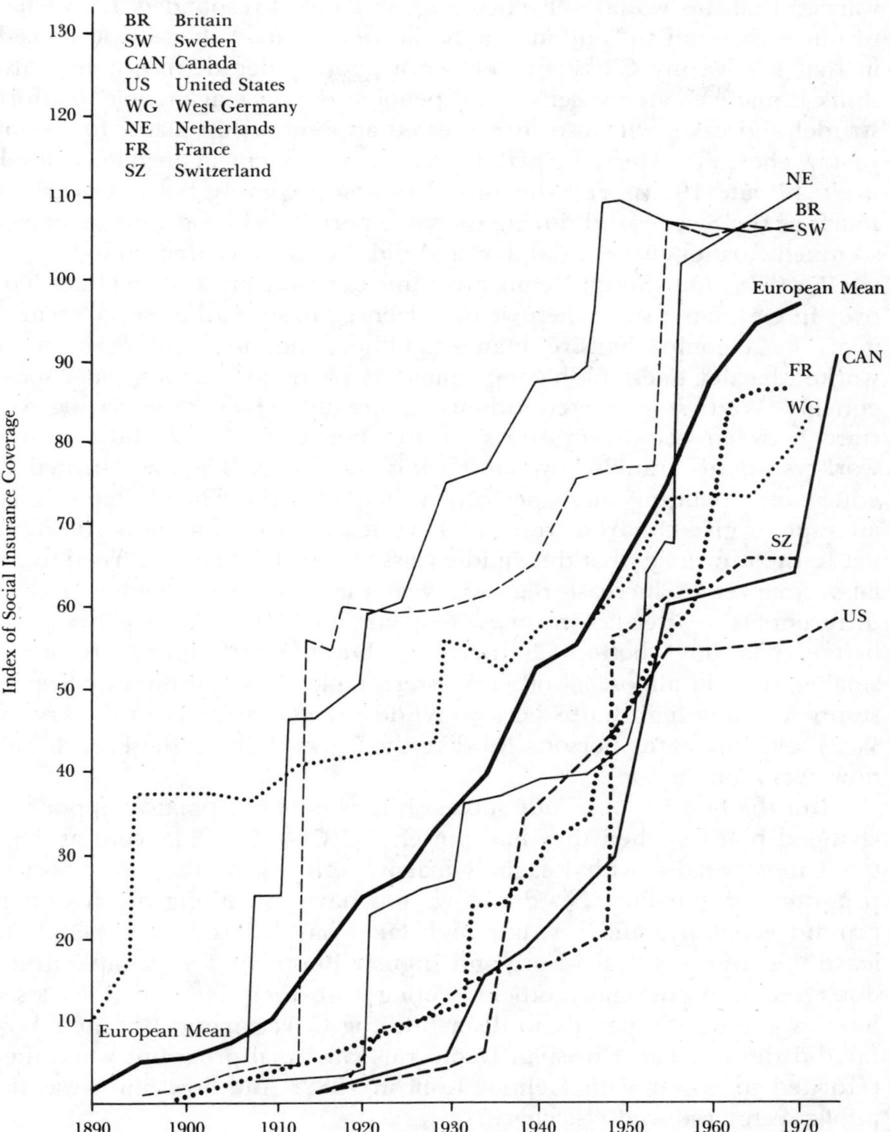

SOURCE Flora and Heidenheimer, *The Development of Welfare States in Europe and America*, p. 55.

pensions by indexing them to wage levels. When my Big Business friends warned that this would only encourage inflation, I responded that we had to put it through to "outbid" the Social Democrats. Politically, it worked, in that it gave my Christian Democrats another decade in power. I also think it made economic sense—old people were once again able to afford strudel and cake, which in turn created apprenticeship places for young pastry chefs . . . which helped keep unemployment at negligible levels until the late 1970s. Yes, this meant raising tax levels, but not nearly as much as the Swedes did during the same period. Why did your people go so much further there, Erlander, and did they achieve their aims?

Erlander: Our Social Democrats came to power just before Hitler took over in Germany; since then we have labored to strengthen social security goals in a comprehensive manner. Others did, too, but perhaps we worked harder to establish complementary prerequisites for greater social equality. We first innovated in housing, greatly reducing the glaring contrast between the living styles of the bourgeoisie and those of the workers—quite frankly, by subsidizing the latter. Then we turned to education, spending more per capita than even the United States, in an attempt to give children from the lower classes the same opportunity to get to the university that the middle-class kids had. Then we turned to the labor market to increase democracy at the work place, and to reduce differentials in after-tax incomes. Yes, our "top 20 percent" still live much better than our "bottom 20 percent," but the differences are surely smaller than in almost all other Western nations. Along the way Swedes stopped calling high-status persons *Ni* (like the German *Sie* or the French *Vous*) and low-status persons *Du* (like the German *Du* or the French *Tu*); now everybody is *Du*.

But the best proof of our success is how little our political opponents changed policies when they had power in 1976–1982. The contrast with the United States, with Reagan's massive rollback of the Great Society programs, is startling. No doubt we too have something of an underground economy; and yes, our high taxes have caused some people to leave the country: Björn Borg and Ingmar Bergman, for example. But I don't see signs of many others "voting with their feet," nor do I see Swedes joining the parade to dismantle Big Government. But then, how far did the German Christian Democrats cut social programs when they returned to power with Helmut Kohl in 1982? And how much was the public sector reduced elsewhere?

Lloyd George: Well, the Thatcherites in Britain and the Reaganites in the United States seem to be giving it quite a good try. But one question is whether their added military expenditures will not more than counterbalance and reductions in social programs. Another question is whether the trend toward increased inequalities—held necessary on economic stabilization grounds—can be effectively resisted. Left-of-center parties in both the United States and Britain seem to be in greater ideological disarray than in Germany or Sweden. What with in-fighting among party leaders, and declining party loyalty among voters, the framework through which policy commitments can achieve progressive results seems more fragile than at any time since the 1930s.

Truman: Here's something that's been puzzling me: Why do government policy responses seem to be so different in the 1980s from what they were in the 1880s? After all, both are decades of economic down-turn after a longer preceding period of growth. Yet, in the former, we see Bismarck expanding the role of the state and increasing the "cash value," if you will, of national citizenship by providing public benefits. Now we see Reagan and Thatcher trying to diminish the scope of state intervention and reducing the protection against extreme inequality which comes as a civic entitlement. We hear so much about this return to market mechanisms—is it a product of tight economic times, or rather a relapse in precisely those countries where the principles of competitive individualism were already more dominant a century ago?

Lloyd George: Perhaps the explanation is that in prosperous times the policy thrusts of capitalist democracies tend to converge, whereas in periods of economic decline they tend to diverge. If you look at periods of relative growth and prosperity, such as the decade before 1914 or the decades up to the mid-1970s, you see a lessening of differences among national policy packages. Most of Europe got social security in the former period, and the cross-national differences in education, health, housing, and other public benefits were lessened in the latter period.

In the depressed 1880s governments reacted quite differently. Germany gave priority to social security, the United States to education; other countries relied just on tariff protection. Now, in the 1980s, we again see governments all trying to control budget growth, but in strikingly different ways. France, Sweden, and other Continental countries are not willing to subordinate social policies to military ones, but are willing to go into debt to maintain the social benefits their citizens now regard as theirs by right. Britain, by contrast, is reducing its level of social and education benefits, even forcing its local governments to sell public housing.

Erlander: The Americans seem willing to go furthest in reducing the level and uniformity of the social and economic benefits. Many programs which were federally administered are to be "returned" to the states, should Reagan get his way. That must lead to greater disparity of benefits, as the states will be even more set against each other to hold taxes and benefits down so as to attract industry and employment opportunities.

Truman: Bismarck would have been surprised to look at Reagan's budget for 1983. Not only did it propose ending construction of low-cost housing units and sharply trimming rent and heat subsidies, but it moved to eliminate summer meal programs for children and reduce food stamp distribution. Federal job-training programs were to end, and day-care centers were to be reduced. Federal funds for improving the schooling of educationally deprived children were to be cut by one third. The White House claimed that these cuts would not really hurt the poor; but not even the Republicans in Congress believed this. In fact, they refused to support the cuts if military expenditures were to be raised even further. So you see we had our rather peculiar American way of celebrating the welfare state centennial. How did you commemorate the occasion in Britain, Lloyd George?

Lloyd George: Well, our Iron Lady was certainly not to be outdone in the Cross-Atlantic Competition. Even with Edward Heath nipping at her heels, she moved strongly into the budget-cutting big league. Her government's projections actually promised to *reduce* the real value of government expenditures during the centennial year . . . back to the levels of a full decade earlier! (See Figure 10.2.) Not only that, but she promised to cut the central civil service, which numbered 732,000 in 1979, by 60,000 in 1983, and by 100,000 by 1984. But as unemployment skyrocketed, each additional 100,000 unemployed required an extra 2,000 civil servants to administer unemployment, social, and welfare benefits. It was far from clear that she would achieve her aims.

Truman: In thinking about the welfare state, I think you have to take the long view. Developing social programs can be a slow and off-again, on-again process—as in the case of American health insurance, for example. Maybe I'm old fashioned, but I don't think liberals have to believe

FIGURE 10.2 BRITISH PUBLIC EXPENDITURES, 1973–1984 (1979 PRICES)

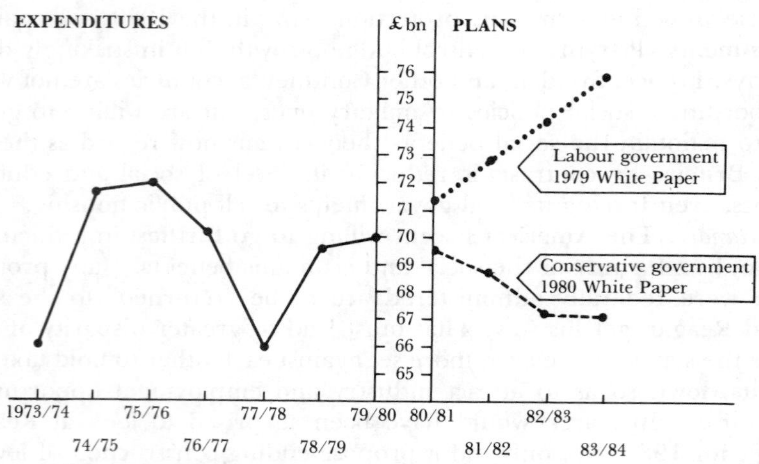

SOURCE *The Government's Expenditure Plans, 1980/81 to 1983/84,* Cmnd 7866, HMSO, 1980

in big spending or big bureaucracies. What we do have to believe is that government has a duty to do what's right and what's fair—and that often means attacking privilege, whether it be in the private or the public sector.

POLICY PATTERNS— NATIONAL, SECTORAL, AND TEMPORAL

The affluence and temper of an era have potent impact on policy development. One writer predicted in the early 1970s that the welfare state "rides the wave of the future," and that apart from some "marginal" American groups, there were "no signs of dispositions to curb it" (Girvetz, p. 520). A decade later the picture is quite different; but the impact of the expenditure crunch has varied greatly in the policy areas. Education and housing have been cut back much more than health; there are many more unemployed teachers than physicians. At the same time, the distribution of resources among sectors and sub-sectors varies considerably from nation to nation. How, therefore, can we analyze the impact of time periods, national settings, and policy sector characteristics on the content of policies? To answer this question, we must examine how they interact in good *and* bad economic climates.

Let us approach this broad subject by drawing on studies which have examined the shaping influences of national system variables, on the one hand, and policy sector variables, on the other. We have identified many discrete differences among nations' handling of various challenges; but to what extent can these habits and experiences be subsumed under consistent national models of policy making? Are these models applied similarly in most policy areas, or do the various sectors develop their own policy-making characteristics? If national institutions help shape national "styles," do the styles remain constant as long as the institutions don't change? To what extent can national policy styles explain why some countries might be more successful in some policy areas than in others?

Some political scientists thus have directly characterized national styles. The British style has been identified with a tendency toward extensive consultation, an avoidance of radical policy changes, and a disposition against actions which would challenge well-entrenched interests. The French style, by contrast, is said to exhibit a greater willingness to enforce radical policy change even against the resistance of strong sectional interests. The Swedish style has also been noted to have a capacity for radical policy innovation, but with widespread consultation and great efforts to wear down and convert opposing interests (Gustafsson and Richardson 1980).

Building on such characterizations, another political scientist developed the extended typology shown in Table 10.1. He ranked three countries on six dimensions. Sweden ranked highest on four of the dimensions. Its policy making was the most consultative and also the most open. Its policy processes were most deliberative but most radical in their proclivities toward sweeping change. The British were ranked lowest on all but two of these dimensions. The French ranked lowest on consultation and highest on centralism and level of conflict. This general policy model was then applied to the area of higher education policies to see if the pattern would hold.

The author found a "high degree of fit" between the generalized national policy style models and the particular case of higher education. In eight of the eighteen cells of the table, the rankings were in full consonance; in four of the cells, the rankings were reversed; and in six cases, the fit was indeterminate or arguable (Premfors). But one could also interpret the data to show that the policy area characteristics probably produced the significant deviations that the author noted.

Analysts of health politics have also examined whether national political systems or policy sector characteristics have had stronger effect on policy making. An influential early study of British medical interest groups concluded that the major determinants of policy in the health sector were functions of the national political system (Eckstein). Other

TABLE 10.1 POLICY STYLES IN BRITAIN, FRANCE, AND SWEDEN

	Britain	France	Sweden
Policy Change	Non-radical (3)	Occasionally radical (2)	Radical (1)
Centralism	Less centralized (3)	Highly centralized (1)	Centralized (2)
Consultation	Quite extensive consultation (2)	Limited consultation (3)	Extensive consultation (1)
Openness	Secretive (3)	Quite secretive (2)	Open (1)
Conflict Level	Quite low (2)	High (1)	Low (3)
Deliberation	Not very deliberative (3)	Quite deliberative (2)	Very deliberative (1)

SOURCE Rune Premfors, "National Policy Styles and Higher Education in France, Sweden and the United Kingdom," *European Journal of Education,* Vol. 16, No. 2 (1981), pp. 253–262.

authors argued that the crucial nature of their services gives physicians in all Western countries overwhelming political resources and that national contexts are comparatively insignificant as determinants of political influence (Marmor and Thomas). A subsequent study of German health politics concluded, more in line with the first study, that "much of the political power of physicians can be accounted for by characteristics of the political system and by political decisions, rather than by the technical nature of medical care or by ideological beliefs and values about health care" (Stone, p. 18).

Another political scientist has examined rule making in the area of occupational safety and health, considering American and Swedish practices to see how institutions embedded in dissimilar political systems handled almost identical problems. For example, how did administrative agencies set tolerance levels for noise, chemical pollution, and construction industry standards? By and large the contents of these regulations turned out to be "surprisingly similar" (Kelman, pp. 51 and 81), even though the legislative processes varied enormously and the values of the bureaucrats were very different in the two national settings. In this instance the characteristics of the policy sector, when combined to some extent with the reform ethos of the period in which the rules were made or changed, outweighed the differences of the national settings.

The findings were quite different when the same political scientist examined the implementation processes of the same rules in the same countries. The enforcement methods applied by health and safety inspectors in similar industrial settings displayed striking differences of style, with much heavier reliance on fines and other punitive methods in the United States. These national characteristics are attributed to the greater reliance in the United States on adversarial relationships and institutions in both the political and judicial systems. The Swedish accommodationist style was evinced both in a greater emphasis on rule making by consensus and in the fact that inspectors modeled their behavior more on that of the teacher and less on that of the policeman. Although differences of national style might have been expected to affect *both* rule making and rule implementation, they left a much sharper imprint on the latter (Kelman, Chapter Five).

One might also compare the relative fit of sectoral patterns to generalized national models. One would scarcely expect to find many situations in which the strength of the national policy style is completely overwhelmed or reversed by the factors peculiar to any one policy sector. After all, many of the key actors, from parliamentarians, to finance ministry officials, to government auditors, serve to extend homogeneity among the policy sectors. However distinct some policy sub-systems are—due to the privileges of a dominant profession as in health or due to the varying autonomy of regional governments or such institutions as central banks—most characteristics of national policy style are likely to be strongly reflected in the individual policy areas.

Up to now there have been very few systematic attempts to compare functionally different policy areas cross-nationally. One could seek to determine, for instance, whether policy processes in housing conform more to general national policy styles than do those in economic management. One difficulty here would be agreeing how to select and measure the relevant indicators. Another would involve the fact that national policy styles change over time. Thus, when many new groups entered into the policy process in Sweden in the late 1970s, some of the differences between Swedish and British policy making that had been clearcut a decade or two earlier were diminished (Gustafsson and Richardson, p. 33).

Another comparative approach identifies policy experiences as either very successful or very unsuccessful, and then asks whether this was because of, or in spite of, the national policy style. Such an inquiry into the recent failures of British economic policy noted that Britain failed to replicate both the links between public and private sectors and the bargaining machinery that weighed social benefits against inflationary debits (instruments used, for example, in France and Germany). These shortcomings were said to reflect some yet more general attributes "embedded in institutional and constitutional rigidities that serve politicians well, but serve the country poorly" (Ashford, p. 121).

The social security sector, by contrast, is one where British policy efforts were judged to be relatively successful. But this was because there partisan deadlock finally led to an interparty compromise which mixed private and public programs in a way that was unusual in general British policy practice (Ashford, p. 287).

VARIATIONS IN SUPPORT FOR PUBLIC POLICIES

How does citizen support for government initiative and activity vary cross-nationally and by policy area? We expect variations, and the results of a 1974 survey administered in four of "our" countries confirm that expectation. Respondents were asked to consider such policy issues as "looking after old people," or "providing a good education," or "supplying adequate housing." They were asked how important these issues were to them, and how much responsibility government had toward that problem. By combining the ratings from these responses, the authors of *Political Action* calculated indices of "agenda support" for public activity in various policy sectors. We will discuss their findings for five policy areas: education, health care, housing, old age security, and employment. On a 1 to 5 scale, the average ratings were (Farah, Barnes, and Heunks in Barnes and Kaase, p. 413):

	Britain	Netherlands	United States	West Germany
Education	4.4	4.5	4.1	4.2
Health Care	4.6	4.3	3.9	4.4
Housing	4.3	4.2	3.3	3.7
Old Age Security	4.3	4.0	3.9	4.3
Employment	4.2	4.1	3.6	4.3

Neither the highest ranking—that for health care in Britain (4.6)—nor the lowest—for housing in the United States (3.3)—should come as a surprise to readers of the preceding chapters. Agenda support in the United States was consistently below that in the European countries. While the gap was smallest in education, it was largest in the areas where the norms of free enterprise support for private initiative come into play most directly—housing and employment. Among the three European countries, we note relatively strong German agenda support for old age security and health care (public programs initiated by Bismarck in the 1880s), and somewhat lower support for education than in Britain and the Netherlands.

FIGURE 10.3 AGENDA SUPPORT FOR HOUSING, EDUCATION, AND HEALTH POLICIES, BY INCOME GROUP

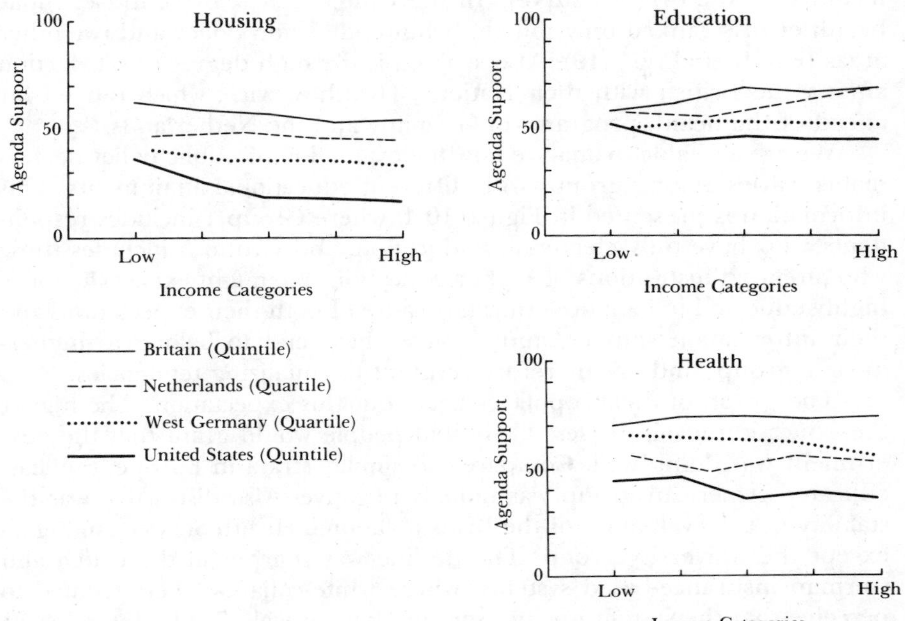

SOURCE *Political Action* Data

We might expect support for public activity to vary by social class. Figure 10.3 confirms this with regard to five income groups. Support in Europe for public housing programs declined slightly among the middle- and higher-income groups, but a much sharper decline occurred in the United States, where lower-middle- and middle-income groups probably perceived their own benefits from government policies less clearly.

Similar agenda support figures in health care and education show some contrasts. British upper-income group support holds up better for the more universal National Health Service than for housing programs. The largest cross-national differences are found in housing, the lowest in education. In these service areas we do not find the Anglo-American vs. Continental contrast which was identified in the economic policy chapter. Here the two Continental systems are bracketed on the high side by the British, on the low side by the Americans. On balance, these patterns are consonant with the finding that on questions regarding the scope of government intervention, "the mass of citizens express views that match their government's behavior" (Wilensky in OECD 1981c, p. 188).

How did *satisfaction* with government performance vary across nations and policy sectors? This can be discerned through analyses of responses to the question, "How well do you think government has been doing?" regarding the various policy sectors. In all three European countries health care was most positively evaluated among the ten policy areas included in the original survey. In the United States, by contrast, public health efforts ranked only fourth, behind education policy and two other areas (Farah et al., p. 419). Also striking is the high degree of satisfaction among the British with their National Health Service, which ranked far ahead of the health programs in Germany and the Netherlands.

We are also able to analyze how the evaluation of public policy performance varies among groups with different educational attainments. This information is presented in Figure 10.4, where Group 1 includes respondents who have only elementary education, and Group 5 includes those who attended institutions of higher education. We might expect the more highly educated to be more critical, because of both their expectations and their information sources, and because they tend to belong to higher-income groups and are therefore resistant to equalizing tendencies.

The graph on health policies bears out this expectation. The higher the education level, the less likely that people would grant that the government was doing well. Compared to similar strata in Europe, the least educated American group was notably negative. Also distinctive was the stability in the evaluation of the British National Health Service among all except the university group. The decline was sharper in the Dutch and German insurance-based systems, where white-collar workers seemed to perceive that the system was not serving them as well. But both the lowest satisfaction levels and the highest inter-group declines were found in the

United States, where both white-collar and professional groups criticized public health programs in whose benefits they largely did not share.

The results are both similar and different when we turn to education policy. Again the more highly educated tended to be more critical. But here it is the Germans who differ sharply from the others. The sharper and more prolonged controversies over reform policies, such as school comprehensivization and university reform, probably contributed to the unusually sharp slope of the German curve. It is interesting to compare the slopes of the second, third, and fourth groups in Germany and Britain. The British medium-education groups regarded recent policy changes fairly positively, whereas the university graduates, whose children were most likely to be attending grammar or private schools, deviated sharply from the evaluations of their countrymen.

Housing policy in all countries is the area where government gener-

FIGURE 10.4 PERFORMANCE EVALUATION OF HOUSING, EDUCATION, AND HEALTH POLICIES, BY EDUCATION

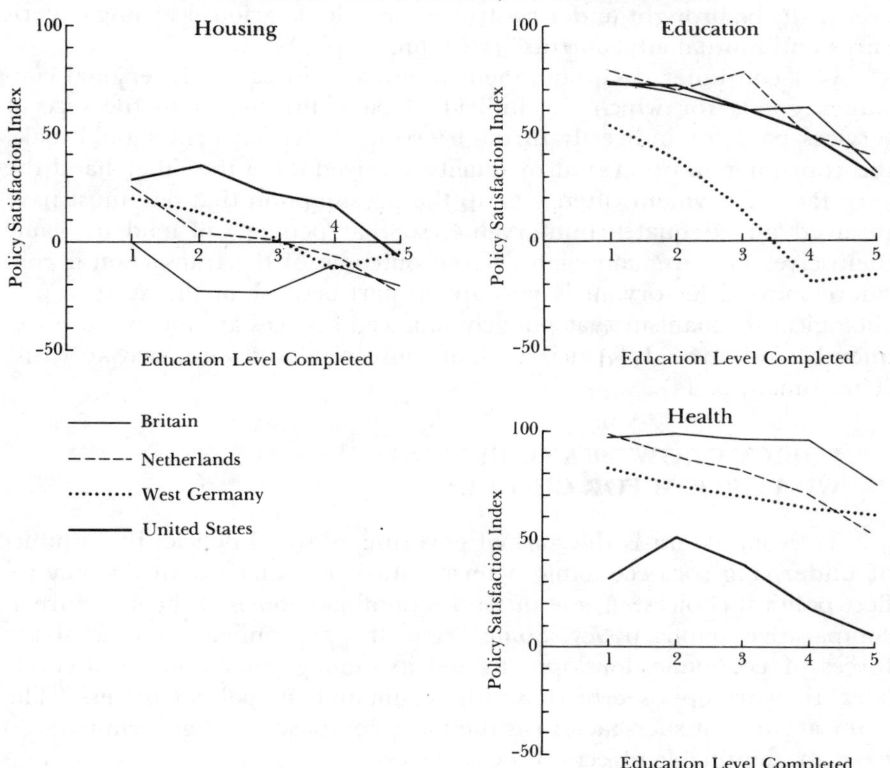

SOURCE *Political Action* Data

ates the most dissatisfaction. At first glance it might appear curious that Americans are less dissatisfied than the Europeans. But the especially negative British response provides the clue: There, government has been most directly involved in actually running, not just subsidizing, a large housing sector. Governmental policies thus become a more likely target for blame in Britain, compared to countries where nonprofit or private developers are more significant.

There may be something to the argument that the quality of services will decline as society makes a determined effort to widen access to them quickly. Disappointment may occur particularly among the first generation of consumers, as upwardly mobile groups painfully learn about the unanticipated high risk and uncertainty associated with such services as education. Should such phenomena be seen as evidence of "policy contradictions," or of "growing pains"? Proponents of the former interpretation perceive inherent conflicts between the legitimation and accumulation functions of the state (O'Connor). The latter interpretation perceives them as "serious, but quite possibly temporary, growing pains. These pains may well cause considerable trouble when first encountered, but can eventually be brought under control as a result of various learning experiences and mutual adjustments" (Hirschman, p. 43).

Will consumer disappointment be greater in cases of personal consumer goods for which the individual pays directly, or in the case of services paid for indirectly through taxes? Direct payment should make the consumer more critical of quality received. "On the other hand the very fact of payment often sets up the presumption that one must have received an adequate countervalue, so that people will tend to blame themselves (and remain silent) if the outcome of the transaction is considered unsatisfactory. It is perhaps in part because of this strange psychological mechanism that publicly financed services are much more frequently and strongly criticized than those rendered on a private basis" (Hirschman, p. 44).

POLICY GROWTH AND DECLINE: WHAT ROOM FOR CHOICE?

To what extent is the *scope* of government social policies the product of underlying socioeconomic determinants? To what extent do they reflect political choices? These questions dominate much of the literature in comparative public policy. Some argue the predominant power of the forces of economic development and its demographic and social correlates; they are opposed by those who maintain that "politics matters." The latter argue that such factors as the party composition of governments do have an identifiable effect on social policy.

> The vehemence of the 'politics matters' debate, and the fact that it is frequently tied in with the conflict of sociological functionalists and Marxist structuralists, on the one side, and the pretensions of a political science discipline premised on the exercise of human choice on the other, suggest that the issues are fundamental, relating to the extent to which the structured socio-economic processes of contemporary societies leave room for conscious agency in reshaping policy and institutional arrangements (Castles 1981, p. 119).

Those who contest the shaping influence of political processes have utilized cross-national studies to demonstrate that per capita GNP and the age structure of populations suffice to explain social security extension, and that one can leave aside discussions of party programs and ideologies (Wilensky 1975). Analyzing similar data differently, their opponents have come to very different conclusions (Cameron 1978, Castles 1979). Economists have asserted that economic and structural variables were predominant in determining such policy output indicators as the cost of health systems, the shape of educational systems, and the nature of urban planning devices. They, too, have been rebuffed by those who believe politics, or social choice, affects policy outcomes.

This debate has further stimulated the array of intellectual challenges which have attracted scholars of different backgrounds to comparative policy studies. Recently, however, one notes tendencies toward some synthesis in the battle of paradigms. Thus a Marxist scholar still holds that those who dominate the institutions of the state are constrained by the imperatives of the capital accumulation process, but he grants that "within these constraints there is room for maneuver, for competing strategies and policies. There is scope for the various organs of the state to initiate policies, to reverse them, to make choices and to make mistakes" (Gough, pp. 43–44). There has been some convergence toward examining policy outcomes by focussing on varying policy patterns and the structural relationships which underlie them. This trend has been viewed as "congenial to the practitioners of a comparative approach to politics and policy for whom an understanding of structured variation is the very essence of their discipline" (Castles 1981, p. 229).

How strongly macro-economic conditions affect public sector growth has been amply demonstrated over the past decade. Where the public sector had attracted increasing proportions of national incomes in all Western countries up to about 1975, there have been standstills and declines since then. But within these strong structural constraints governments have made very different kinds of choices. In Britain and the United States right-wing governments have made heavier cuts in many social policy areas, and used political muscle to force a reprivatization of certain sectors such as public housing. More than their Continental partners in NATO, the United States and Britain have reallocated resources from social welfare to military expenditures. Similarly, they have moved beyond retrenchment to the abolition of programs and agencies which had provided the poor with legal and organizational means to assert their interests (Piven and Cloward).

* * *

How important are the linkages between political, economic, and social systems in conditioning choices of policy *instruments?* The argument that significant differences exist among the Western democracies in the nature of choice-making capacities at the macro level has led social scientists to assess instrumentally the political-economic systems themselves. Some view many European systems as "corporatist democracies" which have relatively greater ability to adapt social policies to economic constraints with less political conflict. This capacity is attributed to three of the countries examined in this volume—the Netherlands, Sweden, and Germany—and also to Austria, Belgium, and Norway. There, consultative relations between employers, workers, governments, and other organized groups are seen as facilitating relatively equitable distributions of costs and benefits. By contrast, the less coordinated political economies of Britain and the United States are seen as being much less able to inhibit conflictual challenges to a political consensus (Wilensky).

Our comparative micro-level discussions of the policy areas strengthen our ability to evaluate the utility of these system-level models, or characterizations. Our probings may suggest that they are more applicable in some areas, such as health and incomes policies, than in others, such as education and urban planning policies. Within a policy area like health corporatist characteristics may be exhibited more where the private sector is still significant, as in Germany, than where it no longer is, as in Sweden. But the contrast between Germany's handling of health cost control and the United States' suggests that corporatist predispositions can help produce different outcomes—in this instance, in good part because of the different positions taken by organized business.

If the so-called democratic corporatist systems were clearly more successful than the others in adapting policies, the discussion might be less extensive than it has become. As is pointed out in Chapter Five, the record of the democratic corporatist systems in the policy area which provides them greatest opportunity to display their structural advantages—incomes policy—has been at best mixed. Only Austria has successfully maintained an incomes policy over a long-term period; even Sweden has recently faltered in its attempts. There the equilibrium between organized labor and business has been threatened by the unions' claims to sharing collectively in the ownership of industrial enterprises, a demand which goes beyond the labor participation in management found in Germany. It remains to be seen, however, whether the higher cooperative potential of the more corporatist systems will engender greater success in meeting Japanese and other Asian competition on international markets than most British and American industries have so far been able to achieve.

When we turn from production to allocation of costs and benefits, the "democratic corporatism matters" thesis is more persuasive. In 1982 and 1983 the officials who manage social services such as education and housing in the "corporatist" systems were in many cases given less ample budgets than they had been a decade earlier. Still, these countries seemed to avoid the widespread—not diminution, but *abolition*—of public agencies, regulatory and social programs, and university-level colleges and departments, which were so prevalent in Britain and the United States during the same years. The most visible factor affecting this contrast in the two latter countries was that conservative politicians were able to intensify their cutbacks in public expenditures because they could count on the consequences of more widespread tax backlash movements.

As we discuss in Chapter Six, it is striking that those democratic corporatist systems with higher tax levels had much weaker antitax movements than Britain and the United States did with their relatively lower tax levels. Tax protests like those of the Danish Glistrup party, the Proposition 13 movement in California, and similar phenomena in other American states were scarcely present and never markedly successful in those Continental countries with stronger corporatist structures. In none of these countries did the right-wing parties go as far in implementing, or even championing, broad income tax reductions as the Tories did under Thatcher and the Republicans under Reagan. In part this can be attributed to their different traditions of responsibility for economic management. But it is also due to the fact that the organizational web underlying the societal consensus was better able to convey to potential middle-class tax protesters what they too stood to lose from lowered social safety nets, the abolition of tenured positions in education and other public services, and the likelihood of a general decline in the quality of public life—perhaps to conditions like those that prevailed during the 1930s.

* * *

Although we are not yet able to base our claims on firm analyses, it appears that the conservative British and American governments made more drastic *distributive* choices in allocating social and economic costs than did the Continental systems. To what extent this pattern is attributable to differences in corporatist structures, and to what extent it is due to broader historical factors, which we discussed at the end of Chapter

One, is still difficult to assess. But it is evident that the Continental countries did not experience to the same degree the recent vilification of bureaucrats, the "fed-hating," and the delegitimization of public services which have been prevalent in the English-speaking countries ever since the Keynesian paradigm was dethroned. Much more discontinuity was generated in Washington between the time that President Nixon declared, "We are all Keynesians now," and when President Reagan tried to enthrone the Laffer Curve, than in the Continental capitals. None of them had to cope with budget-cutting proposals as drastic and "wholly without precedent" as the Thatcher government's proposals of 1980. (Hood and Wright, 24)

In Britain and the United States, politicians were able to carry out more extensive budget-cutting because they were less constrained by agreements with unions and interest groups, and thus could more fully exploit changes in public moods. Because the mood of the war on poverty had passed from the American scene, job-training programs fell victim to more severe cuts than in countries where the programs of the 1960s were more firmly entrenched. The Swedish non-Socialist government of the early 1980s engendered vast deficits rather than reduce such programs. If policy fashions change less quickly in democratic corporatist countries, it is not only because their bureaucracies are more legitimated, but probably because the organizational density tends to perpetuate a stronger sense of recent history. The memories of the unemployment of the 1930s were retained more vividly in the Netherlands and Sweden than in California, where a former union leader, Ronald Reagan, could persuade his more mobile audience that the policy lessons drawn by the preceding generation could be stood on their head with impunity.

Studies show that during a period of budgetary decrementalism, such as the 1980s, those groups whose esteem in public recognition and moods have been least consistent are disproportionately hurt. Among social groups this has meant that the working poor were more easily permitted to slip back under the poverty line than were the elderly, whose claims to social insurance pensions had become more firmly anchored in the English-speaking countries as well. So pensions and health care have not been deeply hurt in the decrementalist era; but it has been different in the case of education. In the 1950s new conceptions of the benefits of educational expansion led to "an astonishing story of public, political, and administrative commitment to, or at least acceptance of, the expansion of service whose products are wholly indirect and invisible." But this was followed by the "erosion of confidence in education's social and productive functions," and the swift deceleration of growth (Kogan in Hood and Wright). Whereas Labour politicians had kept education at least on an even keel, the Conservative government's cutbacks forced the closing of many colleges, the firing of 4,000 tenured university lecturers, and a large-scale curtailment of research. Thus Margaret Thatcher, who as Education Minister had in 1972 issued a White Paper called *Education: A Framework for Expansion,* was, a decade later, presiding over not just the deceleration, but the quantum demolition, of large parts of her previous domain.

CRISES OF POLICIES AND SCALE OF CHOICES

The tendency to view politics as a means of collective social change is likely to grow, not diminish, in the years ahead. There is the obvious sense of growing scarcity in economic and natural resources as well as in the tax revenues to support government programs. Scarcity forces us to be aware of starker choices; some of one thing must be given up to have more of another. This situation has been played out most dramatically in budget-cutting exercises throughout the Western nations in recent years. This setting has clearly evoked another factor in policy options—namely, the size and power of nations.

The United States, as a world power, has pursued a higher level of armaments expenditures at the same time that it has cut federal expenditures in most domestic policy areas. In this it has differed from the middle-sized nations of Europe. In earlier periods, size of military effort generally has not been strongly related to size of social policy effort (Wilensky 1975). In the 1980s, however, the tradeoffs between these two spheres may become more direct. This pressure toward new priorities, from the promotion of individual security through social policy measures to the bolstering of national security through military and strategic measures, is engendering considerable resistance in both Europe and the United States. Considering proposals in NATO countries in the early 1980s that "renewed military effort must be financed from declining economic resources," one Dutch writer assessed the chances that popular opinion would support such a shift, concluding that while such support had earlier been generated during the "coldest" stage of the Cold War, signposts for the 1980s indicated "less popular consensus and support for stressing warfare priorities than for fighting unemployment and preserving welfare programs" (Keman in Castles 1982, p. 217).

Just as the traditional welfare state agenda is feeling the strains of scarcity and belligerence, so its so-called post-materialist goals are also expanding. While public concerns about jobs, schools, and health care remain high, the younger generation seems more interested in seeing other equality-related concerns added to the agenda of political choice (Barnes and Kaase 1979). Quality-of-life issues—such as the meaningfulness of one's work and opportunities for contributing to the preservation of one's environment—do not appear to be replacing traditional bread-and-butter policy topics; but they are lengthening the list of criteria by which public policies are debated and judged in every nation.

From the comparative information available, it appears that public opinion has what can only be called a love-hate relationship with the welfare state. After an exhaustive study of the attitude surveys in the United States and Europe, the most thorough book on this subject to date sums up the results in this way:

> . . . enough evidence currently exists to lend some credibility to the notion of a distinctively "modern" system of mass attitudes, opinions, and beliefs associated with social policy development. The characteristics of this system include, as we have seen, widespread public acceptance of the general principles of the "social rights" of citizenship, entailing positive governmental efforts to promote individual security and social equality, with a simultaneous allegiance to individual freedom, the "free market," and individual responsibility for success or failure in a competitive economic order. In addition, the data firmly establish that some types of social welfare programs are invariably popular in modern society (e.g., old-age pensions), while other categories of programs may be universally problematic (e.g., public assistance) (Coughlin 1980, pp. 155–156).

In other words, public opinion appears to be as inconsistent in its commitment to social policy principles as the welfare state itself. And here we find a key to understanding how democratic politics could create the modern welfare state without satisfying the reasoned requirements of economists or the preferences of ideological purists. Political processes, like public opinion, involve choices that avoid the "big choice" between individual liberty and social equality, between the inequality and insecurity generated by market mechanisms and the flattening equality implied by distributive concepts which arise from uniform definitions of social needs.

By the strict canons of economic reasoning, a democratic welfare state should be impossible. In a brilliant analysis, the economist Kenneth Arrow offered proof that a consistent summation of individual preferences into a collective welfare choice could not be achieved (Arrow, Mackay). Making a number of fairly reasonable assumptions about the distribution of welfare preferences and other constraints, Arrow was able to show the internal contradictions that were bound to arise in any effort to define a democratic social welfare function.

By the less strict, but emotionally charged, canons of ideological reasoning, the welfare state should also be impossible. It fails to satisfy socialist criteria for production organized around social needs rather than profit motives. In fact every Western welfare state is highly ambiguous about how social needs are actually to be defined and who defines them. Yet the welfare state also fails to satisfy conservative criteria for maximizing individual liberty. It does not leave people, as Milton Friedman put it, "free to choose," and it neither fully accepts nor rejects market mechanisms. In terms of ideological clarity, the welfare state is incoherent.

But one need not therefore jump to conclusions about a "system breakdown" or political "overload," for engineering concepts may be no more applicable than economic concepts. Rather, we need to recall that the management of such contradictions is precisely what the politics of social choice is about. If the political choice process had been required to yield a consistent ordering of objectives, the modern welfare state as we know it could never have come into existence.

* * * * *

The welfare state, then, is now going through a period of adjustment, rather than a sharp decline. Marxists might join with social choice theorists to argue that some of the political allocation techniques may prove less effective in a period of greater vulnerability in the Western economies. What one calls acute "capitalist contradictions" the other sees as the pitfalls of destructive regulation and soft-headed protectionism. At the root of all social choices lie values. Ours is a very secularized world, and clearly the values of equality have not been accorded a sacred or unquestioned status in any system—Western capitalist, socialist, or others. It seems entirely appropriate that the broader social consequences of equalizing programs—from Headstart to council housing to free health care—be reviewed in the light of changing economic constraints and altered occupational opportunity. But the long-term study of policy evolution in democratizing political systems shows few instances where the exaltation of inequality has provided clearcut lasting gains for either ruler or ruled. As we approach the end of the second millenium, it somehow does not seem likely that the basic rules of social equity will soon be rewritten to conform to the concept of Thrasymachus, who defined justice as "the interest of the stronger."

BIBLIOGRAPHY

This bibliography serves the dual purpose of providing reference information on sources referred to in this volume and listing some additional cross-national studies relating to the policy areas covered. It is intended to provide an easily accessible overview of the relevant literature, with emphasis on recent English-language publications. Some general references are included in the sections for Chapters One and Ten.

Reference items are generally listed by senior author. Articles in edited volumes are typically cited in the text by author of the article and editor of the volume: (Smith, in Jones). To find reference information in the bibliography you should look under the name of the editor, Jones.

Certain journals are referred to with abbreviations, as follows:

AJS	American Journal of Sociology
APSR	American Political Science Review
BJPS	British Journal of Political Science
Comp Ed Rev	Comparative Education Review
Comp Pol St	Comparative Political Studies
Comp Pol	Comparative Politics
High Ed	Higher Education
Int Jl Urb & RR	International Journal of Urban and Regional Research
Int Jl Hlth Svc	International Journal of Health Services
Jl Hlth PP & L	Journal of Health Politics, Policy and Law
Law & Con P	Law and Contemporary Problems
Mil Mem Q	Milbank Memorial Quarterly

Pol Anal	Policy Analysis
Pol & Pol	Policy and Politics
Pol Stud	Political Studies
Sc Pol Stud	Scandinavian Political Studies
Tijd E & S Geo	Tijdschrift voor Econ. en Soc Geografie
Urb Aff Q	Urban Affairs Quarterly
West Eur Pol	West European Politics

Chapter 1. THE POLITICS OF SOCIAL CHOICE

Anderson, Charles, "System and Strategy in Comparative Policy Analysis: A Plea for Contextual and Experimential Knowledge," in William B. Gwyn and George C. Edwards, III, eds., *Perspective in Public Policy-Making* (New Orleans: Tulane Studies in Political Science, 1975).

Ashford, Douglas E., ed., *Comparing Public Policies: New Concepts and Methods* (Beverly Hills: Sage, 1978).

Barnes, Samuel and Max Kaase, *Political Action* (Beverly Hills: Sage, 1979).

Borcherding, T.E. ed., *Budgets and Bureaucrats: The Sources of Government Growth* (Chapel Hill: Duke, 1977).

Brittan, Samuel, *The Economic Consequences of Democracy* (New York: Holmes and Meier, 1979).

Buchanan, James and Richard Wagner, *Democracy in Deficit* (New York: Academic, 1977).

Cameron, David, "The Expansion of the Public Economy: A Comparative Analysis," *APSR* 72, 4 (December 1978), pp. 1243–1261.

Comstock, Alzada, "Expenditures, Public," *Encyclopedia of the Social Sciences*, Vol. 6 (New York: Macmillan, 1937) pp. 5–10.

Coughlin, Richard M., *Ideology, Public Opinion and Welfare Policy* (Berkeley: Institute of International Studies, 1980) pp. 155–156.

Dyson, Kenneth, *The State Tradition in Western Europe* (New York: Oxford, 1980).

Flora, Peter and Arnold J. Heidenheimer, *The Development of Welfare States in Europe and America* (New Brunswick: Transaction Books, 1981).

Fried, Robert C. and Francine F. Rabinovitz, *Comparative Urban Politics* (Prentice-Hall, 1980).

Graham, Helen, "Implementation through Bargaining," *Public Policy* (Fall 1977).

Groth, Alexander, *Comparative Politics: A Distributive Approach* (New York: Macmillan, 1971).

Gwyn, William B. and George C. Edwards, III, eds., *Perspectives on Public Policy-Making* (New Orleans: Tulane Studies in Political Science, 1975).

Hayward, Jack and Michael Watson, *Planning, Politics and Public Policy: The British, French and Italian Experience* (London: Cambridge, 1975).

Hesse, Hermann, *The Journey to the East* (New York: Farrar, Straus and Giroux, 1956).

Lindblom, Charles, *Politics and Markets* (New York: Basic, 1977).

Moore, Barrington, *The Social Origins of Democracy and Dictatorship* (Boston: Beacon, 1966).

Nordhaus, William, "The Political Business Cycle," *Review of Economic Studies*, Vol. 42 (1975) pp. 169–190.

O'Connor, James, *The Fiscal Crisis of the State* (New York: St. Martin's, 1973).
Piven, Frances F. and Richard A. Cloward, *Regulating the Poor* (New York: St. Martin's, 1973).
Pryor, Frederic L., *Public Expenditures in Communist and Capitalist Nations* (Homewood, IL: Dorsey, 1968).
Rokkan, Stein, "Cities, States and Nations," in S. N. Eisenstadt and Rokkan, eds., *Building States and Nations* (Beverly Hills: Sage, 1974) pp. 73–97.
Rose, Richard, "On the Priorities of Government: A Developmental Analysis," *European Journal of Political Research* 4 (1976) pp. 247–289.
———, ed., *The Dynamics of Public Policy: A Comparative Analysis* (Beverly Hills: Sage, 1976).
Sharkansky, Ira, *Wither the State? Politics and Public Enterprise in Three Countries* (Chatham, NJ: Chatham House, 1979).
Siegel, Richard L. and Leonard B. Weinberg, *Comparing Public Policies: United States, Soviet Union and Europe* (Homewood: Dorsey Press, 1977).
Smith, T. Alexander, *The Comparative Policy Process* (Santa Barbara: ABC–Clio Press, 1975).
Wildavsky, Aaron, *Speaking Truth to Power* (Boston: Little, Brown, 1979).
Wilensky, Harold, *The Welfare State and Equality* (Berkeley: University of California Press, 1975).

Chapter 2. EDUCATION POLICY

Anderson, C. Arnold, "Sweden Examines Higher Education: A Critique of the U-68 Report," *High Ed* 4, 3 (1975) pp. 393–408.
———, "Societal Characteristics Within the School: Inferences from the ISEA Study," *Comp Ed Rev* 23, 3 (October 1979) pp. 408–421.
Archer, Margaret S., *Social Origins of Educational Systems* (London: Sage, 1979).
Banting, Keith G., *Poverty, Politics and Policy* (London: Macmillan, 1979).
Barnes, Samuel and Max Kaase, eds., *Political Action* (Beverly Hills: Sage, 1979).
Bellaby, Paul, *The Sociology of Comprehensive Schooling* (London: Methuen, 1977).
Ben-David, Joseph, *Centers of Learning: Britain, France, Germany, United States* (New York: McGraw-Hill, 1977).
Bereday, George Z.F., "Social Stratification and Education in Industrial Countries," *Comp Ed Rev* 21, 2 (June-October 1977) pp. 195–210.
Bericht der Bundesregierung über die strukturellen Probleme des foederativen Bildungssystem (Bonn: Bundesminister für Bildung und Wissenschaft, 1978).
Boaden, Noel T. and Robert A. Alford, "Sources of Diversity in English Local Government Decisions," *Public Administration* 47 (Summer 1969) pp. 203–223.
Boudon, Raymond, *Education, Opportunity and Social Inequality* (New York, 1974).
———, "The 1970s in France: A Period of Student Retreat," *High Ed* 8 (November 1979) pp. 669–681.
Brickman, Ronald, "The Comparative Political Analysis of Science and Technology," *Comp Pol* 13 (1981) pp. 479–496.
Burn, Barbara, ed., *Access Systems: Youth and Employment* (New York: International Council for Educational Development, 1977).
———, *Admission to Medical Education in Ten Countries* (New York: Interbook, 1978).

Carnegie Council on Policy Studies in Higher Education, *The States and Private Higher Education* (San Francisco: Jossey Bass, 1977).

Clark, Burton, "Academic Differentiation in National Systems of Higher Education," *Comp Ed Rev* 22, 2 (June 1978), pp. 242–258.

Clarke, Alex M. and L. Michael Birt, "Evaluative Reviews in Universities: The Influence of Public Policies," *High Ed* 11, 1 (January 1982) pp. 1–26.

Church, Robert L., *Education in the United States* (New York: Free Press, 1976).

Cremin, Lawrence A., *American Education: The National Experience 1973–1976* (New York: Harper, 1980).

Embling, Jack, *A Fresh Look at Higher Education: European Implications of the Carnegie Commission Reports* (New York: Elsevier, 1974).

Flora, Peter and Arnold J. Heidenheimer, *The Development of Welfare States in Europe and America* (New Brunswick: Transaction, 1981).

Fomerand, Jacques, J. van de Graaff, and Henry Wasser, *Higher Education in Western Europe and North America: A Selected and Annotated Bibliography* (New York: Council on European Studies, Columbia University, 1979).

Geiger, Roger L., "The Changing Demand for Higher Education in the Seventies: Adaptations Within Three National Systems," *High Ed* 9, 3 (May 1980) p. 269.

Goldschmidt, Dietrich, "Participatory Democracy in Schools and Higher Education," *High Ed* 5, 2 (1976) pp. 113–133.

Hearnden, Arthur, *Paths to University: Preparation, Assessment, Selection* (London: Schools Council/ Macmillan, 1973).

_______, *Education in the Two Germanies* (Boulder, CO: Westview, 1979).

Heidenheimer, Arnold J., "Achieving Equality through Educational Expansion: Problems in the Swedish Experience," *Comp Pol St* 10, 3 (October 1977) pp. 413–432.

_______, "Professional Unions, Public Sector Growth and the Swedish Equality Policy," *Comp Pol* 10, 3 (October 1976) pp. 49–73.

_______, "The Politics of Educational Reform: Explaining Different Outcomes of School Comprehensivization Attempts in Sweden and West Germany," *Comp Ed Rev* 18, 3 (October 1974) pp. 388–410.

Husén, Torsten, "Academic Performance in Selective and Comprehensive Schools," in J. Karabel and A.H. Halsey., eds., *Power and Ideology in Education* (New York: Oxford 1977).

_______, *The School in Question* (New York: Oxford, 1980).

_______, "An International Research Venture in Retrospect: The IEA Surveys," *Comp Ed Rev* 23, 3 (October 1979) pp. 371–385.

_______, and Boalt, Gunnar, *Educational Research and Educational Change* (New York: Wiley, 1968).

Inglehart, Ronald, "Post-Materialism in an Environment of Insecurity," *APSR* 75, 4 (November 1981) pp. 880–900.

Kaelble, Harmut, "Educational Opportunities and Government Politics in Europe in the Period of Industrialization," in Peter Flora and Arnold J. Heidenheimer, *The Development of Welfare States in Europe and America* (New Brunswick: Transaction, 1981) Chapter 7.

Koerner, James, *Reform in Education: England and the United States* (New York: Delacorte, 1968).

Kogan, Maurice, *Educational Policy-Making: A Study of Interest Groups and Parliament* (London: Linnett, 1975).

———, *Educational Policies in Perspective: An Appraisal* (Paris: OECD, 1979).

Lavin, David E. *et al.*, "Open Admissions and Equal Access," *Harvard Educational Review* 49, 1 (February 1979) pp. 53–92.

Levin, Henry M., "The Dilemma of Comprehensive Secondary School Reforms in Europe," *Comp Ed Rev* 22, 3 (November 1978) pp. 434–451.

Maier, Hans, "Die Kirchen," in Richard Lowenthal and Hans-Peter Schwarz, eds., *Die Zweite Deutsche Republik; 25 Jahre Bundesrepublik Deutschland: eine Bilanz*, (Stuttgart: Seewald, 1974).

Marshall, T.H., *Sociology at the Crossroads and Other Essays* (London: Heinemann, 1963).

Merritt, Richard L., "Opening up the Universities: The Courts, The Universities and the Right of Admission in the Federal Republic of Germany," *Minerva* 17, 1 (Spring 1979) pp. 1–32.

——— and Fred Coombs, "Politics and Educational Reform," *Comp Ed Rev* 21 (June-October 1977) pp. 247–273.

Neave, Guy, ed., "Changing Links between Secondary and Higher Education," *European Journal of Education* 16, 2 (1981) pp. 141–253.

Organisation for Economic Cooperation and Development, *Reviews of National Policies for Education: Germany* (Paris: OECD, 1972).

———, *Education Statistics in OECD Countries* (Paris: OECD, 1981).

Paulston, Rolland G., *Educational Change in Sweden: Planning and Accepting the Comprehensive School Reforms* (New York: Teachers College Press, 1968).

———, "Social and Educational Change: Conceptual Frameworks," *Comp Ed Rev* 21, 2 (June-October 1977) pp. 370–395.

Podmore, Chris, "Private Schools—An International Comparison," *Canadian and International Education* 6 (December 1977) pp. 8–33.

Premfors, Rune, *The Politics of Higher Education in a Comparative Perspective: France, Sweden, United Kingdom* (Stockholm: Stockholm University, Political Science Department, 1980).

Ringer, Fritz, *Education and Society in Modern Europe* (Bloomington: Indiana University Press, 1979).

Robinsohn, Saul B., ed., *Schulreform im gesellschaftlichen Prozess* (Stuttgart: Klett, 1970).

Selden, William K., *Accreditation* (New York: Harper, 1960).

Trow, Martin, "Aspects of Diversity in American Higher Education," in Herbert J. Gans *et al.*, eds., *On the Making of Americans* (Philadelphia: University of Pennsylvania Press, 1979).

Turner, Ralph H., "Modes of Social Ascent through Education," in A. H. Halsey, ed., *Education, Economy and Society* (Glencoe, IL: Free Press, 1961).

Van de Graaff, John, "West Germany's Abitur Quota and School Reform," *Comp Ed Rev* 11, 1 (February 1967) pp. 75–87.

———, ed., *Academic Power: Patterns of Authority in Seven National Systems of Higher Education* (New York: Praeger, 1978).

White, Dana F., "Education in the Turn-of-the-Century City: The Search for Control," *Urban Education* 4, 2 (July 1969) pp. 169–182.

Wirt, Frederick M., "Comparing Educational Politics: Theory, Units of Analysis and Research Strategies," *Comp Ed Rev* 24, 2 (June 1980) pp. 174–191.

Chapter 3. HEALTH POLICY

Abel-Smith, Brian, "The History of Medical Care," in E.W. Martin, ed., *Comparative Development in Social Welfare* (London: Allen and Unwin, 1972).

Altenstetter, Christa, *Health Policy Making and Administration in West Germany and the United States* (Beverly Hills: Sage, 1974).

———, ed., *Changing National-Subnational Relations in Health* (Washington, DC: National Institutes of Health, 1978).

———, *Innovation in Health Policy and Service Delivery: A Cross National Perspective* (Cambridge: Oelgeschlager, 1981).

Anderson, Odin W., *Health Care: Can There Be Equity?* (New York: Wiley, 1972).

Anderson, Ronald, Bjorn Smedby, and Odin W. Anderson, *Medical Care Use in Sweden and the United States: A Comparative Analysis of Systems and Behavior* (Chicago: Center for Health Administration Studies, Research Series 27, 1970).

Berg, Ole, "The Health Services System: The Interaction of Medical, Socio-Cultural, Economic and Political Logics," *Sc Pol Stud* 3, 3 (1980) pp. 209–234.

Berki, S.E. and B. Kobashigawa, "Education and Income Effects in Use of Ambulatory Services in the United States," *Intl Jl Hlth Svc* 8, 2 (1978) pp. 351–365.

Berlant, Jeffrey L., *Profession and Monopoly: A Study of Medicine in the United States and Great Britain* (Berkeley: University of California Press, 1975).

Blanpain, Jan, ed., *National Health Insurance and Health Resources: The European Experience* (Cambridge: Harvard University Press, 1978).

Brasfield, James, "Health Planning Reform: A Proposal for the Eighties," *Jl Hlth PP & L* 4 (Winter 1982) pp. 718–738.

Brown, Lawrence D., "The Formulation of Federal Health Care Policy," *Bulletin of the New York Academy of Medicine* 54, 1 (1978).

———, "Competition and Health Cost Containment," *Mil Mem Q* 59, 2 (Spring 1981) pp. 145–189.

Bunberry, Jeffrey L., ed., *Lloyd George's Ambulance Wagon: Memoirs of W.J. Braithwaite* (London: Methuen, 1957).

Carder, Mack and Ben Klingeberg, "How 'Swedish' was the Seven Crowns Reform?" in Arnold J. Heidenheimer and Nils Elvander, eds., *The Shaping of the Swedish Health System* (New York: St. Martin's, 1980).

Enthoven, Alan C., *Health Plan* (Reading, MA: Addison Wesley, 1980).

Feldstein, Paul, *Health Associations and the Demand for Legislation* (Ballinger, 1977).

Field, Mark, "The Concept of the 'Health System' at the Macrosociological Level," *Social Science and Medicine* 7, 10 (October 1973) pp. 763–785.

Glaser, William, *Health Insurance Bargaining: Foreign Lessons for America* (New York: Halsted, 1978).

———, *Paying the Doctor: Systems of Renumeration and their Effects* (Baltimore: Johns Hopkins Press, 1970).

Goodman, John C., "NHS: An Ill for All Cures?" *Policy Review* 17 (Spring 1981).

Havighurst, Clark C., "Antitrust Enforcement in the Medical Services Industry: What Does It All Mean?" *Mil Mem Q* 58, 1 (1980) pp. 89–124.

Heidenheimer, Arnold J., Hugh Heclo, and Carolyn Adams, *Comparative Public Policy* (New York: St. Martin's, 1975).

———, "Organized Medicine and Physician Specialization in Scandinavia and West Germany," *West Eur Pol* 3, 3 (October 1980) pp. 373–387.

——— and Nils Elvander, eds., *The Shaping of the Swedish Health System* (New York: St. Martin's, 1980).

Honigsbaum, Frank, *The Division in British Medicine: A History of the Separation of General Practice from Hospital Care, 1911–1965* (London: Kogan Page, 1979).

Kelman, Steven, *Regulating America, Regulating Sweden: A Comparative Study of Occupational Safety and Health Legislation Policy* (Cambridge: MIT Press, 1981).

Kessel, Reuben, "The A.M.A. and the Supply of Physicians," *Law & Con P* 35 (Spring 1970) pp. 267–283.

Klein, Rudolf, "Ideology, Class and the National Health Service," *Jl Hlth PP & L* 4, 3 (Fall 1979) pp. 464–490.

Klein, Rudolf, James Drife, and G.P. McNicol, Comment on NHS Royal Commission Report, *British Medical Journal* (6 October 1979) pp. 840–850.

Krizay, John and Andrew Wilson, *The Patient as Consumer: Health Care Financing in the United States* (Lexington, MA: Lexington Books, 1974).

Landsberger, Henry A., "The Control of Cost in the Federal Republic of Germany: Lessons for America?" (Washington: International Health Planning Series 3, Department of Health and Human Services, 1981).

Leichter, Howard M., *A Comparative Approach to Policy Analysis: Health Care Policy in Four Nations* (New York: Cambridge University Press, 1979).

Lockhart, Charles, "Values and Policy Conceptions of Health Policy Elites in the United States, the United Kingdom, and the Federal Republic of Germany," *JL Hlth PP & L* 6 (1981) pp. 98–119.

Lubove, Roy, *The Struggle for Social Security: 1900–1935* (Cambridge: Harvard University Press, 1968).

Marmor, Theodore, Richard Boyer, and Julie Greenberg, "Medical Care and Procompetitive Reform," in Symposium on Market Oriented Approaches to Health Policy Goals, *Vanderbilt Law Review* 34, 4 (May 1981) pp. 1003–1028.

Marmor, Theodore, *Political Analysis and American Medical Care* (New York: Cambridge University Press, 1983).

Maxwell, Robert J., *Health and Wealth: An International Study of Health Care Spending* (Lexington, MA: Lexington Books, 1981).

Maynard, Alan, *Health Care in the European Community* (Pittsburgh: University of Pittsburgh Press, 1975).

Mechanic, David, *Public Expectations and Medical Care,* (New York: Wiley, 1972).

Moran, Donald W., "HMO's, Competition and the Politics of Minimum Benefits," *Mil Mem Q* 59, 2 (Spring 1981) pp. 190–208.

Newman, John F. *et al.*, "Attempts to Control Health Care Costs: The United States Experience," *Social Science and Medicine* 13A (1979) pp. 529–540.

Office of Technology Assessment, *The Implications of Cost-Effectiveness Analysis of Medical Technology,* OTA Background Paper 4 (Washington, DC: Office of Technology Assessment, October 1980).

Rein, Martin, "Social Class and the Health Service," *New Society* 14, 373 (20 November 1969) pp. 807–810.

Roemer, Milton I., *Comparative National Policies on Health Care* (New York: Denner, 1977).

_______ and Jay W. Friedman, *Doctors in Hospitals* (Baltimore: Johns Hopkins Press, 1971) p. 55.

Sapolsky, Harvey M., Drew Altman, Richard Greene, and Judith Moore, "Corporate Attitudes toward Health Care Costs," *Mil Mem Q* 9, 4 (Fall 1981) pp. 561–585.

Skidmore, Max J., *Medicare and the American Rhetoric of Reconciliation* (University, AL: University of Alabama Press, 1970).

Stevens, Rosemary, *American Medicine and the Public Interest* (New Haven: Yale University Press, 1971).

_______, *Medical Practice in Modern England* (New Haven: Yale University Press, 1966).

Stone, Deborah, "Professionalism and Accountability: Controlling Health Services in the United States and West Germany," *Jl Hlth PP & L* 2 (1977) pp. 32–47.

_______, *The Limits of Professional Power: National Health Care in the Federal Republic of Germany* (Chicago: University of Chicago Press, 1980).

The Swedish Health Service System (Chicago: American Hospital Association, 1971).

Wan, Thomas and Lois Gray, "Differential Access to Preventive Services for Young Children in Low-Income Areas," *Journal of Health and Social Behavior* 9 (September 1978) pp. 312–324.

Witte, Edwin E., *Social Security Perspectives* (Madison: University of Wisconsin Press, 1962).

Vladeck, Bruce C., "The Market vs. Regulation: The Case for Regulation," *Mil Mem Q* 59, 2 (Spring 1981) pp. 209–223.

Chapter 4. HOUSING POLICY

Boaden, Noel, *Urban Policy-Making: Influences on County Boroughs in England and Wales* (Cambridge, Eng.: Cambridge University Press, 1971).

_______ and Robert Alford, "Sources of Diversity in English Local Government," *Public Administration* 47 (London, 1969) pp. 203–223.

Brenner, Joel and Herbert Franklin, *Rent Control in North America and Four European Countries* (Washington, DC: Council for International Urban Liaison, 1977).

British Market Research Bureau, *Housing Consumer Survey* (London: National Economic Development Office, 1977).

Burns, Leland and Leo Grebler, *The Housing of Nations: Analysis and Policy in Comparative Framework* (New York: Wiley, 1977).

Checkoway, Barry, "Large Builders, Federal Housing Programmes, and Postwar Suburbanization," *Int Jl Urb & RR* 4, 1 (March 1980).

Daun, Ake, "Why Do Swedish Suburbs Look the Way They Do?" *Human Environment in Sweden* 9 (February 1979).

Davies, Bleddyn, "Comment on Nicholson and Topham," *Journal of the Royal Statistical Society* 134 (1971) pp. 311–313.

Department of Environment, *Housing Policy—A Consultative Document,* Cmnd. 6851 (London: HMSO, 1977).

Donnison, D. V., *The Goverment of Housing* (Baltimore: Penguin, 1967).

Duclaud-Williams, R.H., *The Politics of Housing in Britain and France* (London: Heinemann, 1978).

Dumouchel, J. Robert, *European Housing Rehabilitation Experience: A Summary and Analysis* (Washington, DC: National Association of Housing and Redevelopment Officials, 1978).

Fainstein, Norman and Susan Fainstein, eds., *Urban Policy Under Capitalism,* Vol. 22, Urban Affairs Annual Reviews (Beverly Hills: Sage, 1982).

Fried, Joseph, *Housing Crisis U.S.A.* (New York: Praeger, 1971).

Frieden, Bernard, "Housing Allowances: An Experiment that Worked," *The Public Interest* 59 (Spring 1980) pp. 15–35.

Frommes, Robert, *Problems Raised by the Individual Subsidization of Accommodation* (The Hague: International Federation of Housing and Planning, 1970).

Grebler, Leo and Frank Mittlebach, *The Inflation of House Prices: Its Extent, Causes, and Consequences* (Lexington, MA: Lexington Books, 1979).

Hallett, Graham, *Housing and Land Policies in West Germany and Britain* (London: Macmillan, 1977).

Harrison, Anthony and Gillian Lomas, "Tenure Preferences: How to Intepret the Survey Evidence," *Centre for Environmental Studies Review* 8 (London: January 1980) pp. 20–24.

Headey, Bruce, *Housing Policy in the Developed Economy: The U.K., Sweden, and the U.S.* (New York: St. Martin's, 1978).

Howenstine, E.J., "The Changing Roles of Housing Production Subsidies and Consumer Housing Subsidies in European National Housing Policy," *Land Economics* 51, (February 1975) pp. 86–94.

International Confederation of Free Trade Unions, *The Housing Situation of Low-Income Groups* (Brussels: ICFTU, 1970).

Katz, Robert, "Is Public Housing Going Out of Business in Great Britain?" *Journal of Housing* 36, 9 (October 1979) pp. 461–464.

Kemeny, James, "Urban Home-ownership in Sweden," *Urban Studies* 15 (1978) pp. 313–320.

———, "Home Ownership and Privatization," *Int Jl Urb & RR* 4, 3 (1980) pp. 372–387.

———, *The Myth of Home Ownership: Private Versus Public Choices in Housing Tenure* (London: Routledge and Kegan Paul, 1981).

Kristof, Frank, "Housing Policy Goals and Housing Market Behavior: Experience in the United States," *Urban Studies* 3, 2 (June 1966).

Lansley, Steward, *Housing and Public Policy* (London: Croom Helm, 1979).

Lett, Monica, *Rent Control: Concepts, Realities, and Mechanisms* (New Brunswick, NJ: Rutgers Center for Urban Policy Research, 1976).

McGuire, Chester, *International Housing Policies: A Comparative Analysis* (Lexington, MA: Lexington Books, 1981).

Merrett, S., *State Housing in Britain* (Boston: Routledge & Kegan Paul, 1979).

Michelson, William, "Reversing the Inevitable Trend: High-Rise Housing in Sweden and Denmark," *Contact: Journal of Urban and Environmental Affairs,* 10, 3 (Winter 1978).

Organisation for Economic Cooperation and Development, Committee on Financial Markets, *Housing Finance: Present Problems* (Paris: OECD, 1974).

———, Committee on Financial Markets, *Flexibility in Housing Finance* (Paris: OECD, 1975).

Pynoos, John *et al.*, eds., *Housing Urban America* (Chicago: Aldine, 1973).
Solomon, Arthur, ed., *The Prospective City* (Cambridge, MA: M.I.T. Press, 1980).
Sternlieb, George *et al., America's Housing: Prospects and Problems* New Brunswick, NJ: Rutgers Center for Urban Policy Research, 1980).
Struyk, Raymond, *Should Government Encourage Homeownership?* (Washington, DC: The Urban Institute, May 1977).
Task Force on Housing Costs, *Final Report* (Washington, DC: Department of Housing and Urban Development, 1978).
Trutko, John, Otto Hetzel, and A. David Yates, *A Comparison of the Experimental Housing Allowance Program and Great Britain's Rent Allowance Program* (Washington, DC: The Urban Institute, April 1978).
Tuccillo, John, *Housing and Investment in an Inflationary World* (Washington, DC: The Urban Institute, 1980).
United Nations, Economic Commission for Europe, *Major Long-term Problems of Goverment Housing and Related Policies* 1 (Geneva, 1966).
Weir, Stuart, "How Labour Failed to Reform Mortgage Relief," *New Society* 5, (October 1978) pp. 14–16.
Wendt, Paul, *Housing Policy—The Search for Solutions: A Comparison of the U.K., Sweden, West Germany, and the U.S.* (Berkeley: University of California Press, 1963).
Wolman, Harold, *Housing and Housing Policy in the U.S. and the U.K.* (Lexington, MA: Lexington Books, 1975).
________, *The Politics of Federal Housing* (New York: Dodd, Mead, 1971).
Young, Ken and John Kramer, *Strategy and Conflict in Metropolitan Housing: Suburbia versus the Greater London Council 1965–1975* (London: Heinemann, 1979).

Chapter 5. ECONOMIC POLICY

Alt, James, *The Politics of Economic Decline* (New York: Cambridge University Press, 1979).
________, and K. Alec Chrystal, "Electoral Cycles, Budget Controls, and Public Expenditure," *International Journal of Public Policy* 1, 1 (1981) pp. 37–59.
________, and K. Alec Chrystal, *Political Economics* (Berkeley: University of California Press, 1983).
Anderson, Terry L. and Peter J. Hill, *The Birth of a Transfer Society* (Stanford: Hoover Institute, 1980).
Andrain, Charles F., *Politics and Economic Policy in Western Democracies* (North Scituate, MA: Duxbury, 1980).
Berger, Suzanne, ed., *Organizing Interest in Western Europe: Pluralism, Corporatism, and the Transformation of Politics* (Cambridge: Cambridge University Press, 1981).
Brittan, Samuel, *The Economic Consequences of Democracy* (London: Temple Smith, 1977).
Bryant, Ralph, *Monetary Policy in Interdependent Nations* (Washington, DC: Brookings, 1980).
Buchanan, James M. and Richard E. Wagner, *Democracy in Deficit* (New York: Academic, 1977).
Cameron, David, "Do Deficits Cause Inflation?" in Lindberg and Maier, *The Politics and Sociology of Global Inflation* (Washington, DC: Brookings, 1983).
________, "On the Limits of the Public Economy" in J. Roger Hollingsworth,

Government and Economic Performance, Annals of the American Academy of Political and Social Science 459 (January 1982).

Castles, Francis G., ed., *The Impact of Parties* (Beverly Hills: Sage, 1982).

Congressional Budget Office, *Incomes Policies in the United States: Historical Review and Some Issues* (Washington, DC: Government Printing Office, 1977).

Corti, G., "Perspectives on Public Corporations and Public Enterprises in Five Nations," *Annals of Public and Co-Operative Economy* 47.

Diebold, William, *Industrial Policy as an International Issue* (New York: McGraw-Hill, 1980).

Drucker, Peter F., "Toward the Next Economics," *The Public Interest,* special issue (1980).

Eckstein, Otto, *The Great Recession,* (Amsterdam: North Holland, 1978).

Feldstein, Martin, ed., *The American Economy in Transition* (Chicago: University of Chicago Press, 1980).

Gilder, George, *Wealth and Poverty* (New York: Basic, 1981).

Ginneken, W. van, "Unemployment: Some Trends, Causes, and Policy Implications: Evidence from Germany, France, and the Netherlands," *International Labour Review* 120, 2 (1981) pp. 165–182.

Goldstein, Walter, ed., *Economic Planning and the Improvement of Economic Policy* (Washington: AEI, 1975).

Goodwin, Craufurd D., ed., *Exhortation and Controls* (Washington, DC: Brookings, 1975).

Green, Diana, "Promoting the Industries of the Future: The Search for an Industrial Strategy in Britain and France," *Journal of Public Policy* 1, 3 (1981) pp. 333–351.

Hancock, M. Donald, "The Political Management of Economic and Social Change: Contrasting Models of Advanced Industrial Society in Sweden and West Germany," *The Annals* 459 (1982), pp. 63–76.

Hartrich, Edward, *The Fourth and Richest Reich* (New York: Macmillan, 1980).

Heisler, Martin O., "Corporate Pluralism Revisited: Where is the Theory?" *Sc Pol Stud* Vol. 2, new series, No. 3 (1979).

Hibbs, Douglas A., "Political Parties and Macroeconomic Policy," *APSR* 71 (1977) pp. 1467–1487.

Hills, Jill, "Government Relations with Industry: Japan & Britain—a Review of Two Political Arguments," *Polity* X14, 2 (Winter 1981), pp. 222–248.

Hollingsworth, J. Rogers, "The Political-Structural Basis for Economic Performance," *The Annals* 459 (1982) pp. 28–45.

Johnson, Nevil and Allan Cochrane, *Economic Policy Making by Local Authorities in Britain and Western Europe* (London: Allen and Unwin, 1981).

Joint Economic Committee of Congress, *Monetary Policy, Selective Credit Policy, and Industrial Policy in France, Britain, West Germany and Sweden,* Staff study issued as Committee Print 26 June 1981, 97th Congress, 1st session (Washington, DC: Goverment Printing Office, 1981).

Katzenstein, Peter, "Conclusion: Domestic Structures and Strategies of Foreign Economic Policy," in Katzenstein, ed., *Between Power and Plenty* (Madison: University of Wisconsin Press, 1978).

Kaufman, Roger, "Why the U.S. Unemployment Rate is So High," *Challenge* (May-June 1978) pp. 155–169.

King, Anthony, "Ideas, Institutions and the Policies of Governments," *BJPS* 3 (1973) pp. 409–423.

Lindberg, Leon and Charles Maier, *The Politics and Sociology of Global Inflation* (Washington, DC: Brookings).

Martin, Andrew, "Political Constraints and Economic Strategies in Advanced Industrial Societies," *Comp Pol St* 10 (1977) pp. 323–354.

McArthur, John H. and Bruce R. Scott, *Industrial Planning in France* (Boston: Graduate School of Business Administration, Harvard University, 1969).

Meltzer, Allan H., "Monetarism and the Crisis in Economics," *The Public Interest*, special issue (1980) pp. 35–45.

Organisation for Economic Cooperation and Development, *The Aims and Instruments of Industrial Policy* (Paris: OECD, 1975).

———, *Main Economic Indicators: Historical Statistics 1960–1979* (Paris: OECD, 1980).

Panitch, "Recent Theorizations of Corporatism," *British Journal of Sociology* 31, 2 (June 1979) p. 159–175.

Schmitter, Philippe C. and Gerhard Lehmbruch, eds., *Trends Towards Corporatist Intermediation* (Beverly Hills: Sage, 1979).

Schnitzer, Martin C. and James W. Nordyke, Comparative Economic Systems (Cincinatti: Southwestern, 1977).

Schwanse, Peter, "Employment Subsidies in Western Europe" in Robert H. Haveman and John L. Palmer, *Jobs for Disadvantaged Workers* (Washington, DC: Brookings, 1982).

Schwerin, Don S., "Norwegian and Danish Incomes Policies and European Monetary Integration," *West Eur Pol* 3 (October 1980) pp. 388–405.

Shanks, Michael, *Planning and Politics: The British Experience* (London: Political and Economic Planning, 1977).

Shonfield, Andrew W. *Modern Capitalism* (London: Oxford University Press, 1969).

Shultz, George P. and Kenneth W. Dam, *Economic Policy Behind the Headlines* (New York: Norton, 1978).

Steward, Michael, *The Jekyll and Hyde Years* (London: Dent and Sons, 1977).

Wachter, Michael L., ed., *Toward a New U.S. Industrial Policy?*, (Philadelphia: University of Pennsylvania Press, 1982).

Wilensky, Harold, *The "New Corporatism," Centralization and the Welfare State* (Beverly Hills: Sage, 1976).

———, "Democratic Corporatism, Consensus and Social Policy," in OECD, *The Welfare State in Crisis* (Paris: OECD, 1981).

Wilson, David E., *The National Planning Ideas in U.S. Public Policy* (Boulder, CO: Westview, 1980).

Woolley, John T., "Monetary Policy Instrumentation and the Relationship of Central Banks and Governments," *The Annals of the American Academy of Political and Social Science* (1978) pp. 151–173.

Chapter 6. TAXATION POLICY

Aaron, Henry, ed., *The Value-Added Tax: Lessons from Europe* (Washington, DC: Brookings, 1981).

———, and Michael J. Boskin, *The Economics of Taxation, Studies of Government Finance* (Washington, DC: Brookings, 1980).

Ardent, Gabriel, *L'Histoire des Impôt* (Paris: Fayard, 1971).
Barnstable, C. F., *Public Finance* (London: Macmillan, 1903).
——— and Colin Clark, "Public Finance and Changes in the Value of Money," *Economic Journal* 55 (December 1945) pp. 371–389.
Barr, N.A., S.R. James, and A.R. Prest, *Self-Assessment for Income Tax* (London: Heinemann, 1977).
Beer, Samuel H., "The Adoption of German Revenue Sharing: A Case Study in Public Politics," *Public Policy* 24 (1976) pp. 127–195.
Beichelt, B. *et al.*, *Steuermentalität und Steuermoral in Grossbritannien, Frankreich, Italien und Spanien* (Cologne: Westdeutscher, 1969).
Bellstedt, Christoph, *Die Steuer als Instrument der Politik* (Berlin: Duncker und Humblot, 1966).
Bennett, R.J., *The Geography of Public Finance: Welfare Under Fiscal Federalism and Local Government Finance* (London: Methuen, 1980).
Boskin, Michael J., ed., *Federal Tax Reform: Myths and Realities* (San Francisco, Institute for Contemporary Studies, 1978).
Bracewell-Milnes, Barry and J.C.L. Huiskamp, *Investment Incentives: A Comparative Analysis of the Systems in the EEC, the USA and Sweden* (Deventer: Kluwer, 1977).
Cnossen, Sijbren, *Excise Systems: A Global Study of Selective Taxation of Goods and Services* (Baltimore: Johns Hopkins Press, 1977).
Eckstein, Otto, *Public Finance* (Englewood Cliffs, NJ: Prentice-Hall, 1964).
Eismeier, Theodore J., "The Political Economy of Tax Reform," paper presented at the 1979 meeting of the American Political Science Association.
Esping-Anderson, Gösta, *Social Class, Social Democracy and State Policy* (Copenhagen: New Social Science Monographs, 1980).
Feige, Edward, *Observer-Subject Feedback: The Dynamics of the Unobserved Economy* (Leyden: Brill, 1982).
Flämig, Christian, *Steuerprotest und Steuerberatung* (Cologne: Arbeitskreis für Steuerrecht, 1979).
Fredersdorf, Herman, *Die Partei der Steuerzahler* (Stuttgart, 1978).
Gold, Steven D., "Scandinavian Local Income Taxation: Lessons for the United States," *Public Finance Quarterly* 5 (October 1977) pp. 471–488.
Gourevitch, Harry G., "Corporate Tax Integration: The European Experience," *The Tax Lawyer* 31, 1 (Fall 1977) pp. 65–112.
Grunow, Dieter, F. Hagner, and Franz Xavier Kaufmann, *Steuerzahler und Finanzamt* (Frankfurt: Campus, 1978).
Hansen, Susan B., "Partisan Realignment and Tax Policy: 1789–1976," in Bruce A. Campbell and Richard J. Trilling, *Realignment in American Politics* (Austin: University of Texas Press, 1980) pp. 288–323.
———, "The Tax Revolt and the Politics of Redistribution," paper presented at the 1981 meeting of the American Political Science Association.
Hibbs, Douglas and Henrik Jess Madsen, "Public Reactions to the Growth of Taxation and Government Expenditure," *World Politics* 33 (April 1981) pp. 413–445.
Institute for Fiscal Studies, *The Structure and Reform of Direct Taxation: Report of Committee Chaired by J.E. Meade* (London: Allen and Unwin, 1978).
Institute of Economic Affairs, *The State of Taxation* (London: 1977).

Johnson, Harry G., "Self-Assessment to Personal Income Tax: The American System," *British Tax Review* (March-April 1971).

Mennel, Annemarie, *Die Finanzverwaltungen in Europa* (Düsseldorf: Union des Finanzpersonals in Europa, 1977).

Minarek, Joseph H., "The Yield of a Comprehensive Income Tax," in Joseph J. Pechman, ed., *Comprehensive Income Taxation* (Washington, DC: Brookings, 1977) pp. 277–298.

Musgrave, Richard A., *Fiscal Systems* (New Haven: Yale University Press, 1969).

________, "Theories of Fiscal Crises: An Essay in Fiscal Sociology," in Henry Aaron and Michael J. Boskin, *The Economics of Taxation, Studies of Government Finance* (Washington, DC: Brookings, 1980).

Organisation for Economic Cooperation and Development, *The Adjustment of Personal Income Tax Systems for Inflation* (Paris: OECD, 1976).

________, *The Tax/Income Composition of Selected Income Groups of OECD Member Countries* (Paris: OECD, 1978).

________, *Revenue Statistics of Member Countries 1965–1980* (Paris: OECD, 1981).

________, *The Taxation of New Wealth, Capital Transfers and Capital Gains of Individuals* (Paris: OECD, 1979).

Peacock, Alan and Francesco Forte, eds., *The Political Economy of Taxation* (New York: St. Martin's, 1981).

Pechman, Joseph J., ed., *Comprehensive Income Taxation* (Washington, DC: Brookings, 1977).

Radian, Alex and Ira Sharkansky, "Tax Reform in Israel: Partial Implementation of Ambitious Goals," *Pol Anal* 5, 3 (1979) pp. 351–366.

Reese, Thomas J., *The Politics of Taxation* (Westport, CT: Quorum, 1981).

Rose, Richard and Guy Peters, *Can Governments Go Bankrupt?* (New York: Basic, 1978).

Roskamp, Karl W. and Francesco Forte, eds., *Reforms of Tax Systems* (Detroit: Wayne State University Press, 1981).

Sabine, B.E.V., *A History of Income Tax* (London: Allen and Unwin, 1966).

Sandford, Cedric T. *et al.*, *Costs and Benefits of VAT* (London: Heinemann, 1981).

Sawyer, Malcolm, "Income Distribution in OECD Countries," *OECD Economic Outlook: Occasional Studies* (July 1976).

Schmoelders, Guenter, "Survey Research in Public Finance—A Behavioral Approach to Fiscal Theory," *Public Finance* 25, 2 (1970).

Shoup, Carl S., "Some Distinguishing Characteristics of British, French, and United States Public Finance Systems," *American Economic Review* 47 (May 1957) pp. 187–219.

Shultz, George and Kenneth W. Dam, *Economic Policy Beyond the Headlines* (New York: Norton, 1977).

Struempel, Burkhard, *Steuersystem und wirtschaftliche Entwicklung* (Tübingen: Mohr, 1968).

Surrey, Stanley S. and Paul R. McDaniel, "The Tax Expenditure Concept and the Legislative Process," in Henry Aaron and Michael J. Boskin, *The Economics of Taxation, Studies of Government Finance* (Washington, DC: Brookings, 1980), pp. 123–144.

Tanzi, Vito, *The Individual Income Tax and Economic Growth: An International Comparison* (Baltimore: Johns Hopkins Press, 1969).

———, *The Underground Economy in the United States and Abroad* (Lexington, MA: Lexington Books, 1982).

———, *Inflation and the Personal Income Tax: An International Perspective* (New York: Cambridge University Press, 1980).

Taxation in France, World Tax Series No. 11 (Chicago: Commerce Clearing House, 1966).

U.S. Congress, *Administrative Procedures of the Interal Revenue Service* (Washington, DC, 1975).

———, *Indexing the Individual Income Tax for Inflation* (Washington, DC: Congressional Budget Office, 1980).

Whalley, John, "Tax Developments Outside the United States and Their Implications for Current U.S. Reform Proposals," in *Federal Tax Reform: Myths and Realities* (San Francisco: Institute for Contemporary Studies, 1978), pp. 211–233.

Wilensky, Harold L., *The Welfare State and Equality* (Berkeley: University of California Press, 1975).

Willis, J.R.M. and P.J.W. Hardwick, *Tax Expenditures in the United Kingdom* (London: Heinemann, 1978).

Wright, L. Hart, ed., *Comparative Conflict Resolution Procedures in Taxation* (Ann Arbor: University of Michigan Law School, 1968).

Chapter 7. INCOME MAINTENANCE POLICY

Aaron, Henry, "Social Security Can Be Saved," *Challenge* (November-December, 1981).

Alber, Jens, "A Crisis of the Welfare State: The Case of West Germany," European Consortium for Political Research Joint Sessions, Florence, Italy, March 1980. German version published in *Zeitschrift fuer Soziologie* 9, 4 (October, 1980) pp. 313–342.

———, *Vom Armenhaus zum Wohlfahrtstaat: Die Entwicklung von Sozialversicherungssysteme in Westeuropa* (Stuttgart: Klett, 1982).

Albritton, R.B., "Social Amelioration through Mass Insurgency." A Re-examination of the Piven and Cloward Thesis," *APSR* 73, 4 (1979) pp. 1003–1011.

Altmeyer, Arthur, *The Formative Years of Social Security,* (Madison: University of Wisconsin Press, 1966).

Beckerman, Wilfred, "The Impact of Income Maintenance Payments on Poverty in Britain, 1975," *Economic Journal* 89, 354 (1976) pp. 261–279.

Bishop, J.H., "Jobs, Cash Transfers and Marital Instability: A Review and Synthesis of the Evidence," *Journal of Human Resources* 15, 3 (1980) pp. 301–334.

Burkhauser, R.V. and T.M. Sneeding, "The Net Impact of the Social Security System on the Poor," *Public Policy* 29, 2, (1981) pp. 159–178.

Boskin, Michael, J., "Social Security and Retirement Decisions," *Economic Inquiry* 15 (January 1977) pp. 1–25.

Boskin, Michael J., *The Crisis in Social Security* (San Francisco: Institute for Contemporary Studies, 1978).

Boye, S., "The Cost of Social Security, 1960–1971: Some National Economic Aspects," *International Labor Review* 115 (1977) pp. 305–325.

Bridges, Benjamin, "Why the Social Insurance Budget is Too Large in a Democracy, A Comment," *Economic Inquiry* 16 (January 1978) pp. 133–142.

Browning, Edgar K., "Why the Social Insurance Budget is Too Large in a Democracy," *Economic Inquiry* 13 (September 1975) pp. 373–387.

Castles, F.G., *The Social Democratic Image of Society* (London: Routledge and Kegan Paul, 1978).

———, "How Does Politics Matter? Structure and Agency in the Determination of Public Policy Outcomes," *European Journal of Political Research* 9 (1981) pp. 119–132.

———, Francis G. and R.D. McKinlay, "Public Welfare Provision, Scandinavia, and the Sheer Futility of the Sociological Approach to Politics," *BJPS* 9 (1979) pp. 157–171.

Cohen, Stephen S. and Charles Goldfinger, "From Permacrisis to Real Crisis in French Social Security," in Leon Lindberg, ed., *Stress and Contradiction in Modern Capitalism* (Lexington, MA: Lexington Books, 1979).

Collier, David and Richard E. Messick, "Prerequisites versus Diffusion: Testing Alternative Explanations of Social Security Adoption," *APSR* 69, 4 (December 1975) pp. 1299–1315.

Copeland, Lois S., "Worldwide Developments in Social Security, 1975–1977," *Social Security Bulletin* (May 1978) pp. 3–8.

Danziger, S. and R. Plotnick, "Income Maintenance Programs and the Pursuit of Income Security," *Annals of the American Academy of Political and Social Science* 453 (1981) pp. 130–152.

Danziger, S., et al., "Retrenchment or Reorientation: Options for Income Support Policy," *Public Policy* 28, 4 (1980) pp. 473–490.

———, "How Income Transfers Affect Work, Savings and the Income Distribution," *Economic Literature* 19, 3 (1981) pp. 975–1028.

Derthick, Martha, *Policymaking for Social Security* (Washington, DC: Brookings, 1979).

Fisher, Paul, "Minimum Old-Age Pensions," *International Labour Review* 102, 3 (September 1970) p.298ff.

Flora, Peter and Arnold J. Heidenheimer, eds., *The Development of Welfare States in Europe and America* (New Brunswick: Transaction, 1981).

Freeman, Gary and Paul Adams, "Social Security and Economic Strategy, A Comparative Analysis," Paper presented to the Second Conference for Europeanists, Council for European Studies, Washington, DC, October 23–25, 1980.

Geiger, Theodore, *Welfare and Efficiency: Their Interactions in Western Europe and Implications for International Economic Relations* (Washington, DC: National Planning Association, 1978).

Gilbert, Bentley, *The Evolution of National Insurance in Great Britain* (London: Michael Joesph, 1966).

———, *British Social Policy, 1914–1939* (London: Batsford, 1970).

Gough, Ian, *The Political Economy of the Welfare State* (London: Macmillan, 1979).

Haanes-Olsen, Leif, "Earnings-Replacement Rate of Old-Age Benefits, 1967–75, for Selected Countries," *Social Security Bulletin* (1978) pp. 3–14.

Havemann, Joel, "In Search of the Truly Needy," *National Journal* (21 March 1982) pp. 492–493.

Heclo, Hugh, *Modern Social Politics in Britain and Sweden* (New Haven: Yale University Press, 1974).

Hewitt, Christopher, "The Effect of Political Democracy and Social Democracy on Equality in Industrial Societies, A Cross-National Comparison," *American Sociological Review* 42 (June 1977) pp. 450–464.

Hockerts, Hans Günter, *Sozialpolitische Entscheidungen im Nachkriegsdeutschland* (Stuttgart: Clett-Cotta, 1980).

Hojer, Karl, *Svensk socialpolitisk historia* (Stockholm: Norstedt, 1952).

Jackman, Robert W., "Socialist Parties and Income Inequality in Western Industrial Societies," *Journal of Politics* 42 (1980) pp. 135–149.

Judge, Ken, "State Pensions and the Growth of Social Welfare Expenditure," Paper presented to the Conference on Post-Keynesian Politics and the Welfare State, Cornell University, September 17–19, 1981.

Katznelson, Ira, "Considerations on Social Democracy in the United States," *Comp Pol* 11 (1978) pp. 77–99.

Kelley, Terence F., *Social Policies in the 1980s* (Paris: OECD, 1981)

Klein, Rudolf, "The Welfare State: A Self-Inflicted Crisis?" *The Political Quarterly* 51 (Janurary-March 1980) pp. 24–34.

Korpi, Walter, "Social Policy and Distributional Conflict in the Capitalist Democracies," *West Eur Pol* (October 1980) pp. 296–316.

Leibfried, Stephan, "Public Assistance in the United States and the Federal Republic of Germany: Does Social Democracy Make a Difference?" *Comp Pol* (October, 1978) pp. 59–76.

Lindberg, Leon, ed., *Stress and Contradiction in Modern Capitalism* (Lexington, MA: Lexington Books, 1979).

Lubove, Roy, *The Struggle for Social Security* (Cambridge: Harvard University Press, 1968).

Lynes, Tony, *French Pensions* (London: G. Bell and Sons, 1967).

Marshall, T.H., *Class Citizenship, and Social Development* (New York: Anchor, 1965).

McArdle, Frank B., "Sources of Revenue of Social Security Systems in Ten Industrial Countries," *Social Security in a Changing World* (Washington, DC: Department of Health, Education, and Welfare, 1979).

Mommsen, W.J., ed., *The Emergence of the Welfare State in Britain and Germany* (London: Croom Helm, 1981).

Munnell, Alicia H., *The Future of Social Security* (Washington, DC: Brookings, 1977).

Organisation for Economic Cooperation and Development, *Public Expenditure on Income Maintenance Programmes,* (Paris: OECD, 1976).

———, *The Welfare State in Crisis* (Paris: OECD, 1981).

Patterson, James T., *America's Struggle Against Poverty, 1900–1980* (Cambridge: Harvard University Press, 1981).

Plotnick, R.D., "Social Welfare Expenditures: How Much Help for the Poor?" *Pol Anal* 5, 3, (1979) pp. 271–289.

Pryor, Frederick, *Public Expenditure in Capitalist and Communist Nations* (Homewood, IL: Irwin, 1968).

Ransom, Roger L., Richard Sutch, and Gary M. Walton, eds., *Explorations in the New Economic History* (New York: Academic, 1981).

Reynolds, Morgan and Eugene Smolensky, *Public Expenditure, Taxes, and the Distribution of Income* (Madison: Institute for Poverty Research, 1977).

Rimlinger, Gaston, *Welfare Policy and Industrialization in Europe, America, and Russia* (New York: Wiley, 1971).

Rimlinger, Gaston V., "The Historical Analysis of National Welfare Systems," in Ransom *et al., Explorations in the New Economic History* (New York: Academic, 1981).

Roberti, P., "Counting the Poor: A Review of the Situation Existing in Six Industrial Nations" in Department of Health and Social Security, *The Measurement of Poverty* (London: Her Majesty's Stationery Office, 1979).

Rosa, Jean-Jacques, ed., *The World Crisis in Social Security* (San Francisco: Institute for Contemporary Studies, 1982).

Samuelsson, Kurt, *From Great Power to Welfare State: 300 Years of Swedish Social Development* (London: Allen and Unwin, 1968).

Saul, K., *Staat, Industrie, Arbeiterbewegung im Kaiserreich* (Dusseldorf, 1974).

Simanis, J.G. "Worldwide Trends in Social Security," *Social Security Bulletin* 43, 8 (1980) pp. 6–9.

Smith, Geoffrey, "Britain Cuts Indexing of Government Benefits," *Journal of the Institute for Socioeconomic Studies* 5 (Summer 1980) pp. 63–72.

Stein, Bruno, *Social Security and Pensions in Transition* (New York: Free Press, 1980).

Steiner, Gilbert Y., *The State of Welfare* (Washington, DC: Brookings, 1971).

Stephens, John D., *The Transition from Capitalism to Socialism* (London: Macmillan, 1979).

Taira, Koji and Peter Kilby, "Differences in Social Security Development in Selected Countries," *International Social Security Review* 22, 2 (Spring 1969) pp. 139–153.

Whiteley, "Public Opinion and the Demand for Welfare," *Journal of Social Policy* 10, 4 (October 1981).

Wilensky, *The Welfare State and Equality* (Berkeley: University of California Press, 1975).

Wilson, Thomas, ed., *Pensions, Inflation and Growth: A Comparative Study of the Elderly in the Welfare State* (London: Heinemann, 1974).

Chapter 8. URBAN PLANNING

Aiken, Michael, "Urban Social Structure and Political Competition: A Comparative Study of Local Politics in Four European Nations," *Urb Aff Q* 11, 1 (September 1975) pp. 82–114.

Anton, Thomas, *Governing Greater Stockholm* (Berkeley: University of California Press, 1975).

Appleyard, Donald, ed., *The Conservation of European Cities* (Cambridge, MA: M.I.T. Press, 1979).

Barnekov, Timothy and Daniel Rich, "Privatism and Urban Development: An Analysis of the Organized Influence of Local Business Elites," *Urb Aff Q* 12, 4 (June 1977) pp. 431–459.

Berry, Brian, *The Human Consequences of Urbanization* (New York: St. Martin's, 1973).

————, ed., *Urbanization and Counterurbanization* (Beverly Hills: Sage, 1976).

Boesler, Klaus-Achim, "Spatially Effective Government Actions and Regional Development in the Federal Republic of Germany," *Tijdschrift voor Econ. en Soc. Geografie* 65, 3 (1974) pp. 208–220.

Brownfield, Lyman, "The Disposition Problem in Urban Renewal," *Law & Con P* 25 (Autumn 1960) pp. 732–776.

Buchanan, Colin *et al., Traffic in Towns: A Study of the Long Term Problems of Traffic in Urban Areas* (London: HMSO, 1963).

Castells, Manuel, *The Urban Question: A Marxist Approach* (Cambridge, MA: M.I.T. Press, 1979).

Cox, Andrew, "Continuity and Discontinuity in Conservative Urban Policy," *Urban Law and Policy* 3 (1980) pp. 269–292.

Department of Environment, *Community Land Scheme—The First Two Years* (London: HMSO, 1979).

Dunham, David, *A Study of the Spatial Planning Process in Britain and the Netherlands* (Amsterdam: Universiteit van Amsterdam, 1971).

Dunn, James A., *Miles to Go: European and American Transportation Policies* (Cambridge, MA: M.I.T. Press, 1981).

Elkin, S.L., *Politics and Land-Use Planning* (New York: Cambridge University Press, 1974).

Evans, H. and L. Rodwin, "The New Towns Program and Why it Failed," *The Public Interest* 56 (Summer 1979) pp. 90–107.

Fainstein, Norman and Susan Fainstein, eds., "Urban Policy Under Capitalism," 22, *Urban Affairs Annual Reviews* (Beverly Hills: Sage, 1982).

Falk, Thomas, "Urban Development in Sweden 1960–1975: Population Dispersal in Progress," in Niles Hansen, ed., *Human Settlement Systems: International Perspectives on Structure, Change, and Public Policy* (Cambridge, MA: Ballinger, 1978), pp. 51–83.

Fried, Robert, "Comparative Urban Policy and Performance," in Fred Greenstein and Nelson Polsby, eds., *Policies and Policymaking* (Reading, MA: Addison-Wesley, 1975) pp. 305–379.

Gale, Dennis, ed., "Symposium: A Comparative View of National Urban Policy," special issue of the *Journal of the American Planning Association* 48, 1 (Winter 1982).

Glickman, Norman and Michelle White, "Urban Land-Use Patterns: An International Comparison," *Environment and Planning* 11 (1979) pp. 35–49.

Gorham, William and Nathan Glazer, eds., *The Urban Predicament* (Washington, DC: The Urban Institute, 1976).

Gottdiener, Mark, *Planned Sprawl: Private and Public Interests in Suburbia* (Beverly Hills: Sage, 1977).

Hall, Peter, *The World Cities* (New York: McGraw-Hill, 1966).

_______ and Dennis Hay, *Growth Centres in the European Urban System* (Berkeley: University of California Press, 1980).

Hamnett, Christopher and Peter Williams, "Social Change in London: A Study of Gentrification," *Urb Af Q* 15, 4 (June 1980) pp. 469–487.

Harloe, Michael, ed., *Captive Cities: Studies in the Political Economy of Cities and Regions* (New York: Wiley, 1977).

Hart, D.A., *Strategic Planning in London: The Rise and Fall of the Primary Road Network* (Oxford, England: Pergamon, 1976).

Harvey, David, *Social Justice and the City* (Baltimore: Johns Hopkins University Press, 1973).

Heinemeyer, W.F. and R.V.E. Gastelaars, "Conflicts in Land Use in Amsterdam," *Tijdschrift voor Econ. en Soc. Geografie* (May-June 1972) pp. 190–199.

Johnson, Nevil and Allen Cochrane, *Economic Policymaking by Local Authorities in Britain and Western Germany* (London: Allen and Unwin, 1981).

Laska, Shirley and Daphne Spain, eds., *Back to the City: Issues in Neighborhood Renovation* (New York: Pergamon, 1980).

Lawless, Paul, *Urban Deprivation and Government Initiative* (London: Faber and Faber, 1979).

Leven, Charles, ed., *The Mature Metropolis* (Lexington, MA: Lexington Books, 1978).

Lottman, Herbert, *How Cities Are Saved* (New York: Universe, 1976).

Madge, C. and P. Willmott, *Inner City Poverty in Paris and London. Reports of the Institute of Community Studies* (London: Routledge and Kegan Paul, 1981).

McKay, John, *Tramways and Trolleys: The Rise of Urban Mass Transport in Europe* (Princeton, NJ: Princeton University Press, 1976).

Mollenkopf, John, "The Post War Politics of Urban Development," in John Walton and Donald Carns, eds., *Cities in Change* (Boston: Allyn and Bacon, 1977) pp. 549–579.

Molotch, Harvey, "The City as a Growth Machine: Toward a Political Economy of Place," *AJS* 82, 2, pp. 309–332.

Mumford, Lewis, *The City in History: Its Origins, Its Transformation, and Its Prospects* (New York: HBJ, 1961).

Organisation for Economic Cooperation and Development, *Managing Transport* (Paris: OECD, 1979).

Pahl, R.E., *Whose City?* (Harlow, England: Longman, 1970).

Pass, David, *Vallingby and Farsta: From Idea to Reality* (Cambridge, MA: M.I.T. Press, 1973).

Peterson, Paul and Paul Kantor, "Political Parties and Citizen Participation in English City Politics," *Comp Pol* 9, 2 (January 1977) pp. 197–217.

Popenoe, David, *The Suburban Environment: Sweden and the United States* (Chicago: University of Chicago Press, 1977).

Public Technology, Inc., *Center City Environment and Transportation: Transportation Innovations in Five European Cities* (Washington, DC: U.S. Department of Transportation, April 1980).

Ratzka, Adolf, *Sixty Years of Municipal Leasehold in Stockholm: An Econometric and Cost-Revenue Analysis* (Stockholm: Swedish Council for Building Research, 1980).

Report of the President's Commission for a National Agenda for the Eighties (New York: NAL, 1981).

Rose, Richard, ed., *The Management of Urban Change in Britain and Germany* (Beverly Hills: Sage, 1974).

Smerk, George, *Urban Transportation: The Federal Role* (Bloomington: Indiana University Press, 1965).

Sorenson, Robert C.A., "Urban Civic Protest Groups in West Germany and Switzerland," paper presented at Ninth World Congress of Sociology, Uppsala, Sweden, August 1978.

Strong, Ann L., *Land Banking: European Reality, American Prospect* (Baltimore: Johns Hopkins University Press, 1979).

Sundquist, James, *Dispersing Population: What America Can Learn from Europe* (Washington, DC: Brookings, 1975).

Thomson, J.M., "The London Motorway Plan," in W.R. Derrick Sewell and J.T. Coppock, eds., *Public Participation in Planning* (New York: Wiley, 1977).

Town and Country Planning Association, Statement on Inner Cities (London: May 1977).

Underhill, Jack, *French National Urban Policy and the Paris Region New Towns* (Washington, DC: U.S. Department of Housing and Urban Development, Office of International Affairs, April 1980).

Valderpoort, W., *The Selfish Automobile* (Amsterdam: Amsterdam Press, 1953).

Walton, John, "Urban Political Economy: A New Paradigm," *Comparative Urban Research* 7, 1 (1979) pp. 5–17.

Warner, Sam Bass, *The Private City* (Philadelphia: University of Pennsylvania Press, 1968).

Wiedenhoeft, Ronald, "Malmö: The People Said No," *Scandinavian Review* 1 (1977) pp. 12–18.

Chapter 9. THE CAPACITY OF LOCAL GOVERNMENTS

Anton, Thomas, "The Pursuit of Efficiency: Values and Structure in the Changing Politics of Swedish Municipalities," in Terry N. Clark, ed., *Comparative Community Politics* (New York: Wiley, 1974) pp. 87–110.

________, *Governing Greater Stockholm* (Berkeley: University of California Press, 1975).

Ashford, Douglas, "The Effects of Central Finance on the British Local Government System," *BJPS* 4 (1974) pp. 305–322.

________ "Territorial Politics and Resource Allocation," *European Studies Newsletter* 8, 2 (November 1978) pp. 1–10.

________ "Territorial Politics and Equality: Decentralization in the Modern State," *Pol Stud* 27 (March 1979) pp. 71–83.

________ ed., *Financing Urban Government in the Welfare State* (New York: St. Martin's, 1980a).

________ ed., *National Resources and Urban Policy* (New York: Methuen, 1980b).

________ and Jean-Claude Thoenig, eds., *Les Aides Financières de l'Etat aux Collectivités Locales en France et à l'Etranger* (Paris: Librairies Techniques, 1981).

Beer, Samuel, "The Adoption of German Revenue-Sharing: A Case Study in Public Politics," *Public Policy* 24 (1976) pp. 127–195.

Benjamin, Roger, *The Limits of Politics* (Chicago: University of Chicago Press, 1980).

Bennett, R.J., *The Geography of Public Finance* (New York: Methuen, 1980).

Bollens, John and Henry Schmandt, *The Metropolis: Its People, Politics, and Economic Life* (New York: Harper, 1975).

Brand, Jack, "Local Government Reform: Sweden and England Compared," in Richard Rose, ed., *The Dynamics of Public Policy: A Comparative Analysis* (Beverly Hills: Sage, 1976) pp. 35–56.

Burgess, Tyrrell and Tony Travers, *Ten Billion Pounds: Whitehall's Takeover of the Town Halls* (London: Grant McIntyre, 1980).

Council of Europe, *Report on the Costs of Urban Concentration and the Financing of the Equipment of Large Towns and Urban Areas,* for the European Conference of Local Authorities, 7th Session, October 1968, Strasbourg.

________ *Study Series: Local and Regional Authorities in Europe: The Development of Central, Regional, and Local Finance Since 1950,* Study No. 13, Vol. 1, Strasbourg, 1975.

Fried, Robert, "Comparative Urban Policy and Performance," in Fred Greenstein and Nelson Polsby, eds., *Policies and Policymaking* (Reading, MA: Addison-Wesley, 1975) pp. 305–379.

Gunlicks, Arthur, "Restructuring Service Delivery Systems in West Germany," in Vincent Ostrom and Frances Bish, eds., *Comparing Urban Service Delivery Systems,* Vol. 12, Urban Affairs Annual Reviews (Beverly Hills: Sage, 1977) pp. 173–196.

________, ed., *Local Government Reform and Reorganization: An International Perspective* (Port Washington, NY: Kennikat, 1980).

Gustafsson, Gunnel, "Modes and Effects of Local Government Mergers in the Scandinavian Countries," *West Eur Pol* 3 (October 1980) pp. 339–357.

Hansen, Tore, "The Financial Problems of European Cities," *Pol & Pol* 6 (1977) pp. 93–95.

Herzlinger, Regina, "Costs, Benefits, and the West Side Highway," *The Public Interest* 55 (Spring 1979) pp. 77–98.

Gorham, William and Nathan Glazer, eds., *The Urban Predicament* (Washington, DC: The Urban Institute, 1976).

Labour Government White Paper, *Reform of Local Government in England* (London: HMSO, 1970).

Local Government Finance, *Report of the* [Layfield] *Committee of Inquiry* Cmnd. 6453 (London: HMSO, 1976).

Lotz, Joergen, "Fiscal Problems and Issues in Scandinavian Cities," in Roy Bahl, ed., *Urban Government Finance: Emerging Trends* (Beverly Hills: Sage, 1981) pp. 221–243.

Maxwell, J.A. and J.R. Aronson, *Financing State and Local Governments* (Washington, DC: Brookings, 1977).

Milch, Jerome, "Urban Government in France: Municipal Policymaking in the Centralized State," *Administration and Society* 9, 4 (February 1978) pp. 467–494.

Newton, Kenneth, *Balancing the Books: Financial Problems of Local Government in West Europe* (Beverly Hills: Sage, 1980).

________, "Is Small Really So Beautiful? Is Big Really So Ugly? Size, Effectiveness, and Democracy in Local Government," *Pol Stud* 30, 2 (June 1982) pp. 190–206.

Oates, Wallace, ed., *The Political Economy of Fiscal Federalism* (Lexington, MA: Lexington Books, 1977).

Rothweiler, R.L., "Revenue Sharing in the Federal Republic of Germany," *Publius* 2 (1972) pp. 4–25.

Salathiel, D., *Local Authority Expenditure Per Head: Variations with Population Decline Per Head* (London: Department of Environment Finance and Local Government Grants Working Group, 1975).

Sbragia, Alberta, "Borrowing to Build: Private Money and Public Welfare," *Int Jl Hlth Svc* 9, 2 (1979a) pp. 207–226.

———, "The Politics of Local Borrowing: A Comparative Analysis," University of Strathclyde Centre for the Study of Public Policy, *Studies in Public Policy* 37 (Glasgow, 1979b).

Sharpe, L.J., ed., *Decentralist Trends in Western Democracies* (Beverly Hills: Sage, 1979).

———, ed., *The Local Fiscal Crisis in Western Europe: Myths and Realities* (Beverly Hills: Sage, 1981).

Simpson, Robin, "Councils Against the Elements," *New Society* (15 November 1979).

Snyder, W.W., "Are the Budgets of State and Local Government Destabilizing? A Six-Country Comparison," *European Economic Review* 4 (1973) pp. 197–213.

Tarrow, Sydney, Pater Katzenstein, and Luigi Graziano, eds., *Territorial Politics in Industrial Nations* (New York: Praeger, 1978).

Thoenig, Jean-Claude, "State Bureaucracies and Local Government in France," in Kenneth Hanf and Fritz Scharpf, eds., *Interorganizational Policymaking: Limits to Coordination and Central Control* (Beverly Hills: Sage, 1978) pp. 167–197.

Chapter 10. POLICY CONTRASTS IN THE WELFARE STATE

Arrow, Kenneth, *Social Choice and Individual Values* (New Haven: Yale University Press, 1963).

Adams, Carolyn T. and Kathryn T. Winston, *Mothers at Work: Public Policies in the United States, Sweden and China* (New York: Longman, 1980).

Ashford, Douglas, *Politics and Policy in Britain* (Philadelphia: Temple University Press, 1980).

Barnes, Samuel and Max Kaase, eds., *Political Action* (Beverly Hills, Sage, 1979).

Berger, Suzanne, *Organizing Interests in Western Europe* (New York: Cambridge University Press, 1981).

Beyme, Klaus von, *Economics and Politics Within Socialist Systems: A Comparative and Developmental Approach* (New York: Praeger, 1982).

Castles, Francis G., "How Does Politics Matter: Structure or Agency in the Determination of Public Policy Outcomes," *European Journal of Political Research* 9 (1981) pp. 119–132.

———, ed., *The Impact of Parties: Politics and Policies in Democratic Capitalist States* (Beverly Hills: Sage, 1982).

Cameron, David, "The Expansion of the Public Economy: A Comparative Analysis," *APSR* 72, 4 (December 1978), pp. 1243–1261.

Coughlin, Richard M., *Ideology, Public Opinion and Welfare Policy* (Berkeley: Institute of International Studies, 1980).

Diamant, Alfred, "Bureaucracy and Public Policy in Neocorporatist Settings: Some European Lessons," *Comp Pol* 14 (1981) pp. 101–124.

Dye, Thomas, "Politics versus Economics: the Development of the Literature on Policy Determination," *Policy Studies Journal* 7 (1979) pp. 652–662.

Eckstein, Harry, *Pressure Group Politics: The Case of the British Medical Association* (Stanford: Stanford University Press, 1960).

Flora, Peter and Arnold J. Heidenheimer, eds., *The Development of the Welfare State in Europe and America* (New Brunswick, NJ: Transaction, 1981).

Freeman, Gary P., *Immigrant Labor and Racial Conflict in Industrial Societies: The French and British Experience 1945–1975* (Princeton: Princeton University Press, 1979).

Fried, Robert R. and Francine Rabinowitz, *Comparative Urban Politics: A Performance Approach.*

Girvetz, Harry, "Welfare State," *International Encyclopedia of the Social Sciences* 16, pp. 512–521.

Gough, L. *The Political Economy of the Welfare State* (London: Macmillan, 1979).

Gustafsson, Gunnel and Jeremy Richardson, "Post-Industrial Changes in Policy Style," *Sc Pol Stud* 3, 1 (1980) pp. 21–37.

Heisler, Martin O. and Guy Peters, "Comparing Social Policy Across Levels of Government, Countries and Time: Belgium and Sweden since 1870," in Douglas Ashford, ed., *Comparing Public Policies* (Beverly Hills: Sage, 1978), pp. 149–172.

Higgins, Joan, *States of Welfare: A Comparative Analysis of Social Policy* (New York: St. Martin's, 1981).

Hirschman, Albert O., *Shifting Involvements: Private Interest and Public Action* (Princeton: Princeton University Press, 1982).

Hood, Christopher and Maurice Wright, eds., *Big Government in Hard Times* (Oxford: Martin Robertson, 1981).

Janowitz, Morris, *Social Control of the Welfare State* (New York: Elsevier, 1976).

Kelman, Steven, *Regulating America, Regulating Sweden: A Comparative Study of Occupational Safety and Health Legislation Policy* (Cambridge, MA: M.I.T. Press, 1981).

King, Anthony, "What Do Elections Decide?" in David Butler, Howard Penniman, and Austin Ranney, eds., *Democracy at the Poles* (Washington, DC: AEI, 1981).

Kjellberg, Francesco, "Do Policies (really) Determine Politics? and eventually how?" *Policy Studies Journal* 5 (1977) pp. 554–570.

Levine, Robert A. *et al.*, eds., *Evaluation Research and Practice: Comparative and International Perspectives* (Beverly Hills: Sage, 1981).

Logue, John and Eric Einhorn, *Welfare States in Hard Times: Problems, Policy, and Politics in Denmark and Sweden*, 2d ed. (Kent: Kent Popular Press, 1982).

Mackay, Alfred, *Arrow's Theorem: The Paradox of Social Choice* (New Haven: Yale University Press, 1980).

Marmor, Theodore and David Thomas, "Doctors, Politics and Pay Disputes: 'Pressure Group Politics' Revisited," *BJPS* 2 (October 1971) pp. 412–442.

Organisation for Economic and Cooperative Development, *The Welfare State in Crisis* (Paris: OECD, 1981).

Piven, Frances Fox and Richard A. Cloward, *The New Class War: Reagan's Attack on the Welfare State and its Consequences* (New York: Pantheon, 1982).

Premfors, Rune, "National Policy Styles and Higher Education in France, Sweden and the United Kingdom," *European Journal of Education* 16, 2 (1981) pp. 253–262.

Rimlinger, Gaston V., *Welfare Policy and Industrialization in Europe, America and Russia* (New York: Wiley, 1971).

Schmitter, Philippe C., "Modes of Interest Intermediation and Models of Social Change in Western Europe," *Comp Pol St* 10 (April 1977) pp. 7–38.

Stone, Deborah A., *The Limits to Professional Power: National Health Care in the Federal Republic of Germany* (Chicago: University of Chicago Press, 1980).

INDEX